W9-ARY-370

UNIX
awk and sed
PROGRAMMER'S
INTERACTIVE WORKBOOK

PETER PATSIS

Prentice Hall PTR
Upper Saddle River, NJ 07458
http://www.phptr.com/phptrinteractive

ISBN 0-13-082675-8

90000

9 780130 826756

Editorial/production supervision: *Mary Sudul*
Acquisitions editor: *Mark L. Taub*
Development editor: *Ralph Moore*
Technical Contributor: *Corinne Gregory*
Marketing manager: *Dan Rush*
Manufacturing manager: *Alexis R. Heydt*
Editorial assistant: *Audri Anna Bazlan*
Cover design director: *Jerry Votta*
Cover designer: *Anthony Gemmellaro*
Art director: *Gail Cocker-Bogusz*
Series design: *Meryl Poweski*
Page layout: *FASTpages*
Web site project manager: *Yvette Raven*

©1999 by Peter Patsis

 Published by Prentice Hall PTR
Prentice-Hall, Inc.
A Simon & Schuster Company
Upper Saddle River, NJ 07458

Prentice Hall books are widely used by corporations and government agencies
for training, marketing, and resale.

The publisher offers discounts on this book when ordered in bulk quantities.
For more information, contact: Corporate Sales Department, Phone: 800-382-3419;
Fax: 201-236-7141; E-mail: corpsales@prenhall.com; or write: Prentice Hall PTR,
Corp. Sales Dept., One Lake Street, Upper Saddle River, NJ 07458.

All products or services mentioned in this book are the trademarks or service marks of their
respective companies or organizations.

All rights reserved. No part of this book may be reproduced, in any form or by any means,
without permission in writing from the publisher.

Printed in the United States of America

10 9 8 7 6 5 4 3 2 1

ISBN   0-13-082675-8

Prentice-Hall International (UK) Limited, *London*
Prentice-Hall of Australia Pty. Limited, *Sydney*
Prentice-Hall Canada Inc., *Toronto*
Prentice-Hall Hispanoamericana, S.A., *Mexico*
Prentice-Hall of India Private Limited, *New Delhi*
Prentice-Hall of Japan, Inc., *Tokyo*
Simon & Schuster Asia Pte. Ltd., *Singapore*
Editora Prentice-Hall do Brasil, Ltda., *Rio de Janeiro*

To my Father, Mother, Brothers and Sisters and
Mary J. for teaching me the most important language.
Hey Greg, it's done next week!!!

CONTENTS

FROM THE EDITOR

Prentice Hall's Interactive Workbooks are designed to get you up and running fast, with just the information you need, when you need it.

We are certain that you will find our unique approach to learning simple and straightforward. Every chapter of every Interactive Workbook begins with a list of clearly defined Learning Objectives. A series of labs make up the heart of each chapter. Each lab is designed to teach you specific skills in the form of exercises. You perform these exercises at your computer and answer pointed questions about what you observe. Your answers will lead to further discussion and exploration. Each lab then ends with multiple-choice Self-Review Questions, to reinforce what you've learned. Finally, we have included Test Your Thinking projects at the end of each chapter. These projects challenge you to synthesize all of the skills you've acquired in the chapter.

Our goal is to make learning engaging, and to make you a more productive learner.

And you are not alone. Each book is integrated with its own "Companion Website." The website is a place where you can find more detailed information about the concepts discussed in the Workbook, additional Self-Review Questions to further refine your understanding of the material, and perhaps most importantly, where you can find a community of other Interactive Workbook users working to acquire the same set of skills that you are.

All of the Companion Websites for our Interactive Workbooks can be found at http://www.phptr.com/phptrinteractive/.

Mark L. Taub
Editor-in-Chief
Prentice Hall PTR Interactive

INTRODUCTION

This book is about three UNIX utilities: grep, sed, and awk. These three utilities enable you to write various terse applications. These UNIX utilities have been around almost as long as the UNIX operating system and yet still are used to solve a variety of tasks even to this day. Grep, awk, and sed can be very useful for file processing; working at the command line, searching within files; working in combination with other UNIX utilities to perform common tasks at the command line; or writing short scripts to solve an application. These are just a few of the tasks for which these utilities can be used. The goal of this book is to introduce and reinforce your expertise in grep, awk, and sed so that you may solve applications that you currently need to implement. In addition, I hope that, by reading this book, when you do have an application to implement, you have enough understanding of the three utilities to consider using them both to solve your application, and to implement a solution. To achieve this goal, the elements of each utility are taught. Each utility's concepts and elements are presented, with detail about the particular syntax, behavior, rules, and nuances of each concept and element. Exercises and exercise discussions then highlight and reinforce the elements and concepts.

All three utilities share common properties. They all can work on standard input, standard output, or user-supplied input files. They may interact with the UNIX environment by utilizing pipes. And all work with regular expressions.

HOW THIS BOOK IS ORGANIZED

Regular expressions are covered first in this book, because all three utilities require a knowledge of them. If you are not familiar with regular expressions, these chapters will introduce them and go over the various metacharacters that are used with them. Although this coverage is extensive, it is not intended to provide the reader with advanced knowledge on the subject. It is meant for beginners or intermediate users of regular expressions. Whenever covering grep, sed, and awk and using regular expressions, I assume that you have not encountered regular expressions before. If you already have encountered regular expressions, then you may skim over the material or skip it altogether.

The next section describes grep. Grep is a utility that is best suited for searching files; thus, I first describe grep with the use of regular expressions. Next, I cover using grep in conjunction with pipes and other UNIX programs. Finally, I discuss the various options with which you may invoke grep.

The next part of the book discusses sed. Sed addressing is covered, as well as the various sed commands that are available within sed. Sed commands provide more functionality than is available in grep and can be used for a variety of applications. Finally, we will discuss more advanced sed commands, such as the multiline pattern space.

Awk is covered last. Awk, as opposed to grep and sed, can be considered more closely tied to a general-purpose language rather than a utility or specialized language. The reason is that awk exhibits more constructs and features that general-purpose languages exhibit. These include:

- The ability to control flow to any part of an awk program
- The ability to store values in user-defined variables that reference general storage locations
- The ability to perform arithmetic operations
- The ability to write functions
- The ability to perform output in a user-specified format

Sed and grep either restrict these features or do not include them. Generally, most books take the approach of teaching awk as a utility and teach solely by giving an example utility using an awk feature. The approach taken in this book is to teach awk as a language rather than a utility. Therefore, we will talk about awk data types, variables, built-in functions, arrays, control statements, input and output, and functions. Many pitfalls occur with teaching awk as a utility and providing examples that use awk to solve that particular utility. First, if all you ever need is to solve those particular utilities, then you are set. However, if you need to implement utilities that are different from those provided, you are left figuring out and understanding the language through the examples on your own. A better approach is to teach awk as a language and give examples that reinforce each particular feature of the language, the rules regarding their use, and the various methods for which they may be used. Various benefits exist to taking this approach.

You cannot anticipate most of the ways in which awk will be used. By learning awk as a language and mastering your understanding of its features, you will reach the goal of this book, quickly determining whether awk can be used to solve a problem and implementing a solution.

If you were to learn awk simply as a utility and not as a language, then if you get an error (especially if learning by example utilities), determining what caused the error is hard. If you understand the language, then by going over the erroneous program, you can more easily determine which statement caused the error, because you understand how each language construct is used to make up the statement. A lot of people complain about the awk error messaging system as being difficult to decipher. My belief is that the problem does not reside in awk's error-messaging system—its run-time error-messaging system is more verbose and informative than GNU C/C++—rather, it resides in not learning the awk language.

Languages are based on very similar principles. Understanding one language can greatly enhance your ability to understand other languages. The reason is that most languages share very similar elements and constructs inherent in the language, such as functions, scoping, coercion, call-by-value, and call-by-reference. (We go over each of these in this book.) If you have already learned a general-purpose language such as C, C++, or Java, then to learn awk will be easier. If you haven't learned a general-purpose language, then the approach taken in this book will help you learn new languages as well as understand this one. In awk, as with most languages, certain design issues go into the creation of the language. One important design issue is orthogonality—which simply means that more than one way of expressing an action must exist. The concept of orthogonality means that more than one language construct (i.e., a `for` loop and `while` loop can both be used to implement a program) can be used to solve a program. Orthogonality is beneficial to the programmer because it gives the programmer flexibility in finding more efficient, compact, and creative coding solutions to any given problem using the language. The impact of orthogonality does not mean that all things are considered equal. Although more than one construct can be used to solve a problem, one construct is better to use than another construct in certain programs. Truly mastering a language is the ability to understand when one construct is better to use than another because, as mentioned, it is more efficient (uses less storage or is faster than another construct) or more compact (requires fewer lines of code or is easier to read). This requires practice. My hope is that while reading this book and after, you will practice writing awk programs. Also think about more than one solution to a problem, write an awk program that implements all solutions, and then test which solution is better (more readable, shorter, quicker, and taking less storage space).

I cannot emphasize enough that the best way to learn computer languages and utilities is by practicing. Try out on your own sample queries. In addition, I have found that sometimes the best way to learn is by making your own mistakes. Try figuring out where you went wrong, and try entering a query that you suspect might not work. You might be surprised at the result.

MY INTENDED AUDIENCE

This book is not a book on languages. Although this introduction has mentioned language details and issues, whether you have encountered languages before or taken a course on programming languages is not important. Also, you do not need to have an advanced understanding of the UNIX operating system. This book is on grep, sed, and the awk programming language. The book is suitable for novice users of UNIX who have never encountered grep, sed, and awk. It is also suitable for intermediate or advanced users of UNIX who have used grep, sed, and awk but do not have advanced knowledge. All you need to go through this book is a general knowledge of the UNIX operating system. In particular, knowledge of how to execute programs from the command line is necessary.

ABOUT THE WEB SITE COMPANION

This book has a companion Web site, located at:

```
http://www.phptr.com/phptrinteractive/
```

The Web site is composed of various modules designed to augment your exposure to awk, sed, and grep. You'll find a student lounge where you can meet and greet other readers of the Interactive Workbooks and share tips and programs. I have an author's corner, where you can find supplemental material to the book and notes from me about it, errata, and so forth. The answers to the "Test Your Thinking" sections from each chapter of the book have their own module. And additional Self-Review Questions reinforce your understanding of the concepts explored in this book.

Visit the Web site periodically to share and discuss your answers.

ABOUT THE AUTHOR

Peter A. Patsis is a Senior Software Engineer at Digital Equipment Corporation, writing software tools for the verification of the Alpha AXP Microprocessors developed at Digital. He earned his B.S in Computer Science from the State University of New York at Potsdam and his M.S. in Computer Science from the Georgia Institute of Technology in Atlanta Georgia. He previously worked as a Software Engineer at the Smithsonian Institute on the AXAF project in collabaration with NASA, MIT, and TRW.

He has worked with the UNIX operating system for over 10 years.

CHAPTER 1

REGULAR EXPRESSIONS AND METACHARACTERS

 Regular expressions are like opinions: Everyone has them, but not everyone uses them wisely.

If you have not encountered regular expressions before, this chapter will help you gain an understanding of how to use and become effective in writing regular expressions. If you have encountered and used regular expressions within the UNIX shell, differences exist between regular expressions used within the shell and regular expressions used within grep, awk, and sed. This chapter does not explain those differences. Rather, we discuss and understand regular expressions as used within grep, sed, and awk. We do explain differences among regular expressions used by grep and sed, and regular expressions used by awk and egrep whenever possible. If you already feel comfortable with regular expressions as used in grep, awk, and sed, you still might want to work out the problems and exercises as a review.

L A B   1.1

USING THE PERIOD AND BACKSLASH METACHARACTERS

LAB OBJECTIVES

After this Lab, you will be able to:

✓ Identify the Operands and Operators of a Regular Expression

✓ Understand the Results of a Regular Expression Consisting of Operands and Operators

✓ Identify When a Regular Expression Is Evaluated

✓ Understand the Results of Evaluating the Expression as a Pattern

✓ Understand the Wildcard Metacharacter

This Lab briefly describes what a regular expression is and lists all the metacharacters used within this book. The best way to learn regular expressions is to learn the functions performed by the metacharacters and the result of using them in a regular expression. Therefore, the best way to learn regular expressions is by example. The chapters that follow show many examples of regular expressions and the metacharacters that are used within them.

OPERANDS AND OPERATORS

Like an arithmetic expression, a regular expression contains operands and operators. Therefore, you can think of a regular expression as an expression like any other expression that contains operands and operators. In arithmetic expressions, operands are numbers, and operators are the plus sign for addition, the minus sign for subtraction, and so forth. In regular expressions, the operands are strings of characters, and the operators are the various metacharacters.

■ FOR EXAMPLE:

Consider the following regular expression:

```
chapter *[0-9]+
```

The operands are the characters "chapter," 0, and 9. The operators are the *, [], -, and + metacharacters. Like arithmetic expressions, the operators use the operands to perform some kind of evaluation that produces some result.

Unlike an arithmetic expression, which usually results in a single value, the result of a regular expression is a list of substrings. The list of substrings form a subset of all substrings that are possibly formed from combining all characters that are printable from length one (single character) to the largest string that can be stored on a computer. Therefore, after evaluating the preceding regular expression, the result would be the list of strings:

```
{chapter 0, chapter 1, chapter 2, chapter 3, chapter
    4, …, chapter9, chapter0, …, chapter9}
```

Here, each value between commas is a substring that results from evaluating the expression. Therefore, you can think of a regular expression as a notation for specifying a subset of strings, or equivalently, a list of substrings. In other words, in our example, the notation chapter *[0-9]+

**LAB
1.1**

specified a list of substrings that begin with the text `chapter` followed by an optional space, followed by at least one occurrence of the digits 0-9.

Now, consider the following regular expression:

```
yes
```

When evaluated, this expression results in a single value:

yes

The regular expression forms a single substring of length three with the letters y followed by e followed by s. In these examples, a single element (in the last example, the single element is `yes`—that is, y literally followed by e followed by s) is selected from a subset of all possible substrings that could have been formed as regular expressions.

When a regular expression that contains metacharacter operators, called a *metacharacter expression*, is evaluated, the result is more than one substring. A regular expression that results in a single element is referred to as a *literal* regular expression, and therefore contains no metacharacter operators. In the preceding examples, the regular expression `chapter *[0-9]+` contains several metacharacters, as you saw, and resulted in more than one substring. The regular expression `yes`, on the other hand, contains no metacharacters and resulted in the single substring yes. Therefore, the simplest notation within regular expressions is to specify a single element from the set of all possible substrings or a literal regular expression.

However, thinking and describing regular expressions just as a means of simply selecting substrings tells half the story; it does not say what it will be used for and how it will be used. The result of a regular expression will be used for matching a possible set of strings. The set of strings to be matched is usually a line of text.

■ FOR EXAMPLE:

Consider the following regular expression:

```
her
```

and the following line of text:

```
feathered,
```

The literal regular expression `her` would match the string `feathered` (the string `her` is contained within the string `feathered` starting at the fifth character). Be sure to understand the view of a regular expression that, when evaluated, results in a string or set of strings that is used for matching (I say string(s) because when you use metacharacters, more than one string results and is used in matching). Also be sure to know that `her` exactly matches `her` as well as longer substrings that contain `her`, such as `feathered`.

Now that we know that regular expressions are used to match another substring, it's time to see where they are used and at what time the regular expression gets evaluated. You will see in more detail when we go over each utility (awk, sed, and grep) in what context regular expressions are used, but for now a couple of examples, without getting into details, should help more clearly define what they are. In grep, you usually want to find out within a line of text from an input file whether a particular string occurs. Therefore, in grep, the particular string to find is a regular expression, and the substring to match is each line in the file.

■ FOR EXAMPLE:

Consider the following:

```
grep her input-file
```

Here, the literal regular expression `her` is determined by grep as a regular expression matching argument to be compared with each line in the file `input-file`. If a match occurs, then the entire line is printed out. Within the grep program the literal regular expression is evaluated as an expression, not at the command line. This fact is important to know, because if the regular expression argument contains any metacharacters that are also interpreted as metacharacters at the command line, then the regular expression argument must be quoted, like so:

```
grep "her*" input-file
```

Here, the asterisk has special meaning at the command line, so to keep its regular expression meaning, it must be quoted.

Don't worry about syntax of grep at this point; that is covered in full detail in later chapters.

MICROCOSM/MACROCOSM

When working with regular expressions, two views are constructed that help determine the results of evaluating regular expressions, understanding what strings the regular expressions match, and finally constructing regular expressions. The two views are the macrocosm and microcosm. You can interpret the views as a partial (microcosm) or a whole (macrocosm) relationship.

In the macrocosm, we are concerned only about the results of evaluating a regular expression as a whole.

■ *FOR EXAMPLE:*

In the previous examples, we are concerned in the macrocosm that the regular expressions `her` and `chapter *[0-9]+` result as a whole in the regular expressions:

```
yes
chapter 1
chapter 2
chapter 3, and so on
```

We are also concerned in the macrocosm with the strings that the regular expressions match. In the macrocosm, the regular expression `chapter 1` matches the following strings:

```
chapter 1
chapter 11.
In chapter 1
```

The previous discussion has centered around the regular expression in the macrocosm. This view centered on a regular expression as an expression in the whole (operands, operators, results as sets).

In the microcosm, we are concerned with the regular expression and the result of each individual operation.

In the previous example, we are concerned with what results when we evaluate [0-9]. The expression results in

```
{0, 1, 2, 3, 4, 5, 6, 7, 8, 9}
```

In other words, in the microcosm, we are concerned how the parts build up and result in the whole, the macrocosm. As another example, consider the regular expression her. In the microcosm, this is constructed by taking the characters h and e and concatenating them to form he, which is then concatenated to the character r to form the regular expression her.

In the microcosm, we are also concerned with the matching process itself. In other words, what in the regular expression matching process did a regular expression character match in the matching substring? In this process, we view regular expressions as patterns; like other patterns, the regular expressions specify a sequence and arrangement of characters that have to appear in the matching substring. In the previous regular expression her, the regular expression specifies that the arrangement of characters or pattern is such that the first character is an h, the second is an e, and the next character is an r, and that taken together they should be used to find out whether another string contains the same pattern. This suggests that, taken as the view of a pattern, a regular expression performs the following algorithm. We assume that the regular expression is her and the matching string is feathered.

1. Start at the leftmost character, f, in the matching string feathered.
2. Ask whether this character, f, is equal to the first character in the regular expression, or h.
3. Because the answer is no, the next leftmost character is used, e.
4. Repeat asking whether the next leftmost character in the matching substring is equal to the first character in the regular expression h.

5. We continue to answer no until we reach the h in the matching string `feathered`.
6. Here, the answer is yes, the next leftmost character in the matching substring is equal to the first character of the regular expression (h is equal to h).
7. We then ask whether the next leftmost character in the regular expression, e, is equal to the next leftmost character in the matching string, `feathered`.
8. Because the answer is yes, we continue to match the next leftmost character until all characters in the regular expression are matched in the matching substring, IN ORDER!!
9. Of course, if we reach the end of the matching substring before we reach the end of the regular expression, then the strings did not match.

At any time if the current leftmost character of the matching substring does not match the current character in the regular expression, then the current character in the regular expression is reset to the first character of the regular expression and the matching continues.

When we use regular expressions in examples and discussions of metacharacters in this chapter and in grep, sed, and awk, the macrocosm is used to show what the result of a regular expression is as a whole and the strings the regular expression matched as a whole. We use the microcosm view to describe each metacharacter and what characters or patterns they create and match and to explain the matching process. Maintain this part/whole view to better understand the functionality of each metacharacter expression and to make constructing and writing your own metacharacter regular expressions easier.

WILDCARD

I briefly mentioned that a metacharacter operator is a mechanism whereby *more* than one element may be selected from a list of all possible substrings. The first one discussed here is the wildcard metacharacter, and you will see what types of patterns the wildcard metacharacter matches. The wildcard metacharacter is denoted by the period character (.). In the previous discussion on literal regular expressions, you selected a single element or pattern from a list of many possible patterns. Sometimes, however, the set of substrings you wish to match is too large to list out individually, so you need some notation that can be used to specify a number of substrings, or patterns, without having to individually list them all out. For example, suppose you wanted to specify all two-character substrings or patterns that start with the letter a. Having to type out aa, ab, ac, ..., az every time you wanted to specify two characters that start with the letter a would be tedious. The wildcard regular expression operator allows you to avoid this tedious task and provides a notation to instruct that when the wildcard is encountered, any character will match it. So the regular expression that provides this instruction is:

    a.

In the macrocosm, the set of substrings from all substrings that will result from the evaluation of this regular expression are:

    aa
    ab
    ac
    az and so on

In the microcosm, the previous wildcard regular expression means that any pattern that contains the letter a followed by any other character will match the regular expression. Therefore, the following substrings will all match a:

    aa
    alfred   - a followed by l, l matches the wildcard
    anytime   - a followed by n, n matches the wildcard

In the following wildcard regular expression, c.i, if the matching substring is chip, then the first character of the regular expression matches the first character of the matching substring. The second character of the regular expression is the wildcard metacharacter, so no comparison needs to be made in the matching substring (it will match), and the comparison moves to the next character position for both the regular expression and matching substring. This is continued until either a match is made or we reach the end of the matching substring. So anytime the wildcard metacharacter is encountered, it acts like a skip function. That is, we can skip the comparison for both the current character in the regular expression and the current character in the matching substring and move on to the next character(s) in both and continue making comparisons. The only exception to the rule is the newline character. The wildcard metacharacter will not match the newline character. So consider the following wildcard regular expression:

```
chapter.
```

and matching substrings that are contained in a file one line after the other:

**chapter
chapter one.**

The regular expression would match only the second line. The reason the first line is not matched is that it contains the string chapter, which is followed by the newline. Because the newline does not match the wildcard metacharacter, the matching string does not match the regular expression (a newline occurs at the end of every line in the input file)

THE BACKSLASH METACHARACTER

Earlier in this chapter, I said that a literal regular expression is a regular expression that contains no metacharacters and results in a single string, and a regular expression that contains a metacharacter results in more than one single string. The backslash metacharacter is the only exception to the rule that any regular expression that contains a metacharacter will result in more than one string. The backslash metacharacter, denoted by the backslash character, \, results in a single literal regular expression.

■ FOR EXAMPLE:

Consider the following string:

```
"chapter."
```

We would like to use the string as a regular expression and match it with all lines containing the word chapter followed by a period. How can we construct this regular expression while at the same time not having the period be evaluated as the wildcard metacharacter, which matches any character? We need some mechanism so that we may interpret the period literally and not as the period metacharacter.

The backslash metacharacter enables us to instruct that the character following the backslash metacharacter be interpreted literally and not as a metacharacter. Any metacharacter operator may be used as a literal character by preceding it with the backslash metacharacter. So in the previous example, we would write our regular expression as follows:

```
chapter\.
```

This would correctly select any substring with the pattern `chapter.`. Again, the backslash character does not result in multiple strings being constructed as a result of the evaluation. Unlike all other metacharacters, it results in a literal or single element and can be interpreted as a literal regular expression. The duality that metacharacters are both operators and literal characters forces the need of the backslash metacharacter.

LAB 1.1 EXERCISES

These exercises will test your understanding of the discussion presented in this chapter. A number of these exercises will not be very difficult. We will challenge and reinforce your knowledge of regular expressions more as we go over more metacharacters. For now, the more important goal is that you understand the basics and answer simple questions before attempting more advanced questions.

1.1.1 IDENTIFY THE OPERANDS AND OPERATORS OF A REGULAR EXPRESSION

What are the operands and operators of the following regular expressions?

a) `Her`

_____

b) `feathered`

_____

c) `Her.`

_____

d) `Feathered\.`

_____

e) `2\*.`

_____

f) `chapter\n`

_____

What type of regular expression is each of the following?

g) `the`

_____

h) `the.`

_____

i) `the\.`

_____

1.1.2 UNDERSTAND THE RESULTS OF A REGULAR EXPRESSION CONSISTING OF OPERANDS AND OPERATORS

What are the results of evaluating the following regular expressions? Think of the expressions as operators and operands, and the results as a set of literal strings.

a) a.b

_____

b) 80.86

_____

c) her

_____

d) \.

_____

e) \\t

_____

1.1.3 IDENTIFY WHEN A REGULAR EXPRESSION IS EVALUATED

a) Identify when the regular expressions in the following code or invocations are evaluated as a regular expression.

```
grep t* input-file

awk { x = 3
     if ($0 ~ x) print $0
     }

grep 't*' input-file
```

_____

_____

1.1.4 UNDERSTAND THE RESULTS OF EVALUATING THE EXPRESSION AS A PATTERN

Use the following regular expressions and matching substrings to answer the questions in this Exercise.

```
reg_expr = her
match string = her, hereafter. Heresy

reg_expr = a.c
match string = abc, acdc, a$c, access

reg_expr = try\.
match string = trying, try$, try.
```

a) Which matching strings match the regular expression?

_____

_____

b) At what character position(s) does the first character of the regular expression match in the matching string?

_____

_____

c) At what character position(s) in the matching string does a match not occur?

_____

_____

1.1.5 UNDERSTAND THE WILDCARD CHARACTER

What strings do the following wildcard regular expressions produce?

a) `the.`

_____

b) `.ed`

_____

LAB 1.1 EXERCISE ANSWERS

This section gives you some suggested answers to the questions in Lab 1.1, with discussions related to those answers. Your answers may vary, but the most important thing is whether or not your answers work. Use these discussions to analyze differences between your answers and those presented here.

If you have alternative answers to the questions in this Exercise, you are encouraged to post your answers and discuss them at the companion Web site for this book, located at:

`http://www.phptr.com/phptrinteractive/`

I cannot emphasize enough that the best way to learn computer languages and utilities is by practicing. Try out sample queries on your own. In addition, I have found that sometimes the best way to learn is by your own mistakes. Try figuring out where you went wrong, and try entering a query that you suspect might not work. You might be surprised at the result.

1.1.1 ANSWERS

What are the operands and operators of the following regular expressions?

a) Her

Answer: Operands: H, e, and `r`   *Operator:* `concatenation`

No explicit operator exists, and the implicit operator concatenation is used to concatenate h with e and then r.

b) feathered

Answer: Operand: `feathered`   *Operator:* `concatenation`

Same reasoning as the previous example.

c) Her.

Answer: Operand: H, e, and r, and all single characters   *Operator:* `concatenation, wildcard`

In this particular expression, we encounter the wildcard operator. The operand to this operator are all single characters, by definition, of the wildcard operator. This is concatenated with the literal expression Her, which was constructed by concatenating h, e, and r.

d) Feathered\.

Answer: Operand: `Feathered.`   *Operator:* `concatenation, backslash`

The backslash operator is encountered next, whose operand is the period. This is concatenated to the literal string Feathered.

e) 2*.

*Answer: Operand: 2, *, all single characters*   *Operator:* `concatenation, backslash, wildcard`

Here, the wildcard operator has as its operands all single characters, which are concatenated to the character *, which is the operand to the backslash, which is then concatenated to the literal character 2.

f) chapter\n

> Answer: *Operand:* `chapter,` *newline character*   *Operator:* `concatena-`
> `tion, backslash`

What type of regular expression is each of the following?

g) the

> Answer: *Literal regular expression, no metacharacters.*

h) the.

> Answer: *Metacharacter regular expression. In particular, a wildcard metacharacter regular expression.*

i) the\.

> Answer: *Literal regular expression; it has a metacharacter but the backslash still evaluates to a literal.*

1.1.2 ANSWERS

What are the results of evaluating the following regular expressions? Think of the expressions as operators and operands, and the results as a set of literal strings.

a) a.b

> Answer: `{aab,…,azb,a1b,  ..,a9b,a!b,  ..,a\fb}`

In other words, all three character strings, including punctuation and non-printable characters like the form feed. Everything except the newline character.

b) 80.86

> Answer: *Again, because the wildcard matches all characters except the newline, the result is the same as before, except that this one is prefixed by* `80` *and suffixed by* `86`.

c) her

> Answer: *{*`her`*} —the single element* `her`.

d) \.

Answer: {.} —the single element period, which was the operand to the backslash. Therefore, the backslash returns the operand following it literally.

e) \\t

Answer: {\t} —the single element consisting of two characters, a backslash, and the character t. The backslash operator has as its operand a backslash. Therefore, the backslash will be taken literally, and the literal character t is concatenated to it.

1.1.3 ANSWERS

a) Identify when the regular expressions in the following code or invocations are evaluated as a regular expression.
```
grep t* input-file
```
Answer: No regular expression exists.

The shell will evaluate the asterisk, because it is not quoted. The shell interprets the expression t* as a filename.

```
awk { x = 3
        if ($0 ~ x) print $0
     }
```

The regular expression x will be evaluated as a regular expression when awk is executing, and awk reaches the line of code if ($0 ~ x) print $0.

In awk, frequently we would like to know whether a string pattern or substring is contained within a line of text from a file. In awk, unlike grep, we would also like to know whether a substring is contained within a portion (or field) of the input line. We might also want to know simply whether a substring or pattern is contained within a variable that contains a string. Therefore, because awk allows string variable assignment, it does not limit the string to which the regular expression will match simply to an input line like grep.

This awk snippet searches for the literal regular expression 3 but further searches whether the regular expression is contained within the string variable $0 and not an entire input line of text. The tilde (~) is an awk regular expression matching operator. When awk encounters the operator, the operator requires that one of its arguments be a regular expression that needs to be evaluated. Because a regular expression is enclosed in slashes in awk, it recognizes the second argument (rightmost operand) /her/ as the regular expression that needs to be evaluated and uses her as the regular expression.

It then determines whether the regular expression her is contained within the substring that is stored in the variable word. In awk, a regular expression is recognized not simply as a string, but as an expression, a regular expression, that needs to be evaluated. We could have rewritten the awk snippet of code as:

```
awk '{reg_expr = "her"
        word ~ reg_expr
    }'
```

This would have returned equivalent results. However, the string her was not evaluated as a regular expression in the assignment statement, but simply as a string. Only when the string is encountered with a regular expression operator is the string recognized as a regular expression to be evaluated. Therefore, the context in which the string is used determines whether it is a regular expression or not.

```
grep 't*' input-file
```

Answer: The regular expression is evaluated when grep is executing.

1.1.4 ANSWERS

Use the given regular expressions and matching substrings to answer the questions in this Exercise.

a) Which matching strings match the regular expression?

Answer: her —matches her and hereafter, but not Heresy; the first character of Heresy is capitalized.

a.c —matches, abc, a$c, and access, but does not match acdc. The pattern of the character a followed by any character and then a c never occurs in acdc.

try\. —matches only try.. The others do not have the period character following the string try.

b) At what character position(s) does the first character of the regular expression match in the matching string?

Answer: her —*the first character,* h, *matches in position 1 in* her *and* hereafter, *and never matches in* Heresy.

a.c —*the first character,* a, *matches in position 1 for all matching strings.*

try\. —*the first character,* t, *matches in all substrings.*

c) At what character position(s) in the matching string does a match not occur?

Answer: her, hereafter —*no positions do not match (positions 1, 2, and 3 are matched and the matching stops).*

Heresy —*no position is a match.*

abc, a$c, access —*no positions match.*

acdc —*positions 2, 3, and 4 do not match.*

1.1.5 ANSWERS

What strings do the following wildcard regular expressions produce?

a) the.

Answer: {thea, ..., thez, theA, .., theZ, the1, .., the9, the$, .., the\f, theaa, theaz, ...}

All strings length four and greater that are prefixed by the string the. Newline cannot follow the string the, but could come after it.

b) .ed

Answer: {aed, .., zed, Aed, ..., Zed, 1ed, .., 9ed, $ed, .., \fed, aeda, .. zeda, ..}

All strings that have any character suffixed by ed, and followed by zero or more characters after the three characters preceding it.

LAB 1.1 SELF-REVIEW QUESTIONS

In order to test your progress, you should be able to answer the following questions.

In each of the following multiple choice questions, the answer may be one or more of the available choices.

1) Which of the following are a result of evaluating the regular expression `123*[a-c]`?

   a) _____ 12
   b) _____ 12a
   c) _____ 123ad
   d) _____ 12cc
   e) _____ 12d

2) What type of regular expression is `chapter\.` ?

   a) _____literal
   b) _____metacharacter
   c) _____it is not a regular expression

3) What characters does `.` match?

   a) _____a letter a-z or A-Z
   b) _____a number
   c) _____a metacharacter

4) What are the operands of the regular expression `cd*e` ?

   a) _____c
   b) _____d
   c) _____e
   d) _____1
   e) _____3

5) Does the string `sentence.` need the backslash metacharacter to be interpreted literally?

   a) _____yes
   b) _____no

   Quiz answers appear in Appendix A, Lab 1.1.

CHAPTER 1

TEST YOUR THINKING

 The projects in this section are meant to have you utilize all of the skills that you have acquired throughout this chapter. The answers to these projects can be found at the companion Web site to this book, located at:

`http://www.phptr.com`

Visit the Web site periodically to share and discuss your answers.

In the rest of this section we will explore additional metacharacters including the asterisk, plus, and question mark metacharacters. These three metacharacters are described in the following table:

Table 1.1 ■ Asterisk, Plus, Question Mark, and Positional Metacharacters

Operator	Description	Usage
Asterisk Metacharacter (*)	`A* matches zero or more occurrences of A in a matching sub-string`	Regular expression a* matches substrings a, aa, after, daal, fred. In the first substring a, the regular expression a*; a occurs one time in a. In the substring aa, the regular expression a*; a occurs twice in aa, and daal. In the substring fred, the regular expression a*; a occurs zero times. (remember that the asterisk metacharacter specifies that zero or more occurrences of the character immediately preceding the asterisk metacharacter may occur in the matching substring
Plus Metacharacter (+)	`A+ matches one or more occurrences of A in a matching substring`	Regular expression a+ matches the same substrings a, aa, after, daal but does not match fred. The plus metacharacter specfies that at least one occurrence of the character immediately preceding the plus metacharacter may occur in the matching substring. The matching substring fred has zero occurrences of a in the string fred.

Table 1.1 ■ Asterisk, Plus, Question Mark, and Positional Metacharacters

Question Mark Metacharacter (?)	`A? matches exactly zero or one occurrences of A in a matching susbtring`	Regular expression a? matches the substrings a, after, and fred but does match aa, and daal. In a, and after the regular expression a? matches one occurrence of a. In fred the regular expression a matches zero occurrences of a.

Positional Metacharacters (^,$)	`^A matches A at the very beginning (first character) of a matching substring`
	
	`A$ matches A at the very end (last character) of a matching substring`
		Regular expression ^a matches the substrings a, after, but does match fred, and daal. In a, and after the regular expression ^a matches the a in the beginning (first character) of the substring a. and after. In fred , and daal, the regular expression ^a does not match an a in the beginning (first character is d and f and not a) of the substrings fred and daal.

Each of the above metacharacters differs from the metacharacters in Lab 1.1 in that the metacharacters in Table 1.1 specify and affect metacharacters and literals not at the current character position but at a position that immediately precedes the metacharacter or immediately follows the metacharacter.

1) For each of the following expressions, identify the subset of values that would result.

   a) AB+C

   b) AB?C

   c) AB*C

   d) ^AB*C

   e) AB*C$

   f) ^AB*C$

2) Explain verbally what the following regular expression produces. Which lines does it match and match?

   " book.* "

Use the following input file called `mic.dat` for this section.

```
There are two principal types of transducers used in
   mics: dynamic and
condensor.   Dynamics  are  often  favored  for  miking
   individual
instruments because they  add  a  favorable  color  to
   the sound.   Condensor
mics  are  generally  more  accurate  than  dynamic  and
   are preferable for
audience recording.
```

1) What is the result of the following regular expressions used within grep?

 Try to figure not only what the regular expression matched when you execute it at the terminal, but what other strings in other files it might match.

a) grep 'dynamic ' mic.dat

b) grep 'dynamic[.?!]' mic.dat

c) grep 'condenser' mic.dat

d) grep '\. *' mic.dat

e) grep '\. *D' mic.dat

f) p [TD]* mic.dat

2) Suppose you wanted to find all matching strings that have a file name that starts with AVL and has a file extension of .h (the rest of the name you do not care about).

g) Write a regular expression that would perform this search.

3) For the following regular expressions, explain verbally what each does.

h) ^.*$

i) ^$

j) "[.?!:] +[a-zA-Z]"

k) ^[+-]?[0-9]+[.]?[0-9]*$

l) ^[0-9][0-9]$

C H A P T E R 2

CHARACTER CLASS, HYPHEN, AND CARET METACHARACTERS

 I never met a metacharacter I didn't like, except in Windows 95.

CHAPTER OBJECTIVES

In this chapter, you will learn about:

✓ The Character Class, Hyphen, and Caret   Page 28
  Metacharacters

In this chapter, additional metacharacters are explored that provide more expressive capabilities in writing regular expressions. You will see that "expressive" means that you have additional operators that increase the number of potential matching patterns that you saw with literal regular expressions. At the same time, you will see that these metacharacters also reduce the number of potential matching patterns compared with the number of matching patterns that were matched with the wildcard metacharacter. The hyphen metacharacter is used only in conjunction with the character class metacharacter. The caret metacharacter, on the other hand, has meaning both within the character class metacharacter and outside it. This chapter discusses the caret metacharacter only as it is used within the character class metacharacter. Later, we will revisit the caret metacharacter outside a character class.

L A B   2.1

THE CHARACTER CLASS, HYPHEN, AND CARET METACHARACTERS

LAB OBJECTIVES

After this Lab, you will be able to:

✓ Understand the Results of the Character Class, Hyphen, and Caret Metacharacters

✓ Recognize the Special Rules Regarding These Three Metacharacters

✓ Write Regular Expressions Using These Three Metacharacters

CHARACTER CLASS

Sometimes we would like to include more characters than can be represented by a literal regular expression and fewer than are represented by the wildcard regular expression. For example, in the last chapter, while discussing the wildcard regular expression, we encountered the following regular expression:

      a.

As mentioned, the wildcard regular expression provided a convenient mechanism over a literal regular expression, in that each literal expression did not have to be specified in the expression, like so:

```
aa
ab
ac
ad
```

LAB
2.1

If we used grep and did not have the wildcard metacharacter, we would have to run grep using each literal regular expression, aa, ab, and so on, until every pattern that contained the letter a followed by any other character was included, as follows:

```
grep aa some-file
grep ab some-file
```

... and so on.

The problem with a literal regular expression is that it matches only a single character at a time. The wildcard metacharacter, on the other hand, matches all characters. Somewhere in between we need a mechanism to reference more than a single character but fewer than all characters. A character class provides this mechanism and is a refinement of the wildcard metacharacter. Instead of matching any character at a specific position using the character class metacharacter, we can list the characters that we wish to include.

■ FOR EXAMPLE:

The character class metacharacter is denoted by opening and closing square brackets, ([,]), and the characters that you wish to include are contained within the square brackets. Suppose, for example, you want to find all occurrences of the word *chapter*, and want to include the possibility that the word *chapter* starts a sentence and is therefore capitalized. You could use the character class metacharacter as follows:

```
[cC]hapter
```

Thus, both the matching patterns *chapter* and *Chapter* would be matched.

**LAB
2.1**

So in the microcosm view of matching patterns, the first character of the regular expression is matched with the matching substring. If the matching substring contains either the lowercase letter "c" or the uppercase letter "C," then a match is made, and the matching continues. Otherwise, a match is not made, and we look at the next character in the matching substring to see if it is "c" or "C." Therefore, the characters inside a character class metacharacter form a concatenation of boolean "or" statements (i.e, is the character a "c" or a "C"). In the macrocosm view, the character class metacharacter returns the list of possible strings, chapter, and Chapter. Although this example does not seem too tedious to write using a literal regular expression, it still saves the trouble of running an extra invocation of a utility or writing another line of code that uses the extra literal regular expression. The following example shows an even broader set of strings that can be matched using the character class metacharacter.

■ *FOR EXAMPLE:*

Suppose you have a text document that contains formatting commands to instruct how the text should appear either on the screen or as output to a printer. One of the tags is a Chapter Number tag. It appears as follows:

```
.CN1 Memory Management
textual discussion of the chapter
.CN2 CPU Scheduling
textual description of the chapter
```

The string .CN signifies that you should interpret the character immediately following the tag as the Chapter Number, and the rest of the line that contains the tag as the Chapter Title. Suppose you want to extract from the Chapter Number tag the integer representing the chapter and the Chapter Title in order to create a book outline. You could accomplish this task using the following character class regular expression:

```
\.CN[123456789]
```

The character class matches the following patterns:

```
.CN1, .CN2, …. .CN9
```

HYPHEN

Suppose further that you have the following regular expression:

    `\.CN[1-9]`

This regular expression would match the following:

   `.CN1, .CN2, .., .CN9`

The dash within the character class metacharacter is called the hyphen metacharacter. It has meaning only within the character class metacharacter and provides an even shorter notation to specify a range of continuous characters within a character class than having to list each character within the range, as we did with the expression `\.CN[123456789]`. By continuous, I mean that each character within the range has an ASCII value that is one greater then the previous character. In the microcosm, an evaluating machine will look at the current character in the matching substring and, upon encountering a character class that contains a hyphen, will see whether the current character in the matching substring occurs within that range. In other words, in our example, it will see whether the current character in the matching substring is greater than or equal to 1 and less than or equal to 9. If yes, then it will continue matching characters; otherwise, no match occurs and the matching process stops.

Remember that the characters inside the character class metacharacter are meant to declare that, at this character position in the pattern, any of the characters in the list within the character class metacharacter are the only characters allowed to occur in the matching substring. If they do not appear, then a match does not occur.

CARET

Normally a character class is used to include all the characters that you wish to match at a particular position in matching a substring. Sometimes specifying characters you want to exclude is more convenient than specifying characters you wish to include. The caret metacharacter regular expression operator is used to specify characters that you wish to exclude in a character class. For example, you could use the caret metacharacter to specify that we would like to match any consonant letter at a particular position in a matching substring with the following regular expression:

```
[^aeiouAEIOU]
```

In this regular expression, we specify that a consonant letter is any letter that is not a vowel. This is easier and less cumbersome to specify than listing out all consonants. In the microcosm, the caret metacharacter, instead of testing for equality, tests that the current character in the substring is not equal to any of the characters in the character class. In other words, it tests for inequality. We can also use the caret metacharacter inside a character class along with other character class metacharacters.

■ FOR EXAMPLE:

To specify a nondigit number, you could write the following caret metacharacter regular expression:

```
[^0-9]
```

The caret is used in conjunction with the hyphen or range metacharacter to specify that the current character in the current position of the matching substring is not included in that range. In the microcosm, this expression amounts to performing the same comparison as we do for the hyphen metacharacter and then negating the result of that comparison. So if the character was a "D," then the hyphen metacharacter result would return false and negating it would return true. If it was a "7," the hyphen metacharacter would return true and negating it would return the expected result false.

I have not yet mentioned what happens when you want to use a character class that contains regular expression metacharacters.

■ FOR EXAMPLE:

Suppose you wanted to specify all the punctuation marks that end a sentence. Earlier in the chapter, we decided that we would like to find and extract all lines that contained the word "chapter," and we used the following regular expression:

```
[cC]hapter
```

Say we now wanted to find and extract only the occurrences of the word "chapter" in which the word ended a sentence. We would write the following character class regular expression:

```
[cC]hapter[!?;:".]
```

The last character class contains characters that are also metacharacters. Notice that we do not have to use the backslash metacharacter to specify each one. The reason for not using the backslash metacharacter is that metacharacters lose their meaning inside a character class ([]), so you do not need to mark them as special characters.

LAB 2.1 EXERCISES

2.1.1 UNDERSTAND THE RESULTS OF THE CHARACTER CLASS, HYPHEN, AND CARET METACHARACTERS

a) Are the following legal character class metacharacter regular expressions?

```
[a-z][A-Z]
```

_____

```
[1-9ABD]
```

_____

b) If so, come up with a couple of matching patterns on your own.

_____

c) What is the result (macrocosm) of each of the following regular expressions?

```
[Ll]ab [1-9]
```

_____

```
[0-1][0-9]-[0-9][0-9]-[0-9][0-9]
```

```
[^a-z]
```

```
"  [A-Z][A-Z]  "
```

```
her[sedbo]
```

Use the following matching lines to answer the next question:

```
Lab 1
Lab Objectives
Understand the view of a regular expression as an expression
Identify the operands and operators of the expression
Understand the results of the expression viewed as an oper-
and, operator expression
Understand and differentiate between a literal regular
expression and a
```

d) What is the result (microcosm) of the preceding regular expressions (from Question c) with the given matching lines? If a match occurs, write the starting position and the ending position within the matching substring where the match occurred. If a match does not occur, state at what position the matching process stops.

Consider the following regular expression:

```
grep a. some-file
```

The contents of `some-file` are as follows:

```
some-file:
after the noon day sun
sets into the distance
```

e) What would the regular expression as given here yield if used with grep and the file `some-file`?

_____

_____

Note that grep reads an entire input line at a time and then uses the whole line to see whether the regular expression matches any string in the line. If so, it prints out the entire line; otherwise, it prints no output if a match is not found.

f) How would you obtain similar results if you did not have the hyphen metacharacter?

_____

_____

g) How would you obtain similar results if you did not have the hyphen and character class metacharacters?

_____

_____

2.1.2 RECOGNIZE THE SPECIAL RULES REGARDING THE THREE METACHARACTERS

a) Are the following regular expressions legal? If so, can you guess what they would match?

[w^]

_____

[-+]

_____

[+-/]

_____

b) Can the following range be used with the hyphen?

[4-7]

_____

[\t-\f]

_____

c) Are the following legal?

[-+][0-9]

_____

[+-*/][0-9

_____

[!\t][0-9]

_____

d) If so, what strings result (macrocosm)?

_____

_____

2.1.3 WRITE REGULAR EXPRESSIONS USING THE THREE METACHARACTERS

a) Write a hyphen character class regular expression that matches the following date strings:

`MM-DD-YY`

_____

`MM/DD/YY`

_____

b) How do you create a regular expression that matches only `.CN1`, ..., `.CN9`, while it simultaneously does not match `.CN10` and greater? Can you come up with a character class that matches just the two following strings?

`.CN12`
`.CN1.1`

_____

c) Write a regular expression that matches the following strings and only the following strings:

`May dd, yy`
`may dd, yy`

_____

LAB 2.1 EXERCISE ANSWERS

 This section gives you some suggested answers to the questions in Lab 2.1, with discussion related to those answers. Your answers may vary, but the most important thing is whether or not your answer works. Use this discussion to analyze differences between your answers and those presented here.

If you have alternative answers to the questions in this Exercise, you are encouraged to post your answers and discuss them at the companion Web site for this book, located at:

http://www.phptr.com/phptrinteractive/

2.1.1 ANSWERS

a) Are the following legal character class metacharacter regular expressions?

`[a-z][A-Z]`

Answer: Yes, this is valid.

The first character class `[a-z]` contains a valid range. By a valid range, we mean that the hyphen has a character immediately before the hyphen whose ASCII value is less than the ASCII value of the character immediately following the hyphen. In our case, the character immediately before the hyphen is a lowercase *a*, whose ASCII value is less than the ASCII value of the character immediately following the hyphen, a lowercase *z*. The same is true for the second character class `[A-Z]`. Notice that no spaces follow any character in the regular expression.

`[1-9ABD]`

Answer: Yes, this is valid.

This character class contains a range alongside three individual characters. That structure means this expands to the following equivalent character class:

`[123456789ABD]`

To verify the validity of a range within a character class, see whether you could expand that range with each value one greater than the previous value for the range only. As seen, this goal is accomplished with the range 1-9. Do not consider characters that appear before or after the character class, ABD, in our example. If this is possible, then the range is valid.

b)   If so, come up with a couple of matching patterns on your own.

Answer: An example for the first expression might be as follows:
`aZ, bC, dEvelop, zZ`

The regular expression matches any matching pattern that contains a lowercase letter followed by an uppercase letter with nothing else, or a lowercase letter followed by an uppercase letter followed by any combination of characters in the ASCII character set. An example of the latter—a lowercase letter followed by a combination of characters in the ASCII character set—is *dEvelop*. It would also match the following:

`dE12\t\t`
`AZ$$$)`

An example for the second expression might be as follows:
`1, ... 9, A, B, D, 1A, .. 9A, 1B, ... 9B, 1D, ... 9D, 1A$,`
`1A<, 1AA, AB, AD`

The regular expression matches a single digit 1 through 9; a single uppercase letter A, B, D; or one or more digits interspersed with any other ASCII character; or A, B, D, interspersed with any other ASCII character.

c)   What is the result (macrocosm) of the following regular expressions?

`[Ll]ab [1-9]`

Answer: This expression would match the following:
`Lab 1, lab 1, Lab 2, lab 2, ....,Lab 10, lab 10, ... Lab`
`laa, lab zed`

In other words, this regular expression matches either `Lab` or `lab`, followed by a space and a digit 1 through 9 followed by zero or more combinations of any other characters in the ASCII character set.

`[0-1][0-9]-[0-9][0-9]-[0-9][0-9]`

This expression would match the following:
`02-05-03, 00-00-00, 12-34-00`

In other words, this regular expression matches two consecutive digits with the first digit either a zero or one, followed by a dash, followed by two consecutive digits, followed by a dash, ending with two consecutive digits. Be careful, as it may also include the following:

`00-05-03aaa, or 00-33-0345`

If you just wanted two consecutive digits at the end of a matching pattern, include a space. This is shown as follows in an example egrep expression:

`egrep '[0-1][0-9]-[0-9][0-9]-[0-9][0-9] ' some-file`

egrep is a utility that extends the capabilities of grep. See Chapter 4, "Using grep with Regular Expressions," for more on egrep.

`[^a-z]`

This expression would match the following:
`A, ..., Z, 0, ... 9, $, *, A*, AB, 1Z`

In other words, this would match any string that did not contain a lower-case letter anywhere in the string. Remember the caret metacharacter says that the characters in the character class are *not* to occur in the matching string. In this expression, this amounts to saying any character but a low-ercase letter is to occur in the matching string.

d) What is the result (microcosm) of the preceding regular expressions (from Question c) with the given matching lines? If a match occurs, write the starting position and the ending position within the matching substring where the match occurred. If a match does not occur, state at what position the matching process stops.

`[Ll]ab [1-9]`

Answer: This expression matches line I starting at position I and ending at 5.

`[0-1][0-9]-[0-9][0-9]-[0-9][0-9]`

This expression does not match anywhere; it stops at the end of the line.

```
[^a-z]
```

This expression matches all lines.

It matches when it encounters any character other than *a-z*. This happens at position 1 for all lines.

**LAB
2.1**

Consider the following regular expression:

```
grep a. some-file
```

The contents of `some-file` are as follows:

> **some-file:**
> **after the noon day sun**
> **sets into the distance**

e) What would the regular expression as given here yield if used with grep and the file `some-file`?

Answer: The expression would match both lines.

In the first line, grep would match the words *after* and *day*. Both of these words contain the letter *a* followed by a lowercase letter *a* through *z*. In the second line, grep would match *distance* for the same reason.

f) How would you obtain similar results if you did not have the hyphen metacharacter?

Answer: The expression would be written as follows:
```
grep a[abcdefghijklmnoprstuvwxyz] some-file
```

g) How would you obtain similar results if you did not have the hyphen and character class metacharacters?

Answer: The expression would be written as follows:
```
grep aa some-file
grep ab some-file
 . . .
grep az some-file
```

Remember that the characters inside the character class metacharacter are meant to declare that, at this character position in the pattern, any of the characters in the list within the character class metacharacter are the only characters allowed to occur in the matching substring. If they do not appear, then a match does not occur.

A character class as demonstrated by the example reduces the extra effort of having to invoke a utility multiple times to find out the result of each occurrence of a character within the character class. All that is needed is one invocation of the utility when using a character class.

Additionally, listing out 26 letters is extremely cumbersome. The hyphen metacharacter inside a character class metacharacter helps alleviate this problem. The hyphen metacharacter within a character class allows you to specify a range of characters to be included in the character class without having to list each value within the brackets explicitly. In the microcosm, an evaluating machine will look at the current character in the matching substring and, upon encountering a character class that contains a hyphen, will see whether the current character in the matching substring occurs within that range. In other words, in our example, it will see if the current character in the matching substring is greater than or equal to 1 and less than or equal to 9. If so, then it will continue matching characters; otherwise, no match occurs and the matching process stops.

2.1.2 ANSWERS

a) Are the following regular expressions legal? If so, can you guess what they would match?

`[w^]`

Answer: Yes, this expression is legal. This matches w or the caret followed by any other combination of ASCII characters. So it could match the following:
were, x^y, or ^y etc.

Why? Before we stated that any metacharacter loses its meaning within a character class. For example, [x*] would match xy, or x*y, or *h. The caret and hyphen are exceptions to this rule. The reason is that they have a function within the character class as we have seen throughout this chapter. Therefore, we need some mechanism to specify that we wish to use the literal meaning of the caret or hyphen metacharacter.

If you wish to retain the literal meaning of the caret, do not put the caret as the first character in the character class. In other words, the caret has functional meaning within a character class only if it is in the first position in the character class. Therefore, the following would create a character class with two characters only:

    [w^]

If you wish to retain the literal meaning of the hyphen, then make sure it is in the first or last position of the character class. A range needs a beginning value and an ending value. If it is first or last, then it cannot create a range and thus is interpreted literally.

    [-+]

This expression is valid for the reasons just stated.

The hyphen is the first character in the character class.

    [+-/]

Yes, this expression is also valid.

This expands to [+,-,/]. Each is continuous in the ASCII character set.

b) Can the following range be used with the hyphen?

    [4-7]

Answer: Yes.

This expands to [4567].

    [\t-\f]

Answer: No.

These overlap. The \t has a greater ASCII value than the \f.

c) Are the following legal?

    [-+] [0-9]

Answer: Yes. It is a two-character regular expression forming all combinations of the characters in the character classes.

    [+-*/] [0-9]

Yes, same as before, but with different characters in the character class. The first character class has four characters.

```
[!\t][0-9]
```

Yes, same as before, but with different characters in the character class. The first character class has three characters.

d) If so, what strings result (macrocosm)?

Answer: The following strings would result:
```
[-+][0-9]
{-0, ..., -9,+0, ..., +9}
[+-*/][0-9]
{-0, .., -9, +0, .., +9, *0, .., *9, .., /0, .., /9}
[!\t][0-9]
{!0, .., !9, \0, .., \9, t0, .., t9}
```

2.1.3 ANSWERS

a) Write a hyphen character class regular expression that matches the following date strings:

MM-DD-YY

MM/DD/YY

Answer: The following expression would work:
```
[0-1][0-9][-/][0-9][0-9][-/][0-9][0-9]
```

The first two consecutive characters come from the first two character classes [0-1][0-9]. Because a month is never greater than 19, we make the first character class [01]. Although this allows for illegal months of 13-19, it is better than allowing 20-99. The next character class allows for a month to be separated only by the two characters - and /, as we desire. The rest follows similarly.

b) How do you create a regular expression that matches only .CN1, ..., .CN9, while it simultaneously does not match .CN10 and greater?

Answer: The following expression would work:
```
"\.CN[1-9] "
```

The quotes are used so that we can match a space after the character class. This regular expression has four parts. The first part matches the period. A backslash is needed so that its metacharacter meaning is not used. The next part makes the literal characters CN together match the next two characters of matching substrings exactly. The third part uses a character class with a hyphen between 1 and 9 so that matching substrings .CN1 through .CN9 are matched. The last part uses a space so that only .CN1 through .CN9 are matched and not .CN10 or greater. Also if the substring .CN1 is part of a larger substring like .CN1AZ, then it will not match as desired.

**LAB
2.1**

Can you come up with a character class that matches just the two following strings?

.CN12
.CN1.1

Answer: "\.CN[2.][1]

We first create the largest literal that will include both matching strings, this is \.CN1. The next character differs in both, and the character class [2.] includes both characters while excluding all others. The next character class [1] includes a space and the digit one to satisfy the last part of both matching strings.

c) Write a regular expression that matches the following strings and only the following strings:

May dd, yy
may dd, yy

Answer: The following expression would work:
[Mm]ay [0-3][0-9], [0-9][0-9]

The first character class solves the upper-, lowercase m. The ay solves the rest of the string may or May. The space is used to separate the month may and the day value as desired. The day can be no larger than 39, because any day greater than 39 is not a valid day. Therefore, the character class combination [0-3][0-9] is used. The rest of the regular expression follows similarly as previous parts of the regular expression.

LAB 2.1 SELF-REVIEW QUESTIONS

In order to test your progress, you should be able to answer the following questions.

For each multiple-choice question, more than one choice may be correct or none at all. Be specific.

**LAB
2.1**

1) What is the character class range metacharacter?
   a) _____ {
   b) _____ [ ]
   c) _____ -
   d) _____ /
   e) _____ ^

2) What is the character class exclusion metacharacter?
   a) _____ -
   b) _____ [ ]
   c) _____ {
   d) _____ !
   e) _____ /

3) What does [a-z] match?
   a) _____ aB
   b) _____ a&
   c) _____ X&
   d) _____ x
   e) _____ UNIX

4) What does [a-z^] match
   a) _____ B
   b) _____ ad
   c) _____ UNIX
   d) _____ x^y

5) What does [1-3A-] match?
   a) _____ x^y
   b) _____ UNIX
   c) _____ aB
   d) _____ x-y
   e) _____ ABLE

6) What does `[w^-)]` match?
   a) _____x^y
   b) _____UNIX
   c) _____aB
   d) _____x-y
   e) _____ABLE

Quiz answers appear in Appendix A, Section 2.1.

LAB
2.1

CHAPTER 2

TᴇST YOUR THINKING

 The projects in this section are meant to have you utilize all of the skills that you have acquired throughout this chapter. The answers to these projects can be found at the companion Web site to this book, located at:

`http://www.phptr.com`

Visit the Web site periodically to share and discuss your answers.

In this section we explore some additional metacharacters. In each of the preceding metacharacters that we covered (*.?+\,^,$), the metacharacter allowed us to specify a single occurrence of a single character (.) or multiple occurrences (0, 1 or more) of a character (*, ?, +). In this section we explore metacharacters that allow us to specify exactly the number of occurrences of any single character. In addition, two of the metacharacters combine regular expressions into larger ones:

Table 2.1 ■ The Spanning, Vertical Bar, and Parentheses Metacharacters

Operator	Description	Usage
Spanning Metacharacter (\{,\})	`A\{n,m\}` matches exactly n, or less than m, occurrences of A in a matching substring `A\{n\}` matches exactly n occurrences of A in a matching substring `A\{n,\}` matches exactly n or more occurrences of A	Regular expression `a\{2,4\}` matches substrings aa, aaa, aaaa, and daal. In the substrings aa, and daal, the regular expression `a\{2,4\};` a occurs exactly twice in aa and daal. In the substring aaa the regular expression `a\{2,4\};` a occurs three times in aaa, In the substring aaaa, the regular expression `a\{2,4\};` a occurs four times in aaaa. Regular expression `a\{2\}` matches substrings aa, and daal, but does not match aaa and aaaa. In the substrings aa and daal the regular expression `a\{2\};` a occurs exactly twice in aa and daal. In the substrings aaa and aaaa the regular expression `a\{2\};` a does not occur exactly twice in aaa, and aaaa.

Table 2.1 ■ The Spanning, Vertical Bar, and Parentheses Metacharacters (Continued)

		Regular expression a\{2,\} matches aa, daal, aaa, and aaaa. In the substrings aa and daal the regular expression a\{2\}; a occurs exactly twice in aa and daal. In the substrings aaa and aaaa the regular expression a\{2\}; a occurs more than 2 times in aaa, and aaaa.
Vertical Bar Metacharacter (|)	r1|r2 matches regular expression r1 or r2	Regular expression a+|b+ matches a, aa, b, and bb. The regular expression a+|b+ matches either a+ or b+. In the substrings a, and aa the regular expression a+; a occurs more than once in a and aa. In the substrings b and bb the regular expression b+; b occurs more than once in b and bb.
Parentheses Metacharacer ()	(r1) matches any string matched by r1 (r1)(r2) matches any string matched by r1 followed immediately by r2 (r1)* matches zero or more occurrences of r1 (r1)+ matches one or more occurrences of r1 (r1)? matches exactly zero or one occurrences of r1	Regular expression (an)+ matches banana, and band. The regular expression (an)+ matches one or more occurrences of an. In the substring banana the regular expression (an)+; an occurs more than once (twice) in banana and once in band. Regular expression (a*)(l?) matches a, aa, daal, and dale. The regular expression (a*)(l?) matches a* and l?. In the substring a and aa the regular expression a*; a and aa occurs one and two times in a* followed immediately by zero times in l? (remember l? is zero or one occurrences. In the substring dale; the regular expression a* occurs one time in dale followed immediately by one occurrence of l in l?.

1) What do the following regular expressions match:

a) `Jazz|Rock|Blues`

b) `(The|That) (Red|Blue|Orange) (Dress|Ball)`

c) `(He)?r`

d) `Lab(oratorie)+s`

e) `[0-9]\{3\}-[0-9]\{2\}-[0-9]\{4\}`

f) `^(\+|-)?[0-9]+\.?[0-9]*$`

2) Evaluate each of the following pairs of expressions to determine if they are valid. If so, do the two always match the same strings?

   a) `Smith(Jones|Kelly)`   and   `(Smith|Jones)Kelly`

   b) `(Smith)(Kelly)*`   and   `SmithKelly*`

   c) `(a)*(bc)*`   and   `a*(bc)*`

   d) `a(bc)*`   and   `abc*`

   Given the following regular expression:

   `be+t`

   This expression correctly matches the following:

   `bet, beet`

   And it matches the following:

   `bt, and beeet`

3) Write a regular expression using the metacharacters in Table 2.1 to match bet and beet but not bt and beeet.

4) Construct a regular expression that will match the following

   a) Match a blank line

   b) Match an entire line

   c) Match a social security number

   d) Match a U.S. telephone number

   e) Match a digit

   f) Match a nondigit

   g) Match a zip code

   h) Match html codes (an html code has an opening angle bracket and closing angle bracket, <,>)

CHAPTER 3

WHAT IS GREP AND WHAT DOES IT DO?

 Grep can be a very powerful utility when used at the command line.

CHAPTER OBJECTIVE

In this chapter, you will learn about:

✓ Getting Started with Grep Page 52

This chapter discusses one of the most widely used UNIX utilities—grep. You will see that grep can be quite powerful when combined with the power of regular expressions. In this chapter, you learn in more detail about grep and all the varied applications for which you may use grep.

L A B   3.1

GETTING STARTED WITH GREP

LAB OBJECTIVES

After this Lab, you will be able to:

✓ Understand How Grep Is Invoked, and the Results of Invoking Grep

✓ Write Simple Grep Invocations

Like many UNIX utilities, such as sed, vi, and awk, grep has its roots on the original UNIX line editor ed. Grep is a utility that performs searches on user-supplied input files and prints matching lines. Hence, you can easily see that a line editor would use a search utility often to globally replace lines given a search string and a replacement string. This capability can be seen by the following command within a line editor:

```
:g/pattern/p
```

This command globally searches for a pattern and whenever it finds it, prints the line out that contained the pattern. This is the function of grep. If you think of the pattern as a regular expression, you can understand where grep obtained its name, (G)lobally search for (R)egular (E)xpression and, if found, (P)rint the entire line out for the line that contained the regular expression. Grep, however, is not invoked within the line editor, but outside it on the UNIX command line. Grep can be a powerful utility when used at the command line. Often, you may like to know whether a file contains a particular pattern. This pattern could be a pattern that somehow uniquely identifies the file. For example, often in a large programming environment, a particular variable may be declared and used in various files. Sometimes if you make a change to the declaration of the variable within the file, you might want to see where that variable is used in other files to avoid possible errors.

■ FOR EXAMPLE:

Grep can be used to print all lines in all files in which the variable is used, with the following command:

```
grep fullname *.c
```

Here, you see a typical command invocation of grep. In this example, three arguments are supplied to grep. The first is the name of the program to invoke (grep). The second argument is a regular expression. The last argument, which is optional, is a file or multiple files. In this case, a file is supplied, which can be more than one file if more than one file has the extension .c. In this example, the regular expression is the literal regular expression, fullname.

Suppose you were supplied with the following files:

main.c

```
main () {  FILE* infile;
   infile = fopen("Employees.dat");
   String fullname;
   String inputLine;
   while (!fgets(inputLine, infile)) {
   getName(fullname, inputLine, 0);
   printName(fullname); }
}
```

getName.c

```
getName(String& fullname, String Input, int pos) {
   while (  ( Input[pos] >= "a" && Input[pos] <= "z")
   ||
```

```
                            ( Input[pos] >= "A"  && Input[pos] <= "Z")
        ||                        Input[pos] == " ") {
                  fullname[pos] = Input[pos];
                  pos++;

        }

    }
```

The output of the example grep invocation would be as follows:

```
main.c String fullname;
main.c getName(fullname, inputLine, 0);
main.c printName(fullname);
getName.c: getName(String& fullname, String Input,
int pos) {
getName.c: fullname[pos] = Input[pos];
```

As you can see, each line that contains the literal regular expression is printed out in its entirety. If the pattern is not found in the specified file(s), then no output is produced.

Grep can also be used with metacharacter regular expressions, as in the following:

```
grep 'AVLm*' *.c
```

Here, the asterisk metacharacter is used. As you may have already noticed, the regular expression is quoted. The reason is to prevent the shell from interpreting the asterisk as its own special metacharacter. The function of the asterisk within the shell is the same as the functionality of the wild-card metacharacter that you saw in the previous chapters; that is, it is used to match any character. Therefore, whenever you construct metacharacter regular expressions, you should enclose the expression within quotes.

Without getting into the particulars, a quote is not always needed whenever a regular expression that contains a metacharacter is used within grep. It depends on the metacharacter; however, to play it safe and avoid errors, it is always best to quote a metacharacter regular expression.

As mentioned previously, the file that is supplied as the third argument is optional. If it is not supplied as an argument, then the input or source file is standard input. In this case, grep pauses while waiting for input from the keyboard until you type something. It stops processing lines when you enter ^d. The following invocation of grep shows that no third argument exists. Therefore, grep is supplied its input from standard input and it continues processing lines until ^d is input.

```
%grep 'ab*c'
abc is
abc is
ad is not
ac is
ac is
^d
%
```

**LAB
3.1**

Here, the % suggests that the grep command was entered at the command prompt. The last % prompt indicates that the command has completed. This happens when ^d is entered as the last line of input to grep. If the line that is input matches, then it is printed in its entirety; hence, the line is printed twice.

Grep, like most other UNIX utilities, returns an exit status that indicates whether it was successful in searching for the regular expression in the supplied file(s). This can be a useful result, in that it may be used to perform some other action based on the success or failure of the search.

■ FOR EXAMPLE:

Consider the following example:

```
%grep 'fullname' *.c
main.c String fullname;
main.c getName(fullname, inputLine, 0);
main.c printName(fullname);
getName.c: getName(String& fullname, String Input,
int pos) {
getName.c: fullname[pos] = Input[pos];
%echo $status
1
```

This example searches for `fullname` in every `.c` file. As shown previously, this invocation successfully finds the literal regular expression `fullname` in two files, as indicated by the output. The last command uses the c-shell shell variable status to print out the result of execution of the grep command. Status always contains the return value from execution of a UNIX program. Here it is 1, indicating that grep was successful in finding the pattern. Grep not only returns 0 (failure) or 1 (success), but it can also return a value of 2. A return status of 2 indicates that grep could not find the file that was supplied as an argument.

**LAB
3.1**

LAB 3.1 EXERCISES

3.1.1 UNDERSTAND HOW GREP IS INVOKED, AND THE RESULTS OF INVOKING GREP

Create the following file, and name it `dop.ini`:

```
[MIDI Cfg]
MidiIn0=TBS Pro External MIDI In 1
MidiOut0=TBS Pro Main Synth Out 1
MidiOut1=TBS Pro Daughter Synth Out 1
MidiOut2=TBS Pro External MIDI Out 1

[DigitalAudio]
EnableWaveSync=1

[PatchSetup]
TBS Pro Main Synth Out 1-1=Pinnacle Sound Banks

[Options]
MidiIsWave=0
RecMode=1

[XfDAGaCompr]
XFDACompres=15 10 50 100 -50
XFDANoiseGa=14 3 40 100 0
XFDALimiter=50 2 61 100 0
XFDAFlag=0
```

Execute the following invocations of grep at your terminal and record the output:

a) `grep Midi dop.ini`

_____

_____

b) `grep Synth dop.ini`

LAB
3.1

_____

_____

What output does each of the following grep commands produce?

c) `grep Enable dop.ini`

_____

_____

d) `grep XFDA dop.ini`

_____

_____

e) `grep TBS Pro dop.ini`

_____

_____

f) `grep compres dop.ini`

_____

_____

g) `grep 1 dop.ini`

_____

_____

3.1.2 WRITE SIMPLE GREP INVOCATIONS

Using the input file `dop.ini` from the preceding Exercise, write a grep command that will output each line that contains the following substrings:

a) `Out`

_____

b) `In`

_____

c) `Midi`, or `Synth`

_____

LAB 3.1 EXERCISE ANSWERS

This section gives you some suggested answers to the questions in Lab 3.1, with discussion related to those answers. Your answers may vary, but the most important thing is whether or not your answer works. Use this discussion to analyze differences between your answers and those presented here.

If you have alternative answers to the questions in this Exercise, you are encouraged to post your answers and discuss them at the companion Web site for this book, located at:

`http://www.phptr.com/phptrinteractive/`

3.1.1 ANSWERS

Using the dop.ini file that you created, execute the following invocations of
grep at your terminal and record the output:

a) grep Midi dop.ini

> *Answer: Each of the following answers match at the beginning of the line; they do not
> match the string MIDI in the line.*
> ```
> MidiIn0=TBS Pro External MIDI In 1
> MidiOut0=TBS Pro Main Synth Out 1
> MidiOut1=TBS Pro Daughter Synth Out 1
> MidiOut2=TBS Pro External MIDI Out 1
> MidiIsWave=0
> ```

Grep is case-sensitive, so an uppercase letter will not match its lowercase
equivalent, and a lowercase letter will not match its uppercase equivalent.

b) grep Synth dop.ini

> *Answer: In each of the following, the literal* Synth *is matched:*
> ```
> MidiOut0= TBS Pro Main Synth Out 1
> MidiOut1=TBS Pro Daughter Synth Out 1
> TBS Pro Main Synth Out 1-1=Pinnacle Sound Banks
> ```

What output does each of the following grep commands produce?

c) grep Enable dop.ini

> *Answer: The output is as follows:*
> **EnableWaveSync=1**

No other input line matches the literal Enable.

d) grep XFDA dop.ini

> *Answer: The output is as follows:*
> **XFDACompres=15 10 50 100 -50**
> **XFDANoiseGa=14 3 40 100 0**
> **XFDALimiter=50 2 61 100 0**
> **XFDAFlag=0**
> [XfDAGaCompr] Wouldn't be returned since the 'f' is
>   lowercase - MCB

e) `grep TBS Pro dop.ini`

Answer: The output is as follows:
Error: File name Pro does not exist

The metacharacter regular expression must be quoted because of the space between TBS and Pro; otherwise, grep will think that TBS is the regular expression and Pro and dop.ini are files to be used as input. Because no file Pro exists, an error is reported. It could have been written correctly as follows:

    grep 'TBS Pro' dop.ini

f) `grep compres dop.ini`

Answer: No output is produced; no line has the matching string compres.

Do not confuse this with matching Compres. The two are different. In the matching substring, the letter C is in uppercase and in the regular expression, the letter c is lowercase.

g) `grep 1 dop.ini`

Answer: This matches one or more occurrences of the number 1, as follows:
MidiIn0=TBS Pro External MIDI In 1
MidiOut0=TBS Pro Main Synth Out 1
MidiOut1=TBS Pro Daughter Synth Out 1
MidiOut2=TBS Pro External MIDI Out 1
EnableWaveSync=1
TBS Pro Main Synth Out 1-1=Pinnacle Sound Banks
RecMode=1
XFDACompres=15 10 50 100 -50
XFDANoiseGa=14 3 40 100 0
XFDALimiter=50 2 61 100 0

3.1.2 ANSWERS

Using the input file dop.ini from the preceding Exercise, write a grep command that will output each line that contains the following substrings:

a) Out

Answer: The command would be written as follows:
`grep Out dop.ini`

b) `In`

Answer: *The command would be written as follows:*
`grep In dop.ini`

c) `Midi` or `Synth`

Answer: *The command would be written as follows:*
`Grep Midi|Synth dop.ini`

In this grep invocation, the vertical bar metacharacter covered in regular expressions performs the *or* of the two literals.

LAB 3.1 SELF REVIEW QUESTIONS

In order to test your progress, you should be able to answer the following questions.
For each of the following multiple choice questions, zero, one, or more answers may be correct.

1) Where does input come from with the grep invocation `grep reg-exp`?
   a) _____`reg-exp`
   b) _____Standard input
   c) _____Nowhere—this invocation is an error

2) When does processing stop when grep is supplied input from standard input?
   a) _____When you enter `ctrl-d`
   b) _____When you enter `:stop`
   c) _____When you enter an empty line

Use the following input file called `some-file` for the next few questions:
```
The rain in spain
ah you know the rest
```

3) What is the output of `grep rain some-file`?
   a) _____`rain`
   b) _____`in spain`
   c) _____`rain in spain`
   d) _____`The rain in spain`
   e) _____no output
   f) _____an error

4) What is the output of `grep The* some-file`?
    a) _____The
    b) _____The rain
    c) _____The rain in spain
    d) _____no output
    e) _____an error

5) What is the output of `grep '[ih]ain' some-file`
    a) _____rain
    b) _____spain
    c) _____The rain in spain
    d) _____no output
    e) _____an error

Quiz answers appear in Appendix A, Section 5.1.

LAB
3.1

CHAPTER 3

TEST YOUR THINKING

 The projects in this section are meant to have you utilize all of the skills that you have acquired throughout this chapter. The answers to these projects can be found at the companion Web site to this book, located at:

```
http://www.phptr.com/phptrinteractive/
```

Visit the Web site periodically to share and discuss your answers.

So far, you have seen that the input to grep has been either from a file or standard input. This section covers grep receiving its input from a pipe. Whenever output from another UNIX utility or program results from executing that utility or program, if that utility or program additionally outputs to standard output, then the data may be used (piped) as input to another utility. In this section, the utility that will work on the piped data is grep—although, in fact, it could be used by any other UNIX utility or program that is able to receive data from standard output as input. Conversely, as you have already seen, grep writes its output to standard output. Therefore, the execution of a grep invocation can also be piped into other UNIX utilities and programs because it writes to standard output. Therefore, in this section, you will also see grep output piped into other UNIX utilities and programs. The pipe symbol in UNIX is the vertical bar (|).

Suppose you wanted to see all file names that were created on May 24. The following grep command used with a pipe, and entered at the command line solves that query.

```
ls -l | grep 'May 24'
```

The pipe symbol, |, is used so that grep may work on the output produced by `ls -l` (output produces all files, along with the files attributes, in the current working directory). Grep takes this input and uses the regular expression `'May 24'` to search for that pattern in the output produced by `ls -l`. Finally, all lines that contain this pattern are produced as output. Notice that the quotes are needed, otherwise grep will think that "May" is the pattern and 24 is a file that is to be used as input, and an error will be produced.

If `ls -l` produced as output

```
drwxrwxr-x  2  patsis  patsis 1024   May 12 11:33 awk
-rw-r--r--  1  root    root    360    May 24 16:43 Xrootenv.0
-rw-r--r--  1  root    root   81779 May 24 16:43 fvwmrca00311
-rw-r--r--  1  root    root    4960  Feb 10 20:35 install.log
```

Then the final output produced by the command `ls -1 | grep 'May 24'` would produce

```
-rw-r--r--  1  root    root    360    May 24 16:43 Xrootenv.0
-rw-r--r--  1  root    root   81779 May 24 16:43 fvwmrca00311
```

grep may also use a pipe to produce output for another utility or program to use as input. This is demonstrated using the dop.ini file in Lab 3.1 Exercises, grep, a pipe, and the `wc -1` program:

`grep '^Midi' dop.ini | wc -1`

The output is thus as follows:

5

The `wc` command counts the number of characters, words, and lines that were input to the command. The `-1` option specifies that only input lines are to be counted. Therefore, because the regular expression `'^Midi'` is supplied to grep, the output is the following five lines:

```
MidiIn0=TBS Pro External MIDI In 1
MidiOut0=TBS Pro Main Synth Out 1
MidiOut1=TBS Pro Daughter Synth Out 1
MidiOut2=TBS Pro External MIDI Out 1
MidiIsWave=0
```

This is input to `wc -1` and the number 5 is printed out.

1) Use the following output produced from executing `ls -1` for a, b, and c of this project:

```
drwxrwxr-x  2     patsis    patsis    1024   May 12 11:33 awk
-rw-r--r--  1     root      root       360    May 24 16:43 Xrootenv.0
-rw-r--r--  1     root      root     81779 May 24 16:43
       fvwmrca00311
-rwxrwxrwx  2     patsis    patsis   99945  May 12 11:45 helper
-rw-r--r--  1     root      root      4960   Feb 10 20:35 install.log
```

a) Find all files owned by patsis.

b) Find all files produced on May 12.

c) Find all files in which the size is greater than 900 but less than 9999.

2) Enter the following query:
```
ls -l | grep '-rw......' >owner-rw
```

a) What is the result?

3) Describe the results of each of the following:

a) `diff file1 file2 | grep patsis`

b) `who | grep patsis`

4) Write a pipe that finds and counts all the different cities in an address file with the following form:
> **First Name Last Name**
> **Address**
> **City, State, Zip**

States are represented by the standard two-letter abbreviation.

5) Write a pipe that finds all unique zip codes and sorts them.

For the next project, use the following file called `test-data`, which is broken down as last name, first name, city, state, brand name, and amount of orders:

```
Smith, John Shrewsbury MA Levinson 20
Craig, Rose Boston MA Krell 12
Potts, Bill Andover MA Apogee 11
Harolds, Jim Brighton MA Theil 5
Ludwig, Rosa Everton MA Avalon 2
Jackson, Bob Cambridge MA Melos 14
Killington, George Boston, PA Altis 9
```

6) Create a grep command that would

a) Find all people who have ordered more than 10 units of any item.

b) Find all people who live in Boston, MA.

c) Find all last names that start with L or more.

d) Find all orders whose brand name is Avalon or who have orders more than 9.

CHAPTER 4

USING GREP WITH REGULAR EXPRESSIONS

 If you thought grep was powerful at the command line, you ain't seen nuthin' yet.

CHAPTER OBJECTIVES

In this chapter, you will learn about:

E arlier in this book, we went over regular expressions but did not see many examples of regular expressions used within other UNIX utilities. This chapter explores regular expressions as they are commonly used within grep. With the power of regular expressions, you are able to express more precisely what you would like to search for in files. As you will see, regular expressions used within grep enable you to perform a variety of different searches.

L A B   4.1

REGULAR
EXPRESSIONS
AND GREP

LAB OBJECTIVES

After this Lab, you will be able to:

✓ Understand the Results of Using Grep with Regular
  Expressions
✓ Understand How to Write Regular Expressions with
  Grep

Throughout this chapter, you will work on the following files. The first is a file that is created as a result of a user submitting a fill-in form from a Web HTML document. It appears as follows:

```
name: inji Nakanomi
email: nakanomi@nipponpaint.co
imsNews: yesSub
narc: yesUnsub
internat: yesSub
spring: yesSub
```

```
scan: yesUnsub
narcOrg: yesSub
narcStab: yesUnsub
narcEmulsion: yesSub
internatOrg: yesSub
internatStab: yesUnsub
internatPigment: yesUnsub
springPigment: yesUnsub
springStab: yesUnsub
springEmulsion: yesUnsub
springAdhesives: yesUnsub
name: Debbie Spartis
email: ds@lexmark.com
scan: yesSub
name: Debbie Berlin
email: db@lexmark.com
spring: yesSub
```

The second file is a typical log file that logs user accesses to Web pages. The first field of information is the Internet domain of the user that accessed the page. The second contains the time and date of the access. The third is the method that the user requested when accessing the page. The fourth is the Web page they requested. The last field contains the version of HTTP that was used to make the request.

```
falgate.fujitsu.com.au - - [29/May/1998:00:02:42 -
0400] "GET /springPigDailySchedule.htm HTTP/1.0" 200
6153

falgate.fujitsu.com.au - - [29/May/1998:00:02:49 -
0400] "GET /bg.gif HTTP/1.0" 200 2586 "http://
www.ims-np.org/springPigDailySchedule.htm"

ts006p3.tlv.netvision.net.il - - [29/June/
1998:01:55:32 -0400] "GET /icdegprg.htm HTTP/1.0"
404 165 "http://av.yahoo.com/bin/query?p=polyethyl-
ene+stabilization&hc=0&hs=0"
```

```
p22.netwide.net - - [29/May/1998:02:03:02 -0400]
"PUT /Petes HTTP/1.0" 301 181 "http://tape-
tracker.com/traderindex/SearchResultsSummary.asp"

gateway.amoco.co.uk - - [29/May/1998:04:00:09 -0400]
"GET / HTTP/1.0" 200 4744

gateway.amoco.co.uk - - [29/May/1998:04:00:10 -0400]
"GET /ConfBkgrd.gif HTTP/1.0" 304 - "http://www.ims-
np.org/"

me-mk-01.jrc.nl - - [29/May/1998:05:14:43 -0400]
"GET /mainContactInfo.htm HTTP/1.0" 200 6378 "http:/
/www.hotbot.com/?_v=2&MT=adhesion+science+profes-
sor&chk=on"

electra03.ciens.ucv.ve - - [29/May/1998:09:35:36 -
0400] "GET /top.gif HTTP/1.0" 200 2329 "http://ims-
np.org/"

electra03.ciens.ucv.ve - - [29/May/1998:09:35:39 -
0400] "GET /greenHorizontalLine.gif HTTP/1.0" 200 89
"http://ims-np.org/"
```

LAB 4.1

The easiest regular expressions to use with grep are literal regular expressions. Suppose that you could not remember the last name of a person in the mailing list file, but you knew their first name. Although multiple names could show up for the first name, you have a vague idea of the last name. You could run the following grep program to find his/her name:

```
grep Debbie mailList
```

The result of executing this is:

```
name: Debbie Spartis
name: Debbie Berlin
```

This obviously returns all lines that contain the literal regular expression "Debbie." From this output, you could deduce the last name you are trying to find.

Now suppose that you want to print all names that are contained within the `mailList` file. You could accomplish this printout with the following grep invocation:

```
grep '^name' mailList
```

The output after execution of this grep command is:

```
name: inji Nakanomi
name: Debbie Spartis
name: Debbie Berlin
```

LAB 4.1

If you recall, the caret metacharacter outside a character class states that the matching must start from the very beginning of the input line. Therefore, the literal characters following the caret metacharacter must occur at the very beginning of the line. If the literal regular expression occurs elsewhere on the line, it will not match. Therefore, in both output lines, the literal characters name occur at the very beginning of each input line. If you notice in the regular expression written previously, the quotes are not necessary. The only time the quotes are necessary is when the character is both a metacharacter of a regular expression and has special meaning within the UNIX shell. However, a good idea is to quote the regular expression just to play it safe, avoid errors, and not have to worry whether a metacharacter has special meaning to the shell also. If it is not understood already, when the shell encounters the quote, it ignores interpreting what is inside the quotes and passes the string as a whole to the program that has been selected by the user to run.

LAB 4.1 EXERCISES

4.1.1 UNDERSTAND THE RESULTS OF USING GREP WITH REGULAR EXPRESSIONS

Use the following file called `input_file` for the first three questions in this Exercise:

LAB 4.1

```
>> lack of power supply. And after listening to the
   tape today, there is an
>> audible difference when using the SBM-1 as opposed
   to without using the
>> SBM-1. The sound is much cleaner, and more crisp,
   and frequency response is
>> much fuller, and powerful in clarity.
>>
>Sounds like a good comparison but it's a bummer when
 you run out of power.
>I've heard you can run both the SBM-1 & a deck off an
 Eco Charge lead acid
>battery. Can you also run a Beyer MV-100 from the
 same Eco Charge or are
>the voltages different?

Nope, the Beyer expects 24v and, as far as I know,
 there isn't an
alternative to the environmentally unfriendly, dual
 9v consumption. I
really hate burning two 9v batteries every time I go
 out. It's such a
waste. I made several attempts (as have others I know)
 to have an
external power supply created for this thing, but,
 from all accounts so
far, it just isn't feasible.
```

What is the result of each of the following invocations of grep?

a) grep 24v input_file

_____

_____

b) egrep Beyer|SBM input_file

_____

_____

c) grep 'Eco Charge' input_file

_____

LAB
4.1

_____

Use the following input file `tape_brand` to answer the next three questions in this Exercise:

```
KAO Gold:      10      $4.00       $40.00
ADS HHS        60      $2.00       $120.00
Sony HHS       50      $5.00       $250.00
Maxell DDS     20      $2.00       $40.00
Maxell ADS     15      $4.00       $60.00
Ampex DDS      60      $5.00       $300.00
Panasonic      50      $3.95       $197.50
```

What is the result of each of the following invocations of grep?

d) grep 5 tape_brand

_____

_____

e) grep '[0-9]\{3,\}\.' tape_brand

_____

_____

f) `egrep '[0-4]?\.  +$[0-9]\{3.\}\.|[0-9]\{3,\}\.'`
`tape_brand`

4.1.2 UNDERSTAND HOW TO WRITE REGULAR EXPRESSIONS WITH GREP

g) Write a regular expression that will find all occurrences of `Max-ell` in the file tape_brand from Exercise 4.1.1.

---

h) Write a regular expression that will find all occurrences of ADS (audio data storage), but not companies with the name ADS, in the file tape_brand from Exercise 4.1.1.

---

i) Write a regular expression that will find all occurrences of `>>` in the file input_file from Exercise 4.1.1.

LAB 4.1 EXERCISE ANSWERS

This section gives you some suggested answers to the questions in Lab 4.1, with discussion related to those answers. Your answers may vary, but the most important thing is whether or not your answer works. Use this discussion to analyze differences between your answers and those presented here.

If you have alternative answers to the questions in this Exercise, you are encouraged to post your answers and discuss them at the companion Web site for this book, located at:

`http://www.phptr.com/phptrinteractive/`

4.1.1 ANSWERS

What is the result of each of the following invocations of grep?

a) `grep 24v input_file`

Answer: *The following line is the only line that contains the literal* `24v`:
```
Nope, the Beyer expects 24v and, as far as I know,
there isn't an
```

b) `egrep Beyer|SBM input_file`

Answer: *The following strings are the only three lines that contain the literals* `SBM` *or* `Beyer`:
```
>> audible difference when using the SBM-1 as
opposed to without using the
>battery. Can you also run a Beyer MV-100 from the
same Eco Charge or are
Nope, the Beyer expects 24v and, as far as I know,
there isn't an
```

LAB
4.1

c) `grep 'Eco Charge' input_file`

Answer: *Because the string is quoted, the literal* `Eco  Charge` *is searched for in* `input_file`. *The following two lines are the only ones that contain the literal* `Eco Charge`:
```
>I've heard you can run both the SBM-1 & a deck off
an Eco Charge lead acid
>battery. Can you also run a Beyer MV-100 from the
same Eco Charge or are
```

What is the result of each of the following invocations of grep?

d) `grep 5 tape_brand`

Answer: *This invocation searches for all lines that contain the literal character* `five`. *All of the following lines contain the literal* `five`:
```
Sony HHS      50      $5.00     $250.00
Maxell DDS    20      $2.00     $40.00
Maxell ADS    15      $4.00     $60.00
Ampex DDS     60      $5.00     $300.00
```

```
Panasonic     50     $3.95    $197.50
```

e) grep `'[0-9]\{3,\}\.'` tape_brand

*Answer: This regular expression searches for a span of three or more (\ {3, \ })
numbers zero through nine ([0-9]), in any combination that is followed by a decimal
point (\ .). In other words, all lines that contain a number greater than 100. All of the
following lines satisfy this criteria:*

```
ADS HHS        60     $2.00    $120.00
Sony HHS       50     $5.00    $250.00
Ampex DDS      60     $5.00    $300.00
Panasonic      50     $3.95    $197.50
```

f) egrep `'[0-4]?\.+$[0-9]\{3.\}\.|[0-9]\{3,\}'` tape_brand

*Answer: This regular expression searches for zero or one numbers zero through four
([0-4] ?), followed by a decimal point (\ .), followed by any number of additional
characters (. *), eventually leading to three or more numbers ([0-9] \ {3, \ }). In
other words, all lines that contain a number zero through four and are also followed by
a number greater than 100. Both of the following lines satisfy this criteria:*

```
ADS HHS        60     $2.00    $120.00
Panasonic      50     $3.95    $197.50
```

4.1.2 ANSWERS

a) Write a regular expression that will find all occurrences of Maxell in
the file tape_brand from Exercise 4.1.1.

Answer: The expression is as follows:
grep Maxell tape_brand

When searching for the literal expression Maxell, no metacharacters are
necessary and no quote is needed.

b) Write a regular expression that will find all occurrences of ADS (audio
data storage), but not companies with the name ADS, in the file
tape_brand from Exercise 4.1.1.

Answer: The expression is as follows:
grep ` ADS' tape_brand

The space as the first character in the regular expression will not match the company name ADS, because the company name ADS always starts at the beginning of the line and cannot match the space.

c) Write a regular expression that will find all occurrences of >> in the file `input_file` from Exercise 4.1.1.

Answer: The expression is as follows:
```
grep '>>' input_file
```

You must quote this grep invocation. The string >> has special meaning to the shell.

LAB 4.1 SELF-REVIEW QUESTIONS

In order to test your progress, you should be able to answer the following questions.

For each of the following multiple choice questions, one or more answers may be correct.

1) Given the grep expression grep 'A\{2\}', which of the following matching patterns matches?
   a) _____No match; it is an error
   b) _____AA
   c) _____AAA
   d) _____AABB

2) The only time that quotes are necessary within a regular expression is when the quoted character is not a metacharacter.
   a) _____True
   b) _____False

3) Given the grep expression `grep '^address' address_book`, which of the following results would you expect?
   a) _____All lines that contain the word `address` in the file `address_book`
   b) _____All lines that contain the word `address` at the very beginning of the line in the file `address_book`
   c) _____All lines that contain the word `address` at the very end of the line in the file `address_book`
   d) _____Nothing; this is an invalid expression

4) Grep recognizes all except which of the following metacharacters?
   a) _____Range metacharacter `\{n,m\}`
   b) _____Positional dollar sign metacharacter `$`
   c) _____Backslash metacharacter `\`
   d) _____Question mark metacharacter `?`
   e) _____Grep recognizes all metacharacters

Quiz answers appear in Appendix A, Section 4.1.

**LAB
4.1**

L A B   4.2

FGREP AND EGREP

**LAB
4.2**

> ## LAB OBJECTIVE
>
> After this Lab, you will be able to:
> ✓ Understand When to Use Grep, Egrep, and Fgrep
>   and the Results of Using Them

So far in the preceding chapters, we have talked many times about regular expressions. In earlier chapters on regular expressions, you saw tables that listed metacharacters and extended metacharacters, which are as follows:

Metacharacters (as used by sed and grep)

- Period metacharacter .
- Asterisk metacharacter *
- Character class metacharacter [ ]
- Positional caret metacharacter ^
- Positional dollar sign metacharacter $
- Range metacharacter \{n,m\}
- Backslash metacharacter \

Extended Metacharacters (as used by egrep and awk)

- Plus metacharacter +
- Question mark metacharacter ?
- Vertical bar metacharacter |
- Parentheses metacharacter ()
- Range metacharacters {n.m}

You may notice that a metacharacter is missing from this list—the anchor metacharacter. The reason the anchor metacharacter hasn't been discussed is that it is not really a metacharacter. It is used only within grep; it is not included within sed, awk, and egrep, and therefore has no equivalent in sed, awk, and egrep. The anchor metacharacter is discussed in Lab 4.3.

In Chapter 3, "What Is Grep and What Does It Do?," none of the examples or exercises used any extended metacharacters with the regular expressions that we constructed. The reason is that grep does not recognize the extended metacharacters. So the following grep command would generate an error:

```
grep 'a+' some-file
```

In this chapter, we talk about two variations of grep called egrep and fgrep. Both perform the same fundamental operations as grep—searching and printing—but differ in their capabilities. Egrep extends the metacharacter operators and fgrep reduces them. Therefore, the names *extended grep* and *fast grep* are used to describe the two grep variations.

■ FOR EXAMPLE:

To correctly run the preceding grep command, you would use the following:

```
egrep 'a+' some-file
```

Therefore, anytime you wish to use any of the extended metacharacters listed previously, you must use egrep. If egrep is not available for some reason, then you can also try the following:

```
grep -e 'a+' some-file
```

The -e option to grep says to grep that you are using an extended metacharacter in your regular expression. The -e option and egrep yield the same results. In this book, we will use egrep anytime we wish to use the extended metacharacters.

Fgrep, sometimes called fast grep or fixed grep, does not recognize any regular expressions. Therefore, any metacharacter will be taken literally.

LAB
4.2

■ *FOR EXAMPLE:*

Consider the following example:

```
fgrep 3+4 input_file
```

This will search for the string "3+4"; the plus metacharacter is not recognized in fgrep. Fgrep obfuscates the need for the backslash metacharacter. It is used when you know you do not need any metacharacters.

Suppose that you want to know all accesses during the month of June from the Web output log file given in Lab 4.1. In addition, you cannot recall the format of a date field. More specifically, does a month begin with a digit, or is the name of the month spelled out? Does the month contain a prefixed zero for months that do not have two digits? Are the day, month, and year separated by slashes or dashes? The following egrep and regular expression invocation executes the preceding query:

```
egrep '[/-][0-1]?[0-9]|[J,j]une' logFile
```

The result would be as follows:

```
ts006p3.tlv.netvision.net.il - - [29/June/
1998:01:55:32 -0400] "GET /icdegprg.htm HTTP/1.0"
404 165 "http://av.yahoo.com/bin/query?p=polyethyl-
ene+stabilization&hc=0&hs=0"
```

The pattern June is found in the output line.

**LAB
4.2**

LAB 4.2 EXERCISES

4.2.1 UNDERSTAND WHEN TO USE GREP, EGREP, AND FGREP AND THE RESULTS OF USING THEM

What is the result of the following commands?

a) grep 'peter?' some-file

b) egrep '[0-9]\{3\}' some-file

---

c) egrep 'Pete' some-file

---

d) fgrep '?' some-file

---

e) grep 'peter*' some-file

LAB 4.2 EXERCISE ANSWERS

This section gives you some suggested answers to the questions in Lab 4.2, with discussion related to those answers. Your answers may vary, but the most important thing is whether or not your answer works. Use this discussion to analyze differences between your answers and those presented here.

If you have alternative answers to the questions in this Exercise, you are encouraged to post your answers and discuss them at the companion Web site for this book, located at:

http://www.phptr.com/phptrinteractive/

4.2.1 ANSWERS

What is the result of the following commands?

a) grep 'peter?' some-file

Answer: This results in an error.

The question mark metacharacter is an extended metacharacter, which grep doesn't recognize, so egrep must be used.

b) `egrep '[0-9]\{3\}' some-file`

Answer: This results in an error.

The \{, \} range metacharacter is not recognized by egrep but is recognized by grep. Therefore, grep must be used.

c) `egrep 'Pete' some-file`

Answer: This results in all lines containing the pattern Pete as output.

You do not need to use egrep only when an extended metacharacter is used. Egrep still works with a literal expression.

d) `fgrep '?' some-file`

Answer: This results in all lines containing the question mark to be output.

Fgrep will interpret any character that it encounters literally. Therefore, it interprets the question mark not as a metacharacter but as a literal.

**LAB
4.2**

e) `grep 'peter*' some-file`

Answer: This results in all lines containing `pete` *or* `pete` *with the* `r` *occurring one or more times.*

Because the asterisk is not an extended metacharacter, the asterisk correctly performs its function when used with grep.

LAB 4.2 SELF-REVIEW QUESTIONS

In order to test your progress, you should be able to answer the following questions.
For each of the following multiple choice questions, one or more answers may be correct.

1) Given the regular expression, A?, which grep version can you use?
    a) _____None
    b) _____grep
    c) _____egrep
    d) _____fgrep

2) Given the regular expression, A*, which grep version can you use?

    a) _____None

    b) _____grep

    c) _____egrep

    d) _____fgrep

3) Given the egrep expression, egrep `A.`, which of the following matching patterns matches?

    a) _____No match; it is an error

    b) _____AB

    c) _____A

    d) _____ABBB

4) The expression fgrep `3+4` input_file and the expression grep -f `3+4` input_file are equivalent.

    a) _____True

    b) _____False

Quiz answers appear in Appendix A, Section 4.2.

**LAB
4.2**

LAB 4.3

USING THE ANCHOR METACHARACTER

LAB OBJECTIVE

After this Lab, you will be able to:

✓ Understand How the Anchor Metacharacter Is Used with Grep

The anchor metacharacter regular expression matches the word within the brackets exactly. It is denoted by the \< and \> characters. The word that you wish to match exactly is contained within the two metacharacter pairs.

■ *FOR EXAMPLE:*

Consider the following expression:

```
grep '\<PUT\>' logFile
```

This would return the following:

```
p22.netwide.net - - [29/May/1998:02:03:02 -0400]
"PUT /Petes HTTP/1.0" 301 181 "http://tape-
tracker.com/traderindex/SearchResultsSummary.asp"
```

However, suppose that you had the following anchor regular expression:

```
grep '\<spring\>' logFile
```

Additionally, suppose that the following line was encountered:

```
falgate.fujitsu.com.au - - [29/May/1998:00:02:49 -
0400] "GET /bg.gif HTTP/1.0" 200 2586 "http://
www.ims-np.org/springPigDailySchedule.htm"
```

This would not match. The reason is that although the string spring does occur within the input line, it is not a word (i.e., it is contained within the larger word springPigDailySchedule). The question remains: "How does the regular expression determine what is a word?" A word as it pertains to the anchor metacharacter is any text that is ended with a space or a punctuation mark. Therefore, because the word springPigDaily-Schedule ends with a period, it is considered a word. However, in our example, this does not match exactly the word spring that we wish to match. The word may occur anywhere in the line (i.e., the beginning of the line, the end of the line, or in between), but it must directly be followed by either a space or a punctuation mark for a match to occur.

The anchor metacharacter regular expression may contain other regular expression metacharacters between the anchors.

LAB 4.3 EXERCISES

4.3.1 UNDERSTAND HOW THE ANCHOR METACHARACTER IS USED WITH GREP

a) Rewrite the grep invocation that you wrote for Exercise 4.1.2, question a, which finds all occurrences of Maxell, so that it also precludes that string from occurring anywhere else but at the beginning of the input line.

_____

_____

What is the result of the following invocations of grep with the following anchors on the tape_brand file from Exercise 4.1.1?

b) `grep '\<$5.00\>' tape_brand`

_____

_____

c) `grep '\<[0-9]\{3\}\.00\>' tape_brand`

_____

_____

LAB 4.3 EXERCISE ANSWERS

This section gives you some suggested answers to the questions in Lab 6.3, with discussion related to those answers. Your answers may vary, but the most important thing is whether or not your answer works. Use this discussion to analyze differences between your answers and those presented here.

If you have alternative answers to the questions in this Exercise, you are encouraged to post your answers and discuss them at the companion Web site for this book, located at:

`http://www.phptr.com/phptrinteractive/`

**LAB
4.3**

4.3.1 ANSWERS

a) Rewrite the grep invocation that you wrote for Exercise 4.1.2, Question a, which finds all occurrences of `Maxell`, so that it also precludes that string from occurring anywhere else but at the beginning of the input line.

Answer: The invocation would be as follows:
`grep '^\<Maxell\>' tape_brand`

The caret is used to make sure that the string following the caret appears nowhere else but at the beginning of the line. The anchor is used to make sure that the string following the caret is the word Maxell.

What is the result of the following invocation of grep with the following anchors on the `tape_brand` file from Exercise 4.1.1?

b)   `grep '\<$5.00\>' tape_brand`

Answer: This invocation matches any line that contains the word $5.00. (Remember the definition of a word as it pertains to an anchor?)

Sony HHS	**50**	**$5.00**	**$250.00**
Ampex DDS	**60**	**$5.00**	**$300.00**

c)   `grep '\<[0-9]\{3\}\.00\>' tape_brand`

Answer: This invocation matches any line that contains a word that consists of exactly three numbers ([0-9]\{3\}), followed by a period (\.) and ending with at least two zeros after the period. In other words, any word that is greater than 100 and less than 999.

ADS HHS	**60**	**$2.00**	**$120.00**
Sony HHS	**50**	**$5.00**	**$250.00**
Ampex DDS	**60**	**$5.00**	**$300.00**
Panasonic	**50**	**$3.95**	**$197.50**

LAB 4.3 SELF-REVIEW QUESTIONS

In order to test your progress, you should be able to answer the following questions.

For each of the following multiple choice questions, one or more answers may be correct.

1) Given the grep expression, `grep '\<[0-9]\{3\}\>'`, which of the following matching patterns matches?
   a) _____No match; it is an error
   b) _____1233
   c) _____12
   d) _____123

2) Given the egrep expression, `egrep '\<[0-9]\{3\}\>'`, which of the following matching patterns matches?
   a) _____No match; it is an error
   b) _____1233
   c) _____12
   d) _____123

3) Regular expression metacharacters within the anchor tags will result in an error.
   a) _____True
   b) _____False

Quiz answers appear in Appendix A, Section 4.3.

C H A P T E R   4

TEST YOUR THINKING

The projects in this section are meant to have you utilize all of the skills that you have acquired throughout this chapter. The answers to these projects can be found at the companion Web site to this book, located at:

```
http://www.phptr.com
```

Visit the Web site periodically to share and discuss your answers.

1) Do the following grep commands produce the same output? Explain why or why not.

```
grep '[0-9][0-9[0-9]-[0-9][0-9][0-9]' some-file
grep '[0-9]\{3\}-[0-9]\{3\}' some-file
```

If the answer is not immediately apparent try the commands with sample input.

Get a text document and run the following command on it

```
grep '[?:.!]' some-file
```

2) What does it do?

A dependency in a makefile has the following form:

```
?.o
```

(where the question mark is some letter denoting a file).

3) Try obtaining a makefile and see all the dependency rules that involve a .c file or an .o file:

If you cannot find a makefile, then find a .c file. A header file in a .c file will look like either of the following:

```
<some-header-file.h>
"some-header-file.h"
```

4)   Find all the header files included in that file.

5)   Find all uppercase letters in a file.

In the rest of this section we will explore grep command options. The grep command options are outlined in Table 4.1.

Table 4.1 ■ Examples of Grep Command Options

Grep Command	Description
grep -w 'reg-exp' file	Prints all lines containing word reg-exp
grep -s 'reg-exp' file	Finds lines containing reg-exp but does not print them
grep -v 'reg-exp' file	Prints all lines that do not contain reg-exp
grep -i 'reg-exp' file	Prints all lines containing reg-exp regardless of case
grep -n 'reg-exp' file	Prints line and line numbers in file that match reg-exp
grep -c 'reg-exp' file	Prints a count of the number of lines that contained reg-exp
grep -l 'reg-exp' file1 file2	Prints all filenames that contain reg-exp

For the following questions we will use a file called `conf.data` which contains reg-istration information for various conferences:

```
Smith      Adhesions     700    200    081098    Digital
Jones      Coatings      900      0    081298    Dow
Phillips   Stabilizers   850    100    080198    Dupont
Kenny      Coatings      900    450    072898    Dow
Patsis     Adhesions     700    350    080198    IBM
Harris     Adhesions     700      0    081198    Digital
Gorge      Stabilizers   850      0    081098    Dupont
Mack       Coatings      900    100    080398    Shell
Jones      Coatings      900      0    080298    Texaco
Denny      Stabilizers   850    200    072998    Chrysler
Pierce     Adhesions     700      0    080398    IBM
```

Jackson	Resins	800	200	080598	Dupont
Taylor	Adhesions	700	0	073098	PPG
Donaldson	Stabilizers	850	200	080998	Dow
Knuth	Resins	800	0	080698	Shell
Harrison	Resins	800	800	080198	Texaco
Patterson	Coatings	900	450	072898	IBM
Aaron	Stabilizers	850	0	081298	Chrysler
Martin	Resins	800	0	081198	PPG
Federicks	Stabilizers	850	100	080898	Dupont
Quinn	Resins	800	500	080298	Dow
Bostic	Coatings	900	900	080198	Digital
Craig	Adhesions	700	0	080598	IBM
Small	Resins	800	0	080998	Dupont

Each column of data in the preceding file represents the following, respectively:

Registered Name

Conference Name

Cost of Conference

Amount Due

Registration Date

Company Name

6) What is the result of each of the following grep invocations:

a) `grep -i coatings conf.data`

b) `grep -i digitaL conf.data`

c) `grep -c coatings conf.data`

d) `grep -c Adhesions conf.data`

e) `grep -l Chrysler conf.data`

f) `grep -n Mack conf.data`

g) `grep -v Resins conf.data`

h) `grep -ic coatings conf.data`

i) `grep -w Chrysler conf.data`

7) Write a grep expression that counts the number of lines that contain conferences in which the fee is 900.

8) Write a grep expression that finds all uppercase or lowercase occurrences of the string `Patsis`.

9) Write a grep expression that finds all lines that do not contain the word `IBM`.

10) Write a grep expression that finds and counts all occurrences of fees that are 700.

CHAPTER 5

INTRODUCTION TO SED

 He sed. She sed. We all sed. Use sed.

CHAPTER OBJECTIVE

In this chapter, you will learn about:

✓ Getting Started with Sed   Page 94

The utilities that I will talk about in the ensuing chapters, sed and awk, are both different from grep in that you can write scripts that perform calculations and produce output. Scripts are sequences of instructions that instruct the computer to perform some collective action. In addition, sed, unlike grep, does not necessarily use only regular expressions as arguments. Sed, as we will see, can perform several text manipulations within a particular line of text. Both sed and grep are UNIX filters. A UNIX filter is any program or utility that reads its input from standard input, does some processing on it, and writes its result to standard output.

Sed originates and has as its descendent the UNIX editor ed. Like all editors, it can perform a variety of functions on the file, such as searching and replacing, inserting and appending text. Rather than performing these functions within the editor, one may wish to invoke these functions outside an editor. If you know that you have a file that you created and edited earlier, to have to invoke the editor would be a nuisance, and then wait for it to load just to replace the text U.S. with United States. A much more convenient approach would be to execute a program telling the program to search for all occurrences of a string and replace it with another string. This is the main purpose and use of sed. Of course, as we will see, this is not the only use of sed. Sed is robust enough to provide other functionality as well.

L A B   5.1

GETTING STARTED
WITH SED

LAB OBJECTIVES

After this Lab, you will be able to:

✓ Understand Simple Substitutions

✓ Understand the Sed Pattern Space

For this Lab, we will use a file similar to the conf.data file that we used in Chapter 4, Test Your Thinking, this file is named conf2.data.

**LAB
5.1**

Smith	Adhesions	700	200	081098	Digital
Jones	Coatings	900	0	081298	Dow
Phillips	Stabilizers	850	100	080198	Dupont
Kenny	Coatings	900	450	072898	Dow
Patsis	Adhesions	700	350	080198	IBM
Harris	Adhesions	700	0	081198	Digital
Gorge	Stabilizers	850	0	081098	Dupont
Mack	Coatings	900	100	080398	Shell
Jones	Coatings	900	0	080298	Texaco
Denny	Stabilizers	850	200	072998	Chrysler
Pierce	Adhesions	700	0	080398	IBM
Jackson	Resins	800	200	080598	Dupont

The easiest and one of the most often used sed commands is the substitution command. The substitution command in its most simplest form is as follows:

```
s/target/replacement/ file
```

When the substitution command is encountered, it searches for the *first* occurrence of the target in the current line and then replaces the target string with the replacement string. In its simplest form, sed, like grep, reads in lines one at a time and processes commands on the read-in line. We will go over the substitution command in more detail in Chapter 7, "Sed Commands." We will also see how sed can read in and process multiple lines in Chapter 8, "Multiline Pattern Space Commands." This chapter covers the processing model of reading in a line at a time.

■ FOR EXAMPLE:

The following is an example of the substitution command:

```
sed s/Adhesions/Adhesive/ conf2.data
```

The output that results from this sed invocation is as follows:

Smith	Adhesive	700	200	081098	Digital
Jones	Coatings	900	0	081298	Dow
Phillips	Stabilizers	850	100	080198	Dupont
Kenny	Coatings	900	450	072898	Dow
Patsis	Adhesive	700	350	080198	IBM
Harris	Adhesive	700	0	081198	Digital
Gorge	Stabilizers	850	0	081098	Dupont
Mack	Coatings	900	100	080398	Shell
Jones	Coatings	900	0	080298	Texaco
Denny	Stabilizers	850	200	072998	Chrysler
Pierce	Adhesive	700	0	080398	IBM
Jackson	Resins	800	200	080598	Dupont

LAB
5.1

As you can see, the first occurrence of the text "Adhesions" that occurs in an input line is replaced by the text "Adhesive." As with any UNIX filter, the input and output may not necessarily come from standard input and output, but to and from a file. Here we have chosen to use the file conf2.data as input and standard output as output. The letter "s" in the command tells sed that the desired command to execute is the substitution command. In essence, the given command sed s/Adhesions/ Adhesive/ conf2.data tells UNIX, in plain English, to use sed to substitute the word Adhesions with the word Adhesive in the file named conf2.data.

In this example, be sure to understand: (1) how to invoke sed, (2) files that can be used as input and output, and (3) the fact that sed does not return only the lines of text that were affected by the command, but all lines.

■ FOR EXAMPLE:

In the following example script, we enter two substitution commands to change all entries of "Adhesions" to "Coatings" and "Coatings" to "Resins."

```
sed s/Adhesions/Coatings/\
s/Coatings/Resins/ conf2.data
```

The output that is produced is as follows:

Smith	Resins	700	200	081098	Digital
Jones	Resins	900	0	081298	Dow
Phillips	Stabilizers	850	100	080198	Dupont
Kenny	Resins	900	450	072898	Dow
Patsis	Resins	700	350	080198	IBM
Harris	Resins	700	0	081198	Digital
Gorge	Stabilizers	850	0	081098	Dupont
Mack	Resins	900	100	080398	Shell
Jones	Resins	900	0	080298	Texaco
Denny	Stabilizers	850	200	072998	Chrysler
Pierce	Resins	700	0	080398	IBM
Jackson	Resins	800	200	080598	Dupont

**LAB
5.1**

Notice the backslash at the very end of the first line in the command. The backslash instructs the shell that the next command continues on the next line. Multiple commands can be entered each on a separate line by using the backslash at the very end of the command. The given substitution command had the unexpected result of changing all occurrences of "Adhesions" *and* "Coatings" to "Resins."

As you can see from these two substitution commands, everywhere the text "Coatings" was encountered, it was replaced by the string "Resins." In addition, everywhere "Adhesions" was encountered, it was also replaced by the string "Resins." If we wanted to replace "Adhesions" with the string "Coatings," and only the original occurrences of "Coatings" with "Resins," then these two substitution commands would not work. Why not? The reason has to do with what sed calls the *pattern space*. The pattern space is a temporary buffer where the current input line is held. Sed takes this input line and applies all commands in the script one after the other in the pattern space. Looking back at the example, we can illustrate the action and the contents of the pattern space after executing the example. They are shown as follows when processing the first line of input:

ACTION: read the current line of input into the pattern space

Pattern Space before Action: **EMPTY**
Pattern Space after Action: `Smith Adhesion 700 200 081098 Digital`
ACTION: apply the first substitution command to the pattern space: `s/Adhesions/`
`Coatings/`
Pattern Space before Action: `Smith Adhesion 700 200 081098 Digital`
Pattern Space after Action: `Smith Coatings 700 200 081098 Digital`
ACTION: sed applies the next command to the pattern space: `s/Coatings/Resins/`
Pattern Space before Action: `Smith Coatings 700 200 081098 Digital`
Pattern Space after Action: `Smith Resins 700 200 081098 Digital`

Because each sed command executes once in a script on the pattern space, that one command may change the pattern space for the next command. The solution to our original example is to simply switch the order of the substitution commands. Therefore, the two substitution commands

```
s/Coatings/Resins/
s/Adhesions/Coatings/
```

would result in

Smith	Coatings	700	200	081098	Digital
Jones	Resins	900	0	081298	Dow
Phillips	Stabilizers	850	100	080198	Dupont
Kenny	Resins	900	450	072898	Dow
Patsis	Coatings	700	350	080198	IBM
Harris	Coatings	700	0	081198	Digital
Gorge	Stabilizers	850	0	081098	Dupont
Mack	Resins	900	100	080398	Shell
Jones	Resins	900	0	080298	Texaco
Denny	Stabilizers	850	200	072998	Chrysler
Pierce	Coatings	700	0	080398	IBM
Jackson	Resins	800	200	080598	Dupont

**LAB
5.1**

LAB 5.1 EXERCISES

5.1.1 UNDERSTAND SIMPLE SUBSTITUTIONS

Using the `conf2.data` file, what is the result for each of the following substitutions?

    a) `sed s/Resins/Coatings/ conf2.data`

    b) `sed s/Resins/Adhesions conf2.data`

    c) `sed s/Coatings/Stabilizers/ conf2.data`

    d) `sed s/Coatings// conf2.data`

    e) `sed s/[1-9][0-9][0-9]/"Too Expensive"/ conf2.data`

Write a substitution command or series of substitution commands that would accomplish each of the following tasks:

**LAB
5.1**

f) Replace "Harris" with "Jacobs"

---

g) Change "Coatings" to "Resins" and separately "Resins" to "Emul-sion"

---

h) Replace every occurrence of zero in the amount due column (fourth column) with the text "Paid in Full."

5.1.2 THE SED PATTERN SPACE

a) For each of the Questions a and c-e in Exercise 5.1.1, show the contents of the pattern space before and after each substitution is made. Do so for the first two input lines.

**LAB
5.1**

b) Run the following commands as a script (i.e., as a group, not individually). What is the pattern space after each of the following commands for the first two lines of the input file `conf2.data`?

```
s/ 0 /Zero/
s/ 0 /Paid/
s/Zero/"In Full"/
```

LAB 5.1 EXERCISE ANSWERS

This section gives you some suggested answers to the questions in Lab 5.1, with discussion related to those answers. Your answers may vary, but the most important thing is whether or not your answer works. Use this discussion to analyze differences between your answers and those presented here.

If you have alternative answers to the questions in this Exercise, you are encouraged to post your answers and discuss them at the companion Web site for this book, located at:

http://www.phptr.com/phptrinteractive/

5.1.1 ANSWERS

Using the conf2.data file, what is the result for each of the following substitutions?

a) sed s/Resins/Coatings/ conf2.data

Answer: The results would be as follows:

Smith	Adhesions	700	200	081098	Digital
Jones	Coatings	900	0	081298	Dow
Phillips	Stabilizers	850	100	080198	Dupont
Kenny	Coatings	900	450	072898	Dow
Patsis	Adhesions	700	350	080198	IBM
Harris	Adhesions	700	0	081198	Digital
Gorge	Stabilizers	850	0	081098	Dupont
Mack	Coatings	900	100	080398	Shell
Jones	Coatings	900	0	080298	Texaco
Denny	Stabilizers	850	200	072998	Chrysler
Pierce	Adhesions	700	0	080398	IBM
Jackson	Coatings	800	200	080598	Dupont

Only the last line is matched by the substitution pattern "Resins." Therefore, the last line has the substitution replacement string "Coatings" as the conference name.

b) `sed s/Resins/Adhesions conf2.data`

Answer: This results in an error. The problem is that the last slash is missing after "Adhesions." The correct command should be:
`sed s/Resins/Adhesions/`

c) `sed s/Coatings/Stabilizers/ conf2.data`

Answer: The result would be as follows:

Smith	Adhesions	700	200	081098	Digital
Jones	Stabilizers	900	0	081298	Dow
Phillips	Stabilizers	850	100	080198	Dupont
Kenny	Stabilizers	900	450	072898	Dow
Patsis	Adhesions	700	350	080198	IBM
Harris	Adhesions	700	0	081198	Digital
Gorge	Stabilizers	850	0	081098	Dupont
Mack	Stabilizers	900	100	080398	Shell
Jones	Stabilizers	900	0	080298	Texaco
Denny	Stabilizers	850	200	072998	Chrysler
Pierce	Adhesions	700	0	080398	IBM
Jackson	Resins	800	200	080598	Dupont

This command replaces the first occurrence of "Coatings" in each input line with the replacement string "Stabilizers." This occurs in lines 2, 4, 8, and 9.

d) `sed s/Coatings// conf2.data`

Answer: The result would be as follows:

Smith	Adhesions	700	200	081098	Digital
Jones		900	0	081298	Dow
Phillips	Stabilizers	850	100	080198	Dupont
Kenny		900	450	072898	Dow
Patsis	Adhesions	700	350	080198	IBM
Harris	Adhesions	700	0	081198	Digital
Gorge	Stabilizers	850	0	081098	Dupont
Mack		900	100	080398	Shell
Jones		900	0	080298	Texaco
Denny	Stabilizers	850	200	072998	Chrysler
Pierce	Adhesions	700	0	080398	IBM
Jackson	Resins	800	200	080598	Dupont

**LAB
5.1**

This command replaces the first occurrence of "Coatings" in every input line with an empty string (""). As we can see, any line that contained "Coatings" was matched.

e) `sed s/[1-9][0-9][0-9]/"Too Expensive"/`
`conf2.data`

Answer: The result would be as follows:

Smith	Adhesions	Too Expensive	200	081098	Digital
Jones	Coatings	Too Expensive	0	081298	Dow
Phillips	Stabilizers	Too Expensive	100	080198	Dupont
Kenny	Coatings	Too Expensive	450	072898	Dow
Patsis	Adhesions	Too Expensive	350	080198	IBM
Harris	Adhesions	Too Expensive	0	081198	Digital
Gorge	Stabilizers	Too Expensive	0	081098	Dupont
Mack	Coatings	Too Expensive	100	080398	Shell
Jones	Coatings	Too Expensive	0	080298	Texaco
Denny	Stabilizers	Too Expensive	200	072998	Chrysler
Pierce	Adhesions	Too Expensive	0	080398	IBM
Jackson	Resins	Too Expensive	200	080598	Dupont

This replaces the first occurrence of three consecutive digits with the replacement string "Too Expensive." This occurs in the third column (conference fee) of every line. Notice that it did not replace the fourth column when that column had three consecutive digits. The reason is that the substitution command does not replace globally. After the first substitution is performed, the command is finished executing, and the next line is read.

Write a substitution command or series of substitution commands that would accomplish each of the following tasks:

f) Replace "Harris" with "Jacobs"

Answer: The command should be as follows:
`sed s/Harris/Jacobs/ conf2.data`

g) Change "Coatings" to "Resins" and separately "Resins" to "Emulsion"

Answer: The command should be as follows:
```
sed s/Resins/Emulsion/\
s/Coatings/Resins/ conf2.data
```

The ordering is important in this substitution. To keep the change "Resins" to "Emulsion" separate from the substitution of "Coatings" to "Resins," this order must be preserved. Otherwise, "Coatings" would have been changed to "Resins," and then changed to "Emulsion" with the first substitution command. Notice the use of the backslash. It is used so that we may continue writing a command on the next line.

h) Replace every occurrence of zero in the amount due column (fourth column) with the text "Paid in Full."

Answer: The command should be as follows:
```
sed s/ 0 /"Paid In Full"/
```

We need a space before and after the zero in the pattern; otherwise, it would match every occurrence of a zero, even when zero is part of a larger number like 100.

5.1.2 ANSWERS

a) For each of the Questions a and c-e in Exercise 5.1.1, show the contents of the pattern space before and after each substitution is made. Do so for the first two input lines.

Answer: For the command `s/Resins/Coatings/`*, the results would be as follows:*

Line 1:

Before:	Smith	Adhesions	700	200	081098	Digital
After:	Smith	Adhesions	700	200	081098	Digital

Line 2:

Before:	Jones	Coatings	900	0	081298	Dow
After:	Jones	Coatings	900	0	081298	Dow

No change occurs before and after each command is executed because no line matched the pattern that was part of the substitution command.

For the command `s/Coatings/Stabilizers/`*, the results would be as follows:*

Line 1:

Before:	Smith	Adhesions	700	200	081098	Digital
After:	Smith	Adhesions	700	200	081098	Digital

Line 2:

Before:	Jones	Coatings	900	0	081298	Dow
After:	Jones	Stabilizers	900	0	081298	Dow

The second line matches the substitution, so the pattern space is changed after execution of the command.

For the command `s/Coatings//`*, the results would be as follows:*

Line 1:

Before:	Smith	Adhesions	700	200	081098	Digital
After:	Smith	Adhesions	700	200	081098	Digital

**LAB
5.1**

Line 2:

Before:	Jones	Coatings	900	0	081298	Dow
After:	Jones		900	0	081298	Dow

Again, only the second line matches, so the pattern space is changed after execution of the substitution command.

For the command s/[1-9][0-9][0-9]/"Too Expensive"/, the results would be as follows:

Line 1:

Before:	Smith	Adhesions	700	200	081098	Digital
After:	Smith	Adhesions	Too Expensive	200	081098	Digital

Line 2:

Before:	Jones	Coatings	900	0	081298	Dow
After:	Jones	Coatings	Too Expensive	0	081298	Dow

Every line matches, so both lines are changed after execution of the substitution command

b) What is the pattern space after each of the following commands for the first two lines of the input file conf2.data?

Answer: For the command s/ 0 /Zero/, the results would be as follows:

Line 1:

Before:	Smith	Adhesions	700	200	081098	Digital
After:	Smith	Adhesions	700	200	081098	Digital

Line 2:

Before:	Jones	Coatings	900	0	081298	Dow
After:	Jones	Coatings	900Zero081298		Dow

The first line is unchanged because no match occurs. The replacement string changes the pattern space of the second line by substituting "0" with "Zero."

For the command s/ 0 /Paid/, the results would be as follows:

Line 1:

Before:	Smith	Adhesions	700	200	081098	Digital
After:	Smith	Adhesions	700	200	081098	Digital

Line 2:

Before:	Jones	Coatings	900Zero081298	Dow
After:	Jones	Coatings	900Zero081298	Dow

Again, the first line is unchanged because no match occurs. In the second line, because the string "0" was changed to the text "Zero" in the preceding substitution command, the pattern "0" here does not match, so the second line is unchanged.

For the command `s/Zero/"In Full"/`, the results would be as follows:

Line 1:

Before:	Smith	Adhesions	700	200	081098	Digital
After:	Smith	Adhesions	700	200	081098	Digital

Line 2:

Before:	Jones	Coatings	900Zero081298	Dow
After:	Jones	Coatings	900In Full081298	Dow

The first line is not changed. Because the pattern space of the second line still contains the text "Zero," this substitution command's pattern matches and the replacement is made.

LAB 5.1 SELF-REVIEW QUESTIONS

In order to test your progress, you should be able to answer the following questions.
For each of the following multiple choice questions, one or more answers may be correct.

1) Where does the substitution command apply a substitution?
   a) _____The input file
   b) _____The pattern space
   c) _____User-Defined buffer

2) What are the contents of the pattern space when a sed script is first started?
   a) _____empty
   b) _____equal to the first input line
   c) _____depends on the sed script started

3) Which of the following statements is true?
   a) _____A command may affect the contents of the pattern space for a subsequent command.
   b) _____A backslash may be used at the command prompt to continue entering another command on the next line.
   c) _____The last slash of a substitution command is not required.
   d) _____Immediately after a line is read in from an input file, sed copies the line to the pattern space.

LAB
5.1

4) What is the result of a substitution command `s/All/Nothing` on the following line:

```
It's All or Nothing
```

a) _____It's All or Nothing

b) _____It's All or All

c) _____It's Nothing or Nothing

d) _____This results in an error

Quiz answers appear in Appendix A, Section 9.1.

CHAPTER 5

TEST YOUR THINKING

The projects in this section are meant to have you utilize all of the skills that you have acquired throughout this chapter. The answers to these projects can be found at the companion Web site to this book, located at:

`http://www.phptr.com/phptrinteractive`

Visit the Web site periodically to share and discuss your answers.

In this section, we will explore various methods by which you may invoke sed that involve multiple sed commands. Four methods are available:

- The first method is to enter the sed commands in a file and invoke sed with the `-f` option.

The command to invoke a sed script is `awk -f script-file-name input-file`. The `-f` option tells awk that the text that follows is to be interpreted as a file name in which the file contains sed commands. The `input-file` is the name of the input file on which sed should process the commands. By *sed script*, we mean the part of the sed program after the command word `sed` and before `input-file`. So in the following command:

```
sed 's/X/Y/' input-file
s/X/Y/ is the script.
```

And in the following:

```
sed 's/X/Y/\
s/Z/V/' input-file
```

the script would be:

```
s/X/Y/
s/Z/V
```

Always use quotes whenever a sed script uses a command line metacharacter.

- The second method is to separate each command with a semicolon. Put the sed script within quotes.
- The third method is to precede each sed command with the -e option.
- Finally, use the backslash (C Shell) after each command except the last command.

1) Use the following commands on the `conf2.data` file and execute the sed script using each of the four methods:

```
s/Smith/Clinton/
s/Digital/Compaq/
```

2) The substitution command substituted the first occurrence of a target string with the replacement string. How would you replace the second or third occurrence of a target string using the substitution command?

3) If we wanted to replace three consecutive digits ([0-9][0-9][0-9]) with ZZZ, how could we use the substitution command to replace the line

```
Smith   Adhesions   700   200   081098   Digital
```

with

```
Smith   Adhesions   ZZZ   ZZZ   ZZZZZZ   Digital
```

C H A P T E R 6

SED SYNTAX AND ADDRESSING

 Without specifying an address, sed processes all lines of the input file. With addressing, you can address which lines should be processed.

CHAPTER OBJECTIVE

In this chapter, you will learn about:

✓ Sed Syntax and Addressing   Page 110

In this chapter, we will look at how addressing works in sed. We saw in Chapter 5 how sed applied commands to every line in the file. Previous commands may have an effect on what subsequent commands will see in the pattern space. In this chapter, you will learn how to specify particular lines for subsequent commands to work on instead of every line. Thus, by sed addressing, we mean specifying on which lines we would like sed commands to work. I will also mention the comment character, and how to comment your sed scripts.

L A B   6.1

SED SYNTAX AND ADDRESSING

LAB OBJECTIVES

After this Lab, you will be able to:

✓ Specify Addresses by Using No Address

✓ Specify Addresses by Using One Address

✓ Specify Addresses by Using Two Addresses

✓ Understand Grouping Commands

COMMENTS

Comments vary, depending on which version of sed you are using. In System V, a comment is allowed only in the first line of a script. In SUNOS 4.1x and in GNU sed, the version that is supplied with RedHat's distribution of Linux, a comment can appear anywhere in a script. The version that I will talk about is GNU sed. The comment character is the octothorpe character (#). The following is an example of a comment:

```
# This is a comment
```

SED ADDRESSING

For this Lab, we will again use the `conf2.data` file that we used in Chapter 5, Lab 5.1. You can also download the file from this book's Web companion.

As we have seen in sed, we can specify an address by specifying no address! In this case, the commands will be applied to every line in the input file.

■ *FOR EXAMPLE:*

Consider the following command:

```
sed s/Adhesions/Coatings/ conf2.data
```

For every line that contains the string "Adhesions," this command replaces the string "Adhesions" with the string "Coatings." In other words, by specifying no address, the substitution will potentially occur at every line.

To restrict the lines in which to apply a sed command, one can specify particular lines instead of all lines. You can do so by specifying one or more addresses. To specify a single address, you have two methods. The first is specifying a regular expression.

■ *FOR EXAMPLE:*

The simplest regular expression is a literal regular expression, and it can be used to specify a single address, as in the following:

**LAB
6.1**

```
sed /Smith/s/Adhesions/Coatings/ conf2.data
```

With this command, while all lines are output, not all lines that contain the string "Adhesions" are replaced by "Coatings." Only the lines that additionally contain the string "Smith" are changed. As a result, only the line

| **Smith** | **Adhesions** | **700** | **200** | **081098** | **Digital** |

is changed to

```
Smith            Coatings       700   200    081098    Digital
```

In the above example, two criteria need to be met for the replacement to occur: (1) the line must contain the address specified by the regular expression ("Smith"), and (2) the line must contain the target string ("Adhesions"). If both of these are true, then the replacement is made.

The second method in which you specify one address is giving a specific line number.

■ FOR EXAMPLE:

Consider the following command:

```
sed 1s/Adhesions/Coatings/ conf2.data
```

This would result in:

```
Smith            Coatings       700   200    081098    Digital
```

As you can see, single addressing restricts the lines to which the substitution command may be applied. This illustrates what we mean by addressing in sed. An address is referred to or defined by a line number. Be careful, because if more than one file is supplied, as in the following script, the second file does not reset the line numbering.

```
sed 1s/Adhesions/Coatings/ conf2.data conf.data
```

LAB 6.1

In other words, line number 1 refers only to the first line in `conf2.data` but *not* also to the first line in `conf.data`. Only one substitution is made, because line number addressing refers to unique addresses. [Of course, if you are using a single regular expression, you may make a substitution may be made in both files.] Sed also uses a special metacharacter for referring to an address. The dollar sign, $, is used to address the last line in an input file. Thus, the following command:

```
sed '$s/Resins/Coatings/' conf2.data
```

would change only the last line

Jackson	Resins	800	200	080598	Dupont

to

Jackson	Coatings	800	200	080598	Dupont

The last method of addressing is to specify a range of addresses. This is accomplished by specifying two addresses separated by a comma.

■ FOR EXAMPLE:

Consider the following command:

```
sed 1,5s/Adhesions/Coatings/ conf2.data
```

The output is as follows:

Smith	Coatings	700	200	081098	Digital
Jones	Coatings	900	0	081298	Dow
Phillips	Stabilizers	850	100	080198	Dupont
Kenny	Coatings	900	450	072898	Dow
Patsis	Coatings	700	350	080198	IBM
Harris	Adhesions	700	0	081198	Digital
Gorge	Stabilizers	850	0	081098	Dupont
Mack	Coatings	900	100	080398	Shell
Jones	Coatings	900	0	080298	Texaco
Denny	Stabilizers	850	200	072998	Chrysler
Pierce	Adhesions	700	0	080398	IBM
Jackson	Resins	800	200	080598	Dupont

**LAB
6.1**

The range of addresses is specified by inserting a comma between the starting address and the ending address. As you can see, the substitution command is applied only to that range. Regular expressions can also be specified as a starting and ending address. Thinking of a regular expression as a starting and an ending address is harder than with line number ranges. However, if we had a sorted file of conference names, as follows:

```
Adhesions    600
Coatings     700
Emulsion     800
Resins       900
Stabilizers  850
```

then we could specify a range:

```
sed /A/,/E/s/[67]/8/
```

This would result in the following output:

```
Adhesions    800
Coatings     800
Emulsion     800
Resins       900
Stabilizers  850
```

In this example, the regular expression "A" is the starting address and "E" is the ending address. Be careful with the way sed handles ranges. The starting address "A" and ending address "E" does not mean that only addresses A and E will match. If we had the same script and ran it on the following file:

```
Adhesions    600
Coatings     700
Stabilizers  850
Emulsion     800
Resins       900
Stabilizers  850
```

then the third line, which contains the address Stabilizers, would also match. Ranges are activated or deactivated. Whenever a starting address is matched in the pattern space, the range is activated. All subsequent lines will match until the ending address is matched in the input line. When the ending address is matched in the pattern space, the range is deactivated. All subsequent lines will not match in the pattern space until the starting address in the range is matched in the pattern once again. This process, activating and deactivating the range, may occur multiple times when processing an input file. In this example, the range was activated when the first line was read into the pattern space. For the first line, the starting address "Adhesions" matched "Adhesions 800." All subsequent lines matched the range until the ending address "Emulsion" was matched in the line "Emulsion 800." All subsequent lines do not match. For each address that is matched by the range, if the line contains a 6 or 7, then sed replaces that number with an 8. This replacement occurs within the first two lines. As a result, only the first two lines within the range of three addresses is changed.

GROUPING COMMANDS

In all of the previous examples, each address was tied to a single substitution.

■ *FOR EXAMPLE:*

Consider the following example:

```
sed /Digital/s/Adhesions/Coatings/ conf2.data
```

This command substitutes "Coatings" for "Adhesions" only when the current pattern space contains the address "Digital." The same is true for a range of addresses:

```
sed /Dow/,/Digital/s/Adhesions/Coatings/ conf2.data
```

Sometimes we would like to apply multiple commands at a particular address. We could list each command individually, as in the following:

```
sed'/Digital/s/Adhesions/Coatings/;/Digital/s/700/777//' conf2.data
```

**LAB
6.1**

Having to repeat the address every time we wish to apply multiple commands to an address is tedious, and is harder to read as more commands are added. Also, as we will see in Chapter 7, it limits the types of applications we can design, and limits the full set of commands that we may use. Sed allows us to apply multiple commands to a single address or range of addresses by using a grouping operator.

■ *FOR EXAMPLE:*

The previous two substitutions could be designed using the grouping command operator:

```
/Digital/{
    s/Adhesions/Coatings/
    s/700/777/
}
```

In this example, everything within the braces will be executed if the address "Digital" specified before the opening brace is matched. The grouping command operator is the opening and closing braces. Its syntax is as follows:

```
address{
    command
    command
    ...
}
```

The first command can be placed on the same line as the opening brace. However, the closing brace must be on a line by itself. Multiple commands can be on the same line when a semicolon is used to separate them. However, they should be avoided. I recommend that you start each command on a separate line. This includes the first command, which may also be on the same line as the opening brace.

The pattern space is not output after each command is executed, nor is a new line read. Rather, the pattern space is output and a new line is read when control reaches the top of the script once again. As we will see in Chapters 7 and 8, some commands may transfer control to the top of the script before all commands within the braces are executed. Later on, we will also see that many different types of commands will occur within the grouping operator. For now, the important goal is to understand that the contents of the pattern space may change for the next command within a grouping operator, and additionally, to understand the syntax and rules of using the grouping operator.

**LAB
6.1**

LAB 6.1 EXERCISES

6.1.1 SPECIFY ADDRESSES BY USING NO ADDRESS

Because this topic is straightforward, I have only a single question.

> **a)** What address does the following specify?
> ```
> s/x/X/
> ```

_____

_____

6.1.2 SPECIFY ADDRESSES BY USING ONE ADDRESS

Enter the following commands using the `conf2.data` file:

```
sed '$s/Resins/Stabilizers/' conf2.data
sed '1s/Smith/Kaplan/' conf2.data
```

a) What is the output?

_____

_____

 Try the preceding with and without the single quotes and note the output.

**LAB
6.1**

What addresses (lines) do the following specify from the `conf2.data` file?

> **b)** `2s/../../ conf2.data`

_____

_____

c) /Smith/s/../../ conf2.data

d) /^$/s/../../ conf2.data

e) 4s/../../ conf2.data

f) /^$/s/../../ some_file1 some-file2

g) /.*es.*/[0-9][0-9][0-9]/600/ conf2.data

Are the following equivalent (i.e., do they result in the same output)?

LAB
6.1

h) /X/s/X/Y/ and s/X/Y/

i) /X/s/Y/X/ and s/Y/X/

j) `1s/X/Y/` and `^/s/X/Y/`

k) Write a single address substitution command that will replace each occurrence of "Digital" with "Compaq."

l) Write a single address expression that, for every line that contains "Digital," if the conference fee is 700, replaces it with 600.

6.1.3 SPECIFY ADDRESSES BY USING TWO ADDRESSES

What output does each of the following produce on the `conf2.data` file?

    a) `1,5s/Coatings/Adhesions/`

    b) `/Adhesions/, /Coatings/s/Adhesions/Resins/`

**LAB
6.1**

    c) `'/700 */, /850 */s/900/875/'`

d) `/Coatings/,/Adhesions/s/Coatings/Resins/`

Are the following equivalent?

e) `1,$s/../../` and `s/../../`

f) `/Adhesions/, /Stabilizers/s/../../` and `s/../../`

6.1.4 UNDERSTAND GROUPING COMMANDS

a) Is each of the following a legal grouping command?

```
address {
    command1
    command2
}
```

LAB 6.1

```
address{ command1
command2
}
```

```
address{command1
command2
}
```

_____

_____

```
address{command1;command2}
```

_____

_____

```
address{
    command1
    command2}
```

_____

_____

```
address{
    command1;command2
}
```

_____

_____

b) For each of the following, show the contents of the pattern space both before commands within the grouping command are executed and after each command is executed:

```
/Digital/{
s/Coatings/Adhesions/
s/ 0 /Paid/
}
```

_____

_____

```
/Resins/, ${
s/Dupont/Digital/
s/Jackson/Paul/
}
```

_____

_____

LAB 6.1 EXERCISE ANSWERS

This section gives you some suggested answers to the questions in Lab 6.1, with discussion related to those answers. Your answers may vary, but the most important thing is whether or not your answer works. Use this discussion to analyze differences between your answers and those presented here.

If you have alternative answers to the questions in this Exercise, you are encouraged to post your answers and discuss them at the companion Web site for this book, located at:

```
http://www.phptr.com/phprinteractive/
```

6.1.1 ANSWERS

a) What address does the following specify?
   s/x/X/

   Answer: No address is specified, so all addresses are valid. Therefore, every line that is read from the input file will be matched and the substitution made when the pattern x is also matched.

6.1.2 ANSWERS

Enter the following commands using the conf2.data file:
```
sed '$s/Resins/Stabilizers/' conf2.data
sed '1s/Smith/Kaplan/' conf2.data
```

a) What is the output?

Answer: The first command replaces the last line of `conf2.data` *with the following line:*
Jackson Stabilizers 800 200 080598 Dupont.

The rest of the file is output without modification.

Without the quotes, it results in an illegal variable name error. Why? Without the quotes, the "$" is interpreted as a shell metacharacter; therefore, "$s" is interpreted as a shell variable. Because we haven't defined "s," no values are returned, and the computer thinks you are sending the command

```
sed /Resins/Stabilizers/ conf2.data
```

which is an illegal command.

The second command replaces the first line of `conf2.data` *with the following line:*
Kaplan Adhesions 700 200 081098 Digital

The rest of the file is output without modification

Without the quotes, it results in the same output as with the quotes, because no characters in this sed command are special to the shell.

What addresses (lines) do the following specify from the `conf2.data` file?

b) `2s/../../  conf2.data`

Answer: Line 2 is specified.

c) `/Smith/s/../../  conf2.data`

Answer: Line 1. Only line 1 is specified by the single address regular expression Smith.

LAB 6.1

d) `/^$/s/../../  conf2.data`

Answer: No lines are specified.

This address will match any line that is a blank line. Any address surrounded by slashes will be interpreted as a regular expression. The caret, as you will recall from the chapters on regular expressions, matches from the very beginning of a line, and the dollar sign matches the very end. So if these two metacharacters are side by side with nothing between them surrounded by slashes, then the address matches a blank line.

e) `4s/../../ conf2.data`

Answer: This matches the fourth line.

f) `/^$/s/../../ some_file1 some-file2`

Answer: This matches any blank line in either `some_file1` *or* `some_file2`. *Sed will process* `some_file1` *first.*

g) `/.*es.*/[0-9][0-9][0-9]/600/ conf2.data`

Answer: This matches line 1 (Adhesions), line 2 (Jones), line 5 (Adhesions), line 6 (Adhesions), line 9 (Jones), line 11 (Adhesions), line 12 (Resins).

The address regular expression `.*es.*` matches any line that contains any number of characters, followed by the string `es`, ending in any number of characters. This matches the pattern "Jones" and "Adhesions" and "Resins." A shorter regular expression can be used; see if you can come up with it.

Are the following equivalent (i.e., do they result in the same output)?

h) `/X/s/X/Y/` and `s/X/Y/`

Answer: These two are equivalent.

In the first command, the address specifies any line that contains the regular expression "X." If it contains the regular expression, the substitution pattern string "X" will be replaced by "Y." This is the same as specifying no address and seeing whether the pattern "X" exists, and if so, then substituting with "Y." In the second case, every line matches since no address is specified, and if "X" exists in the line, then "Y" is substituted. In other words, if "X" exists, then the address specified by "X" will match.

i) `/X/s/Y/X/` and `s/Y/X/`

Answer: These two are not equivalent.

If a line contains the regular expression Y but does not contain the regular expression X, then the second substitution command will be made but the first will not, since the address must already contain X. In the second, every address is matched, since no address is provided.

j) `1s/X/Y/` and `^s/X/Y/`

Answer: These two are not equivalent.

"`1s/X/Y/`" will be applied only to the first line of a file. "`^s/X/Y/`" will result in an unrecognized command error. The reason is that sed does not recognize the caret metacharacter as an address metacharacter. One might think that because the dollar sign has a regular expression meaning and the caret has the opposite regular expression meaning—and furthermore, that the dollar sign is an address metacharacter that can address the last line of an input file—that the caret would be an address metacharacter that can address the first line. This assumption is not so.

k) Write a single address substitution command that will replace the first occurrence of "Digital" with "Compaq."

Answer: The command should be as follows:
`S/Digital/Compaq/`

l) Write a single address expression that, for every line that contains "Digital," if the conference fee is 700, replaces it with 600.

Answer: The expression should be as follows:
`/Digital/s/700/600/`

The address `/Digital/` satisfies the query for every line that contains "Digital." The substitute command satisfies the query that if the conference fee is 700, 600 replaces it.

6.1.3 ANSWERS

What output does each of the following produce on the `conf2.data` file?

a) `1,5s/Coatings/Adhesions/`

Answer: The output is as follows:

Smith	Adhesions	700	200	081098	Digital
Jones	Adhesions	900	0	081298	Dow
Phillips	Stabilizers	850	100	080198	Dupont
Kenny	Adhesions	900	450	072898	Dow
Patsis	Adhesions	700	350	080198	IBM
Harris	Adhesions	700	0	081198	Digital
Gorge	Stabilizers	850	0	081098	Dupont

Mack	Adhesions	900	100	080398	Shell
Jones	Adhesions	900	0	080298	Texaco
Denny	Stabilizers	850	200	072998	Chrysler
Pierce	Adhesions	700	0	080398	IBM
Jackson	Resins	800	200	080598	Dupont

Only lines 1 through 5 are matched by this range.. Therefore, in the first five lines, whenever "Coatings" occurs, it is replaced by "Adhesions" (lines 2 and 4).

b) /Adhesions/, /Coatings/s/Adhesions/Resins/

Answer: The output is as follows:

Smith	Resins	700	200	081098	Digital
Jones	Coatings	900	0	081298	Dow
Phillips	Stabilizers	850	100	080198	Dupont
Kenny	Coatings	900	450	072898	Dow
Patsis	Resins	700	350	080198	IBM
Harris	Resins	700	0	081198	Digital
Gorge	Stabilizers	850	0	081098	Dupont
Mack	Coatings	900	100	080398	Shell
Jones	Coatings	900	0	080298	Texaco
Denny	Stabilizers	850	200	072998	Chrysler
Pierce	Resins	700	0	080398	IBM
Jackson	Resins	800	200	080598	Dupont

In this example, the pattern "Adhesions" is used as the starting range address, and "Coatings" is the ending range address. Therefore, whenever "Adhesions" is matched in the pattern space, then the range is activated and all subsequent lines will match until either "Coatings" (ending address) is matched in the pattern space or the end of file is reached. Whenever "Coatings" is matched in the pattern space, then the range is deactivated and all subsequent lines will not match until either "Adhesions" is matched in the pattern space or the end of file is reached. Each input line, and whether the range is activated or deactivated after it is read into the pattern space, appears here:

**LAB
6.1**

Smith Adhesions 700 200 081098 Digital (Activated—starting address matched)
Jones Coatings 900 0 081298 Dow (Deactivated—ending address matched)
Phillips Stabilizers 850 100 080198 Dupont (Remains deactivated)
Kenny Coatings 900 450 072898 Dow (Deactivated—ending address matched)
Patsis Adhesions 700 350 080198 IBM (Activated—starting address matched)
Harris Adhesions 700 0 081198 Digital (Activated—starting address matched)

```
Gorge Stabilizers 850 0 081098 Dupont (Remains activated)
Mack Coatings 900 100 080398 Shell (Deactivated—ending address matched)
Jones Coatings 900 0 080298 Texaco (Deactivated—ending address matched)
Denny Stabilizers 850 200 072998 Chrysler (Remains deactivated)
Pierce Adhesions 700 0 080398 IBM (Activated—starting address matched)
Jackson Resins 800 200 080598 Dupont (Remains activated)
```

The substitution command is applied only to addresses that are activated (lines 1, 5, 6, 7, 11, and 12) and that match the regular expression "Adhesions" (lines 1, 5, 6, and 11). Therefore, only in lines 1,5, 6, and 11 is "Adhesions" replaced by "Resins."

c)   `'/700 */, /850 */s/900/875/'`

Answer: The output is as follows:

Smith	Adhesions	700	200	081098	Digital
Jones	Coatings	875	0	081298	Dow
Phillips	Stabilizers	850	100	080198	Dupont
Kenny	Coatings	900	450	072898	Dow
Patsis	Adhesions	700	350	080198	IBM
Harris	Adhesions	700	0	081198	Digital
Gorge	Stabilizers	850	0	081098	Dupont
Mack	Coatings	900	100	080398	Shell
Jones	Coatings	900	0	080298	Texaco
Denny	Stabilizers	850	200	072998	Chrysler
Pierce	Adhesions	700	0	080398	IBM
Jackson	Resins	800	200	080598	Dupont

This example substitution command creates a range from the numbers 700 followed by a space and then followed by zero or more characters (*), to 850 followed by a space and any other character. The lines that are matched are lines 1, 2, 5, 6, 11, and 12. Only line 2 matches the substitution pattern and it is the only line changed. Although this range expression could be simplified, the point of the discussion is to emphasize that metacharacters can be used in range expressions. Notice the quotes. They are needed to prevent the shell from interpreting the asterisk.

LAB 6.1

d)   `/Coatings/,/Adhesions/s/Coatings/Resins/`

Answer: The output is as follows:

Smith	Adhesions	700	200	081098	Digital
Jones	Resins	900	0	081298	Dow
Phillips	Stabilizers	850	100	080198	Dupont
Kenny	Resins	900	450	072898	Dow

Patsis	Adhesions	700	350	080198	IBM
Harris	Adhesions	700	0	081198	Digital
Gorge	Stabilizers	850	0	081098	Dupont
Mack	Resins	900	100	080398	Shell
Jones	Resins	900	0	080298	Texaco
Denny	Stabilizers	850	200	072998	Chrysler
Pierce	Adhesions	700	0	080398	IBM
Jackson	Resins	800	200	080598	Dupont

This exercise is meant to reinforce the idea that ranges that use regular expressions as a starting address and ending address are not meant to create a range that selects lines that fall between the starting address and ending address in alphabetical order. In this range, the starting address "Coatings" appears after the ending address "Adhesions" in alphabetical order. Therefore, if ranges specified alphabetical order, nothing could come between "Coatings" and "Adhesions"; yet lines 2, 3, 4, 8, 9, and 10 are matched. As stated, sed ranges are either activated or deactivated by a starting or ending address. Lines 2, 4, 8, and 9 activate the range, and lines 1, 5, 6, and 11 deactivate the range. Only lines 4, 8, and 9 are substituted.

Are the following equivalent?

e) `1,$s/../../` and `s/../../`

Answer: Yes, these two are equivalent.

The first matches every line from line number 1 to the last line number ($). This is equivalent to specifying no address.

f) `/Adhesions/, /Stabilizers/s/../../` and `s/../../`

Answer: These two are not equivalent.

LAB
6.1

In the first command, the range from "Adhesions" to "Stabilizers" specifies lines 1-3, 5-7, 11-end of file (EOF). The second command matches every line.

6.1.4 ANSWERS

a) Is each of the following a legal grouping command?
```
address {
    command1
    command2
}
```
Answer: Yes, this is legal.

The space after the address and before the opening brace is legal, and the closing brace is contained on a line by itself.

```
address{ command1
command2
}
```
Answer: Yes, this is legal.

No space occurs between the address and opening brace, which is legal. A command may appear on the line containing the opening brace. More than one command is legal, and the closing brace is on a line by itself.

```
address{command1
command2
}
```
Answer: Yes, this is legal.

The reason is the same as the immediately preceding grouping command, except in this grouping no space occurs between the opening brace and the command. This is legal.

```
address{command1;command2}
```
Answer: This is not legal.

The closing brace must be on a line itself.

```
address{
    command1
    command2}
```
Answer: This is not legal.

The closing brace must be on a line itself.

**LAB
6.1**

```
address{
    command1;command2
}
```

Answer: Yes, this is legal.

b) For each of the following, show the contents of the pattern space both before commands within the grouping command are executed and after each command is executed:

```
/Digital/{
s/Coatings/Adhesions/
s/ 0 / Paid/
}
```

Answer: The results are as follows:

```
Pattern space
```
Smith Adhesions 700 200 081098 Digital

1st Command: `s/Coatings/Adhesions/`
After: **Smith Adhesions 700 200 081098 Digital**

2nd Command: `s/ 0 / Paid/`
After: **Smith Adhesions 700 200 081098 Digital**

```
Pattern space
```
Harris Adhesions 700 0 081198 Digital

1st Command: `s/Coatings/Adhesions/`
After: **Harris Adhesions 700 0 081198 Digital**

2nd Command: `s/ 0 / Paid/`
After: **Harris Adhesions 700 Paid081198 Digital**

```
/Resins/, ${
s/Dupont/Digital/
s/Jackson/Paul/
}
```

Answer: The results are as follows:

```
Pattern space
```
Jackson Resins 800 200 080598 Dupont

1st Command: `s/Dupont/Digital`
After: **Jackson Resins 800 200 080598 Digital**

2nd Command: `s/Jackson/Paul/`
After: **Paul Resins 800 200 080598 Digital**

LAB 6.1 SELF-REVIEW QUESTIONS

In order to test your progress, you should be able to answer the following questions.
For each of the following multiple choice questions, one or more answers may be correct.

1) In the range /A/, /Z/ , if the range has already been activated, then which of the following lines will match?
   a) _____U
   b) _____V
   c) _____X
   d) _____Y
   e) _____Z

2) Which of the following addresses specifies only the last line of an input file?
   a) _____1
   b) _____/$/
   c) _____$
   d) _____15
   e) _____^

3) Which of the following specifies only the first line of an input file?
   a) _____^
   b) _____15
   c) _____/^/
   d) _____/$/
   e) _____None of the above

4) Which of the following addresses matches a line that contains the text "Jackson"?
   a) _____J
   b) _____4
   c) _____/J/
   d) _____/Jackson/
   e) _____/.*/

5) Which of the following is a valid address?

    a) _____5

    b) _____`1, 4`

    c) _____`/Adhesions/`

    d) _____`/A/, /D/`

    e) _____`^`

Quiz answers appear in Appendix A, Section 6.1.

C H A P T E R 6

TEST YOUR THINKING

 The projects in this section are meant to have you utilize all of the skills that you have acquired throughout this chapter. The answers to these projects can be found at the companion Web site to this book, located at:

```
http://www.phptr.com/phptrinteractive/
```

Visit the Web site periodically to share and discuss your answers.

1) What happens when a starting address and ending address in a range both occur in the same input line?

Use the `conf2.data` file and use the following range command:
```
/Adhesions/, /0/{
s/0/Paid/
s/Adhesions/Adhesive/
}
```

2) Are the following two equivalent? Explain your answer.
```
/Resins/, ${
s/Dupont/Digital/
s/Jackson/Paul/
}

/Resins/, $s/Dupont/Digital/
s/Jackson/Paul/
```

3) Why do you suppose that sed surrounds addresses that are regular expressions with slashes?

4) Why do you suppose that sed has the dollar sign to refer to the last line but does not allow the caret to refer to the first line?

5) Write a sed program that will take Chapter 7 and write a table of contents.

CHAPTER 7

SED COMMANDS

*Sed commands allow the user to perform more powerful text manipula-
tions.*

CHAPTER OBJECTIVES

In this chapter, you will learn about:

In this chapter, we will talk about sed commands. Sed commands allow the user to perform more powerful text manipulations. The main purpose of sed is to read an input file, perform some manipulation on the text, and output the results. The various commands provide mechanisms so that the user may direct the computer to perform these manipulations. In Chapter 6, you saw some rudimentary search and replace examples. In this chapter, we will explore the search and replace command more thoroughly as well as other commands such as delete, list, and print, to name a few. After this chapter, you will be able to perform the majority of applications that you will write using sed.

L A B   7.1

THE SUBSTITUTION
COMMAND

LAB OBJECTIVES

After this Lab, you will be able to:

✓ Understand the Options to the Substitute Command

✓ Understand the Replacement String Characters to the Substitute Command

We saw simple substitution commands in Chapter 6. At this point, I will formally introduce the substitute command and the various options and examples with which the substitute command may be used. The syntax of the substitute command is as follows:

```
[address]s/pattern/replacement/flags
```

■ *FOR EXAMPLE:*

**LAB
7.1**

We have seen an example of the substitute command:

```
s/Adhesions/Coatings/
```

As the example suggests, the address is optional, specified by the brackets in the syntax shown. If it is not provided, then the address is matched by every line. Therefore, every line in the file is matched.

You'll notice that I use the phrase "a line is matched in the input line," or "the current line is matched," or even simply "a line is matched." In most of the examples and exercises, these phrases are true. However, the precise phrase is "the pattern space is matched." We have seen that a command may change the pattern space for a subsequent command, and in Chapter 8, when we go over multiline pattern spaces, we will see that a pattern space may contain multiple input lines. Therefore, a line and the pattern space may not be the same.

We will not go over the various addressing schemes, because we discussed them before, but will just mention that an address can be a number, a regular expression, or a range separated by commas. If a regular expression is specified as an address but no pattern in the syntax shown in the beginning is supplied, the substitute command matches what is matched by the address. We will see the use of this in a later chapter. If no replacement string is given, then an empty string is replaced at the address matched by the address expression and pattern expression. The slashes (the delimiter) are required after the command, after the pattern, and after the replacement. Addresses that are regular expressions are required to be delimited by the slash. Unlike addresses, the command, the pattern, and the replacement may be delimited by a character other than the slash. This option is useful if both the pattern and replacement contain a slash within their strings.

■ FOR EXAMPLE:

This is shown in the following example:

```
s^/usr/home/p^/usr/home/s^
```

In this example, the caret symbol is used as the delimiter, and /usr/home/s replaces /usr/home/p at whatever line /usr/home/p occurs. The first character after the command will determine what the delimiter is. The delimiter cannot be a space or a tab. The delimiter is required to separate the command, pattern, and replacement strings. Not to provide all three is an error. The following command is a common error:

```
s/Adhesions/Coatings
```

LAB
7.1

This will result in an error because the third delimiter that ends the replacement string was not provided.

A number of optional flags may also appear in the substitute command. The following are the available flags that we will cover in this chapter:

- n—specify the nth occurrence to replace
- g—make changes globally on all occurrences in the pattern space
- p—print the contents of the pattern space
- w—write the contents of the pattern space
- n—a number (1 to 512) that specifies that the replacement should occur for the nth pattern that was matched in the pattern space.

Consider the following line of text contained in the pattern space:

```
Mr. Smith was looking forward to his trip although
Mr. Smith had never made the trip before.
```

If we use the following substitution command:

```
's/Mr. Smith/Mrs. Smith/2'
```

it would result in the following substitution:

```
Mr. Smith was looking forward to his trip although
Mrs. Smith had never made the trip before.
```

As we can see by specifying 2 as a flag to this substitution command, only the second occurrence of the pattern Mr. Smith is replaced by the string Mrs. Smith. Any decimal from 1 to 512 may be specified as the option.

The g flag simplifies the nth occurrence flag; it replaces every occurrence of the pattern in the pattern space by the replacement string. Therefore, with the g flag, you do not have to guess how many occurrences of the pattern will occur in the pattern space; all will be replaced. Using the same line that we saw previously, the following g flag substitution command:

```
's/Mr. Smith/Mrs. Smith/g'
```

produces the following:

> **Mrs. Smith was looking forward to his trip although**
> **Mrs. Smith had never made the trip before.**

Every occurrence of the string `Mr. Smith` is replaced by `Mrs. Smith`.

The `p` flag is used to immediately print out the contents of the pattern space. The following command will do so:

    's/Mr. Smith/Mrs. Smith/p'

The output is the following:

> **Mrs. Smith was looking forward to his trip although**
> **Mr. Smith had never made the trip before.**

The `w` flag is similar to the `p` flag except that the contents of the pattern space are not provided as output but are written to a file. If the file doesn't exist, the `w` flag will create it.

■ FOR EXAMPLE:

Consider the following:

    's/Mr. Smith/Mrs. Smith/w sed.output'

And the line:

> Mrs. Smith was looking forward to his trip although
>   Mr. Smith had never made the trip before.

This is written to `sed.output` as well as printed to the screen. Notice that the name of the output file, `sed.output`, must be contained within the apostrophes and one space must be between the `w` flag and the output file.

Flags may also be combined, so the following is also legal:

    s/Mr. Smith/Mrs. Smith/gp

And `Mrs. Smith` will replace `Mr. Smith` globally and be printed twice.

The replacement string is any string of characters that is to be used as a replacement to the pattern. In the replacement string, the following characters have special meaning. Additionally, in no other context except in the replacement string do the following characters have meaning:

- `&`—replaced by the string matched by the regular expression in the pattern
- `\n`—matches the nth (single digit) substring specified in the pattern by `\( \)`
- `\`—used to escape in the replacement string, the ampersand (`&`), the backslash (`\`), and the substitution command delimiter when it is used literally in the replacement string (again, the three above characters have meaning only in the replacement section; therefore, they need to be backslashed only within the replacement string)

Because only these three metacharacters have meaning in the replacement string, you can use the period, asterisk, or any other character that has meaning in addresses or patterns without having to backslash them in the replacement string.

Consider the following sed command:

```
's/Dupont/& Corporation/g'
```

If the following input line was in the pattern space:

```
Dupont is a leader in the chemical industry
```

then the following would result:

```
Dupont Corporation is a leader in the chemical industry
```

The ampersand would match the pattern `Dupont` and in the replacement string when the ampersand is encountered, it is expanded with the pattern `Dupont`. The ampersand is therefore useful when an entire pattern is to be matched in the replacement string.

The /n metacharacter encountered within the replacement string means that the nth occurrence within a pattern that is surrounded by parentheses will be replaced in the replacement string. This will be clearer as we go over an example; however, keep in mind that this is a way to match portions of a pattern instead of entire patterns, as with the ampersand.

Suppose that a file of addresses has a regular mail format, as follows:

```
Peter Patsis
75 Center St.
New Paltz, New York 12561
```

If we want to replace the text for the state of New York with its two-letter abbreviation, we can successfully execute this with the following sed command:

```
's/\(.*,\) New York \(.*\)/\1 NY \2/'
```

The slash opening and closing parentheses in the pattern are meant to instruct the computer to save whatever pattern or portion of the regular expression that is matched between the parentheses for later recall in the replacement string.

In this example, we have two pairs of opening and closing parentheses that are preceded by a backslash.

1. `\(.*,\)`
2. `\(.*\)`

Each is considered a different instance, although they are similar regular expressions (notice the comma in the first, which is not in the second). Therefore, in the example, New Paltz, matches the first instance of the parentheses in the pattern. Next, the literal regular expression " New York " is matched in the input line by " New York ". Finally, the ZIP code 12561 is matched by the second instance of parentheses (\.*\). Each instance is saved for later recall in the order it was encountered, starting at the beginning of the line. Therefore, in the replacement string, the special replacement string metacharacter \1 recalls New Paltz,. The string " NY " (notice the spaces around NY) is then taken literally. Finally, the special replacement string metacharacter \2 recalls the ZIP code 12561. The replacement string then becomes New Paltz, NY 12561. And the output produced by the input line:

LAB 7.1

```
Peter Patsis
75 Center St.
New Paltz, New York 12561
```

becomes:

```
Peter Patsis
75 Center St.
New Paltz, NY 12561
```

Up to nine saves are allowed when using the special replacement string metacharacter \n and the pattern special metacharacter \(, \). Remember that numbering starts with the leftmost occurrence of a pair of opening and closing parentheses preceded by a backslash.

The last special replacement metacharacter is the backslash. It is used whenever you wish to use a special replacement metacharacter literally in the replacement string. It was used previously in the discussion of save and recall but could also be used to protect other metacharacters.

■ FOR EXAMPLE:

Consider the following:

```
's/Coltrane/Medeski, Martin \& Wood/g'
```

This would replace every occurrence of Coltrane with Medeski, Martin & Wood. Notice that if we had not backslashed the ampersand, then the replacement string would be Medeski, Martin, Coltrane Wood. The ampersand would have matched Coltrane in the replacement string.

The backslash can also be used to specify escape characters. We've seen one example with the \(,\) set.

Another use of the backslash is when you wish to use the newline character, \n, literally in the replacement string. Using the newline in the replacement string literally creates a multiline replacement string, with each occurrence of newline causing the text that follows the newline to be output on the next line. Suppose that we wish to replace each occurrence of an adjacent first name and last name, as in the following:

```
Peter Patsis
```

Into a displayable database format which each field on a separate line pre-fixed by the field name as in the following:

```
First Name: Peter
Last Name: Patsis
```

The following sed command implements this goal:

```
`s/\(.* \)\(.*\)/First Name: \1\
Last Name: \2/'
```

We use the special metacharacter parentheses in the pattern to save the first name and then the last name in the input line Peter Patsis. To do so, we use the regular expression ".* ". Notice the space in the regular expression; the space acts as a separator between the first name and last name. Convince yourself that if the space wasn't used as a separator, then the first .* would have matched the entire line. The second regular expression that is saved is the last name. The replacement string first prints the literal "First Name: ," after which it uses the saved first name to print the string Peter. The replacement then uses the backslash special meta-character to print a newline (To create this multiline replacement string, enter a backslash at the point where you want the text that follows to appear on the next line. Then press the Enter key and enter the text that you want to appear on the next line.). Lastly, it prints Last Name and the string Patsis using the saved last name in the pattern. The effect is that whenever a first name and last name are encountered, they are replaced by the multiline pattern:

```
First Name: ?????
Last Name: ?????
```

Also note that this example is limited, because it would also perform the following replacement:

```
First Name: 2
Last Name: Center St.
```

**LAB
7.1**

when presented with the following line:

```
2 Center St.
```

LAB 7.1 EXERCISES

7.1.1 UNDERSTAND THE OPTIONS TO THE SUBSTITUTE COMMAND

Use the following file to answer Questions a through e of this Exercise:

> To fully understand the cypriot crisis, one needs to first understand the nature of greek-turkish relations. After understanding the greek-turkish relationship, then one must understand the undermining and self-interest in cyprus from world powers before and after the cold war. Namely, the british, the americans, and the russians.

a) What is the output of the following command?

```
sed s/greek/Greek/g cyprus.txt
```

_____

_____

b) What is the output of the following command?

```
sed s/turkish/Turkish/g cyprus.txt
```

_____

_____

c) What is the output of the following command?

```
sed 's/greek-turkish/greek and turkish/1' cyprus.txt
```

_____

_____

d) What is the output of the following command?
```
sed 's/greek-turkish/greek and turkish/2' cyprus.txt
```

_____

_____

e) What is the output of the following command?
```
sed s/cypriot/Cypriot/p cyprus.txt
```

_____

_____

f) Using the previous file, write a substitution command that replaces every occurrence of one needs with should. For each modification made, create a file called modify.out that will contain each line that was modified.

_____

_____

7.1.2 UNDERSTAND THE REPLACEMENT STRING CHARACTERS TO THE SUBSTITUTE COMMAND

Use the same file as in Exercise 7.1.1 to answer questions a through d in this Exercise.

Try to figure out the output without entering the command at the computer first. Then enter the command and figure out whether the results were different from what you expected. This approach helps give you a better understanding of working with commands.

LAB
7.1

a) What is the output of the following command?
```
sed 's/greek-turkish/greek \& turkish/' cyprus.txt
```

_____

_____

b) What is the output of the following command?

```
sed s/greek-turkish/greek \& turkish/ cyprus.txt
```

c) What is the output of the following command?

```
sed '1s/.*/<p>&/' cyprus.txt
```

d) What is the output of the following command?

```
sed 's/\(.*the \).*,\( the \).*,\(.* the \).*\./
     \1United Kingdom\2United States\3Soviet Republic/'
     cyprus.txt
```

Suppose that we have a file like the following:

```
<H1>Section 1. Sed Commands</H1>
<H2>Section 1.1. Substitution Command<H2>
```

Each section is indicated by the starting and ending element tag `<H1>`, `</H1>` and each subsection is indicated by the starting and ending element tag `<H2>,</H2>`.

e) Write a sed script that will strip away the element tags along with the text Section and create a table of contents as follows:

```
1.      Sed Commands
1.1 Substitution Command
```

f) After creating a script for the preceding problem, reverse the problem. Take a table of contents and format it with the proper element tags.

_____

_____

g) Write a substitution command that will take each occurrence of `greek-turkish` and switch it with the text `turkish` and `greek`. Use parentheses expressions.

_____

_____

h) Write an expression that will reverse the order of three numbers that appear in a line one after the other and are separated by a space, as follows:

`20 15 10`

_____

_____

LAB 7.1 EXERCISE ANSWERS

 This section gives you some suggested answers to the questions in Lab 7.1, with discussion related to those answers. Your answers may vary, but the most important thing is whether or not your answer works. Use this discussion to analyze differences between your answers and those presented here.

If you have alternative answers to the questions in this Exercise, you are encouraged to post your answers and discuss them at the companion Web site for this book, located at:

`http://www.phptr.com/phptrinteractive/`

LAB 7.1

7.1.1 ANSWERS

Use the given file to answer Questions a through e of this Exercise.

a) What is the output of the following command?
```
sed s/greek/Greek/g cyprus.txt
```

Answer: The string Greek *replaces* greek *everywhere it occurs (*g *option) in the pattern space.*

b) What is the output of the following command?
```
sed s/turkish/Turkish/g cyprus.txt
```

Answer: The string Turkish *replaces* turkish *everywhere it occurs (*g *option) in the pattern space.*

c) What is the output of the following command?
```
sed 's/greek-turkish/greek and turkish/1' cyprus.txt
```

Answer: The string greek and turkish *replaces the first occurrence only of* greek-turkish. *Notice that the quotes were necessary to stop the space from being evaluated by the shell.*

d) What is the output of the following command?
```
sed 's/greek-turkish/greek and turkish/2' cyprus.txt
```

Answer: The string greek and turkish *replaces the second occurrence only of* greek-turkish *in the pattern space. Again, notice that the quotes were necessary to stop the space from being evaluated by the shell.*

e) What is the output of the following command?
```
sed s/cypriot/Cypriot/p cyprus.txt
```

Answer: The first input line is printed twice. The first line that is printed is the result of a successful substitute command in combination with the p *flag to the substitute command.*

In line one, a successful substitution was made changing cypriot *to* Cypriot.

f) Using the previous file write a substitution command that replaces every occurrence of one needs with should. For each modification made, create a file called modify.out that will contain each line that was modified.

Answer: The command would be as follows:

```
sed 's/one needs/should/gw modify.out' cyprus.txt
```

The command matches the first line, makes the substitution, prints the matching line to `Modify.out`, and then prints the default output. Since default output is not suppressed, each line is printed out.

7.1.2 ANSWERS

Using the same file as in Exercise 7.1.1 to answer questions a through d in this Exercise.

a) What is the output of the following command?

```
sed 's/greek-turkish/greek \& turkish/' cyprus.txt
```

Answer: The results would be as follows:

To fully understand the cypriot crisis, one needs to first understand the nature of

greek & turkish relations. After understanding the greek-turkish relationship, then one must understand the undermining and self-interest in cyprus from world powers before and after the cold war. Namely, the british, the americans, and the russians.

The command replaces the first occurrence (not second, third, or every) of the string `greek-turkish` with `greek  &  turkish`. Notice two things. First, the command is quoted to protect the spaces in the replacement string from being interpreted by the shell. Second, the ampersand (&) is preceded by the backslash so that the ampersand may be interpreted literally and printed out properly.

b) What is the output of the following command?

```
sed s/greek-turkish/greek \& turkish/ cyprus.txt
```

Answer: The results would be as follows:

Error unterminated s command

LAB
7.1

The error results because the substitution command, in this case, was not quoted (protected from the shell interpreting the substitution command as an argument to pass to sed). The shell in this case contains the following arguments:

```
sed
s/greek-turkish/greek
\&
turkish/
cyprus.txt
```

(A space to the shell acts as an argument delimiter when parsing).

Because sed interprets the second argument passed to it as a command, in this case, the command is s/greek-turkish/greek. Since this command is missing the closing slash, it is unterminated, hence the above error.

c) What is the output of the following command?
```
sed '1s/.*/<p>&/' cyprus.txt
```

Answer: The substitution command addresses only the first line. In that line, we match the entire line by the pattern, (. *). This pattern matches the entire first line:
To fully understand the cypriot crisis, one needs to first understand the nature of

In the replacement string, we use the ampersand to recall the entire matched pattern and prefix it with the string <p>. Thus the pattern space becomes:

<p>fully understand the cypriot crisis, one needs to first understand the nature of

after the substitution command. It is printed as default output when the script reaches the bottom.

d) What is the output of the following command?
```
sed  's/\(.*the \).*,\(  the \).*,\(.*  the \).*\./
    \1United  Kingdom\2United  States\3Soviet  Republic'
    cyprus.txt
```

Answer: The results would be as follows:
To fully understand the cypriot crisis, one needs to first understand the nature of

```
greek-turkish relations. After understanding the
greek-turkish relationship, then one must
understand the undermining and self-interest in
cyprus from world powers before and after the
cold war. Namely, the United Kingdom the United
States and the Soviet Republic
```

The pattern and replacement string in this substitution command is a little more complex, because we are using a more involved parenthesized save and recall pattern. Let's break it down into parts. We will just describe the command for the line that matches the entire pattern. This is the last line:

```
cold war. Namely, the british, the americans, and
the russians.
```

The first part of the pattern, `\(.*the \)`, matches the following snippet of the last line and is the first argument saved for later recall:

```
cold war. Namely, the
```

(`.*` matches `cold war. Namely,` and "`the `" is matched literally).

The second part of the pattern, `.*,`, matches the string `british,`.

The third part of the pattern, `\( the \)`, matches the string " `the `." It is saved second for later recall.

The fourth part, `.*,`, matches the string `americans,`.

The fifth part of the pattern, `\(.* the \)`, matches the string " `and the `." It is saved third for later recall.

The last part of the pattern, `.*\`, matches the string `russians`.

To recap, the saved portions are:

```
\1 "cold war. Namely, the "
\2 " the "
\3 " and the "
```

The replacement string "\1United Kingdom\2United States\3Soviet Republic" thus results in:

cold war. Namely, the United Kingdom the United States and the Soviet Republic

Suppose that we have a file like the following:

```
<H1>Section 1. Sed Commands</H1>
<H2>Section 1.1. Substitution Command</H2>
```

Each section is indicated by the starting and ending element tag <H1>, </H1>, and each subsection is indicated by the starting and ending element tag <H2>, </H2>.

e) Write a sed script that will strip away the element tags along with the text `Section` and create a table of contents as follows:
   1. Sed Commands
   1.1 Substitution Command

   Answer: The script would be as follows:
   ```
   s/<H1>Section \(.*\)<\/H1>/\1/
   s/<H2>Section \(.*\)<\/H2>/   \1/
   ```

Let's go over the first substitute command.

We would like to output the following:

1. Sed Commands

So given the following input string:

<H1>Section 1. Sed Commands</H1>

We like to strip off "`<H1>Section `" and output everything else up to the string </H2>. This action is equivalent to saving only the bolded part below:

<H1>Section **1. Sed Commands**</H1>

In the substitute command pattern (or target) part, the literal regular expression "`<H1>Section `"

```
s/<H1>Section \(.*\)<\/H1>/\1/
```

is matched in the input line by:

`<H1>Section` `1. Sed Commands</H1>`

In the pattern, the rest of the regular expression

```
s/<H1>Section \(.*\)<\/H1>/\1/
```

is matched in the input line by:

`<H1>Section` **`1. Sed Commands</H1>`**

However, the save portion "`\(.*\)`" of "`\(.*\)<\/H2>`" matches

`1. Sed Commands`

The reason is that we have the regular expression `.*`, which matches 0 or more of any characters. It is bounded by the literal regular expression `<\/H2>` (the backslash in `<\/H2>` is used to prevent sed from thinking that the slash is the slash that is part of the substitute command). Because the regular expression `\(.*\)` is bounded by `<\/H2>`, everything is matched up to that string. So the first and only saved portion is

`\1 = 1. Sed Commands`

In the replacement string, `\1` is recalled, so the whole line is replaced and output by the following:

`1. Sed Commands`

which is what we want. The only difference between the first and second substitute commands is that in the second command in the replacement string, we prefix three spaces before recalling `\1`.

LAB 7.1

f) After creating a script for the preceding problem, reverse the problem. Take a table of contents and format it with the proper element tags.

Answer: This script is as follows:
```
s/\(^[0-9].*\)/<H1>Section \1<\/H1>/
s/^   \([0-9].*\)/<H2>Section \1<\/H2>/
```

To do the reverse, suppose that you have the following input:

1. Sed Commands
1.1 Substitution

Further, suppose that you wish to output the following:

```
<H1>1. Sed Commands</H1>
<H2>1.1 Substitution</H2>
```

All you have to do is save in the pattern the entire input line

1. Sed Commands

and replace the input line entirely by recalling the shown saved input line and then precede the saved input line with "<H1>Section " and succeed it with </H2>. In the replacement string of the first substitute command, the bolded section precedes the saved portion:

<H1>Section \1<\/H1>

And in the following, the bolded text succeeds the saved portion:

<H1>Section \1**<\/H1>**

\1 recalls the saved portion. The difference between the first command and the second is the tags <H2> and </H2>, and in the pattern of the substitution command, three spaces precede the regular expression.

**LAB
7.1**

g) Write a substitution command that will take each occurrence of greek-turkish and switch it with the text turkish and greek. Use parentheses expressions.

Answer: The command is as follows:
```
's/\(greek\)-\(turkish\)/\2 and \1/g'
```

h) Write an expression that will reverse the order of three numbers that appear in a line one after the other and are separated by a space, as follows:

```
20  15  10
```

Answer: The command is as follows:
```
'sed s/\([0-9]. \)\([0-9]. \)\([0-9].\)/\3 \2\1/'
```

LAB 7.1 SELF-REVIEW QUESTIONS

In order to test your progress, you should be able to answer the following questions.

1) In the following table, match each flag with the text description that correctly describes the function of the flag:

    a) Replaces each occurrence of the pattern globally within the pattern space   i) p flag

    b) Replaces the third occurrence of the pattern within the pattern space   ii) g flag

    c) Writes out the contents of the pattern space immediately after a successful substitution   iii) w flag

    d) Prints out the contents of the pattern space immediately after a successful substitution   iv) 3

2) Which of the following needs to be backslashed in the replacement string so that it may be interpreted literally?
    a) _____ .
    b) _____ *
    c) _____ &
    d) _____ +
    e) _____ \

3) Which of the following statements is true?
    a) _____The last slash in the substitute command is optional.
    b) _____The slash must be used to separate the substitute command, pattern, and replacement string.
    c) _____The ampersand is used in a replacement string to exactly match the pattern.
    d) _____The slash followed by an opening parenthesis in combination with a slash and closing parenthesis is used in the pattern of the substitute command for later recall in the replacement string.

**LAB
7.1**

Use the following line of input for questions 4 through 6:
650x555x1201
Use the following substitute command for questions 4-6:
s/\(650\)x\(555\)x\([0-9][0-9][0-9]\)/(\1)\2\3

4) What is \1 in the replacement string after the substitute command?
     a) _____555
     b) _____650x
     c) _____555x
     d) _____1201
     e) _____x1201
     f) _____None of the above

5) What is \2?
     a) _____650
     b) _____650x
     c) _____555x
     d) _____555
     e) _____1201

6) What is \3?
     a) _____650
     b) _____650x
     c) _____555
     d) _____555x
     e) _____1201

Quiz answers appear in Appendix A, Section 7.1.

**LAB
7.1**

L A B   7.2

THE DELETE COMMAND

LAB OBJECTIVE

After this Lab, you will be able to:

✓ Understand the Delete Command

The delete command removes the contents of the pattern space of the address that the command matches. The command's syntax is given as follows:

```
[line-address]d/
```

■ FOR EXAMPLE:

Suppose that you have the following lines:

```
<H1>This is a header one</H1>
<H2>This is a header two</H2>
<H3>This is a header three</H3>
```

Then the delete command

```
/H2/d
```

**LAB
7.2**

would result in:

```
<H1>This is a header one</H1>
<H3>This is a header three</H3>
```

The regular expression pattern H2 addresses the second line. The entire pattern space that contains the address of H2 is deleted and the next line is processed. Note that the delete command does not result in the pattern space partially becoming deleted, but the entire line is deleted. So the previous command did not result in the second line becoming

```
<H1>This is a header one</H1>
This is a header two</H2>
<H3>This is a header three</H3>
```

or

```
<H1>This is a header one</H1>
This is a header two
<H3>This is a header three</H3>
```

Rather, the entire line is deleted. For partial deletion, you can use the substitution command with an empty replacement string, as we have already seen.

Once the pattern space is deleted, any subsequent commands that are to be executed on the matched address are skipped. So if you have an HTML file that contains a table element, then the following commands would delete all lines that contain a header tag within the file and would change images from no-border to border:

```
/<table>/,/<\/table>/{
    /h[1-9]*/d
    s/border=0/border=1/
}
```

Using the following segment from an HTML file:

```
<table>
     <tr>
     <td>
          <h2>This is an image <img src="pic.gif"  border=0></h2>
          <h3>This is just a header</h3>
          <img src="pic.gif" border=0>
     </td>
     <tr>
</table>
```

The output that would result is:

```
<table>
     <tr>
     <td>
          <img src="pic.gif" border=1>
          </td>
     <tr>
</table>
```

Here, the delete and substitution commands are executed whenever the tag `<table>` occurs in the file. The commands are executed repetitively until another matching address `</table>` is found or the end of file is reached. Consider the following line:

```
<h2>This is an image <img src="pic.gif"  border=0><h2>
```

The substitution command following the delete is not executed, because the delete command deletes the pattern space of the line. Therefore, the substitution command has nothing to process; however, it continues with the rest of the file. Finally, the next line is also deleted, and in the last line a substitution is executed.

LAB 7.2 EXERCISES

7.2.1 UNDERSTAND THE DELETE COMMAND

Use the following file called `drums.dat` for each of the questions in this Exercise:

```
<p>
<TD>
        <IMG SRC="traps.gif">This is a picture of my percussion garden

        <IMG SRC="djembe.gif">This is a picture of my djembe
        <IMG SRC="conga.gif">This is a picture of my quinto and conga
</TD>
```

a) What is the output of the following command?
```
sed '/^$/d' drums.dat
```

b) What is the output of the following command?
```
sed '/<TD>/, /<\/TD>/{
\/^$/d\
s/traps/percAll/\
}' drums.dat
```

c) What is the output of the following command?
```
sed '/<TD>/,/<\/TD>/{\
d\
}' drums.dat
```

LAB 7.2 EXERCISE ANSWERS

This section gives you some suggested answers to the questions in Lab 7.2, with discussion related to those answers. Your answers may vary, but the most important thing is whether or not your answer works. Use this discussion to analyze differences between your answers and those presented here.

If you have alternative answers to the questions in this Exercise, you are encouraged to post your answers and discuss them at the companion Web site for this book, located at:

```
http://www.phptr.com/phptrinteractive/
```

7.2.1 ANSWERS

Use the given file to answer each of the questions in this Exercise.

a) What is the output of the following command?
```
sed '/^$/d' drums.dat
```

Answer: the output is as follows:
```
<p>
<TD>
        <IMG SRC="traps.gif">This is a picture of my percussion garden
        <IMG SRC="djembe.gif">This is a picture of my djembe
        <IMG SRC="conga.gif">This is a picture of my quinto and conga
</TD>
```

The regular expression /^$/ searches for all lines that have a beginning-of-line (BOL) character, ^, and an end-of-line (EOL) character, $, with nothing in between (i.e., a blank line). Once matched, the script deletes the line. In our example, the blank lines between the `<img src>` tag lines are deleted.

b) What is the output of the following command?
```
sed /<TD>/, /<\/TD>/{
\/^$/d\
    s/traps/percAll/\
}' drums.dat
```

Answer: The output is as follows:
```
<p>
<TD>
```

```
<IMG SRC="percAll.gif">This is a picture of my percussion garden
<IMG SRC="djembe.gif">This is a picture of my djembe
<IMG SRC="conga.gif">This is a picture of my quinto and conga
</TD>
```

Notice first in this example that the range expression /\/TD> has a backslash in it. It is needed because the slash might be interpreted by sed as a range delimiter. This example creates a range from the starting table column element tag <TD> to the ending table element tag </TD>. Within this range, every blank line is deleted. The next command substitutes the pattern traps with percAll. The control steps that sed takes when encountering commands that do not affect the normal control flow (unlike the delete command, which changes the normal control flow) are as follows:

1. Preprocessing step—Read the next line into the pattern space
2. Processing step—Process all commands directly on the pattern space
3. Postprocessing step—Print out the pattern space and return control to Step 1

This process is continued until the end-of-file is reached.

The delete command, on the other hand, immediately stops the processing step and passes control to the postprocessing step, which prints out the pattern space. Because the pattern space is empty as a result of the delete command, nothing is printed.

Therefore, when the delete command is encountered, if the pattern space matches the address that is part of the delete command (i.e., a blank line), then the contents of the pattern are deleted, and control passes directly to the postprocessing step. The substitution command is bypassed.

c) What is the output of the following command?
```
sed /<TD>/,/<\/TD>/{\
d\
}' drums.dat
```

Answer: The output is as follows:
```
<p>
```

In this example, everything within the beginning and ending table column tag is deleted, including the beginning and ending table column element tags, which are considered within the range.

LAB 7.2 SELF-REVIEW QUESTIONS

In order to test your progress, you should be able to answer the following questions.

1) The delete command cannot operate on a range of addresses.
    a) _____True
    b) _____False

2) The delete command can work on a single address.
    a) _____True
    b) _____False

3) Control passes to the postprocessing step immediately after the delete command is encountered.
    a) _____True
    b) _____False

4) The pattern space is immediately deleted after the delete command is encountered.
    a) _____True
    b) _____False

5) The pattern space is empty after the delete command.
    a) _____True
    b) _____False

Quiz answers appear in Appendix A, Section 7.2.

LAB
7.2

L A B   7.3

THE APPEND, INSERT, AND CHANGE COMMANDS

LAB OBJECTIVES

After this Lab, you will be able to:

✓ Understand the Append and Insert Commands

✓ Understand the Change Command

The syntax for these three commands is as follows:

```
[line address]a\
text

[line address]i\
text

[line address]c\
text
```

Here, the a, i, and c stand for append, insert, and change, respectively. They are different from the syntax we have previously encountered. The command does not appear entirely on a single line as it does with the substitution command. The append, change, and insert commands each have their commands on one line and the replacement text on the subsequent line(s).

The change command removes the contents of the pattern space and replaces them with the text following the command. The append and insert commands append and insert the text following the command when the pattern space is printed at the postprocessing step.

All three commands have a backslash at the end of the first command line and precede the text to escape the end of line. Remember that the pattern space does not match the end of line.

■ FOR EXAMPLE:

Suppose that we have forgotten the ending tag of all level-two headers in an HTML file. We could use the following command to append the end tag to every line that contains the level-two header, as follows:

```
/<H2>/a\
</H2>
```

For every line that contains a level-two header (matched by the regular expression <H2>), we append </H2> to the end of the line with the append command. Again, the text that we wish to append appears on the line following the append command; in our case, it is </H2>. The line that contains the append command is followed by the backslash to match the end-of-line (EOL) character.

The output of the example append command would appear as follows:

```
<H2>This is a level two header
</H2>
```

As you can see, the text that we append always appears at the beginning of the next line, because the text is appended at the postprocessing step. In the postprocessing step, the pattern space is output first. Because the pattern space contains a newline by default (this newline cannot be matched; think of it as a hidden newline), the newline is printed and then the appended text is output. Notice that the text that is part of the append command has an embedded newline on the same line as the command name a. This newline is also printed so that any subsequent output appears at the beginning of the next line.

As another example, consider the following insert command:

```
/Peter Patsis/i\
Mr.
```

The result would be that for every address that matches the pattern Peter Patsis, the text Mr. is inserted before the whole pattern space that matched that address. Therefore, the lines containing:

```
Peter Patsis
75 Center St.
New Paltz, NY 12561
```

would now be:

```
Mr.
Peter Patsis
75 Center St.
New Paltz, NY 12561
```

As you can see, the text that we insert always appears at the beginning of a line by itself before the contents of the pattern space. Like the append command, the text that is inserted is inserted at the postprocessing step, in which the pattern space is output first. Unlike the append command, in the postprocessing step, the text that is supplied with the insert command is printed first, and then the contents of the pattern space are printed. Because the text that is supplied to the insert command has an embedded newline that immediately follows the command name i, the inserted text is printed, then the embedded newline, and finally the pattern space.

The text that follows the insert and append command cannot be matched. Subsequent commands cannot affect the appended or inserted text. The text is printed during the postprocessing step when output is printed. Regardless of whether default output is suppressed or not, the inserted or appended text will be output.

Consider the following command:

```
/<Recipient>/c\
Dear Jack Clark
```

If we execute the command on the following form letter:

```
<Name>
<Address>
<City> <State> <Zip>

Dear <Recipient>,

It has come to our attention that you have an out-
standing balance of <amount>. Please call us to
arrange payment.
```

the result would be:

```
<Name>
<Address>
<City> <State> <Zip>

Dear Jack Clark,

It has come to our attention that you have an out-
standing balance of <amount>. Please call us to
arrange payment.
```

The change command takes the text `Dear Jack Clark` and replaces each line that is matched by the address <Recipient>. The change command, like the delete command, deletes the entire contents of the pattern space and returns control to the postprocessing step. However, unlike the delete command, the change command has a newline following the command, followed by the text to change. The change command prints the supplied text, then the newline, and finally the pattern space (which is empty).

No subsequent commands after the change command are executed. Control is passed to the postprocessing step.

The append and insert commands do not work on a range of addresses. Therefore, the following are not valid insert and append commands:

```
/<table>/, /<\/table>/i\
   <table>
/<table>/, /<\/table>/a\
   </table>
```

Because /<table>/, /</table>/ specifies a range of addresses, it is not a valid insert command. In other words, to interpret the preceding script, we cannot nest <table> and </table> tags around another table with an insert and append command.

■ FOR EXAMPLE:

The change command differs from the insert and append command in that it can be applied to a range of addresses. Therefore, the following is legal:

```
/<table>/, /<\/table>/c\
<Line Deleted>
```

This would replace all text starting from a beginning table tag, <table>, to the ending table tag </table>, with the single line <Line Deleted>. Thus, consider the following table:

```
<table>
     <tr>
     <td>
         <h2>This is an image <img src="pic.gif"  border=0>
         <h3>This is just a header</h3>
         <img src="pic.gif" border=0>
     </td>
     <tr>
</table>
```

After executing the example change command, the result would be:

```
<Line Deleted>
```

The change command text is printed once for the entire range of addresses, which in our example is a beginning and ending table element pair. Note that the change command text was not printed for each line; it was printed only once.

This behavior is different from when the change command is used within a pair of braces. The change command within a pair of braces will replace each line within the range of addresses with the supplied text in the change command. Therefore, using the previous table, if we replace the command

```
/<table>/, /<\/table>/c\
<Line Deleted>
```

with

```
/<table>/, /<\/table>{
c\
<Line Deleted>
}
```

then the output would be:

```
<Line Deleted>
<Line Deleted>
<Line Deleted>
<Line Deleted>
<Line Deleted>
<Line Deleted>
<Line Deleted>
<Line Deleted>
<Line Deleted>
/New York$/a\
 12561
s/12561$/10012/
```

If given the following two lines:

```
New Paltz, New York
New Paltz, NY 12561
```

the output would be

New Paltz, New York
12561
New Paltz, NY 10012

In the first line, the pattern space contains New Paltz, New York. Because this address in the pattern space matches the address expression New York$, the append command is applied to the pattern space. The pattern space remains unchanged; it is still New Paltz, New York. However, after the last command is executed, then the text 12561 will be appended to the pattern space. This will appear on a new line. Therefore, as this example suggests, you cannot match the appended text—it does not affect the contents of the pattern space. The appended text was not altered by the subsequent substitution command, which changes the text 12561 to 10012.

In the second line, the address that is specified by the append command (New York$) does not match the address New Paltz, NY 12561 (the line does not end with the text New York). Therefore, the append is not applied and the substitution command is evaluated. The pattern space does indeed end in the text 12561 (remember, the dollar sign matches the end of the line), so the text 12561 is changed to 10012. The exercises in this Lab will help clarify this discussion.

LAB 7.3 EXERCISES

7.3.1 UNDERSTAND THE APPEND AND INSERT COMMANDS

Use the file conf2.data from Lab 5.1 to answer Questions a through c of this Exercise:

a) What is the output of the following command?
```
sed '/ 0 /a\
#####  PAID IN FULL #####' conf2.data
```

b) What is the output of the following command?

```
sed 'a\
Inc.' conf2.data
```

_____

_____

c) What is the output of the following command?

```
sed 'i\
Ms. ' conf2.data
```

_____

_____

d) Assume that a new paragraph is always preceded by a blank line. Write a script that will insert a <P> tag before the start of each paragraph.

_____

_____

After each of the following commands is executed, show what the pattern space is for each of the following input lines:

Line 1: Smith Adhesions 700 200 081098 Digital

Line 2: Jones Coatings 900 0 081298 Dow

e) The commands are as follows:

```
s/08\(..\)\(..\)/Aug \1,19\2/
a\
Inc
/Aug/i\
Month
```

_____

_____

7.3.2 UNDERSTAND THE CHANGE COMMAND

Use the following lines to answer Questions a and b of this Exercise:

```
Peter Patsis
75 Center St.
New Paltz, NY 12561
```

a) What is the result of the pattern space after executing the following command?

```
/New Paltz, NY 12561/c\
Newburgh, NY 12601
s/NY/New York/
```

_____

_____

b) What is the result of the pattern space after executing the following command?

```
/Peter Patsis/c\
James Uribe\
s/Peter/Mr. Peter/
```

_____

_____

Use the following form letter to answer Question c of this Exercise.

```
<Name>
<Address>
<City> <State> <Zip>

Dear <Recipient>,

It has come to our attention that you have an out-
standing balance of <amount>. Please call us to
arrange payment.
```

c) Write a script that changes each of the tags (<>) with the follow-ing text values:

     <Name> = Peter Patsis
     <Address> = 75 Center St.
     <City> <State> <Zip> = Wallkill, NY 12876
     <Recipient> = Peter Patsis
     <amount> = $1000.00

LAB 7.3 EXERCISE ANSWERS

This section gives you some suggested answers to the questions in Lab 7.3, with discussion related to those answers. Your answers may vary, but the most important thing is whether or not your answer works. Use this discussion to analyze differ-ences between your answers and those presented here.

If you have alternative answers to the questions in this Exer-cise, you are encouraged to post your answers and discuss them at the companion Web site for this book, located at:

```
http://www.phptr.com/phptrinteractive/
```

7.3.1 ANSWERS

Use the `conf2.data` file to answer Questions a through c of this Exercise.

a) What is the output of the following command?
```
sed '/ 0 /a\
#####   PAID IN FULL #####' conf2.data
```
Answer: The output is as follows:
```
Smith Adhesions 700 200 081098 Digital
Jones Coatings 900 0 081298 Dow
#####   PAID IN FULL   #####
Phillips Stabilizers 850 100080198 Dupont
```

```
Kenny Coatings 900 450 072898 Dow
Patsis Adhesions 700 350 080198 IBM
Harris Adhesions 700 0 081198 Digital
#####  PAID IN FULL  #####
Gorge Stabilizers 850 0 081098 Dupont
#####  PAID IN FULL  #####
Mack Coatings 900 100 080398 Shell
Jones Coatings 900 0 080298 Texaco
#####  PAID IN FULL  #####
Denny Stabilizers 850 200 072998 Chrysler
Pierce Adhesions 700 0 080398 IBM
#####  PAID IN FULL  #####
Jackson Resins 800 200 080598 Dupont
```

The expression appends the string #### PAID IN FULL ##### for every line that contains a space followed by zero followed by another space. The only place this occurs is if the person paid their balance in full (fourth column equals zero). Notice that the text to append, ##### PAID IN FULL #####, begins on a new line when the pattern space is output and not on the same line as the pattern. In the following:

```
Jones Coatings 900 0 080298 Texaco
#####  PAID IN FULL  #####
```

PAID IN FULL ##### appears on a new line after the text Jones Coatings 900 0 080298 Texaco. When each line is read into the pattern space, each line in the input file has a newline at the end. Therefore, the pattern space has a newline at the end. This newline will not be matched, but it will be output. As a result, any line (or pattern space) will always start on a separate line when output. The append command places its text after this newline. Thus the text ##### PAID IN FULL #### is output on the next line.

b) What is the output of the following command?
```
sed 'a\
Inc.' conf2.data
```

Answer: This command appends the word "Inc." on a new line after each line of the input file, like so:
```
Smith Adhesions 700 200 081098 Digital
Inc.
```

```
Jones Coatings 900 0 081298 Dow
Inc.
Phillips Stabilizers 850 100080198 Dupont
Inc.
```

And so on.

c) What is the output of the following command?
```
sed 'i\
Ms. ' conf2.data
```

Answer: This command inserts the word "Ms." on its own line preceding each line of the input file, like so:

```
Ms.
Smith Adhesions 700 200 081098 Digital
Ms.
Jones Coatings 900 0 081298 Dow
Ms.
Phillips Stabilizers 850 100080198 Dupont
```

And so on.

Because we do not specify an address to the insert command, every address is matched.

d) Assume that a new paragraph is always preceded by a blank line. Write a script that will insert a <P> tag before the start of each paragraph.

Answer: The script should be as follows:
```
/^$/i\
<P>
```

After each of the following commands is executed, show what the pattern space is for each of the following input lines:
Line 1: Smith Adhesions 700 200 081098 Digital
Line 2: Jones Coatings 900 0 081298Dow

e) The commands are as follows:

Line 1:
```
s/08\(..\)\(..\)/Aug \1,19\2/
```
Answer: For Line 1, the pattern space is as follows:
Smith Adhesions 700 200 Aug 10, 1998 Digital

The pattern in the substitute command matches if a number contains the number 08 followed by four alphanumeric text digits between 0 and 8. The save feature (\(, \)) is used to save the first four numbers after the pattern 08. The first two numbers correspond to the day, and the last two the year. The day and year are recalled in the replacement string to print a more readable date, done only, as we said, for the month of August.

```
a\
Inc
```

Answer: For Line 1, the pattern space is as follows:
Smith Adhesions 700 200 Aug 10, 1998 Digital

Remember that even though the append command is performed, this does not affect the pattern space. It will be appended after the end of the script is reached.

```
/Aug/i\
Month
```

Answer: For Line 1, the pattern space is as follows:
Smith Adhesions 700 200 Aug 10, 1998 Digital

Again, as with the append command, the pattern space is not affected by the insert command.

The output that results for Line 1 is:

**Month
Smith Adhesions 700 200 Aug 10, 1998 Digital
Inc**

The append and insert are applied at the end of the script.

```
Line 2:
s/08\(..\)\(..\)/Aug \1,19\2/
```

Answer: For Line 2, the pattern space is as follows:
Jones Coatings 900 0 Aug 12, 1998 Dow

The reasoning is the same as for the first line.

```
a\
Inc
```

Answer: For Line 2, the pattern space is as follows:
Jones Coatings 900 0 Aug 12, 1998 Dow

The reasoning is the same as for the first line.

```
/Aug/i\
Month
```

For Line 2, the pattern space is as follows:
Jones Coatings 900 0 Aug 12, 1998 Dow

Again, the reasoning is the same.

The output that results is:

Month
Jones Coatings 900 0 Aug 12, 1998 Dow
Inc

7.3.2 ANSWERS

Use the given lines to answer Questions a and b of this Exercise.

a) What is the result of the pattern space after executing the following
command?
```
/New Paltz, NY 12561/c\
Newburgh, NY 12601
s/NY/New York/
```

Answer: The pattern space is as follows:
Newburgh, NY 12601

The change command replaces the entire contents of the pattern space
with the text following the command. Therefore, in this change command, New Paltz, NY 12561 is changed to Newburgh, NY 12601. Just
like the append and insert commands, subsequent sed commands do not
affect the modifications made by the change command.

The full output is as follows:

Peter Patsis
75 Center St.
Newburgh, NY 12601

b) What is the result of the pattern space after executing the following command?

```
/Peter Patsis/c\
James Uribe\
s/Peter/Mr. Peter/
```

Answer: The pattern space is as follows:
James Uribe

Again, a match is specified by the address in the change command, and Peter Patsis is changed to James Uribe. Control is passed to the postprocessing step, and the changed pattern space is printed. The substitute command is skipped.

The full output is as follows:

James Uribe
75 Center St.
New Paltz, NY 12561

Use the given form letter to answer Question c.

c) Write a script that changes each of the tags (<>) with the following text values:

```
<Name> = Peter Patsis
<Address> = 75 Center St.
<City> <State> <Zip> = Wallkill, NY 12876
<Recipient> = Peter Patsis
<amount> = $1000.00
```

Answer: All that is required for each answer is to match the correct angle bracket tag with the appropriate text for the command.

```
/<Name>/c\
Peter Patsis
/<Address>/c\
75 Center St,
/<City> <State> <Zip>/c\
Wallkill, NY 12876
s/<Recipient>/Peter Patsis/
s/<amount>/$1000.00/g
```

We provided the substitute command for the above two angle bracket tags because they occur interspersed with other text. The change command would have replaced the entire line, a result we do not want. Also, we use the g option to the substitute command, in case <amount> might appear more than once in a line.

LAB 7.3 SELF-REVIEW QUESTIONS

In order to test your progress, you should be able to answer the following questions.

1) The change command affects the contents of the pattern space.
    a) _____True
    b) _____False

2) The append and insert command affects the contents of the pattern space.
    a) _____True
    b) _____False

3) The append command prints the text following the command on a newline following the output of the pattern space.
    a) _____True
    b) _____False

4) The change command always prints the text following the command once every time the command is executed.
    a) _____True
    b) _____False

5) The insert command inserts the text following the command on a newline following the output of the pattern space.
    a) _____True
    b) _____False

6) Subsequent commands can match the appended or inserted text after executing an append or insert command.
    a) _____True
    b) _____False

Quiz answers appear in Appendix A, Section 7.3.

L A B   7.4

THE LIST AND TRANSFORM COMMANDS

LAB OBJECTIVES

After this Lab, you will be able to:

✓ Understand the List Command
✓ Understand the Transform Command

The list command syntax is as follows:

```
l
```

At the command line prompt, it can be executed by:

```
sed -n "l" input-file
```

In this example, the quotes are optional.

Otherwise, it can be executed in a script by entering the character l on a line by itself, as follows:

```
#sed script showing l command
l
```

As with other sed commands, the list command accepts addresses:

```
sed -n /Patsis/l conf2.data
```

That command produces:

Patsis Adhesions 700 350 080198 IBM

Also, this command:

```
sed -n 7l conf2.data
```

produces:

Gorge Stabilizers 850 0 081098 Dupont

The list command displays the contents of the pattern space. Additionally, it displays nonprintable characters as their two-digit ASCII values. The –n option suppresses the default output that sed produces after each line is processed. We use the –n option in the first example because the list command causes immediate output. If we do not suppress the default output, then the list command would display the contents of the pattern space twice.

■ *FOR EXAMPLE:*

Suppose that we have the following script:

```
sed -n 'l
s/^[/Escape/'
```

If we were given the following file:

This is the ^[character

then executing sed, with default output suppressed, on the above script and file would produce:

This is the \33 character

Try this example without the -n option.

As you can see, the list command prints the contents of the pattern space immediately with all nonprintable characters displayed as their ASCII values. In our case, the escape character, ^[, is represented by its two-digit ASCII value by the list command, which is \33. The substitute then substitutes the escape character with the word Escape.

TRANSFORM

The syntax of the transform command is as follows:

```
[line-address]y/abc/ABC/
```

The command transforms each occurrence of a with A, each occurrence of b with B, and each occurrence of c with C in the specified lines. The replacement occurs regardless of whether a precedes b and c. In other words, each replacement is independent of the other replacement. One useful way to use this command is to replace each occurrence of a lowercase letter with its uppercase equivalent.

■ *FOR EXAMPLE:*

Suppose that you have the following airline itinerary file:

Passenger	Departure Date	Airline	Flight	City	Time
Marley	Nov14	NW	413	NEW	10:15 am
Newton	Nov15	AM	1187	BOS	9:04 am
Nittinger	Nov15	NW	413	NEW	10:15 am

In the third line, you need to change the Airline from AM to NW. This goal can be accomplished with the following command:

```
3y/AM/NW
```

Simple enough. However, you can see the limitations of the transform command if you needed to, for example, change all airlines to AM. You might think the following command would work:

```
y/NW/AM
```

It would, of course. But keeping in mind that each replacement is independent of any other replacement, you'd get the following output:

```
Passenger    Departure Date   Airline   Flight   City    Time
Marley       Aov14            AM        413      AEM     10:15 am
Newton       Aov15            AM        1187     BOS      9:04 am
Nittinger    Aov15            AM        413      AEM     10:15 am
```

Each instance of an uppercase N is transformed to an uppercase A and each instance of an uppercase W is transformed to an uppercase M, regardless of whether they occur next to each other.

LAB 7.4 EXERCISES

7.4.1 UNDERSTAND THE LIST COMMAND

Use the file `conf2.data` from Lab 5.1 for Questions a through e in this Exercise:

a) What is the output of the following command?
```
sed -n '1' conf2.data
```

_____

_____

b) What is the output of the following command?
```
sed 1 conf2.data
```

_____

_____

c) What is the output of the following command?
```
sed '1
s/Adhesions/Coatings/' conf2.data
```

_____

_____

d) What is the output of the following command?

```
sed  -n '1
s/Adhesions/Coatings/' conf2.data
```

e) Write a debugging script that lists the pattern space after each of the following substitution commands. Use the `conf2.data` file.

```
s/Adhesions/Coatings/
```

```
s/Digital/Compaq/
```

7.4.2 UNDERSTAND THE TRANSFORM COMMAND

Use the `conf2.data` file for Questions a and b of this Exercise.

a) What is the output of the following commands?

```
y/abcdefghijklmnopqrstuvwxyz/ABCDEFGHIJKLMNOPQRSTU-
VWXYZ/
```

and

```
y/ABCDEFGHIJKLMNOPQRSTUVWXYZ/abcdefghijklmnopqrstu-
vwxyz/
```

b) Do the two following scripts produce the same output?

```
s/b/c/
y/abcdefghijklmnopqrstuvwxyz/ABCDEFGHIJKLMNOPQRSTU-
  VWXYZ/
```

and

```
y/abcdefghijklmnopqrstuvwxyz/ABCDEFGHIJKLMNOPQRSTU-
  VWXYZ/
s/b/c/
```

_____

_____

c) Write a script that uses only the transform command to convert the conference name and *only* the conference name to uppercase.

_____

_____

LAB 7.4 EXERCISE ANSWERS

This section gives you some suggested answers to the questions in Lab 11.4, with discussion related to those answers. Your answers may vary, but the most important thing is whether or not your answer works. Use this discussion to analyze differences between your answers and those presented here.

If you have alternative answers to the questions in this Exercise, you are encouraged to post your answers and discuss them at the companion Web site for this book, located at:

```
http://www.phptr.com/phptrinteractive/
```

7.4.1 ANSWERS

Use the file `conf2.data` for questions a through e in this Exercise:

**LAB
7.4**

a) What is the output of the following command?
```
sed -n 'l' conf2.data
```
Answer: Each line in the pattern space is output once:

In this sed invocation, only one command exists and it is the list command, which immediately outputs the contents of the pattern space. The default action outputs the contents of the pattern space. Since default output is suppressed, no output is printed, and the output above is due to the list command.

b) What is the output of the following command?
```
sed l conf2.data
```
Answer: Here, the default output is not suppressed, so the contents of the pattern space are output twice, once due to the list command and once due to the default action of outputting the contents of the pattern space during postprocessing.

c) What is the output of the following command?
```
sed 'l
s/Adhesions/Coatings/' conf2.data
```
Answer: The output is as follows:
```
Smith Adhesions 700 200 081098 Digital
Smith Coatings 700 200 081098 Digital
Jones Coatings 900 0 081298 Dow
Jones Coatings 900 0 081298 Dow
Phillips Stabilizers 850 100080198 Dupont
Phillips Stabilizers 850 100080198 Dupont
```
And so on.

Let's examine the first two lines:

```
Smith Adhesions 700 200 081098 Digital
Smith Coatings 700 200 081098 Digital
```

The first action is for sed to read in a line of input from the input file and copy it to the pattern space. The first command encountered is the list command. The list command causes immediate output of the contents in the pattern space, which is the first line. The script then substitutes Coatings for Adhesions. The bottom of the script is reached, and since default output is not suppressed, the second line is output. The rest of the pairs of output follow this same reasoning.

d) What is the output of the following command?
```
sed   -n  'l
s/Adhesions/Coatings/' conf2.data
```

Answer: The output is as follows:
```
Smith Adhesions 700 200 081098 Digital
Jones Coatings 900 0 081298 Dow
Phillips Stabilizers 850 100 080198 Dupont
Kenny Coatings 900 450 072898 Dow
Patsis Adhesions 700 350 080198 IBM
Harris Adhesions 700 0 081198 Digital
Gorge Stabilizers 850 0 081098 Dupont
Mack Coatings 900 100 080398 Shell
Jones Coatings 900 0 080298 Texaco
Denny Stabilizers 850 200 072998 Chrysler
Pierce Adhesions 700 0 080398 IBM
Jackson Resins 800 200 080598 Dupont
```

In this example, default output is suppressed; we do not see the second line output (the line that would have been output after the substitute). The only line that is output is a result of the list command, and as a result, we cannot see the changes from the substitution.

e) Write a debugging script that lists the pattern space after each of the following substitution commands. Use the `conf2.data` file.
```
s/Adhesions/Coatings/
s/Digital/Compaq/
```

Answer: The script is as follows:
```
sed -n 's/Adhesions/Coatings/
1
s/Digital/Compaq/
1' conf2.data
```

All that is required is to immediately execute the list command after the substitute command is performed. This will cause immediate output of the pattern space, and since no other command is placed between the list and substitute command, the list command will show the changes, or lack of changes, of the substitute commands. Of course, a line of output that is not altered because of the substitute commands will be printed out twice, because all four commands are executed for every line. The two substitute commands may not alter the pattern space.

7.4.2 ANSWERS

Use the `conf2.data` file for Questions a and b of this Exercise.

a) What is the output of the following command:
```
y/abcdefghijklmnopqrstuvwxyz/ABCDEFGHIJKLMNOPQRSTU-
    VWXYZ/
```

and
```
y/ABCDEFGHIJKLMNOPQRSTUVWXYZ/abcdefghijklmnopqrstu-
    vwxyz/
```

Answer: In the first command, the transform command replaces every lowercase letter with its uppercase equivalent. In the second, it replaces every uppercase letter with lowercase. The transform command is useful for converting files from lowercase to uppercase, or uppercase to lowercase.

b) Do the two following scripts produce the same output?
```
s/b/c/
y/abcdefghijklmnopqrstuvwxyz/ABCDEFGHIJKLMNOPQRSTU-
    VWXYZ/
```

and
```
y/abcdefghijklmnopqrstuvwxyz/ABCDEFGHIJKLMNOPQRSTU-
    VWXYZ/
s/b/c/
```

Answer: No

In the first, a substitution is made and then the line is transformed. In the second, the transformation converts to uppercase first. The substitution then is not performed because the b is lowercase. Because the transform command just converted b to B, no match is made. However, if the file contains no occurrences of the lowercase letter b, then the two are equivalent. The important point is that the transform command affects the contents of the pattern space, and subsequent commands work on the transformed pattern space.

c) Write a script that uses only the transform command to convert the conference name and *only* the conference name to uppercase.

Answer: You cannot.

At first glance, you might want to write the following transform command:

```
/Adhesions/y/abcdefghijklmnopqrstuvwxyz/ABCDEF-
   GHIJKLMNOPQRSTUVWXYZ/
```

However, this would be incorrect, because it would cause the whole line to be transformed to uppercase. The address just narrows down the conditions. The transform command will not work, because you have no way to isolate the command to work only on certain words. The transform will globally look at every character in its target and will replace that target character with the replacement character that positionally corresponds.

LAB 7.4 SELF-REVIEW QUESTIONS

In order to test your progress, you should be able to answer the following questions.

1) The command `y/abc/ABC/` would only change the word `abc` to uppercase.
   a) _____True
   b) _____False

2) If output is not suppressed and a sed script contains the list command, the pattern space will be output once.
   a) _____True
   b) _____False

3) The transform command does not affect the contents of the pattern space.
   a) _____True
   b) _____False

4) If output is suppressed and a sed script contains the list command, then the pattern space will be output once.
   a) _____True
   b) _____False

Quiz answers appear in Appendix A, Section 7.4.

L A B 7.5

THE PRINT AND NEXT COMMANDS

LAB OBJECTIVES

After this Lab, you will be able to:

✓ Understand the Print Command

✓ Understand the Next Command

PRINT COMMAND

Like the list command, the print command (p) immediately prints the contents of the pattern space. As always, if the default output is not suppressed, then a duplicate of the pattern space will be printed. The print command does not change the contents of the pattern, nor does it alter the flow of control within a sed script.

■ *FOR EXAMPLE:*

An example of a print statement is as follows:

```
/[0-9][0-9][0-9][0-9][0-9]/p
```

This example will print every line that contains a five-digit ZIP code.

The print flag found in the substitute command differs from the print statement found here, in that the print flag within the substitute command prints only if a successful substitution occurs. If no substitution occurs, then the print does not occur.

When used with the substitute command, the p *flag with output suppressed prints only those lines in which a substitution occurs.*

■ FOR EXAMPLE:

Consider the following script:

```
/<table>/{
p
y/abcdefghijklmnopqrstuvwxyz/ABCDEFGHIJKLMNOPQRSTU-
  VWXYZ/
p
}
```

This script capitalizes all characters found on the same line as `<table>`. It shows the contents of the pattern space immediately before the transformation occurred and after it. In this way, anyone can determine the results of a command on the pattern space by surrounding the command with a pair of print statements.

Another command that can be used for printing is the equal sign (=), which can be used for two purposes. First, if you combine it with the -n option to suppress the default output, = will print only the line number in which a match occurs. However, a more useful approach is to not suppress the default output so that both the matching line and its line number are printed.

Note that the equal sign (=) command does not work on a range of addresses.

■ *FOR EXAMPLE:*

Consider the following file:

```
Peter Patsis
75 Center St.
New Paltz, NY 12561
```

Suppose that we use the following script:

```
/Patsis/{
=
p
}
```

The output will thus be:

```
1
Peter Patsis
```

if default output is suppressed, or if default output is not suppressed, then the following is printed:

```
1
Peter Patsis
Peter Patsis
```

```
75 Center St.
New Paltz, NY 12561
```

The pattern matches only the first line. Once the match is made, the equal sign prints the line number. Next, the print command outputs the match. Finally, default output prints the line again. No other matches are made, so the default output spews out the rest.

NEXT COMMAND

The syntax of the next command is as follows:

```
[line-address]n
```

The next command (n) is used to read the next line of input into the pattern space. Like the delete command, the next command causes control to pass directly to the postprocessing step. Unlike the delete command, the contents of the pattern space are untouched and subsequently output. Control then reaches the preprocessing step, where the next line is read into the pattern space.

■ FOR EXAMPLE:

LAB
7.5

Consider the following command:

```
/Adhesions/n
s/ [0-9][0-9][0-9] /900/
```

The output is as follows:

Smith	Adhesions	700	200	081098	Digital
Jones	Coatings	900	0	081298	Dow
Phillips	Stabilizers	900	100	080198	Dupont
Kenny	Coatings	900	450	072898	Dow
Patsis	Adhesions	700	350	080198	IBM
Harris	Adhesions	700	0	081198	Digital
Gorge	Stabilizers	900	0	081098	Dupont
Mack	Coatings	900	100	080398	Shell
Jones	Coatings	900	0	080298	Texaco
Denny	Stabilizers	900	200	072998	Chrysler
Pierce	Adhesions	700	0	080398	IBM
Jackson	Resins	900	200	080598	Dupont

In this script, the next command contains the address regular expression Adhesions. Therefore, whenever the pattern space contains the address Adhesions, the next command causes control to pass to the postprocessing step, and the contents of the pattern space are output. Otherwise, the next command is not executed and the substitution command substitutes the conference fee to 900 for all other conferences.

LAB 7.5 EXERCISES

7.5.1 UNDERSTAND THE PRINT COMMAND

Use the `conf2.data` file to answer Questions a through e of this Exercise.

LAB 7.5

a) What is the result of the following command?

```
sed p conf2.data
```

_____

_____

b) What is the result of the following command?

```
sed -n 'p' conf2.data
```

_____

_____

c) What is the result of the following command?

```
sed -n '=' conf2.data
```

_____

_____

d) What is the result of the following command?

```
sed '/^/, /$/=' conf2.data
```

_____

_____

e) What is the result of the following command?

```
sed '/Adhesions/, /Coatings/p' conf2.data
```

_____

_____

f) Are the following two commands equivalent?
```
1,$p
```
and
```
1,$1
```

In the previous Lab, we had an exercise as follows:

Write a debugging script that lists the pattern space after each of the following substitution commands. Use the `conf2.data` file.

```
s/Adhesions/Coatings/
s/Digital/Compaq/
```

g) Answer the same question but use the print command.

7.5.2 UNDERSTAND THE NEXT COMMAND

Use the following lines for Question a of this Exercise:

```
<table>

<td>This is column number 1
<td>This is column number 2
</table>
```

a) What are the contents of the pattern space after the following command?
```
/<table>/{
n
/^$/d
}
```

b) Write a script that will substitute the conference name Adhesions with Coatings, except for the name Pierce in the conf2.data file.

_____

_____

LAB 7.5 EXERCISE ANSWERS

This section gives you some suggested answers to the questions in Lab 7.5, with discussion related to those answers. Your answers may vary, but the most important thing is whether or not your answer works. Use this discussion to analyze differences between your answers and those presented here.

If you have alternative answers to the questions in this Exercise, you are encouraged to post your answers and discuss them at the companion Web site for this book, located at:

`http://www.phptr.com/phptrinteractive/`

7.5.1 ANSWERS

Use the conf2.data file to answer Questions a through e of this Exercise.

a) What is the result of the following command?
```
sed p conf2.data
```
Answer: Each line is printed twice, once because of the print command and again because default output has not been suppressed.

b) What is the result of the following command?
```
sed -n 'p' conf2.data
```
Answer: Each line is printed once as a result of execution of the print statement.

c) What is the result of the following command?
```
sed -n '=' conf2.data
```
Answer: Because the equal command is used, the line numbers are output. Because default output is suppressed, nothing else is printed.

d) What is the result of the following command?
```
sed '/^/, /$/=' conf2.data
```
Answer: The result is as follows:
Error: Sed command uses only one address

The error results because the equal sign does not work on ranges, only single addresses or no address.

e) What is the result of the following command?
```
sed '/Adhesions/, /Coatings/p' conf2.data
```

LAB
7.5

Answer: The result is as follows:
```
Smith Adhesions 700 200 081098 Digital
Smith Adhesions 700 200 081098 Digital
Jones Coatings 900 0 081298 Dow
Jones Coatings 900 0 081298 Dow
```

At this point, the range condition has been turned off and the print command is not executed.

```
Phillips Stabilizers 850 100080198 Dupont
Kenny Coatings 900 450 072898 Dow
Patsis Adhesions 700 350 080198 IBM
```

At this point, the range condition is satisfied, and the print command will continue to execute until the range condition is turned off once again, at which point it finds a pattern with the ending condition Coatings or the end of file is reached.

```
Patsis Adhesions 700 350 080198 IBM
Harris Adhesions 700 0 081198 Digital
Harris Adhesions 700 0 081198 Digital
Gorge Stabilizers 850 0 081098 Dupont
Gorge Stabilizers 850 0 081098 Dupont
Mack Coatings 900 100 080398 Shell
Mack Coatings 900 100 080398 Shell
Jones Coatings 900 0 080298 Texaco
```

At this point, the range ending condition was encountered, and the print command will continue to not execute until a pattern that contains the starting pattern Adhesions is found or the end of file is reached.

```
Denny Stabilizers 850 200 072998 Chrysler
Pierce Adhesions 700 0 080398 IBM
```

At this point, the range condition is turned on:

```
Pierce Adhesions 700 0 080398 IBM
Jackson Resins 800 200 080598 Dupont
Jackson Resins 800 200 080598 Dupont
```

As you can see, the print command will execute as long as the range criteria is met (we encountered the starting range address and have not encountered the end address yet); otherwise, the print command will not execute. Regardless of whether we have encountered the print statement or not, because the default output is not suppressed, then the default action to print out the pattern space at the postprocessing step is performed. For this reason, patterns that encounter the print statement are output twice.

f) Are the following two commands equivalent?
```
1,$p
```
and
```
1,$l
```

Answer: No.

They may be equivalent if one file contains no characters like ^[. Remember that the list command will print the numeric character code equivalent of ^[, which is \33. The print command does not. It will print out the contents of the pattern space as they are visible.

In the previous Lab, we had an exercise as follows:
Write a debugging script that lists the pattern space after each of the following substitution commands. Use the conf2.data file.
```
s/Adhesions/Coatings/
s/Digital/Compaq/
```

g) Answer the same question but use the print command.

Answer: The script is as follows:
```
s/Adhesions/Coatings/
p
s/Digital/Compaq/
p
```

All that is required is to immediately execute the print command after the substitute command is performed. This will cause immediate output of the pattern space and, because no other command is placed between the print and substitute command, the print command will show the changes of the substitute commands. Of course, a line of output that is not altered because of the substitute commands will be printed out twice.

**LAB
7.5**

7.5.2 ANSWERS

Use the given lines for Question a of this Exercise.

a) What are the contents of the pattern space after the following command?
```
/<table>/{
n
/^$/d
}
```

Answer: Whenever the line contains a begin table tag, `<table>`, the next command is executed and the contents of the pattern space before it is executed is `<table>`.

After executing the next command, the pattern space is output and the next line is read into the pattern space, which is a blank line. After executing the command, control is passed to the bottom of the script, and the delete command is executed.

The pattern space is exactly the same as the input for all other cases.

b) Write a script that will substitute the conference name `Adhesions` with `Coatings`, except for the name `Pierce` in the `conf2.data` file.

Answer: The script is as follows:
```
/Pierce/n
s/Adhesions/Coatings/
```

In order to satisfy the previously stated condition, we use the next command. The next command first checks whether the line contains the pattern `Pierce`. If so, the next command skips it and reads the next line; otherwise, the "Adhesions/Coatings" substitution is performed.

LAB 7.5 SELF-REVIEW QUESTIONS

In order to test your progress, you should be able to answer the following questions.

1) The print command works exactly like the list command.
    a) _____True
    b) _____False

2) The print command causes immediate output of the pattern space.
    a) _____True
    b) _____False

3) The next command passes control immediately to the postprocessing step.
    a) _____True
    b) _____False

4) The next command causes the next line to be read into the pattern space immediately.
    a) _____True
    b) _____False

5) After the next command is executed, subsequent commands that appear after the next command will execute.
    a) _____True
    b) _____False

6) The print command does not operate on a range of addresses.
    a) _____True
    b) _____False

    Quiz answers appear in Appendix A, Section 7.5.

L A B   7.6

THE READ AND
WRITE COMMANDS

LAB OBJECTIVES

After this Lab, you will be able to:

✓ Understand the Read Command

✓ Understand the Write Command

READING FROM FILES

The syntax of the read command, which reads specified lines from a file, is as follows:

```
[line-address]r file
```

■ FOR EXAMPLE:

Suppose that we have a file that contains all the conferences that are to be offered this year, called conf98.dat. The contents of the file are as follows:

```
Coatings
Resins
Stabilizers
```

We also have the following file, which we'll call `memofile`:

```
The conferences that we are offering this year are
as follows

Adhesions

Please contact the Institute for further informa-
tion.
```

With this file as input, let's see what happens if we run the following sed read command on the `conf98.dat` file:

```
sed '/Adhesions/r conf98.dat' memofile
```

 Note that a space must separate the `r` command from the file name. Sed will issue an error if the file does not exist. Because a space separates the `r` command from the file name, the command must be enclosed in quotes to protect the space from being interpreted by the shell.

This would result in the following:

```
The conferences that we are offering this year are
as follows

Adhesions
Coatings
Resins
Stabilizers

Please contact the Institute for further informa-
tion.
```

As this example shows, the read command outputs the entire contents of the `conf98.dat` file into the `memofile` immediately *after* the matching line. In our example, this action occurred on the address that contained Adhesions.

As you can see, the address string that was matched, `Adhesions`, was output in its entirety. This fact demonstrates that the read command does not affect the contents of the pattern space. Because the read command does not affect the pattern space, the pattern space may be used by subsequent commands, whereas input lines may not. Suppose the Adhesions conference was no longer offered by the Institute. Let's use the same two files and execute them on the following script:

```
/Adhesions/r conf98.dat
/Adhesions/d
```

The output would thus be:

```
The conferences that we are offering this year are
as follows

Coatings
Resins
Stabilizers

Please contact the Institute for further informa-
tion.
```

Because the read command does not affect the pattern space, the delete command is applied to the current pattern space `Adhesions`.

The read command cannot operate on a range of lines, nor can you make any changes to the lines that were read in.

WRITING TO FILES

The write command (w) is similar to the read command, except instead of reading lines from one file into another, it writes the contents of the pattern space into a separate file. Its syntax is as follows:

```
[line-address]w file
```

■ FOR EXAMPLE:

Suppose that we have the following file:

Smith	Adhesions	700	200	081098	Digital
Jones	Coatings	900	0	081298	Dow
Phillips	Stabilizers	850	100	080198	Dupont
Kenny	Coatings	900	450	072898	Dow
Patsis	Adhesions	700	350	080198	IBM
Harris	Adhesions	700	0	081198	Digital
Gorge	Stabilizers	850	0	081098	Dupont
Mack	Coatings	900	100	080398	Shell
Jones	Coatings	900	0	080298	Texaco
Denny	Stabilizers	850	200	072998	Chrysler

**LAB
7.6**

Now, suppose that we want to create three separate files, one for each of the conferences, that will contain information specific only to that conference. This task is one function of the write command, as follows:

```
/Adhesions/w adhesions.dat
/Coatings/w coatings.dat
/Stabilizers/w stabilizers.dat
```

Note that, as with the read command, a space must separate the w command from the file name.

In this script, each time the pattern space matches Adhesions, that entire line is output to a new file, adhesions.dat. The same holds true for Coatings, whose lines are written to coatings.dat, and Stabilizers, whose lines are written to stabilizers.dat.

If a script attempts to write to a file that already exists, that file will be overwritten each time you run the script. However, if a single existing file is written to multiple times within the same script, that file is simply appended with each new write command.

Again, like the read command, because the pattern space is not affected by the write command, subsequent commands can work on the pattern space. In addition, if a previous command works on the pattern space, then the changes will be output by the write command. Therefore, the write command does not output when the end of the script is encountered, but instead it writes the output immediately.

■ FOR EXAMPLE:

Suppose that we wish to replace the conference name from the preceding example with the word Confirmed so that it appears where the conference name appeared in the file. We could do so with the following script:

```
/Adhesions/{
    s/Adhesions/Confirmed/
    w adhesions.dat
}
/Coatings/{
    s/Coatings/Confirmed/
    w coatings.dat
}
/Stabilizers/{
    s/Stabilizers/Confirmed/
    w stabilizers.dat
}
```

The contents of the file adhesion.dat would be:

Smith	Confirmed	700	200	081098	Digital
Patsis	Confirmed	700	350	080198	IBM
Harris	Confirmed	700	0	081198	Digital

The command s/Adhesions/Confirmed/ substitutes the current matching address /Adhesions/ with the word Confirmed. Therefore, the write command writes out Confirmed instead of the string Adhesions.

LAB 7.6 EXERCISES

7.6.1 UNDERSTAND THE READ COMMAND

Use the following files for the questions in this Exercise:

```
register.data
Smith      Adhesions     081098    Digital
Jones      Coatings      081298    Dow
Phillips   Stabilizers   080198    Dupont
Kenny      Coatings      072898    Dow
adhesions.data
700 London, England
coatings.data
850 Frankfurt, Germany
stabilizers.data
650 Boston, MA
```

a) What is the output of the following sed script?
```
sed '/Adhesions/r adhesions.data\
/Coatings/r coatings.data\
/Stabilizers/r stabilizers.data' register.data
```

b) What is the output of the following sed script?
```
sed '/Adhesions/r adhesions.data\
s/700/800/' register.data
```

c) What is the output of the following sed script?
```
sed -n '/Adhesions/r' adhesions.data
```

7.6.2 UNDERSTAND THE WRITE COMMAND

a) What is the output of the following command? What is written to the file?

```
/Adhesions/, /Coatings/w test.out
```

_____

_____

b) What is the output of the following command? What is written to the file?

```
/Adhesions/w test.out
```

_____

_____

c) What is the output of the following command? What is written to the file?

```
/Adhesions/{
s/Adhesions/Coatings/
w test.out
}
```

_____

_____

LAB 7.6 EXERCISE ANSWERS

This section gives you some suggested answers to the questions in Lab 7.6, with discussion related to those answers. Your answers may vary, but the most important thing is whether or not your answer works. Use this discussion to analyze differences between your answers and those presented here.

If you have alternative answers to the questions in this Exercise, you are encouraged to post your answers and discuss them at the companion Web site for this book, located at:

```
http://www.phptr.com/ptrinteractive/
```

7.6.1 ANSWERS

Use the files called `register.data`, `adhesions.data`, `coatings.data`, and `stabilizers.data` for the questions in this Exercise.

a) What is the output of the following sed script?
```
sed '/Adhesions/r adhesions.data\
/Coatings/r coatings.data\
/Stabilizers/r stabilizers.data' register.data
```

Answer: The output is as follows:
Smith Adhesions 081098 Digital
700 London, England
Jones Coatings 081298 Dow
850 Frankfurt, Germany
Phillips Stabilizers 080198 Dupont
650 Boston, MA
Kenny Coatings 072898 Dow
850 Frankfurt, Germany

LAB 7.6

Whenever the pattern `Adhesions` is found, the file `adhesions.data` is appended to the pattern space when control reaches the postprocessing step. The entire contents of `adhesions.data` would be appended, but because only one line of input exists from `adhesions.data`, the single line 700 London, England is appended. Notice that the line read in always starts on a newline. The same reasoning applies to coatings.data and stabilizers.data.

b) What is the output of the following sed script?
```
Sed '/Adhesions/r adhesions.data\
s/700/800/' register.data
```

Answer: The output is as follows:
Smith Adhesions 081098 Digital
700 London, England
Jones Coatings 081298 Dow
Phillips Stabilizers 080198 Dupont
Kenny Coatings 072898 Dow

Because the contents of the pattern space are not changed by the read command, the substitution won't affect them. The substitution affects only the original line read in from `register.data`, changing 700 to 800, which never occurs.

c) What is the output of the following sed script?

```
sed -n '/Adhesions/r' adhesions.data
```

Answer: The output is as follows:

700 London, England

Because default output is suppressed, the original line is not output. The only line that is output is the result of the read command.

7.6.2 ANSWERS

a) What is the output of the following command? What is written to the file?

```
/Adhesions/, /Coatings/w test.out
```

Answer: The output to the screen is as follows:

Smith	Adhesions	081098	Digital
Jones	Coatings	081298	Dow
Phillips	Stabilizers	080198	Dupont
Kenny	Coatings	072898	Dow

The output that is written to `test.out` *is as follows:*

Smith	Adhesions	081098	Digital
Jones	Coatings	081298	Dow

LAB
7.6

Every line is output to the screen because default output is not suppressed; however, `test.out` contains only lines that met the range criteria. (Ranges can be used with the write command.)

b) What is the output of the following command? What is written to the file?

```
/Adhesions/w test.out
```

Answer: The output to the screen is as follows:

Smith	Adhesions	081098	Digital
Jones	Coatings	081298	Dow
Phillips	Stabilizers	080198	Dupont
Kenny	Coatings	072898	Dow

The output that is written to `test.out` *is as follows:*

```
Smith        Adhesions        081098        Digital
```

Every line is output to the screen because default output is not suppressed, and `test.out` contains only lines that met the address criterion that the address contains the pattern `Adhesions`.

c) What is the output of the following command? What is written to the file?

```
/Adhesions/{
s/Adhesions/Coatings/
w test.out
}
```

Answer: The output to the screen is as follows:

```
Smith        Adhesions        081098        Digital
Jones        Coatings         081298        Dow
Phillips     Stabilizers      080198        Dupont
Kenny        Coatings         072898        Dow
```

The output that is written to `test.out` *is as follows:*

```
Smith Coatings 081098 Digital
```

Every line is output to the screen because default output is not suppressed. Therefore, we see the result of the substitute command whenever it is applied. `Test.out` contains the result of the substitution because the substitution occurs first. Notice that because we have a brace expression, the script is invoked only when the line read in contains the address pattern `Adhesion`.

LAB 7.6 SELF-REVIEW QUESTIONS

In order to test your progress, you should be able to answer the following questions.

1) The read command changes the contents of the pattern space.
   a) _____True
   b) _____False

2) The write command changes the contents of the pattern space.
   a) _____True
   b) _____False

3) The read command causes control to pass immediately to the postpro-cessing step.
   a) _____True
   b) _____False

4) The read command does not operate on a range of addresses.
   a) _____True
   b) _____False

5) The write command does not operate on a range of addresses.
   a) _____True
   b) _____False

Quiz answers appear in Appendix A, Section 7.6.

LAB
7.6

CHAPTER 7

TEST YOUR THINKING

 The projects in this section are meant to have you utilize all of the skills that you have acquired throughout this chapter. The answers to these projects can be found at the companion Web site to this book, located at:

`http://www.phptr.com/phptrinteractive/`

Visit the Web site periodically to share and discuss your answers.

1) When appending, how would you have the appended text appear on the same line as the pattern space to which it was appended?

In Lab 7.4, we had the following debug script:

```
sed -n 's/Adhesions/Coatings/
l
s/Digital/Compaq/
l' conf2.data
```

The problem was that the list command printed the contents of the pattern space out twice when no substitution was performed.

2) Fix this problem to print out the contents of the pattern space only if a change is made.

3) The MS-DOS operating system ends all lines with the character code ^M. It is invisible to MS-DOS and also invisible when the file is output with the more command. Inside UNIX, how would you discover all lines that contain the ^M character?

CHAPTER 8

MULTILINE PATTERN SPACE COMMANDS

 The commands you will see in this chapter are the same as those you have already seen, except that they are uppercase.

CHAPTER OBJECTIVE

In this chapter, you will learn about:

In Lab 7.2, we described the normal flow of control of a sed script in three steps: Preprocessing, processing, and postprocessing.

The commands we looked at did not alter this flow of control within a sed script. In this chapter, you will look at commands that change the normal flow of control and work on more than one line at a time from the input file. They provide the ability to match and manipulate multiple lines to delete, substitute, print, or transform. Each of the multiline commands (N, D, P) have the same character that represents the single-line command character, and also have similar functionality. The representation of the multiline commands differs from the single-line commands in that the multiline commands are written in uppercase and the single-line commands are written in lowercase.

L A B   8.1

THE MULTILINE NEXT, DELETE, AND PRINT COMMANDS

LAB OBJECTIVES

After this Lab, you will be able to:

✓ Understand the Multiline Next Command

✓ Understand the Multiline Delete Command

✓ Understand the Multiline Print Statement

MULTILINE NEXT COMMAND

The multiline next command (N) appends the next line in the input file to the pattern space after the current line that is contained in the pattern space. The original contents of the pattern space are separated from the next line read in by a newline.

■ *FOR EXAMPLE:*

Consider the following script:

```
1{
N
}
```

Suppose that we used the following input file:

The UNIX operating system comes in
many flavors. There are AIX, DUNIX, Solaris,
Linux, and many others.

The next command is executed for the first line of input that is matched by the address 1. In this example, the result of the pattern space is as follows:

The UNIX operating system comes in\nmany flavors.
There are AIX, DUNIX, Solaris,\n

Here, \n represents a newline. As can be seen from the example, the first line is read into the pattern, and the pattern space becomes:

The UNIX operating system comes in

**LAB
8.1**

When the multiline next command is executed, the second line is read in, and the two lines are separated by a newline. The pattern thus becomes:

The UNIX operating system comes in\nmany flavors.
There is AIX, DUNIX, Solaris,\n

The important distinction to make is that the two lines can be thought of as a single line and can be matched in their entirety by subsequent commands. The difference between the single-line next command and multiline next command is that the single-line next command outputs the current contents of the pattern space and then reads the next line and does not append it to the current line.

■ FOR EXAMPLE:

As another example, suppose that we wish to protect against word wrap in a file. More specifically, suppose that we wish to replace "UNIX operating system" with "DOS operating system" everywhere it occurs in a file. Furthermore, suppose that the text "UNIX operating system" may be split across lines. The following sed script will perform the replacement:

```
/UNIX/{
s/UNIX operating system/DOS operating system/
N
s/ *\n/ /
s/UNIX operating system */DOS operating system\
/
}
```

How does this script work? Let's look at two groups of lines:

The UNIX operating system is very robust.
The UNIX operating system was developed in the 70s.

The UNIX operating
system is very robust

In the first group, the first line read in matches the address /UNIX/, and the inner commands are executed. The first one substitutes "UNIX operating system" with "DOS operating system," as expected. The line thus becomes:

The DOS operating system is very robust.

The following line is the multiline next command. Therefore, the next command reads the next line, appends it to the last line, and separates the two with the newline character. The pattern space then becomes:

The DOS operating system is very robust.\nThe UNIX
operating system was developed in the 70s.\n

The next substitute command substitutes a space, / /, whenever it encounters a newline (zero spaces) or one or more spaces followed by a newline, represented by the pattern / *\n/ (the asterisk specifies zero or more spaces). Because the substitute command replaces only the first occurrence of a match, the pattern space becomes, after executing the second command:

```
The DOS operating system is very robust. The UNIX
operating system was developed in the 70s.\n
```

The last command

```
s/UNIX operating system */DOS operating system\
```

substitutes the last occurrence of the UNIX operating system with the DOS operating system and appends the newline character after the text system. The line then becomes:

```
The DOS operating system is very robust. The DOS
operating system\n
was developed in the 70s.\n
```

After the first substitution, the next group becomes:

```
The UNIX operating
system is very robust.
```

**LAB
8.1**

In other words, no match occurs. The next command reads the next line of input, appends it to the first line read in, and separates it with a newline. After executing the next command, it becomes:

```
The UNIX operating\nsystem is very robust.\n
```

The substitution command then replaces the space and newline with a space. The pattern space becomes:

```
The UNIX operating system is very robust.\n
```

The next substitution then replaces the string "UNIX operating system" (remember that the asterisk matches the space after the letter m) with the string "DOS operating system" and appends a newline (remember the backslash). The pattern space then becomes:

```
The DOS operating system
is very robust.\n
```

MULTILINE DELETE

The multiline delete command deletes from the start of the pattern space up to the first embedded newline character. It does not cause a newline to be read; it deletes the front part (and only the front part) of a multiline pattern space. This differs from the single-line delete command, which deletes the entire pattern space, and returns control to the postprocessing step.

■ FOR EXAMPLE:

As an example of the multiline delete, let's look at the following:

```
/<\/*table>/{
N
D
}
```

Suppose that we have the following as an input file:

```
<table>
    <tr>
    <td>
      <h2>This is an image <img src="pic.gif"  border=0>
        <h3>This is just a header</h3>
        <img src="pic.gif" border=0>
    </td>
    <tr>
</table>
```

The output would be:

```
<tr>
<td>
   <h2>This is an image <img src="pic.gif"  border=0>
     <h3>This is just a header</h3>
     <img src="pic.gif" border=0>
</td>
<tr>
```

LAB
8.1

The commands within the braces are executed whenever the input line contains the pattern `/</*table>/`. This execution happens in the first and last input line when it encounters the patterns `<table>`, `</table>`. At that point, the next command is executed first within the braces. The pattern space thus becomes:

`<table>\n<tr>`

When the multiline delete command is encountered, then the pattern space becomes:

`<tr>`

because the delete command deletes only the front part (i.e., everything before `\n`) of the pattern space. Because no commands are left to process, the postprocessing step prints the contents of the pattern space `<tr>/`. The script continues reading until the ending tag is encountered. The element `</table>` matches `/</*table>/` and the multiline next statement is executed. It reads the next line of input. No more input exists, so the pattern space remains:

**LAB
8.1**

`</table>`

The multiline delete command then deletes the entire pattern space, and performs the postprocessing step of printing the contents of the pattern space. Because the pattern space is empty, nothing is printed.

The multiline delete command always returns control to the outermost block. If a grouping command exists, as in the following:

```
/Adhesions/{
N
D
s/Coatings/VVV/
}
s/Coatings/ZZZ/
```

then the outermost block is the command following the closing brace (the end of the group), the second substitute command. If the multiline delete command is outside a grouping statement, as in the following:

```
N
D
s/Coatings/ZZZ/
```

then control is always returned to the postprocessing step. In the previous multiline delete command, the substitution would be skipped.

Be careful to understand what is deleted by the multiline delete and what statement is evaluated after the command is executed.

MULTILINE PRINT COMMAND

The multiline print command (P) outputs the first part of the pattern space up to the newline character. If the default output is suppressed, then the contents of the pattern space are not output.

**LAB
8.1**

■ *FOR EXAMPLE:*

An example of the multiline print statement is as follows:

```
sed 'N\
P'
```

Suppose that we are to use the following table:

```
<table>
    <tr>
    <td>
        <h2>This is an image <img src="pic.gif"  border=0>
        <h3>This is just a header</h3>
        <img src="pic.gif" border=0>
    </td>
    <tr>
</table>
```

Then the output would be:

```
<table>
 <table>
<tr>
```

```
<td>
<td>
        <h2>This is an image <img src="pic.gif"  border=0>
        <h3>This is just a header</h3>
        <h3>This is just a header</h3>
        <img src="pic.gif" border=0>
    </td>
    </td>
     <tr>
</table>
</table>
```

For the first line, the pattern space before the multiline next command is executed is:

```
<table>
```

After the multiline next command is executed, the pattern space is:

**LAB
8.1**

```
<table>\n<tr>
```

The multiline print command prints up to the first newline:

```
<table>
```

Because default output is not suppressed, the pattern space is printed out in the postprocessing step, which results in:

```
<table>
<tr>
```

The newline in the pattern space causes the tag <tr> to appear on the next line. The next line read in is:

```
<td>
```

Notice in the last line that the multiline next command does not change the pattern space, because no next line to read exists (end-of-file is reached). Therefore, the multiline print statement prints up to the first newline character it encounters, which is the newline that is always at the end of a pattern space.

LAB 8.1 EXERCISES

8.1.1 UNDERSTAND THE MULTILINE NEXT COMMAND

For the first two questions in this Exercise, use the `conf2.data` file from Lab 5.1:

Run each of the following sed commands:

```
sed '/Adhesions/{
N
s/Adhesions 700/ /2
}' conf2.data
```

a) What is the output?

_____

_____

```
sed 'N' conf2.data
```

b) What is the output?

_____

_____

In the discussion in this Lab, you saw the following sed script:

```
/UNIX/{
s/UNIX operating system/DOS operating system/
N
s/UNIX operating system */DOS operating system\
/
}
```

c) What is the output of the script using the following line?

```
The UNIX operating system is very robust. The UNIX
operating system was developed in the 70s.
```

_____

_____

Use the following input lines to answer the following question:

```
<Table>

<tr>This is a row
<td width=50%>This is a column</td>
<td>This is another column</td>
</tr>
<tr>
<Table>


<tr>This is another row</tr>
</table>
</tr>
</table>
```

d) What is the output of the following sed script on those input lines?

```
/Table/{
N
s/\n/ /
}
```

_____

_____

8.1.2 UNDERSTAND THE MULTILINE DELETE COMMAND

Using the `conf2.data` file, run the following sed commands:

```
sed -n '/Adhesions/D' conf2.data
```

a) What is the output?

_____

_____

```
sed '/Adhesions/D' conf2.data
```

b) What is the output?

_____

_____

```
sed '/Adhesions/{
s/[0-9]\{6\}/\
/
D
}' conf2.data
```

c) What is the output?

_____

_____

Use the following file, called `table.in`, for the next question:

```
<Table>

<tr>This is a row
<td width=50%>This is a column</td>
<td>This is another column</td>
</tr>
<tr>
<Table>


<tr>This is another row</tr>
</table>
</tr>
</table>
```

d) What is the output of the following sed script?

```
/<Table>/{
N
/^$/D
}
```

_____

_____

8.1.3 UNDERSTAND THE MULTILINE PRINT STATEMENT

Using the `conf2.data` file, run the following sed commands:

```
sed '/Adhesions/{
N
P
}' conf2.data
```

LAB
8.1

a) What is the output?

_____

_____

```
sed -n /Adhesions/{
N
P
}' conf2.data
```

b) What is the output?

_____

_____

```
sed -n 's/Adhesions/Coatings/
N
P' conf2.data
```

c) What is the output?

_____

_____

Suppose that you would like to take a line of input that may extend over one or more lines and print that line of input as a single line.

The line of input is as follows:

```
!AddressHistory[1]   =   R   D   ASM   0x4:0x1111..0x2222
     phys:0x3333..0x4444!
```

At the very longest, it may be extended over two lines. In the single-line or two-line case, each address history line will be enclosed within exclamation points. One of the many two-line extensions is as follows:

```
!AddressHistory[2]= R D ASM
0x4:0x1111..0x2222 phys:0x3333..0x4444!
```

For these two lines of input, the output would be as follows:

```
AddressHistory[1] = R D ASM 0x4:0x1111..0x2222
phys:0x3333..0x4444
```

d) Write a script that would perform the given function.

_____

_____

LAB 8.I EXERCISE ANSWERS

This section gives you some suggested answers to the questions in Lab 8.1, with discussion related to those answers. Your answers may vary, but the most important thing is whether or not your answer works. Use this discussion to analyze differences between your answers and those presented here.

If you have alternative answers to the questions in this Exercise, you are encouraged to post your answers and discuss them at the companion Web site for this book, located at:

`http://www.phptr.com/phptrinteractive/`

8.I.I ANSWERS

For the first two questions in this Exercise, use the `conf2.data` file. Run each of the following sed commands:

```
sed '/Adhesions/{
N
s/Adhesions 700/ /2/
}' conf2.data
```

a) What is the output?

Answer: The output would be as follows:

```
Smith Adhesions 700 200 081098 Digital
Jones Coatings 900 0 081298 Dow
Phillips Stabilizers 850 100 080198 Dupont
Kenny Coatings 900 450 072898 Dow
Patsis Adhesions 700 350 080198 IBM
Harris    0 081198 Digital
Gorge Stabilizers 850 0 081098 Dupont
Mack Coatings 900 100 080398 Shell
Jones Coatings 900 0 080298 Texaco
Denny Stabilizers 850 200 072998 Chrysler
Pierce Adhesions 700 0 080398 IBM
Jackson Resins 800 200 080598 Dupont
```

Whenever the input line contains the address `Adhesions`, the script within the braces is executed. The first command encountered is the multiline next command. It causes the next line of input to be read and appended to the pattern space. Therefore, when the following line is encountered, the script within the braces is executed:

```
Patsis Adhesions 700 350 080198 IBM
```

The multiline next command is executed next, and it causes the next line to be read in and appended to the current contents of the pattern space, and then it separates the line read and the pattern space with a newline. Therefore, the pattern becomes:

```
Patsis Adhesions 700 350 080198 IBM\nHarris Adhe-
sions 700 0 081198 Digital
```

**LAB
8.1**

The next command is the substitute command. The pattern in the substitute command matches any pattern space that contains the pattern `Adhesions 700`. Because the pattern space above contains this pattern, it is matched and replaced by a space for the second occurrence of the pattern "Adhesions 700" only. Therefore, after the substitution, the pattern space becomes:

```
Patsis Adhesions 700 350 080198 IBM\nHarris 0 081198
Digital
```

When the end of the script is reached, the pattern is output. The output that results is:

```
Patsis Adhesions 700 350 080198 IBM
Harris 0 081198 Digital
```

In other words, because an embedded newline exists, when that character is output, it causes the string following that character in the pattern space to be output on a new line.

Notice that the substitution occurs for only two lines that contain an occurrence of `Adhesions 700`, where one line immediately follows the previous occurrence in the input file.

```
Sed 'N' conf2.data
```

b) What is the output?

Answer: The output is as follows:
```
Smith Adhesions 700 200 081098 Digital
Jones Coatings 900 0 081298 Dow
Phillips Stabilizers 850 100080198 Dupont
Kenny Coatings 900 450 072898 Dow
Patsis Adhesions 700 350 080198 IBM
Harris Adhesions 700 0 081198 Digital
Gorge Stabilizers 850 0 081098 Dupont
Mack Coatings 900 100 080398 Shell
Jones Coatings 900 0 080298 Texaco
Denny Stabilizers 850 200 072998 Chrysler
Pierce Adhesions 700 0 080398 IBM
Jackson Resins 800 200 080598 Dupont
```

The multiline next command causes the next line to be appended to the pattern space and separates the two with a newline. Because nothing else is done to the pattern, it results in both lines being output. Because an embedded newline separates the two, it causes the second line to be output on a new line. This is equivalent to performing output a line at a time.

**LAB
8.1**

In the discussion in this Lab, you saw the following sed script:
```
/UNIX/{
s/UNIX operating system/DOS operating system/
N
s/UNIX operating system */DOS operating system\
/
}
```

c) What is the output of the script using the following single line?
```
The UNIX operating system is very robust. The UNIX
operating system was developed in the 70s.
```

Answer: The output would be as follows:
```
The DOS operating system is very robust. The DOS
operating system
was developed in the 70s.
```

The first substitute command substitutes the first occurrence of "UNIX operating system" with "DOS operating system." Therefore, the pattern space before and after the substitute command is as follows:

Before: **The UNIX operating system is very robust.**
The UNIX operating system was developed in the 70s.
After: **The DOS operating system is very robust. The**
UNIX operating system was developed in the 70s.

The next command encountered is the multiline next command. It appends the next line, which doesn't exist, to the pattern space separated by a newline. The pattern space then becomes unchanged.

The substitute command then substitutes the string "DOS operating system" followed by a newline whenever the pattern space contains "UNIX operating system." As a result, the pattern space before and after becomes:

Before: **The DOS operating system is very robust. The**
UNIX operating system was developed in the 70s.
After: **The DOS operating system is very robust. The**
DOS operating system\nwas developed in the 70s.

The pattern space causes the output given in this answer.

d) What is the output of the following sed script using the given input lines?

```
/Table/{
N
s/\n/ /
}
```

Answer: The output would be as follows:
<Table>
<tr>This is a row
<td width=50%>This is a column</td>
<td>This is another column</td>
</tr>
<tr>
<Table>

```
<tr>This is another row</tr>
</table>
</tr>
</table>
```

The first line read in matches the address /Table/. Therefore, the script contained within the braces is executed. The first command encountered is the multiline next command. Before executing the command, the pattern space is as follows:

<Table>

The next line that is read in as a result of the multiline next command is blank. As a result, after executing the multiline next command, the pattern space becomes:

<Table>\n

Be sure to distinguish between the embedded newline that was appended as a result of executing the multiline next command and an end-of-line (EOL) character. A newline character can be an EOL, but an EOL cannot be a newline character; as such, sed matches newline characters only if they are not also EOLs.

After the substitution command, which replaces the embedded newline with a space, the pattern space becomes:

"<Table> "

This is subsequently output. As a result, the script removes the blank line and prints the two lines (the line with the text <Table> and the blank line) in the input file as a single line.

This is also done a second time when the text <Table> occurs later in the input file.

**LAB
8.1**

8.1.2 ANSWERS

Using the `conf2.data` file from Exercise 8.1.1, run the following sed commands:
```
sed -n '/Adhesions/D' conf2.data
```

a) What is the output?

Answer: No output occurs.

The multiline delete command deletes everything until the first embedded newline is encountered. It does not print out the line it deleted. Since no embedded newline is encountered in each line, whenever it encounters the address Adhesions that is supplied to the multiline delete command, it will delete the entire input line. Furthermore, since default output is suppressed, no output is produced for each of the other lines that are read in.

```
sed '/Adhesions/D' conf2.data
```

b) What is the output?

Answer: The output would be as follows:
```
Jones Coatings 900 0 081298 Dow
Phillips Stabilizers 850 100080198 Dupont
Kenny Coatings 900 450 072898 Dow
Gorge Stabilizers 850 0 081098 Dupont
Mack Coatings 900 100 080398 Shell
Jones Coatings 900 0 080298 Texaco
Denny Stabilizers 850 200 072998 Chrysler
Jackson Resins 800 200 080598 Dupont
```

Because default output is not suppressed, every line that does not match the multiline delete command is output, unlike the previous example. Every line that matches the address Adhesions is deleted in its entirety, as described in the previous example. Therefore, no line that contains the address Adhesions is output.

```
sed '/Adhesions/{
s/[0-9]\{6\}/\
/
D
}' conf2.data
```

c) What is the output?

Answer: The output would be as follows:

```
Digital
Jones Coatings 900 0 081298 Dow
Phillips Stabilizers 850 100 080198 Dupont
Kenny Coatings 900 450 072898 Dow
  IBM
Digital
Gorge Stabilizers 850 0 081098 Dupont
Mack Coatings 900 100 080398 Shell
Jones Coatings 900 0 080298 Texaco
Denny Stabilizers 850 200 072998 Chrysler
  IBM
Jackson Resins 800 200 080598 Dupont
```

Let's look at the first line of the input file:

```
Smith Adhesions 700 200 081098 Digital
```

The address `Adhesions` is matched in the first line, and the group command enclosed within the braces is executed. The first command encountered is a substitution command. The substitution command replaces any string that contains six consecutive digits with no characters, separating the digits with a newline. The pattern that contains six consecutive digits is "081098." The pattern space then becomes:

```
Smith Adhesions 700 200 \n Digital
```

The multiline delete commands deletes everything up to the first embedded newline. Therefore, the pattern space becomes:

```
Digital
```

This is subsequently output. The same logic is applied on lines 4, 5, and 10.

Use the file `table.in` for the next question.

d) What is the output of the following sed script?

```
/<Table>/{
N
/^$/D
}
```

Answer: Whenever the line that contains the address <Table> is encountered, the script within the braces is executed. This occurs in the first line read in. The first command in the script is the multiline next command. It causes the next line, which is blank, to be read in, and the two lines are separated by an embedded newline. The pattern space after the multiline next command is executed becomes:

`<Table>\n`

The command that is executed following the multiline next command is the multiline delete command. The multiline delete command is executed whenever it encounters a pattern space that is empty. The pattern space will never be empty whenever the multiline delete command is encountered, because the previous command is the multiline next command. At the very least, the multiline next command will always append an embedded newline. Therefore, the end result of executing this entire sed command is to output each line in the input file as it was read in initially.

**LAB
8.1**

8.1.3 ANSWERS

Using the `conf2.data` file from Exercise 8.1.1, run the following sed commands:

```
sed '/Adhesions/{
N
P
}' conf2.data
```

a) What is the output?

Answer: The output is as follows:

```
Smith Adhesions 700 200 081098 Digital
Smith Adhesions 700 200 081098 Digital
Jones Coatings 900 0 081298 Dow
Phillips Stabilizers 850 100 080198 Dupont
```

```
Kenny Coatings 900 450 072898 Dow
Patsis Adhesions 700 350 080198 IBM
Patsis Adhesions 700 350 080198 IBM
Harris Adhesions 700 0 081198 Digital
Gorge Stabilizers 850 0 081098 Dupont
Mack Coatings 900 100 080398 Shell
Jones Coatings 900 0 080298 Texaco
Denny Stabilizers 850 200 072998 Chrysler
Pierce Adhesions 700 0 080398 IBM
Pierce Adhesions 700 0 080398 IBM
Jackson Resins 800 200 080598 Dupont
```

Whenever a line that contains the pattern /Adhesions/ is encountered, the script within the braces is executed. The first line contains this pattern:

```
Smith Adhesions 700 200 081098 Digital
```

The first statement within the braces is the multiline next command, which causes the input line to be appended to the pattern space, separating each with an embedded newline. The pattern space then becomes:

```
Smith Adhesions 700 200 081098 Digital\nJones Coat-
ings 900 0 081298 Dow
```

The multiline print command causes the pattern space to be output, up to the first embedded newline. This results in the following output:

```
Smith Adhesions 700 200 081098 Digital
```

When the end of the script is reached, the default action is to output the entire pattern space. The embedded newline, when output, causes the text after it to be output on a newline. Therefore, the two following lines are output:

```
Smith Adhesions 700 200 081098 Digital
Jones Coatings 900 0 081298 Dow
```

**LAB
8.1**

Therefore, each time the script within the braces is executed, three lines of output result.

```
sed -n /Adhesions/{
N
P
}' conf2.data
```

b) What is the output?

Answer: The output is as follows:
Smith Adhesions 700 200 081098 Digital
Patsis Adhesions 700 350 080198 IBM
Pierce Adhesions 700 0 080398 IBM

Because default output is suppressed, the only output that is seen is a result of executing the multiline print command. The script within the braces follows the same logic as the previous example.

```
sed -n 's/Adhesions/Coatings/
N
P' conf2.data
```

c) What is the output?

Answer: The output is as follows:
Smith Coatings 700 200 081098 Digital
Phillips Stabilizers 850 100 080198 Dupont
Patsis Coatings 700 350 080198 IBM
Gorge Stabilizers 850 0 081098 Dupont
Jones Coatings 900 0 080298 Texaco
Pierce Coatings 700 0 080398 IBM

Because default output is suppressed, the only output occurs as a result of the multiline print command. The multiline print command prints everything up to the first embedded newline. Therefore, only the first line of every two lines read in (the second line is read into the pattern space as a result of the multiline next command) is output. In other words, the first, third, fifth, seventh, ninth, and eleventh lines are output. For each line that contains the pattern Adhesions, the pattern Adhesions is replaced by Coatings.

Suppose that you would like to take a line of input that may extend over one or more lines and print that line of input as a single line.

d) Write a script that would perform the given function.

Answer: The script would be as follows:
```
sed 's/!//
/!/{
s/!//
n
}
N
s/\n/ /
s/!//g'
```

In the first command, we substitute the first exclamation point we encounter with an empty character, effectively deleting the first exclamation point. The following command is the next command. If another exclamation point exists, then the entire address history is contained within a single line. In this case, the next line is read into the pattern space and control is returned to the postprocessing step, which prints the address history and then causes another line to be read. If no other exclamation point exists, then the address history is contained within two lines. In this case, we use the multiline next command to read in the remaining address history on the next line into the pattern space. We subsequently replace the embedded newline that is inserted as a result of the multiline next command with a space. We then replace the last exclamation point with an empty character.

**LAB
8.1**

LAB 8.1 SELF-REVIEW QUESTIONS

In order to test your progress, you should be able to answer the following questions.

For each of the following multiple choice questions, one or more answers may be correct.

Use the following file for these questions:

XXX

YYY

ZZZ

1) If the pattern space contains the first line XXX and a multiline next command is executed, what are the contents of the pattern space?
    a) _____XXX\nYYY
    b) _____XXX
    c) _____XXXYYY
    d) _____XXXZZZ

2) If the pattern space contains XXX\nYYY and the multiline delete command is executed, what are the contents of the pattern space?
    a) _____XXX\n
    b) _____XXX
    c) _____YYY\n
    d) _____YYY

3) If a multiline delete command exists within a grouping statement, then which of the following is the next command to be executed?
    a) _____the command after the closing brace
    b) _____the postprocessing step
    c) _____the preprocessing step
    d) _____no command executes

4) If no grouping command occurs, then which of the following is the next command to be executed?
    a) _____no command
    b) _____the postprocessing step
    c) _____the preprocessing step
    d) _____the next command after the multiline delete command

Quiz answers appear in Appendix A, Section 8.1.

LAB
8.1

C H A P T E R   8

TEST YOUR THINKING

The projects in this section are meant to have you utilize all of the skills that you have acquired throughout this chapter. The answers to these projects can be found at the companion Web site to this book, located at:

`http://www.phptr.com/phptrinteractive/`

Visit the Web site periodically to share and discuss your answers.

1) Given a file that contains information regarding errata of various Pentium processors, write the information pertaining to each errata in a separate file. The file is formatted as follows (the file is provided at the Web companion site).

```
Errata 1
Xeon

... .


Errata 2
Triton II

... .
```

The dots represent the text between each errata that is to be written out in a separate file. The first line of each file contains the name of the processor.

In the rest of this section, we will examine commands that use a temporary buffer and the pattern space to move data back and forth between the buffer and the pattern space. All the sed commands that we encountered in the last chapter worked on the pattern space. For the following exercises, we will use the following file called `example.txt`.

```
Smith 123 Adhesions
Jones 245 Adhesions
Grace 356 Coatings
```

HOLD SPACE

Besides the pattern space that contains the input line, there is another temporary space called the *hold space*. The hold space, as its name implies, can be used to hold the contents of the pattern space at any given time. Therefore, the hold space acts as a temporary buffer in which the contents of the pattern space can be stored.

HOLD COMMAND

The hold command is used to perform the function of copying the contents of the pattern space into this temporary buffer, which we call the hold space. The hold command has two variations: an uppercase and a lowercase version(H, h). The syntax of the hold command is as follows:

```
[line-address]h
```

or:

```
[line-address]H
```

The `line-address` can take on no address, one address, or a range of addresses. In either version, if a subsequent sed command is encountered, then the command works on the pattern space, and does not work on the contents of the hold space. Therefore, the contents of the hold space are not altered by any subsequent sed command. The difference between the lowercase version and uppercase version is that the lowercase version overwrites what currently resides in the hold space with the contents of the pattern space, while the uppercase version appends the contents of the pattern space to what currently resides in the hold space. The uppercase version of the hold command (H) appends the contents of the pattern space to the hold space, it inserts a newline after the current contents of hold space.

For each line read in, what are the contents of the hold space and pattern space at the end of executing each of the following commands:

2)   The command is as follows:

```
sed '/Adhesions/h' example.txt
```

3) The command is as follows:

```
sed '/Adhesions/h

s/Adhesions/Coatings/' example.txt
```

4) The command is as follows:

```
sed '/Adhesions/H

s/Adhesions/Coatings/' example.txt
```

5) The command is as follows:

```
sed '/Adhesions/{

H

N

}' example.txt
```

THE GET COMMAND

The get command is used to perform the opposite function of the hold command. It copies the contents of the hold space back to the pattern space. This is done presumably after a previous hold command was encountered. Like the hold command, the get command command has both a lowercase and uppercase variation (G, g). The syntax of the get command is:

```
[line-address]g
```

or:

```
[line-address]G
```

As with the hold command, there can be no address, one address, or a range of addresses. Of course after executing the get command, the pattern space is altered and any subsequent command will then work on the contents of the hold space that were copied to the pattern space. The difference between the lowercase get command and the uppercase version is that the lowercase get command (g) overwrites the contents of the pattern space with the contents of the hold space. The uppercase get command (G) appends the contents of the hold space onto the contents of the pattern space and inserts a newline between them.

For each line read in, what are the contents of the hold space and pattern space at the end of executing each of the following commands.

6) The command is as follows:

```
sed '/Adhesions/g

s/Adhesions/Coatings/' example.txt
```

7) The command is as follows:

```
sed '/Adhesions/G

s/Adhesions/Coatings/' example.txt
```

8) The command is as follows:

```
sed '/$/{

H

G

s/Adhesions/Coatings/g

}' example.txt
```

THE EXCHANGE COMMAND

The exchange command (x) , as its name suggests, is used to swap the contents of the hold space and pattern space. The contents of the pattern space will be the contents of the hold space and the contents of the hold space will be the contents of the pattern space. The exchange command does not perform any modifications on either buffer and does not use the newline. Unlike the hold and get commands, the exchange command has only one version and its syntax is shown as follows:

```
[line-address]x
```

As with the hold and get commands, there can be no address, one address, or a range of addresses. Of course, after executing the exchange command, the pattern space is altered and any subsequent command will then work on the contents of the hold space that were copied to the pattern space.

For each line read in, what are the contents of the hold space and pattern space at the end of executing the following commands.

9) The command is as follows:

```
sed  '/Adhesions/h

s/Adhesions/Coatings

x' example.txt
```

10) The command is as follows:

```
sed '/Adhesions/h

/Coatings/x' example.txt
```

CHAPTER 9

AN AWK PROGRAM

 I cannot emphasize enough that the best way to learn computer languages and utilities is by practicing. Try out some sample queries on your own. In addition, I have found that sometimes the best way to learn is by your own mistakes. Try figuring out where you went wrong, and try entering a query that you suspect might not work. You might be surprised at the result.

CHAPTER OBJECTIVES

In this chapter, you will learn about:

This chapter is meant to introduce awk using a simple example, one that demonstrates what an awk program looks like, gives a very brief introduction to the various types of applications for which awk is useful, and illustrates the basic operation of an awk program. This basic operation is performed, simplistically, from the viewpoint of a generalized awk program that reads your input awk program, parses it, and then executes it. Through this three-step process, the awk language elements are introduced. Next, the structure of an awk program is given, generalizing the example awk program into this structure and explaining the major structural elements that all programs must have. Finally, the various ways an awk program can be run from the command line and the fashion in which awk reports errors are explained.

L A B   9.1

AN EXAMPLE AWK PROGRAM

LAB OBJECTIVES

After this Lab, you will be able to:

✓ Understand the Results of a Simple Awk Program

✓ Write a Simple Awk Program

**LAB
9.1**

Before proceeding into the meat of the awk language, a short tour of awk is necessary. When learning new languages and utilities, this approach can be easier to grasp because it gives greater context for more advanced subject matter. Additionally, all languages have to be compiled, linked, and executed, as is the case for static-compiled languages like C/C++, or dynamically invoked at the command line, like awk, which is only interpreted. If you first learn how to invoke awk at the command line using simple examples before you get into functions or control structures, you will have an easier time learning the concepts of functions or control structures by invoking awk on a program that uses language elements.

 Before getting into some exercises, let's briefly go over an awk program and explain its input, processing, and output. We'll use our `conf.data` file, which is found in Lab 4.1 (Chapter 4, "Grep Command Options"). You can also download this file from the companion Web site for this book, located at:

`http://www.phptr.com/phptrinteractive/`

As a reminder, this file contains six columns, each representing, from left to right: the name of the registrant, the name of the conference, the conference fee, amount owed or balance due, the date the registrant registered, and the company for which the registrant works.

In simple terms, each line of the input file is called a *record* in awk, and each record consists of *fields*. The `conf.data` file has six columns, with each one in each record representing a field. You'll see in Lab 11.3 how records and fields are identified by awk. For now, take a look at the following line (or record) from the file:

```
Jones     Coatings      900      0      081298      Dow
```

In this example, each word represents a new field to awk (by default, fields are separated by either multiple spaces or tabs). Fields are referenced in awk by using the field operator $. So the first field is represented by $1 (its value in the example line is `Jones`), the second is $2 (its value is `Coatings`), and so forth. You will use fields often throughout the rest of this book; they are explained in greater detail in Chapter 11, "Variables."

■ FOR EXAMPLE:

LAB
9.1

Suppose that for each registrant who still has an amount owing, you would like to print the name of the registrant, the conference they wish to attend, and the amount that they owe. The following awk program provides this information:

```
awk '$4 > 0 {print $1, $2, $4}' conf.data
```

In this example, the expression $4 > 0 is called a *pattern*, and the statement {print $1, $2, $4} is called an *action*. Patterns may consist of regular expressions or operators. Actions consist of one or more statements, separated by either semicolons or newlines, and are always enclosed in curly braces. Both patterns and actions are optional.

Simplistically, what this awk program says is: using the `conf.data` file, select the lines in the file for which the value of the fourth field is greater than 0, and from those lines print the first, second, and fourth fields. In our specific example, this translates to: for lines in which the amount owed is greater than 0, print the attendee name, conference name, and amount owed to the output device. In this case, the (default) standard output is the screen. The output resulting from this query is:

```
Smith Adhesions 200
Phillips Stabilizers 100
Kenny Coatings 450
Patsis Adhesions 350
Mack Coatings 100
Denny Stabilizers 200
Jackson Resins 200
Donaldson Stabilizers 200
Harrison Resins 800
Patterson Coatings 450
Federicks Stabilizers 100
Quinn Resins 500
Bostic Coatings 900
```

Let's take a closer look at what's going on here. One can think of awk working internally as follows:

1. Read in an input line.
2. Store the input line as field 0 (or more formally, $0).
3. Parse the input line and break it into fields.
4. After breaking up the input line into fields, execute the pattern. The pattern can be any expression. If the expression yields a non-zero number then the action is executed. In our case, it is a conditional and asks whether the fourth field of the input line is greater than 0. If so, awk executes the action. If the pattern is matched (in our case, if the condition is true), continue with Step 5. Otherwise, continue at Step 1.
5. Execute the action with the input line and separated fields. The action may involve one or more statements. These statements could involve many possible actions, including input, output, arithmetic, and reordering of the fields.
6. Continue processing at Step 1 until all input lines have been read in.

Although this process is not the actual way awk works internally, it provides a simpler abstraction to think about patterns and actions and how fields are instantiated.

The types of applications that awk is meant for involve quick, easy file or query processing. In the preceding example, you can easily see that the one-line awk program doesn't contain complicated logic and constructs. All it contains are a simple selection mechanism and a simple print statement to print the results. However, awk is not limited to just simple selection and printing statements. It has an abundance of rich expressions and statements. Similarly, it is not limited to simple query and file processing. As stated earlier, awk provides many constructs and elements that can be used to program more advanced applications such as database processing, data validation, text processing, and World Wide Web CGI scripting. Within a software development environment, it can provide various utilities to assist a team of developers writing a software application. And more commonly, it enables system administrators to perform common tasks. In more advanced sections, we go over some of these applications using awk.

Don't worry if you don't completely understand some of the terms or concepts explored in this chapter. The intent here is to introduce you to some actual awk programming. These ideas will be explained in further detail as you work through the remaining chapters on awk.

**LAB
9.1**

LAB 9.1 EXERCISES

These exercises are meant to test your knowledge of basic awk elements. Because this section has not described the constructs in full, you are not expected to be able to answer these questions instantly. Do not get discouraged and do not spend too much time trying to answer the questions. They are just meant to be a cursory attempt at thinking about how to write and understand one-line awk programs. In addition, because the various ways to invoke awk at the command line have not been described, you may not understand how to test these exercises at the command line. Don't despair; I will go over how to do so within the exercises. These exercises should be able to be run on any UNIX operating system. If you cannot execute awk on your system, consult your system administrator.

These exercises work on the conf.data file from Lab 4.1. You can input this file, or retrieve it from this book's companion Web site, located at:

http://www.phptr.com/phptrinteractive/

9.1.1 UNDERSTAND THE RESULTS OF A SIMPLE AWK PROGRAM

Enter the following query:

```
awk '$4 > 0 {print $0}' conf.data
```

a) What does this program do?

_____

_____

Enter the following query:

```
awk '$4 == 0 {print $6, $1, $2}' conf.data
```

b) What does this program do?

_____

_____

Enter the following query:

```
awk '$4 > 0 && $2 == "Coatings" {print $1, $4}' conf.data
```

c) What does this program do?

_____

_____

9.1.2 WRITE A SIMPLE AWK PROGRAM

Write an awk program to print the names of all registrants who don't owe any money for the Adhesions conference.

      a) What is the program?

_____

_____

Write an awk program to print the names of all registrants for the Stabilizers conference.

      b) What is the program?

_____

_____

Write an awk program to print the names, the conference name, the cost of the conference, and the amount owed for registrants of the Coatings conference.

      c) What is the program?

**LAB
9.1**

_____

_____

Write an awk program to print the complete `conf.data` file.

      d) What is the program?

_____

_____

Lab 9.1 Exercise Answers

This section gives you some suggested answers to the questions in Lab 9.1, with discussion related to those answers. Your answers may vary, but the most important thing is whether or not your answer works. Use this discussion to analyze differences between your answers and those presented here.

If you have alternative answers to the questions in this Exercise, you are encouraged to post your answers and discuss them at the companion Web site for this book, located at:

```
http://www.phptr.com/phptrinteractive/
```

The most important thing to realize is whether your answers work. You should note the implications of the answers here and what the effects are from any variations in any answers you may devise.

9.1.1 Answers

Enter the following query:

```
awk '$4 > 0 {print $0}' conf.data
```

a) What does this program do?

Answer: This program prints each record from the `conf.data` *file for which the fourth field is greater then 0 (i.e., for which an amount is owed).*

Stepping through this program, here's what essentially happens: awk examines field number four looking for a value greater than zero (`$4 > 0`), and for each record that meets that criterion, it prints the entire record (`{print $0}`) from the `conf.data` file (`conf.data`).

Note that the field variable `$0` represents an entire record. By default, this program would have produced the same output if it had read:

```
awk '$4 > 0 {print}' conf.data
```

Enter the following query:

```
awk '$4 == 0 {print $6, $1, $2}' conf.data
```

b) What does this program do?

Answer: This program prints field numbers six (company name), one (registrant's name), and two (conference name) for every record in the `conf.data` *file for which* `$4` *(amount owed) is equal to 0.*

Enter the following query:

```
awk '$4 > 0 && $2 == "Coatings" {print $1, $4}' conf.data
```

c) What does this program do?

Answer: For every record in which the conference name is Coatings and the amount due is greater than 0 in the `conf.data` *file, this program prints the name of the registrant and the amount owed.*

Again, this translates in awk to: print field number one (registrant's name) and field number four (amount owed) for every line in the `conf.data` file in which field number four is greater than 0 and field number two is equal to `Coatings`.

9.1.2 ANSWERS

Write an awk program to print the names of all registrants who don't owe any money for the Adhesions conference.

a) What is the program?

Answer: The program is as follows:
```
awk '$4 == 0 {print $1}' conf.data
```

If your program doesn't match this one, go back and review the questions and answers in Exercise 9.1.1.

Very simply, this program checks field four of each record for a value that is equal to 0 (`$4 == 0`), and for each record that matches that criterion, it prints the first field (`{print $1}`) in the `conf.data` file.

Write an awk program to print the names of all registrants for the Stabilizers conference.

b) What is the program?

Answer: The program is as follows:
```
awk '$2 == "Stabilizers" {print $1}' conf.data
```

The action '{print $1}' performs the part of the query that prints the names of the registrants. $1 is the first field, which contains the registrants' names. The $2 == "Stabilizers" part selects those lines in which the second field (conference name) is equal to **STABILIZERS**. The last part of the program is the input file on which to perform the query.

Write an awk program to print the names, the conference name, the cost of the conference, and the amount owed for registrants of the Coatings conference.

c) What is the program?

Answer: The program is as follows:
```
awk '$2 == "Coatings" {print $1, $2, $3, $4}' conf.data
```

The action '{print $1, $2, $3, $4}' performs the part of the query that selects and prints the registrants' names, conference name, cost of the conference, and the amount owed by the registrant for the conference. The $2 == "Coatings" selects those lines from the input file for which the second field (conference name) matches Coatings. The last part of the query names the file to use as input for processing the query.

Write an awk program to print the complete conf.data file.

**LAB
9.1**

d) What is the program?

Answer: The program is as follows:
```
awk '{print}' conf.data
```

This may not be entirely obvious, because the examples and discussion so far have not suggested how one might write an awk program to accomplish this task. All the previous examples have used an action that prints a particular field. An alternative result could have been written as:

```
awk '{print $1, $2, $3, $4, $5, $6}' conf.data
```

Another variation is:

```
awk '{print $0}' conf.data
```

All yield the same results. Convince yourself by entering both at the command line if you haven't already done so. The big question is: why are these three programs equivalent? In awk, an action with a single print statement with no fields after it means that awk prints all fields that are contained within the line. So in the first awk program, the single-action `print` prints all the fields contained within the `conf.data` file. In the last variation, the single-action `print $0` also prints all fields in a line of the input file.

LAB 9.1 SELF-REVIEW QUESTIONS

In order to test your progress, you should be able to answer the following questions.
For each of the following multiple choice questions, one or more answers may be correct.

1) In the awk program awk `'x == 5 {print $2}'` some-file, which part of the program is the pattern?
   a) _____`{print $2}`
   b) _____`x == 5`
   c) _____no pattern
   d) _____`x == 5 {print $2}`
   e) _____These are all patterns of this program

2) Using the `conf.data` file, which program prints the conference name for every line?
   a) _____awk `'$5 > 0 {print $2}'` conf.data
   b) _____awk `'{print}'` conf.data
   c) _____awk `'{print $2}'` conf.data
   d) _____awk `'{print $3}'` conf.data
   e) _____None of the above

3) Which program prints the name of a registrant who registered for the Coatings conference?
   a) _____awk `'{print $1}'` conf.data
   b) _____awk `'$2 == "Coatings" {print}'` conf.data
   c) _____awk `'$1 == "Smith" {print $2}'` conf.data
   d) _____awk `'$3 == "Coatings" {print $2}'` conf.data
   e) _____None of the above

Quiz answers appear in Appendix A, Section 9.1.

L A B   9.2

THE STRUCTURE OF AN AWK PROGRAM

LAB OBJECTIVE

After this Lab, you will be able to:

✓ Understand the Components of an Awk Program

What is meant by the statement *an awk program*? This section examines what an awk program consists of structurally, the syntax of an awk program, and a couple of variations on this structure. We have already touched upon the ideas contained within this section informally, but here is where we develop a more formal understanding of the structure of an awk program.

■ *FOR EXAMPLE*

So far in this chapter, we have seen a number of awk programs. Almost all of the programs have been of the following form:

```
awk 'query {action}' input-file
```

Formally, query would be replaced by the word pattern:

```
awk 'pattern {action}' input-file
```

Between the single quotes lies what is considered the awk program. The awk program in the preceding example consists of a single pattern-action statement. An awk program may take the following form:

```
awk 'pattern {action}
      pattern {action}
         ...' input-file
```

Therefore, an awk program may consist of one or more pattern-action statements inside a pair of single quotes. When awk interprets an awk command line, it takes everything inside the quotes and processes the program on the passed-in input file. The dots mean that any number of additional pattern-actions may exist up to the closing quote.

Either the pattern or the action may be omitted in an awk program, but not both. Therefore, an awk program may have the following structure:

```
awk '{action}
      pattern {action}
      pattern' input-file
```

An awk program may additionally contain a BEGIN and END pattern. The structure of an awk program that uses the BEGIN and/or END pattern looks like the following:

```
awk 'BEGIN {action}
pattern {action }
. .
END {action}' input-file
```

LAB 9.2

```
awk 'BEGIN {action}
      pattern {action}
      ....' input-file
```

```
awk 'pattern {action}
      ....
      END {action}' input-file
```

One can think of the BEGIN pattern as performing preprocessing before any pattern-action statement has been encountered, or before any input line has been read or processed. Some typical uses are printing column headers and titles on tables, pre-initializing variables, or altering the values of built-in variables. The END statement can be thought of as a postprocessor. It performs awk actions after every input line has been read and processed. Typical uses of the END pattern are for totaling and performing calculations at the end of a run.

LAB 9.2 EXERCISES

9.2.1 UNDERSTAND THE COMPONENTS OF AN AWK PROGRAM

For Question a of this Exercise, analyze the following program:

```
awk '$4 == 0' conf.data
```

a) Is this a valid awk program? If not, why?

_____

_____

For Question b of this Exercise, analyze the following program:

```
awk '{print $2, $3}' conf.data
```

b) Is this a valid awk program? If not, why?

_____

_____

For Question c of this Exercise, analyze the following program:

```
awk $3 == 750 '{print $1}' conf.data
```

c) Is this a valid awk program? If not, why?

_____

_____

For Question d of this Exercise, analyze the following program:

```
awk $3 '{print $1}' conf.data
```

d) Is this a valid awk program? If not, why?

_____

_____

For Question e of this Exercise, analyze the following program:

```
awk 'BEGIN {print "This is all names in the conf.data
   input file"}
   {print $0}' conf.data
```

e) Is this a valid awk program? If not, why?

_____

_____

For Question f of this Exercise, analyze the following program:

```
awk 'BEGIN
{print $1, $3, $3 - $4}' conf.data
```

f) Is this a valid awk program? If not, why?

_____

_____

LAB
9.2

For Question g of this Exercise, analyze the following program:

```
awk '{print $1, $3 - $4}
END' conf.data
```

g) Is this awk program valid? If not, why?

_____

_____

h) Why does awk use braces to separate an action from a pattern?

_____

_____

i) Why does awk use quotes to represent an awk program?

_____

_____

LAB 9.2 EXERCISE ANSWERS

 This section gives you some suggested answers to the questions in Lab 9.2, with discussion related to those answers. Your answers may vary, but the most important thing is whether or not your answer works. Use this discussion to analyze differences between your answers and those presented here.

If you have alternative answers to the questions in this Exercise, you are encouraged to post your answers and discuss them at the companion Web site for this book, located at:

```
http://www.phptr.com/phptrinteractive/
```

9.2.1 ANSWERS

For Question a of this Exercise, analyze the following program:

```
awk '$4 == 0' conf.data
```

a) Is this a valid awk program? If not, why?

Answer: It is a valid awk program.

It consists of the single pattern $4 == 0. As you can tell from the output, when awk encounters a single pattern with no action, it prints all fields for which the pattern matches. In this case, it matches when field number four, amount owed, is equal to zero.

For Question b of this Exercise, analyze the following program:

```
awk '{print $2, $3}' conf.data
```

b) Is this a valid awk program? If not, why?

Answer: It is a valid awk program.

It consists of the single action {print $2, $3}. As you can also tell from the output, when awk encounters a single action with no pattern, then the pattern matches for every input line. Therefore, awk prints field number two, conference name, and field number three, conference fee, for every input line.

For Question c of this Exercise, analyze the following program:

```
awk $3 == 750 '{print $1}' conf.data
```

c) Is this a valid awk program? If not, why?

Answer: It is not a valid awk program. The problem with this program is that the pattern is not contained within the quotes. The solution is to move the first quote mark to just before the $3.

For Question d of this Exercise, analyze the following program:

```
awk $3 '{print $1}' conf.data
```

d) Is this a valid awk program? If not, why?

Answer: It is a valid awk program.

**LAB
9.2**

This is a tricky program. At first glance, in light of the preceding program examples, this program appears invalid. However, with awk, the opening quote does not need to be encountered first. This approach works because awk tries to recover from errors. In this case, awk tries to interpret what the user might have wanted to type. In other words, awk is assuming that the user does not intend to enter a pattern and that the $3 was mistakenly entered. The program, therefore, skips over the $3 and continues processing as if no pattern was provided. When no pattern is provided, every input line matches or awk interprets the pattern $3 which is non-zero interpreted as tru for all records and processes the action on all records. This result is validated by the output produced—namely, the first field for each input line is output.

For Question e of this Exercise, analyze the following program:

```
awk 'BEGIN {print "This is all names in the conf.data
    input file"}
{print $0}' conf.data
```

e) Is this a valid awk program? If not, why?

Answer: This is a valid awk program.

It consists of a valid BEGIN pattern followed by an action that prints a header. As you can see from the output, no blank line occurs between the BEGIN action print statement and the first line of output. Later, you will see how to make the output more readable by inserting blank lines.

The second line contains a valid awk statement, which contains a single action to print the entire line of input matched by the pattern. Because no pattern exists, the action is matched for every input line. So the output produced is simply the entire conf.data file line by line, with the first line of output being the string contained in the BEGIN pattern-action statement.

For Question f of this Exercise, analyze the following program:

```
awk 'BEGIN
{print $1, $3, $3 - $4}' conf.data
```

f) Is this a valid awk program? If not, why?

Answer: This is not a valid awk program. The reason is that a BEGIN pattern must have an associated action. Recall that the purpose of a BEGIN pattern is to perform preprocessing prior to the execution of the body of the program. In this example, the BEGIN statement refers to no action. Instead, the next statement in the program is a pattern/action combination instead of the expected pattern for the BEGIN.

Attempting to execute this awk program will produce errors, the syntax of which depends on your specific type and version of UNIX. For my version, the error is as follows:

awk: cmd. line:2: warning: BEGIN blocks must have an action part

For Question g of this Exercise, analyze the following program:

```
awk '{print $1, $3 - $4}
END' conf.data
```

g) Is this awk program valid? If not, why?

Answer: *Again, this is not a valid awk program, for reasons similar to those in the preceding example discussing* BEGIN. *To have an* END *pattern that performs no action doesn't make sense.*

Once again, your output will vary. My output is as follows:

awk: cmd. line:3: warning: END blocks must have an action part

h) Why does awk use braces to separate an action from a pattern?

Answer: *The reason that awk requires braces is that a pattern or action may be optionally omitted. Awk needs some way to recognize that a construct is an action. Otherwise, without the braces, awk does not know that it has encountered an action, because it is optional.*

i) Why does awk use quotes to represent an awk program?

Answer: *The quotes are used so that the shell does not interpret special characters such as the dollar sign character, $, and other special characters in awk that have special meaning to the shell.*

LAB 9.2 SELF-REVIEW QUESTIONS

In order to test your progress, you should be able to answer the following questions.

1) Is awk `''` input-file a legal awk program?

    a) _____yes

    b) _____no

2) Can a pattern or action be omitted?

    a) _____yes

    b) _____no

3) Can a begin or end statement have no action?

    a) _____yes

    b) _____no

LAB
9.2

Use the following awk program for the remaining questions:

```
awk 'END {print $1}
{print $3}
BEGIN {x=3}' some-file
```

4) What is executed first?

   a) _____END {print $1}
   b) _____{print $3}
   c) _____BEGIN {x=3}
   d) _____None; the program is invalid

5) What is executed second?

   a) _____END {print $1}
   b) _____{print $3}
   c) _____BEGIN {x=3}
   d) _____None; the program is invalid

6) What is executed last?

   a) _____END {print $1}
   b) _____{print $3}
   c) _____BEGIN {x=3}
   d) None; the program is invalid

Quiz answers appear in Appendix A, Section 9.2.

**LAB
9.2**

L A B   9.3

INVOKING AN AWK PROGRAM

LAB OBJECTIVE

After this Lab, you will be able to:

✓ Understand the Various Ways to Invoke Awk at the Command Line

---

INVOKING AWK FROM WITHIN A FILE

We have seen one way that awk is invoked at the command line prompt. Another way is possible: The awk program may be contained within a file and then invoked with the following command at the command line prompt:

```
awk -f name-of-program-file input-file
```

The -f option tells awk to open the program file and execute the program within. The awk program inside the file does not need the beginning and ending quotes that we have seen in previous exercises. So suppose that the following awk program is contained in the file confAwkPrograms:

```
$4 > 0 {print $1, $2}
```

To execute this program, you would enter the following at the command line prompt:

```
awk -f confAwkPrograms conf.data
```

This would execute the program residing within `confAwkPrograms` and output the first two fields of each record for which the pattern proves true.

Of course, for a program of this size, to write this program in a file and then execute it using the `-f` option is not advantageous, because entering this program at the command line is just as easy. However, if you have a large awk program that may be used more than once, a more sensible approach is to store the program in a file and then invoke that program from the command line. In addition, if you have developed a number of awk programs that make up a larger application, to store those applications in a file would also make sense.

MULTIPLE INPUT FILES

Although we have not seen such an example so far, you may also supply more then one input file for an awk program to process. In the following example, you have two input files. The first file is the `conf.data` file. The second is a file called `courses.data`. This file is similar to the `conf.data` file, except that instead of conference names, it contains course names. Every other field in the new file is similar to the one in the `conf.data` file.

The `courses.data` file is as follows:

```
Leonard Adhesions 300 200 081098 Digital
Johnson Coatings 200 0 081298 Dow
Peters Stabilizers 250 100 080198 Dupont
Koenig Coatings 200 50 072898 Dow
Moore Adhesions 300 200 080198 IBM
Oreilly Adhesions 300 0 081198 Digital
Samuals Stabilizers 250 0 081098 Dupont
Henry Coatings 200 100 080398 Shell
```

To direct awk toward more than one input file, simply reference all of the necessary input files in the program, like so:

```
awk '$4 > 0 {print $1, $2}' conf.data courses.data
```

The output after executing this program would be the first and second fields for each input line in which the fourth field is greater than zero in *both* the conf.data and courses.data files.

INVOKING AWK WITHOUT AN INPUT FILE

Another way to invoke awk is to not supply an input file. In all our examples so far, awk has been invoked with the conf.data as the input file. However, an input file is not a requirement. If the input file(s) is(are) omitted, awk reads from standard input. This result is true of many UNIX commands. The default source for standard input is the keyboard; with shell notation, standard input can be redirected to come from a file or pipe. So you can enter awk input lines at the keyboard one line at a time until awk encounters the end-of-file character. In Linux and UNIX, the end-of-file character is Control-d. An example of an awk program that does not take an input file is:

```
awk '$4>0 {print $1, $2}'
```

Assuming that the user enters the following lines from the keyboard, the output from this program is:

> **Input:** Smith Adhesions 700 200 081098 Digital
> Output: **Smith Adhesions**
> **Input:** Jones Coatings 900 0 081298 Dow
> Output: None. Note that no match occurs for the pattern $4>0 for this input line.
> **Input:** Phillips Stabilizers 850 100 080198 Dupont
> Output: **Phillips Stabilizers**
> **Input:** Kenny Coatings 900 450 072898 Dow
> Output: **Kenny Coatings**

**LAB
9.3**

The ability to enter one line of input at a time is especially useful for testing an awk program. You can enter input lines at the command line prompt and see how awk processes the line. The output will tell you whether awk accepts the program as entered or whether errors exist in the program, and you can interactively correct your entry and rerun the program.

LAB 9.3 EXERCISES

9.3.1 UNDERSTAND THE VARIOUS WAYS TO INVOKE AWK AT THE COMMAND LINE

For the following question, enter this awk program into a file called `script.awk`:

```
{print $1, $2}
```

Save the file, and run the script on the `conf.data` file.

a) What command did you use?

_____

_____

b) What is the output?

_____

_____

For the following question, enter the following awk program at the command line:

```
awk '{print $2}'
```

After entering this command, enter the following two lines, one after the other:

```
10 20 40
^d
```

(^d means to press the Control key and the letter d simultaneously)

c) What is the output?

_____

_____

LAB 9.3 EXERCISE ANSWERS

This section gives you some suggested answers to the questions in Lab 9.3, with discussion related to those answers. Your answers may vary, but the most important thing is whether or not your answer works. Use this discussion to analyze differences between your answers and those presented here.

If you have alternative answers to the questions in this Exercise, you are encouraged to post your answers and discuss them at the companion Web site for this book, located at:

```
http://www.phptr.com/phptrinteractive/
```

9.3.1 ANSWERS

For the following question, enter the awk program into a file called `script.awk`:

```
{print $1, $2}
```

Save the file, and run the script on the `conf.data` file.

a) What command did you use?

Answer: The command is as follows:
```
awk -f script.awk conf.data
```

To run an awk program that is contained within a file (an awk script), you must use the `-f` option.

b) What is the output?

Answer: Awk outputs the first two fields of each record in the `conf.data` file.

For the following question, enter the following awk program at the command line:

```
awk '{print $2}'
```

After entering this command, enter the following two lines, one after the other:

```
10 20 40
^d
```

c) What is the output?

Answer: The output is as follows:
```
10 20 40
```
20

The first line is the line that you entered. The next line is the result of the awk program on that input line. If no file is provided to an awk program, then awk expects its input from standard input.

LAB 9.3 SELF-REVIEW QUESTIONS

In order to test your progress, you should be able to answer the following questions.

For each of the following multiple choice questions, one or more answers may be correct.

1) Which of the following awk programs invokes an awk script at the command line?
    a) _____awk `{print $1}'` conf.data
    b) _____awk -f awk.script conf.data
    c) _____awk -f awk.script
    d) _____None of the above

2) Which of the following are legal awk invocations?
    a) _____awk -f awk.script
    b) _____awk `{print $1}'` conf.data address.dat
    c) _____awk `{print $1}'`
    d) _____awk -f awk.script conf.data address.dat
    e) _____None of the above

Quiz answers appear in Appendix A, Section 9.3.

**LAB
9.3**

C H A P T E R   9

TEST YOUR THINKING

The projects in this section are meant to have you utilize all of the skills that you have acquired throughout this chapter. The answers to these projects can be found at the companion Web site to this book, located at:

```
http://www.phptr.com/phptrinteractive/
```

Visit the Web site periodically to share and discuss your answers.

In this chapter, you have been introduced to awk, its structure, and some concepts regarding its operation. What has not really been covered is how awk handles error reporting. Recall from Lab 9.2 that various flavors of UNIX report errors differently. In this section, you are going to intentionally enter some invalid awk programs to become familiar with how your version of UNIX handles errors.

Using the `conf.data` file as input, execute the following program exactly as shown:

```
awk '$4 > 0 [print $2, $3}' conf.data
```

1) You can probably immediately see what's wrong with this program – that is, we've used an opening square bracket to enclose the `print` statement instead of an opening curly bracket. This is an example of a parse error, which results from a problem with a program's syntax. What type of error message did you receive? Did it help you understand what was wrong with the program?

2) Try entering the preceding program without the input file. Instead, manually enter the first few lines of the `conf.data` file to see what results. What happened?

Another type of error is a run-time error, which results from a problem with a program's logic. Using the `conf.data` file as input, execute the following program:

```
awk 'BEGIN { x=1 }
END {while x>1
X=x+1
}' conf.data
```

While we haven't yet seen an example quite like this program so far, see whether you can determine what's wrong with it, based on the message you get.

3) What type of error message did you receive? Did it help you understand what was wrong with the program? Was the information that was included in the message, not including the text description of the error, different from problem 1?

4) Enter the preceding example without specifying the input file. As in Project 2 of this section, manually enter the first few lines of the `conf.data` file. What happened?

5) Write a program that generates an itemized invoice for Dupont using the `conf.data` and `courses.data` files. This program should accomplish the following:

a) Print the string "The following Dupont employees have a balance due for the Stabilizers conference or course:" as the first line of output.

b) Print the name of the registrant and the amount owed for all Dupont employees registered for the Stabilizers conference who have a balance due from the `conf.data` file and all Dupont employees registered for the Sta- bilizers course who have a balance due from the `course.data` file.

c) Print the name of the file from which the resulting data is taken, before listing the results from each file.

d) Print the string "Payment is expected 10 days prior to attendance." at the end of the output.

Be careful of what you include in your BEGIN *and* END *blocks in this program.*

C H A P T E R 10

BASIC AWK LANGUAGE ELEMENTS

One's language has a considerable effect on the way that one thinks; indeed on what one can think.

—Benjamin Wharf

This chapter introduces the awk programming language more formally and in greater detail than in Chapter 9. The approach taken in this book is to describe awk as a programming language, and to teach awk using the methods taken in describing traditional programming languages. This method first describes basic elements in the language, data types, expressions, statements, constants, and the assignment operators. You will understand this as you work through this chapter.

L A B   10.1

AWK STATEMENTS AND EXPRESSIONS

LAB OBJECTIVE

After this Lab, you will be able to:

✓ Identify Statements and Expression Components

A statement consists of one of the following, followed by a statement separator:

    1. A primary expression (described below)
    2. An operator that combines primary expressions (described below)
    3. One of the following:

```
break
continue
next
exit [Expression]

if (Expression) then
    action
[else action]

while (Expression)
```

```
      action

do
   action
while (Expression)

for (counter; test; increment)
     action

for (variable in array)
     action

delete array-element

return [Expression]

input-output statement
```

In this chapter we will explore expressions (1 and 2 above); number 3 we will explore in Chapters 14, 15, and 16.

STATEMENT SEPARATOR

Statements are separated by a semicolon or a newline or both. A statement that has two statement separators next to each other creates an empty statement.

In awk, an expression is formed either by a single primary expression or by combining primary expressions with an operator that combines expressions. The types of primary expressions in awk are:

- constants
- variables
- field variables
- function calls
- array elements

The following operators combine expressions:

- assignment operators: =, +=, -=, *=, /=, %=, ^=
- conditional expression: ?:

**LAB
10.1**

- logical operators: | |, &&, !
- matching operators: ~, !~
- relational operators: <, <=, ==, !=, >, >=
- concatenation: (no explicit operator)
- arithmetic operators: +, −, *, /, %, ^
- unary: +, −
- increment, decrement operators: ++, −−
- parentheses for grouping

■ FOR EXAMPLE:

The following is an expression in awk:

```
$1 + $2
```

It consists of two expression components, or *primary* expressions—both field variables and expressions in their own right—that are combined using the combining operator "addition." The following is also an expression:

```
($1 + $2) / 3
```

This expression consists of the three primary expressions—two field variables and a constant—and two operators that combine expressions, addition and division.

Any primary expression can be used as an operand of any operator. So the following is a valid awk expression:

```
a = b + function(a, b) - array[i]
```

In this example, a, b, function(a, b), and array[i] are primary expressions. The overall format of the expression is very flexible. Blank lines may be inserted before or after any statement, pattern-action statement, or function definition. Spaces and tabs may be inserted around operators or operands. Similar to the UNIX shell, a long statement in awk may be broken by a backslash, and continued on the next line. However, the opening brace of an action must be put on the same line as the pattern it accompanies.

**LAB
10.1**

COMMENTS

As with any programming language, be sure to comment your awk code so others can understand your logic. A comment in awk begins with the # sign and ends at the end of a line. The comment character can appear on a line by itself or it can be used at the end of a statement.

■ *FOR EXAMPLE:*

The following is a segment of commented code:

```
awk '{print $1        # print name
x=$3; print x;   # print last name

# print Social Security number

print $2}'
```

Use white space and comments liberally when coding. They make your programs easier to read and maintain.

CONSTANTS AND LITERALS

Constants and literals are used frequently in awk, as well as in general-purpose programming languages, to represent values that will not change in one or more statements, or will be used once in a calculation. We have already seen many examples of constants in previous chapters.

Two types of constants are in awk: string constants and numeric (or number) constants. As we have seen, a string constant is created by inserting characters between a pair of quotes, like so:

```
"Hello World"
"Adhesions"
```

**LAB
10.1**

String constants may also contain escape sequences, which are special characters that are used for specific purposes that cannot be represented using a character found on the keypad (see Lab 10.2), as in the following conditional:

```
$1 == "\n"
```

Numerical or number constants are created simply by listing their value. Number constants may be whole numbers, decimal values, or real values represented in scientific notation. Examples of numeric constants are as follows:

```
10
10.0
10e-1
```

A string or number constant may have any representation described in Labs 10.2 and 10.3. All numbers are stored as floating points, and the highest number constant that can be represented is machine dependent.

LAB 10.1 EXERCISES

10.1.1 IDENTIFY STATEMENTS AND EXPRESSION COMPONENTS

What are the primary expressions, what types of primary expressions are they, and what are the operators that combine the primary expressions in the following?

a) `$1 + sort(x, y) / (3 + 4)`

_____

_____

b) `array[x] / calc(y, z)`

_____

_____

c) Is the following statement valid?
`awk '{ $1 = 3; print }' some_file`

_____

_____

d) Is the following statement valid?
```
awk '{$1 = 3
print
}' some_file
```


e) Is the following statement valid?
```
awk '{$1}' some-file
```


LAB 10.1 EXERCISE ANSWERS

This section gives you some suggested answers to the questions in Lab 10.1, with discussion related to those answers. Your answers may vary, but the most important thing is whether or not your answer works. Use this discussion to analyze differences between your answers and those presented here.

If you have alternative answers to the questions in this Exercise, you are encouraged to post your answers and discuss them at the companion Web site for this book, located at:

```
http://www.phptr.com/phptrinteractive/
```

10.1.1 ANSWERS

What are the primary expressions, what types of primary expressions are they, and what are the operators that combine the primary expressions in the following?

a) `$1 + sort(x, y) / (3 + 4)`

   Answer: $1 Primary expression, Field

`sort(x, y)` *Primary expression, Function Call*

`x, y` *Primary expressions, Variable*

`3, 4` *Primary expression, Constant*

`+, /, +,` *and* `()` *Combining Expression Operators*

b) `array[x] / calc(y, z)`

Answer: `array[x]` *Primary expression, Array Element*

`x` *Primary expression, Variable*

`calc(y, z)` *Primary Expression, Function Call*

`y, z` *Primary expressions, Variable*

`/` *Combining Expression Operator*

c) Is the following statement valid?
```
awk '{ $1 = 3; print }' some_file
```
Answer: Yes, it is valid.

A print statement can appear on a line after another statement, as long as they are separated by a semicolon. The print statement does not have to have arguments provided to it.

d) Is the following statement valid?
```
awk '{$1 = 3
print
}' some_file
```
Answer: Yes, it is valid.

Multiple statements may appear in an awk program, with each statement beginning on a newline. In this case, the semicolon is not necessary.

e) Is the following statement valid?
```
awk '{$1}' some-file
```
Answer: Yes, it is valid.

**LAB
10.1**

A primary expression can be a statement on a line by itself.

LAB 10.1 SELF-REVIEW QUESTIONS

In order to test your progress, you should be able to answer the following questions.

For each of the following multiple choice questions, one or more answers may be correct.

1) Which of the following data types does awk support?
  a) _____string
  b) _____char
  c) _____numbers
  d) _____floating
  e) _____pointer

2) Which of the following are statement separators in awk?
  a) _____ ;
  b) _____ .
  c) _____ ,
  d) _____ \n
  e) _____None of the above

3) Which of the following are combining expressions?
  a) _____3 + 4
  b) _____$1
  c) _____sort(x)
  d) _____(3 / 4)

4) What type of constant is x="Hello"?
  a) _____string
  b) _____literal
  c) _____number
  d) _____character

5) What is the largest number constant that can be represented?
  a) _____1000000
  b) _____1000000000
  c) _____100000000
  d) _____None of the above

Quiz answers appear in Appendix A, Section 10.1.

**LAB
10.1**

L A B   10.2

AWK STRINGS

LAB OBJECTIVES

After this Lab, you will be able to:

✓ Understand Strings and Escape Sequences

✓ Understand String Initialization

✓ Understand String Concatenation

STRINGS

A string in awk is defined as a sequence of zero or more characters. Words, digits, regular expressions . . . these are all strings when enclosed in double quotes. Some examples might be as follows:

`"Hello, World"`	a string with 12 characters; note that a blank character space is considered a character
`"\t"`	a string with 1 character (escape sequence)
`"John Smith\n"`	a string with 11 characters
`""`	a string with zero characters, the null string
`"0123"`	a string with four characters, the digits 0123
`"(-|+)?[0-9]*"`	a string containing 12 characters, a regular expression

Note that a string with zero characters is the null string, which is empty.

One important use of the null string is to initialize variables that may later be used to concatenate strings. This we'll see later in this Lab. The null string is also useful with conditionals to represent that a variable hasn't been initialized by a previous assignment. Null strings are also used by conditionals to test the result of a string comparison.

ESCAPE SEQUENCES

The string "\t" contains what is called an escape sequence. Escape sequences are special characters that are used for specific purposes that cannot be represented using a regular character on the keypad. An escape character is recognized when it is preceded by the backslash (\ ) character. You may have encountered these escape characters if you have programmed in other general-purpose programming languages such as C/C++, Pascal, Basic, and so on. These characters along with their functions are listed in Table 10.1.

Table 10.1 ■ Awk Escape Characters

Character	Function
\b	backspace
\f	formfeed
\n	newline (line feed)
\r	carriage return
\t	tab
\ddd	octal value ddd, where ddd is one to three digits between 0 and 7
\c	any other character c where c is interpreted literally (e.g., \\ for backslash)

In the case of the first five functions, the function is performed when the escape sequence is printed. Additionally, these functions may be used as field separators but are rather uncommon. The last two are used for specific purposes. For example, \& could be used as the \c escape sequence. This would be used so that the & character could be interpreted by its textual meaning instead of interpreted by the awk language as its regular expression meaning. You will see the uses of the ampersand and other escape sequences throughout this text.

STRING INITIALIZATION

In awk, strings are initialized to the null string by default. Therefore, if a variable is used in a program before it is given an initial specific string value, it is initialized to the null string. As a programmer, you do not have to worry about initialization. It comes for free and allows for less time spent programming. You don't have to write extra lines of code to initialize a string. It makes the code more efficient and more compact.

STRING CONCATENATION

String concatenation allows a user to join more than one string to create a list of strings. Concatenation occurs at the end of the first string used. In other words, additional strings are appended to the first one. The string concatenation in awk is accomplished by writing two or more operands (that are primary expressions) one after the other with a space separating each operand. For example:

```
full_name = "Peter " last_name
```

Here, the operands (primary expressions) are a string constant and a variable. If the last name is "Patsis," the operation concatenates the two strings and assigns "Peter Patsis" to the variable `full_name`. The `last_name` variable contains a string value. If the variable contained a number, then the number would be converted to a string and then concatenated with "Peter." We will go over how numbers are converted to strings in Lab 10.4.

As you can see, no explicit operator is used. All that is required to perform string concatenation is to list one string value after another string value.

■ FOR EXAMPLE:

Suppose that you have an application that prints all the unique conferences (conference name) you are offering for the current year in sorted order. The output could then be used to update a database or be used in a report. The following program implements this problem.

```
awk '{print $1}' conf.data | sort | awk 'names != $1 {names = $1 \
                                    allnames = allnames $1 " "} \
                                    END {print allnames}'

awk '{print $1}' conf.data | sort
```

This part of the application produces a sorted list of conference names and sends this as input to the second awk program. This task is accomplished by using a UNIX pipe for both input and output. Pipes were covered in sed and grep and in Chapter 16, "Advanced Input and Output," but are introduced here to hint at the power of using pipes in your awk program. The second awk program is:

```
awk 'names != $1 {names = $1 \
allnames = allnames $1 " "} \
END {print allnames}'
```

This program takes the sorted list as input. The variable names is used to store the current conference being processed. If names != $1, then we are processing a new conference, and we must append the new conference being to names (names = $1), and we must concatenate the new conference to the allnames string variable. The allnames variable keeps a list of all unique conference names. To demonstrate the algorithm when we process the first record:

```
first record = "Adhesions
$1 = "Adhesions"
names = " "
allnames = " "

names ! = $1 => " " != "Adhesions" => True and the
    action is executed
names = $1 => "Adhesions"

allnames = allnames $1 " "
```

Since three operands are listed side by side with a space in between, string concatenation is performed:

LAB
10.2

```
allnames = allnames $1 "" => "" "Adhesions" " " =>
   "Adhesions "
```

The second record and $1 is "Adhesions."

Here, $1 ("Adhesions") is equal to $1 ("Adhesions") and the action is not performed. The action is not performed again until the input record and $1 are "Coatings."

The final value of allnames that is output is "Adhesions Coatings Stabilizers Resins."

 Since string concatenation has no operator symbol and is distinguished by placing operands side by side with a space in between, it can result in unintentional errors. For example, say that you intended to divide two numbers, sum / total, and you forgot the division symbol (/). The expression would be sum total. This would be interpreted as string concatenation and would produce erroneous results. Be careful to avoid this type of error.

LAB 10.2 EXERCISES

10.2.1 UNDERSTAND STRINGS AND ESCAPE SEQUENCES

Create some-file with just one line of input and execute the following programs:

```
awk '{print "Hello Ther\be, Peter"}' some-file
awk '{print "Hello There, Peter\f"}' some-file
awk '{print "Hello There, Peter\n"}' some-file
awk '{print "Hello There,\r Peter"; print "Yes sir"}' some-file
awk '{print "Hello There,\t Peter"; print "Yes sir"}' some-file
```

a) What do the programs produce as output?

_____

_____

b) Write an awk program that prints the characters *, &, and \, one after the other.

_____

_____

10.2.2 UNDERSTAND STRING INITIALIZATION

Use the following file, called `input-file`, for question a:

```
30000 Jones
45000 Peters
40000 Smith
300000 Harold
25000 Grier
```

a) What does the following awk program produce as output, given the file `input-file`?

```
awk ' BEGIN {testvalue = 40000} $1 > testvalue {names
    = names + $2 " "}
```

_____

_____

Consider the following awk program:

```
awk 'BEGIN {count = 1; name = $1}
        name  != $1 {name = $1; count = count +1}'
    input_file
```

b) What is wrong with the program?

_____

_____

10.2.3 UNDERSTAND STRING CONCATENATION

For the following questions, what is the value of `result` after the following single line is read in?

> `45000 Peters`

a) `result = "Jones" $1`

_____

_____

b) Using the `conf.data` file from Lab 5.1, write an awk program that prints out in a single line the names of all participants who have registered for conferences that cost more than $800.

_____

_____

LAB 10.2 EXERCISE ANSWERS

This section gives you some suggested answers to the questions in Lab 10.2, with discussion related to those answers. Your answers may vary, but the most important thing is whether or not your answer works. Use this discussion to analyze differences between your answers and those presented here.

If you have alternative answers to the questions in this Exercise, you are encouraged to post your answers and discuss them at the companion Web site for this book, located at:

`http://www.phptr.com/phptrinteractive/`

Create `some-file` with just one line of input and execute the given programs.

a) What do the programs produce as output?
```
awk '{print "Hello Ther\be, Peter"}' some_file
```

Answer: This program outputs the following:
Hello Thee, Peter

The reason that the character `r` in `there` is not printed is that the next character in the string `Ther\be` to be printed is `\b`, which is the backspace character. When printed, it executes its function, which backspaces over the character `r`.

```
awk '{print "Hello There, Peter\f"}' some-file
```

Answer: This program outputs the following:
Hello There, Peter

followed by a form feed.

The form feed causes the system to output a preset number of blank lines to the default output device. On a printer, the effect would be for the paper to advance to the next page. If the default output device is the screen or a file, you would simply see the same number of blank lines that would correspond to a "page."

```
awk    '{print "Hello There, Peter\n"}' some-file
```

Answer: This program outputs the following:
Hello There, Peter

followed by 2 newlines.

Any subsequent output would print on the line following the next line. The extra newline is printed because of the `\n` escape sequence in the string. The print statement prints a newline as a default, so two newlines are printed.

```
awk '{print "Hello There,\r Peter"; print "Yes sir"}'
    some-file
```

Answer: The program outputs the following:

```
Peter There,
Yes sir
```

followed by a carriage return.

```
Hello There,
  Peter
```

Any text appearing after the carriage return escape sequence that are part of the same print statement as the escape sequence will print at the start of the first character position in the current line. The reason is that the function of the carriage return is to move the cursor to the start of the current line. The string " Peter" is part of the same print statement in which the carriage return is encountered. Therefore, the carriage return is executed, returning the cursor to the first character in the current line, and the string " Peter" overwrites the characters "Hello." Because the default action of the print statement is to print a newline after executing the print statement, the next print statement "Yes sir" prints on the next line.

```
awk '{print "Hello There,\t Peter"; print "Yes sir"}'
  some-file
```

Answer: This program outputs the following:

```
Hello There, Peter
Yes sir
```

The same reasoning as the last applies in this program, except instead of a carriage return, a tab is printed before the string "Peter" is printed.

b) Write an awk program that prints the characters *, &, and \, one after the other.

Answer: The program is as follows:

```
awk '{print "\* \& \\"}' some-file
```

Because the asterisk, ampersand, and backslash have special meaning to awk, they must be preceded by a backslash.

10.2.2 ANSWERS

a) What does the following awk program produce as output, given the file `input-file?`

```
awk ' BEGIN {testvalue = 40000} $1 > testvalue {names
  = names + $2 " "}
```

Answer: The output is as follows:

```
"Peters Harold "
```

The action `names = names + $2 " "` will be executed for every line in which the pattern `$1 > 40000` is true. This action happens whenever the first field in the current line is greater than 40000. Lines 2, 3, and 4 all have the first field greater than 40000.

For each of these lines, the action is executed. The action uses string concatenation to append the variable names with the value of the second field and a space. Together, this concatenation is then assigned back to the variable names. Therefore, names contains a list of string names for which the value of the first field is greater than 40000. Because names is never explicitly initialized, it is implicitly initialized with the null string. Therefore, before the second line of the input file is processed, names contains

```
Names  = ""
```

The action is executed for the second line because 45000 > 40000. The values of the string concatenation are:

```
Names = "" "Peters" " " and after the string concat-
enation
Names = "Peters "
Names = "Peters Harold "
```

Notice the space at the very end of the output.

Consider the following awk program:

```
awk 'BEGIN {count = 1; name = $1}
        name != $1 {name = $1; count = count +1}'
  input_file
```

**LAB
10.2**

is wrong with the program?

Cannot access a field variable ($1) in a BEGIN pattern

...tle tricky because of a subtlety that occurs when using BEGIN. BEGIN is executed before *anything* is read from the input file. Therefore, $1, which has assigned its value to name, does not exist and results in an error.

10.2.3 ANSWERS

For the following question what is the value of result after the following single line is read in?

45000 Peters

a) result = "Jones" $1

Answer: result = "Jones45000"

b) Using the conf.data file from Lab 5.1, write an awk program that prints out in a single line the names of all participants who have registered for conferences that cost more than $800.

Answer: The program is as follows:
```
awk 'BEGIN {names = ""}
$3 > 800 {names = names $1}
END {print names}' conf.data
```

In this program, names is explicitly initialized to the null string in the BEGIN pattern. The string variable names is then concatenated with the first field (registrant's name) whenever the third field in the current line (conference fee) is greater than 800. The variable names, which contains the list of all registrants, is then printed out in the END pattern.

LAB 10.2 SELF-REVIEW QUESTIONS

In order to test your progress, you should be able to answer the following questions.

For each of the following multiple choice questions, one or more answers may be correct.

1) What is a string initialized to if it wasn't explicitly initialized?
    a) _____ " "
    b) _____ ""
    c) _____ "\n"
    d) _____ "\0"
    e) _____None of the above

2) What is the string concatenation operator?
    a) _____ /
    b) _____ &
    c) _____ +
    d) _____ *
    e) _____None of the above

3) What is the result of names after the statement result = "Smith" 12?
    a) _____Smith
    b) _____Smith 12
    c) _____Smith12
    d) _____12
    e) _____None of the above

Quiz answers appear in Appendix A, Section 10.2.

L A B   10.3

AWK NUMBERS

LAB OBJECTIVES

After this Lab, you will be able to:

✓ Understand the Various Representations of Numbers

✓ Understand How Numbers Are Initialized

The only other data type used in awk is numbers. Awk differs from most languages in that no concept of various types of numerical data types exists. In this Lab, you will learn the various representations that are allowed in awk, how awk interprets the various representations, and how awk initializes numbers.

In awk, numbers can be represented as follows:

- As an integer or whole number, preceded by an optional sign value, such as the following:

    ```
    1
    +5
    001
    ```

- As a real number (decimal and fractional part) preceded by an optional sign value, such as in the following:

    ```
    10.12
    +5.3
    ```

- In scientific notation, like so:

```
-5.2e-1
```

The scientific notation—also known as an "exponential" number—may have a decimal and fractional part preceding the letter e. This possibility is seen in the example with the number 5.2. In addition, you may have an optional sign before the digit after the letter e. This may be seen with the negative sign before the number 5.2 and after the letter e. The letter e may be in either upper- or lowercase.

The value shown above is equal to the real number –.052.

All the following are additional examples of scientific notation:

```
5e0
5e+2
0.1e+1
```

In awk, the following values are interpreted as the same value:

```
5
5.0
+5
5e0
0.5e+1
5E-1
5e-1
005
```

In awk, all numbers are initialized to the value 0 if they are not given an initial explicit value.

■ FOR EXAMPLE:

Consider the following:

```
awk 'name == "Sommers" {count = count + 1}' some-file
```

The variable `count` has not been explicitly initialized to any number. Therefore, awk uses implicit initialization to initialize `count` to zero and then it adds 1 to it. This approach is especially helpful in that it eliminates the need to declare initial values to 0 in a `BEGIN` pattern, when otherwise the `BEGIN` pattern would not be used. This is commonly the case when using accumulator values. Typically, accumulator values start at the value 0 and are used for running totals. For example, accumulator values are commonly used in the case of calculating averages or printing totals in a report.

All numbers in awk are stored internally as floating-point numbers. The maximum value is machine dependent.

LAB 10.3 EXERCISES

10.3.1 UNDERSTAND THE VARIOUS REPRESENTATIONS OF NUMBERS

Create a file called `input_file`, containing the following data:

```
10.9
+10
8E3
8e
8e+2
8b2
8.3e+2
-3.2e+1
+08e-2
```

Now run the following program:

```
awk 'BEGIN  {expr  =   "^[+-]?([0-9]+[.]?[0-9]*|[.][0-
    9]+)([eE][+-]?[0-9]+)?$"}
$1 ~ expr {print $1, "  Is A Valid Number"}
$1 !~ expr {print $1, "  Not A Valid Number"}'
    input_file
```

a) What is the output?

Create a file called `input_file`, containing the following data:

```
5.0 +5.0
5 5.00
5E0 +5
5E2 +500
"5E2" 500
```

Run the following program.

```
awk '$1 == $2 {print $1, "Equal To", $2}
$1 != $2 {print $1, "Not Equal To", $2}' input_file
```

b) What is the output?

10.3.2 UNDERSTAND HOW NUMBERS ARE INITIALIZED

Use the following program for Questions a–c of this Exercise.

```
awk 'BEGIN {x = values_below }
{print x}' some_file
```

What is the output of the program, given the following values for `values_below`?

a) `values_below = +5`

b) `values_below = "50.3"`

_____

_____

c) `values_below = 5E3`

_____

_____

In the Lab discussion, you saw the following program:

```
awk 'name == "Sommers" {count = count + 1}' some-file
```

d) Write an equivalent program that uses a BEGIN pattern.

_____

_____

Use the following file, called `number.data`, to answer the next question:

```
5
4
3
8
```

e) What is the result of the following program?
```
awk '{sum = sum + $1}
END {print sum/count}' number.data
```

_____

_____

LAB 10.3 EXERCISE ANSWERS

This section gives you some suggested answers to the questions in Lab 10.3, with discussion related to those answers. Your answers may vary, but the most important thing is whether or not your answer works. Use this discussion to analyze differences between your answers and those presented here.

If you have alternative answers to the questions in this Exercise, you are encouraged to post your answers and discuss them at the companion Web site for this book, located at:

```
http://www.phptr.com/phptrinteractive/
```

10.3.1 ANSWERS

Run the following program using the file `input_file` that you created:

```
awk ' BEGIN {expr = "^[+-]?([0-9]+[.]?[0-9]*|[.][0-
    9]+)([eE][+-]?[0-9]+)?$"}
$1 ~ expr {print $1 "  Is A Valid Number"}
$1 !~ expr {print $1 " Not A Valid Number"' input_file
```

a) What is the output?

Answer: The program produces the following output:

10.9 Is A Valid Number

+10 Is A Valid Number

8E3 Is A Valid Number

8e Not A Valid Number

8e+2 Is A Valid Number

8b2 Not A Valid Number

8.3e+2 Is A Valid Number

-3.2e+1 Is A Valid Number

+08e-2 Is A Valid Number

The only invalid numbers are 8e and 8b2. For 8e, it must have either a number or a sign or just a whole number following the e. 8b2 cannot have a b, it must be a, e, or E.

Run the following program using the second `input_file` that you created:

```
awk '$1 == $2 {print $1, "Equal To", $2}
     $1 != $2 {print $1, "Not Equal To", $2}' input_file
```

b) What is the output?

Answer: The output is as follows:
5 Equal To 5

Awk strips the leading plus sign.

5 Equal To 5

Awk strips the zeros after the decimal point.

5 Equal To 5

Awk prints the whole number representation of the equivalent scientific notation.

500 Equal To 500
5E2 Equal To 500

Notice that awk does not print the whole number equivalent of the scientific form, because awk forces the value from string to number, leaving the original scientific notation representation. This forcing of one type of value to another is known as *coercion*. Coercion is described more fully in Lab 10.4.

10.3.2 ANSWERS

Using the program given, what is the output, given the following values for `values_below`?

a) `values_below = +5`

Answer: 5

A number is printed as a whole number if no decimal portion exists, and no leading and trailing characters are displayed.

b) `values_below = "50.3"`

Answer: 50.3

c) `values_below = 5E3`

Answer: 5E3

In the Lab discussion, you saw the following program:

```
awk 'name == "Sommers" {count = count + 1}' some-file
```

d) Write an equivalent program that uses a BEGIN pattern.

Answer: The program is as follows:
```
awk 'BEGIN {count =0 }
name == "Sommers" {count = count + 1}' some-file
```

The point of this program is to illustrate the advantage of implicit initialization. Implicit initialization eliminates the need for extra statements that would be required to explicitly initialize values. In the example, we do not need the BEGIN pattern, thus resulting in more compact, shorter, and faster programs.

Use the given file, called `number.data`, to answer the next question:

e) What is the result of the following program?

```
awk '{sum = sum + $1}
END {print sum/count}' number.data
```

Answer: The result is as follows:

**awk: cmd. line:2: (FILENAME=number.data FNR=8)
fatal: division by zero attempted**

The reason that we get a divide-by-zero error is that count is not explicitly initialized. Because awk implicitly initializes number values that have not been initialized before to zero, count is initialized to zero in the division. This example shows how implicit initialization can cause unexpected behavior such as division by zero. Make sure that if you intend a variable to have a certain value, you explicitly assign the value correctly.

LAB 10.3 SELF-REVIEW QUESTIONS

In order to test your progress, you should be able to answer the following questions.

For each of the following multiple choice questions, one or more answers may be correct.

1) How are numbers stored internally in awk?
   a) _____floating point
   b) _____whole number
   c) _____string
   d) _____scientific notation
   e) _____None of the above

2) What is the largest number that may be stored in awk?
   a) _____1E+20
   b) _____1E+25
   c) _____-1E+20 to +1E+20
   d) _____-1E+25 to +1E+25
   e) _____None of the above

3) What are numbers implicitly initialized to?
   a) _____ ""
   b) _____ 1
   c) _____ 0
   d) _____machine dependent

Quiz answers appear in Appendix A, Section 10.3.

L A B   10.4

COERCION

LAB OBJECTIVES

After this Lab, you will be able to:

✓ Understand When a Coercion Is Performed

✓ Understand the Result of a Coercion

✓ Understand Explicit and Implicit Coercions

The process by which one data type is converted to another type is called *coercion*. It is performed by the compiler (or in this case, the interpreter) when an expression requires a certain type to be evaluated. An example is the addition operator. The addition of two numbers requires both types on either side of the operator to be numbers. If one of the variables is of a different type, then the language coerces the nonnumber into a number. The rules for converting from one type to another are language specific. In this Lab, we explore the rules and issues involved in coercing one data type to another. Because awk has only two data types, numbers and strings, this activity entails coercing from a string value to a number value, or from a number value to a string value. The rules for coercion and the results of coercion from one data type to another are important to understand. Often, coercion is the source of many potential errors in programming. Expecting one value and receiving another can result in unexpected errors. In C/C++, coercion is often referred to as implicit and explicit casting.

When an awk programmer encounters the following statement, the types of the two field variables are unknown:

```
$1 == $2
```

Only when the input line is read in is the type known to both the reader and awk. The reason is that a field variable may be assigned any type. Therefore, $1 may be a string or a number. Furthermore, no hard-and-fast rule exists that the current line may contain a string for the first field and that in the next line, the first field may contain a number.

■ FOR EXAMPLE:

Consider the following file:

```
Smith 20 NY
10 Jones 30 CA
```

In this file, $1 is a string in the first line and a number in the second.

In awk, a field variable is assigned a string unless the field variable is a recognizable representation of a number. These representations were described in Lab 10.3. If both types in the comparison are numbers, then a numerical comparison is made. If either one of the operands is a string or both are strings, then a string comparison is made.

■ FOR EXAMPLE:

Because the following operation is numeric, then both values must be numeric:

```
pi + 3
```

So if pi is not already a number, then it is coerced to a number.

Because the following string concatenation is a string operation, if name and ssn are not already strings, they are coerced into strings:

```
name ssn
```

Then consider the following situation:

```
a = b
```

In this case, the type of the operation cannot be determined solely from the operator. Here, both the assignment and the variable a acquire the type of the expression b. Therefore, in the following awk statement, both the value of the statement and the variable a acquire a string value (in this case, the string "Hello").

```
a = "Hello"
```

One might be curious as to the importance of a statement having a value. It will be clear when we talk about relational operators and control-flow in Lab 12.3 and Chapter 14, "Awk Control Flow," in which the statement value is used to determine a branch. Again, in the statement a = b, the value of a can be determined only from context and may in fact be undetermined. It can be determined only when the value of b is assigned.

■ FOR EXAMPLE:

Consider the following statement:

```
x = $5
```

Now suppose that we have the following two input lines:

```
Smith 20 NY
10 Jones 30 CA
```

In this case, $5 would not exist, because only three fields are in the first line and four in the second. Nonexistent fields are always initialized with the string value of null, or "". Therefore, $5 is initialized with a null value because it is nonexistent. If a variable that is nonexistent is subsequently used in a numeric operation, and furthermore because a nonexistent variable (like $5 in this case) is initialized with the null string value, then a rule must coerce that null value into a number. As a rule, awk always coerces a null value to the number zero. Thus, consider the following awk statement:

```
count = count + 1
```

If count was not previously assigned with a string or number value, then count on the right-hand side of the equal sign is initialized with the string value of null, and finally coerced to 0, because the operator to the right of it is the numeric addition operator. In Lab 13.4, we will go over which operators have priority over other operators, and whether they are evaluated from right to left or left to right. For this example, the addition operator has higher precedence than the assignment operator; therefore, the addition operator is evaluated first.

Again, to recap, if the operation requires one of its operands to be of a certain type and the operand is not of that type, then the operand will be coerced to the correct type. We have seen three types of operations so far: string (string concatenation), number (addition), and undetermined (assignment). A complete list of operations and the type of the operands that the operations require are given in Table 15-1. Note that a U stands for undetermined, an S stands for string, and an N stands for a number.

Table 10.2 ■ Operations and their Operand

Operation Type	Operator	Type of Operand	Operation Result
Assignment	=	U (can be both)	U
Assignment	+=, -=, *=, /=, %=, ^=	N	N
Conditional	?:	U	U
Logical OR	||	U	N
Logical AND	&&	U	N
Array Membership	in	S	N
Relational Matching	~, !~	S	N
Relational	<, <=, >, >=, ==, !=	U	N
Concatenation	"a" "b"	S	S
Arithmetic, Add, Subtract	+, -	N	N
Arithmetic, Mult, Div, Mod	*, /, %	N	N
Unary Plus, Minus	+, - -3 negation of 3	N	N
Logical Not	!	U	N
Exponentiation	^	N	N
Increment, Decrement	++, --	N	N
Field	$	N	N
Grouping	()	Doesn't apply	Doesn't apply

In this table, if the type of the operand and the operation result are of the same type (for example, both are N for addition), then if one or both of the operands are of a different type, coercion will be performed, and the rules described previously for converting from a string to a number or a number to a string will be applied. In the assignment operator, the type of operand may be either a string or a number, and the type of the result of the assignment is determined by the type of the right-hand side of the assignment statement. A relational operator may take a string or a number, but only if both operands are a number will a numerical comparison be made. Note that regardless of the type of the comparison, the result will be numerical. The same is true for the logical operators as is for the relational operators. The conditional operator is a little bit trickier, and we will talk about it in Lab 12.3. We will talk about the rest of the operators in more detail in Chapter 12, "Operators."

LAB
10.4

All of above examples in this Lab were coercions that were performed implicitly by the awk interpreter. However, at times, an awk programmer may wish to coerce operands in an operation explicitly. Following are examples that explain the rules and issues on performing explicit coercions. Two rules or ways exist to coerce or convert a number to a string and string to a number. These rules keep the values intact; in other words, if a string has a value of "1," the rule for converting to a number retains the numeric value 1. Conversely, the rule for converting to a string retains the numeric value as a string. Thus, the number 123 retains its value "123" as a string.

```
number ""
```

And the string value "123" retains its numeric value 123, after the addition below:

```
string + 0
```

In the first rule, by using string concatenation and appending a null value, the resulting string retains its numeric representation as a string. In the second example, by using addition by 0, the string value is coerced to its numerical value represented by the string, and addition by 0 yields the identical value.

To summarize: the rules for coercing (implicit or explicit) a string into a number are as follows:

1. If the first left-most character does not have a numerical equivalent (it is not a digit 0-9), it is assigned the value 0.
2. Otherwise, the first character is a digit 0-9. Continue moving left until the next left-most character is not a digit or until the end of the string is reached. The number that is represented will be the number starting at the first character continuing left until the first nondigit is encountered (the exception to this is scientific notation, which may have an e or E, as discussed in Lab 10.3).

LAB 10.4 EXERCISES

10.4.1 UNDERSTAND WHEN A COERCION IS PERFORMED

Use the following file called some-file for this Exercise:

```
5 10 1.2
5 10 Smith
5 Jones Smith
Peters Moore Jones
Peters 7 10
```

a) What is the output of the following program?

```
awk '{print (!$1)
print ($2 < $3)
print $2 $3
print ($1 || $2 $3)
$1 = $2 + $3
print $1
}' some-file
```

10.4.2 UNDERSTAND THE RESULT OF A COERCION

What would be the number that results if the following strings were converted to a number?

LAB
10.4

a) "123.0"

_____

_____

b) "Smith"

_____

_____

c) ""

_____

_____

d) "35 Dollars"

_____

_____

e) "$12 Dollars"

_____

_____

Use the following conditional statement to answer Questions f through j in this Exercise:

```
$1  ==  $2
```

If the two operands are equal, the result of the equal comparison is 1 and zero. Otherwise, the result is zero.

f) What would the result of the comparison be, given the following pair of operands?

```
$1 = 5
$2 = 5.0
```

_____

_____

g) What would the result of the comparison be, given the following pair of operands?

```
$1 = 5
$2 = +5
```

_____

_____

h) What would the result of the comparison be, given the following pair of operands?

```
$1 = 5e0
$2 = 5.0e0
```

_____

_____

i) What would the result of the comparison be, given the following pair of operands?

```
$1 = " "
$2 = 0
```

_____

_____

j) What would the result of the comparison be, given the following pair of operands?

```
$1 = ""
$2 = 0.0
```

Use the following addition operation to answer Questions k through o in this Exercise:

```
result = $1 + 1
```

What would the value of the variable result be, given the following values for $1?

k) `$1 = "2E2"`

l) `$1 = 1.234`

m) `$1 = ""`

n) `$1 = "3x2"`

o) `$1 = "Smith"`

10.4.3 UNDERSTAND EXPLICIT AND IMPLICIT COERCIONS

Use the following conditional statement to answer the questions in this Exercise:

```
$1 + 0 == $2 + 0
```

a) What would the result of the comparison be, given the following pair of operands, and why?

```
$1 = " "
$2 = 0
```

b) What would the result of the comparison be, given the following pair of operands, and why?

```
$1 = "5e0"
$2 = 5
```

c) What would the result of the comparison be, given the following pair of operands, and why?

```
$1 = "2ab3"
$2 = 2
```

d) What would the result of the comparison be, given the following pair of operands, and why?
```
$1 = " "
$2 = 1
```

LAB 10.4 ANSWERS

 This section gives you some suggested answers to the questions in Lab 10.4, with discussion related to those answers. Your answers may vary, but the most important thing is whether or not your answer works. Use this discussion to analyze differences between your answers and those presented here.

If you have alternative answers to the questions in this Exercise, you are encouraged to post your answers and discuss them at the companion Web site for this book, located at:

```
http://www.phptr.com/phptrinteractive/
```

10.4.1 ANSWERS

Use the given file called `some-file` for this Exercise:

a) What is the output of the following program?
```
awk '{print (!$1)
print ($2 < $3)
print $2 $3
print ($1 || $2 $3)
$1 = $2 + $3
print $1
}' some-file
```

Answer: The output is as follows:
```
0
```

**LAB
10.4**

Taking the negation of any other value except zero is false (or zero).

    0
    101.2

String concatenation takes string arguments. Both operands are numbers. Therefore, both operands are coerced into strings. The coercion results in $2 = "10" and $3 = "1.2". These strings are then concatenated together.

    1

The operands to the or statement are 5 and "101.2" (string concatenation from the previous print statement). The string "101.2" is coerced to a number because the or statement expects number operands. The or statement then becomes 5 || 101.2. Awk interprets any positive number as true; therefore, the result of the or statement is a 1 or true.

    11.2
    10 + 1.2 = 11.2
    0
    1

This example illustrates the need to carefully consider the potential for unexpected results when operating with variables. The greatest pitfall comes when data in a numeric field is actually an alphanumeric string (e.g., intended data 5.3 might be entered as T.3). Whenever a relational comparison is made, if one of the operands is a string, then a string comparison is made. (This is the reason for the U in the previous discussion in this Lab for the type of operand.) Because the digit 1 is less than the first character S in the string "Smith," a 1 (or true) result is returned.

    10Smith
    1

Because one of the operands in the or statement is always a string (I say "always" because string concatenation is performed on the right-hand side of the or statement), a logical or is performed on strings. Therefore, the first operand is always converted to a string. Because a string has a numerical value associated with it (its ASCII value), this or statement will always evaluate to true. The only way an or statement that has string operands can evaluate to false is if the following comparison is made: \0 || \0;. In other words, "" || "" (an or statement with both operands being the null string)

```
10


0
1
JonesSmith
1
0
```

Because addition takes number operands only, the strings "Jones" and "Smith" are coerced to numbers. Any string that does not have a number equivalent is coerced to zero.

```
0
```

No coercion to a number occurs, because a logical negation that has a string operand will be treated as a string. However, the string's value is recognized by its ASCII value. Therefore, this statement amounts to the following:

```
!50   (50 is the ASCII value for the capital letter P
- the P in the string "Peters")
0
MooreJones
1
0

0
1
710
1
17
```

10.4.2 ANSWERS

What would be the number that results if the following strings were converted to a number?

a) "123.0"

Answer: 123

The trailing zero after the decimal is stripped off. It drops the trailing zero because it interprets only the significant digits.

b) "Smith"

Answer: 0

Be careful with this coercion. If the string "Smith" is used as an operand to a relational expression, the string is coerced to its ASCII value, and the ASCII value that results is used in the comparison. Therefore,

```
!"Smith" = !83 = 0 (83 is the ASCII value in decimal
of the character "S")
```

However, if the string "Smith" is used in an arithmetic operation, it is coerced to zero. Therefore,

```
0 + "Smith" = 0 + 0 = 0
```

So the coercion is based on the context in which the string is used.

c) ""

Answer: 0

The null string is the only string (or character) whose coercion to a number does not depend on the context in which the string is used. The null string is coerced to zero, regardless of whether it is used in an arithmetic or relational expression. Therefore,

```
!"" = !0 = 1 (ASCII value of the null string (or
character) is zero)
0 + "" = 0
```

d) "35 Dollars"

Answer: 35

Starting at the first left-most character, 3, and continuing right, find the first nondigit character. The space between the character 5 and the character D is the first nondigit character. The number that results is everything from the digit 3 up to but not including the space. This number is 35.

e) "$12 Dollars"

Answer: 0

Starting at the first leftmost character, $, this character is not a digit. Therefore, the string is coerced to 0. Notice again that the value used in an arithmetic expression is different from the value used in a relational expression.

Use the following conditional statement to answer Questions f through j in this Exercise:

```
$1 == $2
```

f) What would the result of the comparison be, given the following pair of operands?
```
$1 = 5
$2 = 5.0
```
Answer: 1

The result would be true. The comparison $1 == $2 for the values 5 and 5.0 would be a comparison of numeric values or numbers. The values 5 and 5.0 are both the same, so they are equal.

g) What would the result of the comparison be, given the following pair of operands?
```
$1 = 5
$2 = +5
```
Answer: 1

The result would be true. The comparison $1 == $2 for the values 5 and +5 would be a comparison of numeric values or numbers. The values 5 and +5 represent the same value, and are therefore equal.

h) What would the result of the comparison be, given the following pair of operands?

```
$1 = 5e0
$2 = 5.0e0
```

Answer: I

The result would be true. `5e0` and `5.0e0` represent the same values.

i) What would the result of the comparison be, given the following pair of operands?

```
$1 = ""
$2 = 0
```

Answer: 0

The result would be false. The comparison would be a comparison of string values. The first string operand is not equal to the second string operand. In other words,

```
"" != "0"
0 != 48 ( 0 and 48 are the ascii values of the null
character and digit 0)
```

j) What would the result of the comparison be, given the following pair of operands?

```
$1 = ""
$2 = 0.0
```

Answer: 0

Again, the result would be false. The comparison would be one of string values. The first string operand is not equal to the second string operand.

Use the following addition operation to answer Questions k through o in this Exercise:

```
result = $1 + 1
```

What would the value of the variable result be, given the following values for $1?

k) `$1 = "2E2"`

Answer: 201.

2E2 would be recognized when coercing as the scientific notation representation of the value 200.

l) `$1 = 1.234`

Answer: 2.234.

m) `$1 = " "`

Answer: I.

The null string is coerced to 0.

n) `$1 = "3x2"`

Answer: 4.

The largest substring that is recognized as a number is 3; adding one yields four.

o) `$1 = "Smith"`

Answer: I

The string "Smith" is coerced to zero, because no numerical representation exists for this string. Adding 1 to it yields 1.

10.4.3 ANSWERS

Use the following conditional statement to answer the questions in this Exercise:

```
$1 + 0 == $2 + 0
```

a) What would the result of the comparison be, given the following pair of operands, and why?
```
$1 = " "
$2 = 0
```

Answer: I

The result would be true. The first operand would be coerced to a number, because the operator is addition, which is performed on numbers. The result of the coercion would be 0, because the null string is by definition coerced to 0 for arithmetic operations. The second operand is 0, so 0 + 0 = 0 + 0, and the result is true.

b) What would the result of the comparison be, given the following pair of operands, and why?

```
$1 = "5e0"
$2 = 5
```

Answer: 1

The result would be true. The first operand is coerced to 5e0, which is 5, so $5 + 0 = 5 + 0$.

c) What would the result of the comparison be, given the following pair of operands, and why?

```
$1 = "2ab3"
$2 = 2
```

Answer: 1

The result would be true. The first operand would be coerced to a number. The result of that coercion would be 2. By definition, when a number is coerced, awk starts at the left-most character of the string and continues left, finding the longest substring that is still a number. Because a cannot be represented as a number (e and E are the only letters that could possibly be part of a number), the largest substring that can be represented is two. $2 + 0 = 2 + 0$, so the comparison is true.

d) What would the result of the comparison be, given the following pair of operands, and why?

```
$1 = ""
$2 = 1
```

Answer: 0

The result is false. The first operand is a string and is coerced to zero. 0 + 0 is not equal to 0 + 1.

LAB 10.4 SELF-REVIEW QUESTIONS

In order to test your progress, you should be able to answer the following questions.

For each of the following multiple choice questions, one or more answers may be correct.

LAB 10.4

1) What type of operand does the operator = take?
    a) _____number
    b) _____string

2) What type results from relational operator ==?
    a) _____number
    b) _____string

3) What results from `0 + "Smith"`?
    a) _____0
    b) _____50
    c) _____1
    d) _____error

4) What type of coercion results from `"" 123.45`?
    a) _____implicit
    b) _____explicit
    c) _____string
    d) _____number

Quiz answers appear in Appendix A, Section 10.4.

L A B   10.5

AWK ASSIGNMENT OPERATOR

LAB OBJECTIVES

After this Lab, you will be able to:

✓ Identify Rvalues and Lvalues

✓ Write a Program Using the Assignment Statement

An assignment statement is one of the most widely used constructs in all programming languages, and awk is no exception. An assignment statement has many behind-the-scenes implications for a compiler or interpreter, some of which are discussed in this Lab. I also present some programming language terminology when explaining the assignment statement. In Lab 12.2, we revisit some specialized assignment statements that are offered in awk. Here, I describe the most basic assignment statement. We have already seen the assignment statement in many examples throughout previous sections and Chapter 9, "An Awk Program." In this Lab, I will explain the function of the assignment statement, briefly revisit coercion, explain the terms and difference between an rvalue and an lvalue, and finally state some of the rules regarding the assignment statement in awk.

In its most basic form, the assignment statement can be represented as follows:

```
lvalue = rvalue
```

The rvalue in this statement can be a constant, a variable (Chapter 11, "Variables"), an array (Chapter 15, "Awk Arrays and Functions"), a conditional expression (Chapters 12, "Operators," and 14, "Awk Control Flow"), or more generally, any expression that is allowed in awk.

You have seen the assignment statement before in the following form:

```
name = $1
$1 = 1.2
name = "Smith"
count = count + 1
```

**LAB
10.5**

Generally, you have seen that the assignment statement is used whenever you want to store a value with a referenced value. This reference has usually been by means of a named variable, or by providing a string or numeric constant.

In programming languages, when you talk about assignments, you mention whether a variable, constant, operand, or expression can be an lvalue or an rvalue. These values refer to whether a value appears on the left side of an assignment statement or the right side. If a value can be an lvalue, you can write to the value. In all cases, lvalues are variables. For a constant to be an lvalue would not make sense, because that would violate the principle by which it is used—namely, as a constant value that doesn't change. If we could write to a constant, then it wouldn't be constant but would instead change its value. In addition, functions, conditional, arithmetic, and string operators do not make much sense being written to and do not appear as lvalues. If a value appears on the right-hand side of an assignment statement, the value can be referenced or read. Most expressions can appear as an rvalue, including constants, variables, conditionals, arrays, the result of an operation, and functions. To recap:

- An lvalue is a programming construct that can appear on the left-hand side of an assignment statement, and a value can be written to the programming construct.
- An rvalue is a programming construct that can appear on the right-hand side of an assignment statement, and its value can be referenced or simply the programming construct can be referenced.

In the first example listed previously, name = $1, name is an lvalue, which suggests that variables can appear as an lvalue (you can write to them). $1 in that statement appears as an rvalue, which suggests that a field variable can be an rvalue (its value read).

LAB 10.5 EXERCISES

10.5.1 IDENTIFY RVALUES AND LVALUES

Identify complete and component rvalues, lvalues, both, or neither (invalid assignment), for values involved in the following assignments.

a) a = sqrt(16)

_____

_____

b) a = a + 1

_____

_____

10.5.2 WRITE A PROGRAM USING THE ASSIGNMENT OPERATOR

Use the following file to write a program that calculates how many records are contained within the file and prints the first two fields:

```
01/02/98 Digital 12
01/03/98 IBM 13
02/04/97 Sun 15
03/05/97 HP 24
04/09/98 TRW 20
04/10/97 Netscape 20
02/11/98 Compaq 10
```

a) What is the program?

_____

_____

b) What is the output?

_____

_____

LAB 10.5 ANSWERS

 This section gives you some suggested answers to the questions in Lab 10.5, with discussion related to those answers. Your answers may vary, but the most important thing is whether or not your answer works. Use this discussion to analyze differences between your answers and those presented here.

If you have alternative answers to the questions in this Exercise, you are encouraged to post your answers and discuss them at the companion Web site for this book, located at:

```
http://www.phptr.com/phptrinteractive/
```

10.5.1 ANSWERS

Identify complete and component rvalues, lvalues, both, or neither (invalid assignment), for values involved in the following assignments.

a) `a = sqrt(16)`

Answer: The values are as follows:
```
rvalue = 16   - Constant Value
rvalue = sqrt(16) - Function result
lvalue a = 4 - Assignment to variable a
```

Remember that rvalues are values that are read or referenced. A constant can be an rvalue. Therefore, the value 16 that is passed to the sqrt function is an rvalue. The result of the function is used as an rvalue to the assignment statement.

b) `a = a + 1`

Answer: The values are as follows:
```
rvalue = 1 - A constant
rvalue = a - Original variable value
lvalue = a - The new value in a after the expression
is evaluated and assigned.
```

a is both an rvalue and an lvalue.

10.5.2 ANSWERS

Use the given file to write a program that calculates how many records are contained within the file and prints the first two fields:

a) What is the program?

Answer: The program is as follows:
```
awk '{print $1, $2
count = count + 1
}
END {print "The total is ", count}
```

The statement `print $1, $2` prints the first two fields. The statement `count = count + 1` keeps a running total of the number of lines read in. `count` is implicitly assigned the value 0 the first time it is referenced. This assignment happens when the first line is read in. Because no pattern exists, the action is executed for every input line. Therefore, `count` will correctly contain the number of lines read in.

b) What is the output?

Answer: The output is as follows:
```
01/02/98 Digital
01/03/98 IBM
02/04/97 Sun
03/05/97 HP
04/09/98 TRW
04/10/97 Netscape
02/11/98 Compaq
The total is 7.
```

LAB 10.5 SELF-REVIEW QUESTIONS

In order to test your progress, you should be able to answer the following questions.

For each of the following multiple choice questions, one or more answers may be correct.

1) Which of the following is true of an rvalue?
   a) _____They can be read.
   b) _____They can be written.
   c) _____They appear on the right-hand side of an assignment.
   d) _____They appear on the left-hand side of an assignment.

LAB
10.5

2) Which of the following is true of an lvalue?
   a) _____They can be read.
   b) _____They can be written.
   c) _____They appear on the right-hand side of an assignment.
   d) _____They appear on the left-hand side of an assignment.

3) Which value is an rvalue in the statement `z = array[z] + 1`?
   a) _____`1`
   b) _____`=`
   c) _____`array[z]`
   d) _____`z`

4) Which value is an lvalue in the statement `array[x] = array[y] = 13`?
   a) _____`x`
   b) _____`y`
   c) _____`array[x]`
   d) _____`array[y]`
   e) _____`13`

Quiz answers appear in Appendix A, Section 10.5.

C H A P T E R 10

TEST YOUR THINKING

 The projects in this section are meant to have you utilize all of the skills that you have acquired throughout this chapter. The answers to these projects can be found at the companion Web site to this book, located at:

http://www.phptr.com/phptrinteractive

Visit the Web site periodically to share and discuss your answers.

So far, we have two ways to invoke an awk program:

```
awk 'awk program' [datafile(s)]
awk -f scriptfilename [datafile(s)]
```

The brackets indicate that the parameter inside the brackets is optional.

In the first method, the awk program (as described in Chapter 9, "An Awk Program," as one or more pattern-action statements) is written at the command line. In the second, the awk program is contained within a file called scriptfilename. A datafile(s) is optional. If a datafile is not specified, then input comes from standard input.

Awk command-line arguments and options may also be specified when awk is invoked. In this "Test Your Thinking," we explore awk command-line arguments.

The complete awk invocation syntax at the command line is the following:

```
awk [-v variable=value] [-Fvalue] [--] 'awk program'
    variable=value [datafile(s)]
awk [-v variable=value] [-Fvalue] [--] -f scriptfile-
    name variable=value [datafile(s)]
```

We will use the following two files to go over each command-line argument that we have not covered in Chapters 9 and 10:

```
Transaction.dat
w 10
d 20
w 10
d 20
w 10
```

```
Transaction.csv
w,10
d,20
w,10
d,20
w,10
```

The first field of both files is a transaction type (w—withdrawal, d—deposit). The second field is a transaction amount.

The following sets an awk variable on the command line that enables the variable to be used within the awk program:

```
[-v variable=value]
```

The variable name is listed after the -v, followed by the equal sign and the value for the variable. You cannot set the value of a built-in variable (FS, NF, OFS, and so forth) using the -v option.

1) Write the following program into a file called finalbal.scr:

```
$1 == w { balance = balance - $2 }
$2 == d {balance = balance +$2}
END { print "Final balance is ", balance }
```

2) Enter a starting balance of $1200.12 at the command line using the -v option. (Use the -f finalbal.scr command-line option to instruct awk to use the awk program in the finalbal.scr file. Also use the Trans-action.dat file.)

a) What is the output?

3) Enter a starting balance of 1200.12 and FS = "," at the command line using the -v option. (Use the -f finalbal.scr command-line option to instruct awk to use the awk program in the finalbal.scr file. Also use the Transaction.csv file.)

a) What is the output?

-Fvalue—Sets the FS (Field Separator) to value. No space exists between the -F option and the value following the -F option.

4) Enter the awk program `finalbal.scr` with the `-f` option at the command line using the `-v` option with a starting balance of 1200.12. In addition, use the `-F` option to set FS and the file `Transaction.csv`, which separates each field by a comma to compute the final balance.

`variable=value`—Provides the same function as the `-v` option, but with differences. The `-v` option specifies that the variable is to be set to value before the `BEGIN` pattern is even executed. Without the `-v` option, the value is set after the first line of input is read. Therefore, in the `-v` option, a built-in variable cannot be used, but setting the variable on the command line without the `-v` option allows you to set the value of any variable. The value without the `-v` option can be any value, shell variable, or pipe value. It must be quoted if it contains spaces or tabs.

5) Enter a starting balance of $1200.12 at the command line using the `variable=value` parameter. (Use the `-f finalbal.scr` command-line option to instruct awk to use the awk program in the `finalbal.scr` file. Also use the `Transaction.dat` file.)

a) What is the output?

6) Enter a starting balance of 1200.12 and `FS = ","` at the command line using the `variable=value`. (Use the `-f finalbal.scr` command-line option to instruct awk to use the awk program in the `finalbal.scr` file. Also use the `Transaction.csv` file.)

a) What is the output?

VARIABLES

Just mentioning a variable in your awk program causes it to exist. You have seen examples of both user-defined and field variables in previous labs throughout this book.

CHAPTER OBJECTIVES

In this chapter, you will learn about:

A wk variables are used as a convenient mechanism to refer to values. Therefore, a discussion of the way awk uses them is essential. The goal of this chapter is to define variables and the rules by which we may create variables.

L A B   11.1

FIELD VARIABLES

**LAB
11.1**

LAB OBJECTIVES

After this Lab, you will be able to:

✓ Understand How Awk Splits an Input Line into Field Variables

✓ Access Field Variables

✓ Assign Values to Field Variables

A field variable is recognized by a dollar sign, which prefixes the variable.

The awk programming model consists of reading in an input line and breaking the input line into fields. When awk breaks the line into fields, the fields of the current line are called $1, $2, and so on, up to the total number of fields that the current line contains (let's call that $N). Fields are broken up or separated by a field delimiter, such as spaces or tabs, by default (field separators are dealt with in Lab 11.3). $0 refers to the entire current input line.

Fields share the same properties as variables. They may be used in any expression where a value is expected. In addition, they may be either an *rvalue* or an *lvalue*. In other words, they may be referenced on the right-hand side of an assignment statement or assigned on the left-hand side of an assignment statement.

Awk applies special processing rules when it encounters a field variable on the left-hand side of an assignment operator. If you assign a new value to a field variable, awk automatically recreates $0 using the built-in variable OFS (the output field separator, which is discussed further in the next Lab). Therefore, for each input line read in, you will always get the current value of the input line after changes are made and before the next input line is read in. Likewise, when $0 is changed, then each of the fields $1, $2,...,$N is recomputed using the built-in variable FS (field separator) as the delimiter. The default field separator is a blank.

■ *FOR EXAMPLE:*

In awk, you can create a new field by prefixing the field number with a dollar sign. The field number must be greater than $N (the total number of fields that were separated from the input line). Awk initializes or assigns a newly created field or nonexistent field with a null value. Thus, if four fields were in the current input line, $1 through $4, and we wanted to create a fifth field containing the value of $3 multiplied by the value of $4, we could write the following awk program to perform that task:

```
awk '{result = $3 * $4
         print  result
      }' some_file
```

LAB 11.1 EXERCISES

11.1.1 UNDERSTAND HOW AWK SPLITS AN INPUT LINE INTO FIELD VARIABLES

a) What is the value of each field variable given in the following input line?

```
Smith 23 Confirmed Adhesions
```

_____

_____

b) Write a program that calculates the average amount paid by all participants in the `conf.data` file (from Lab 4.1). In addition, calculate the average amount owed by each participant, and print these values.

_____

_____

11.1.2 ACCESS FIELD VARIABLES

For each of the following programs, use `courses.data` (from Lab 9.3) as the input file. The file is also available at the companion Web site for this book:

**LAB
11.1**

```
http://www.phptr.com/phptrinteractive/
```

a) What is the output of the following program?
```
awk '$6 == "Digital" {print $1.25}' courses.data
```

_____

_____

b) What is the output of the following program?
```
awk 'END { print $3 }' courses.data
```

_____

_____

c) What is the output of the following program?
```
awk '$6 == "Digital" {print $(2-3)}' courses.data
```

_____

_____

d) What is the output of the following program?
```
awk '{ print $(6+1) }' courses.data
```

_____

_____

11.1.3 ASSIGNING VALUES TO FIELD VARIABLES

For each of the following programs, use `conf.data` (from Lab 4.1) as the input file. The file is also available at the companion Web site for this book:

```
http://www.phptr.com/phptrinteractive/
```

a) What is the output of the following program?
```
awk '{$7 = $3 * $4; print $0}' conf.data
```

LAB
11.1

b) What is the output of the following program?
```
awk 'BEGIN { i = 3 }
{$0 = $0 i}' conf.data
```

c) What is the output of the following program?
```
awk '{$3 = $3 + 50}' conf.data
```

d) What is the output of the following program?
```
awk 'BEGIN {i = 3}
{$0 = ($0 " ") i + 1
print $1, $7
}' conf.data
```

e) Write an awk program that calculates the amount owed in the `conf.data` file and stores that calculation as field number seven ($7) in the file. In addition, after calculating that number, output the maximum value from field seven.

_____

_____

f) Rewrite the program in question a of this Exercise without assigning a field variable (i.e., without assigning $7).

_____

_____

LAB 11.1 EXERCISE ANSWERS

This section gives you some suggested answers to the questions in Lab 11.1, with discussion related to those answers. Your answers may vary, but the most important thing is whether or not your answer works. Use this discussion to analyze differences between your answers and those presented here.

If you have alternative answers to the questions in this Exercise, you are encouraged to post your answers and discuss them at the companion Web site for this book, located at:

http://www.phptr.com/phptrinteractive/

11.1.1 ANSWERS

a) What is the value of each field variable given in the following input line?
Smith 23 Confirmed Adhesions

Answer: The values are as follows:
$0 = **Smith 23 Confirmed Adhesions**
$1 = **Smith**
$2 = **23**
$3 = **Confirmed**

$4 = **Adhesions**

$0 contains the contents of the input line read in. $1 contains all the characters up to the first delimiter (a space by default). $2 contains all the characters from the first delimiter to the next delimiter, and so on.

b) Write a program that calculates the average amount paid by all participants in the conf.data file (from Lab 4.1). In addition, calculate the average amount owed by each participant, and print these values.

Answer: The program is as follows:
```
awk '{paid = paid + ($3 - $4)
        count = count + 1
        owed = owed + $4
      }
      END {print "Average amount paid is ", paid/count
           print "Average amount owed is ", owed/count
      }' conf.data
```

In the first statement in the action, paid is assigned the previous value of paid plus the value of the third field (conference fee) minus the fourth field (amount owed). The values of these fields are assigned by awk when each line is read in and split into fields. Paid contains a running total of the amount paid by all registrants up to the current line. In the second statement, count is incremented by one each time an input record is read, and therefore is a count of the total number of input lines that have been read up to the current input line. In the last statement, the variable owed contains a running total of the total amount owed by all registrants up to the current input line. Finally, in the END pattern, the average amount paid is paid/count. This number is printed. The average amount owed is owed/count, and that number is printed as well.

11.1.2 ANSWERS

For each of the following programs, use courses.data (from Lab 9.3) as the input file.

a) What is the output of the following program?
```
awk '$6 == "Digital" {print $1.25}' courses.data
```

Answer: The output is as follows:
Leonard
Oreilly

Note from this Exercise that floating-point numbers are allowed when referring to fields, but awk truncates them, thus resulting here in print $1.

b) What is the output of the following program?
```
awk 'END { print $3 }' courses.data
```

Answer: The output is as follows:
200

A field variable retains its value in an END statement, however program
processing is finished. As a result, its value is never again changed by
awk—only by the programmer. In this Exercise, because the last input
record in the course.data file is as follows, field variable three retains its
value from the very last assignment, which is 200:

Henry Coatings 200 100 080398 Shell

This value was produced when awk split the input record into fields.

c) What is the output of the following program?
```
awk '$6 == "Digital" {print $(2-3)}' courses.data
```

Answer: The output is as follows:
Fatal error attempt to access field -1

Any expression may be used when trying to reference a particular field.
Thus, for example, the second field could be referenced with the expression $(3 - 1), or $(3 - i), where i=1. However, field numbers start at
zero, and numbering is continued up to the number of fields. Therefore,
negative field numbers do not exist, and an attempt to reference one
results in an error.

d) What is the output of the following program?
```
awk '{ print $(6+1) }' courses.data
```

Answer: The program results in eight blank lines.

Six fields are in the courses.data file. Because the expression $(6+1)
equates to the expression $7, this number is greater than the number of

current fields. When awk encounters a field number that is referenced that is greater than the number of fields currently split up, it creates a new field assigning it, in this case, $7. However, because no assignments to $7 exist, its value is a null string (i.e., nothing). So printing $7 for each line in courses.data results in a blank line for each.

> **Contrast this with the following two lines:$(6+1) = 3**
> **print $(6+1)**

Now you've assigned a value to field $(6+1), so the result would print eight lines containing the value 3.

Field splitting is discussed further in Chapter 12, "Operators."

11.1.3 ANSWERS

For each of the following programs, use conf.data (from Lab 4.1) as the input file.

a) What is the output of the following program?
awk '{$7 = $3 * $4; print $0}' conf.data

Answer: The following is an example of the output:
Smith Adhesions 700 200 081098 Digital 140000
Jones Coatings 900 0 081298 Dow 0
Phillips Stabilizers 850 100 080198 Dupont 85000

. . . and so on.

Here, the temporary field $7 is created and assigned the value of field number three ($3) multiplied by field number four ($4). Because a new field is created, awk recomputes $0. The print statement then prints out the recomputed field $0. This results in the value of $7 output at the end of each line.

b) What is the output of the following program?
awk 'BEGIN { i =3 }
{$0 = $0 i}' conf.data

Answer: For the first three lines, the value of $0 is:
$0 = Smith Adhesions 700 200 081098 Digital 3
$0 = Jones Coatings 900 0 081298 Dow 3

```
$0 = Phillips Stabilizers 850 100 080198 Dupont 3
```

In the BEGIN pattern, i is assigned the value 3. Because no pattern to match exists, the action is performed for every input line. The action causes the value of i to be concatenated to $0. Additionally, because $0 has been assigned a value—the old $0 value appended with the value 3— the input line is resplit into fields. The last field in the line, $7, now contains the value 3 for every input line. Although the above values for $0 are only for the first three input records, the rest of the input lines follow the same logic.

c) What is the output of the following program?
   awk '{$3 = $3 + 50}' conf.data

Answer: The first three lines of output are as follows:
   Smith Adhesions 750 200 081098 Digital
   Jones Coatings 950 0 081298 Dow
   Phillips Stabilizers 900 100 080198 Dupont

The number 50 is added to the current value of $3; $0 is recreated with the third field containing this sum for all records in conf.data.

d) What is the output of the following program?
   awk 'BEGIN {i = 3}
   {$0 = ($0 " ") i + 1
   print $1, $7
   }' conf.data

Answer: The first three lines of output are as follows:
   Smith 4
   Jones 4
   Phillips 4

The user-defined variable i is assigned the value 3 in the BEGIN pattern. The program then uses this value to concatenate i plus one into field variable $0, with a blank concatenated to the end of the original $0 value. Remember that string concatenation has no operator, so variables and expressions next to each other with no operator in between denote concatenation. The parentheses mean that the first concatenation $0 "" is evaluated first.

Similar to the previous example, $0 is reconstructed whenever it is an lvalue in an assignment statement. As a result, by concatenating a blank between the end of the original value of $0 and i+1, awk interprets that blank as a field separator and creates a seventh field with the value i+1. Don't worry if you do not understand this field-splitting entirely; it is more fully covered in Lab 11.3. For now, understand that when $0 changes, its associated value changes and fields are recomputed as well.

e) Write an awk program that calculates the amount owed in the conf.data file and stores that calculation as field number seven ($7) in the file. In addition, after calculating that number, output the maximum value from field seven.

Answer: The program is as follows:
```
awk '{paid = $3 - $4
$7 = paid
}
$7 > max { max = $7}
END {print max}' conf.data
```

The first action is performed for every input record. It calculates the paid amount in the first statement and then assigns it to a newly created field seven. After that, $0 is reconstructed and that value can be referenced. The second action is performed if the value of $7 is greater than the current value of max. Remember that the first time around, max will be zero, because it has not been initialized. If $7 is greater than the current value of max, then max is assigned the maximum value seen so far. This process is continued until all input records have been read in and compared. Lastly, the maximum value is printed out.

f) Rewrite the program in Question a of this Exercise without assigning a field variable (i.e., without assigning $7).

Answer: The program is as follows:
```
awk '{paid = $3 * $4}
paid > max { max = paid}
END {print max}' conf.data
```

Advantages and disadvantages exist to creating and assigning new field variables. Some of the disadvantages are:

1. When creating a new field variable, instead of using a user-defined variable, the code may be longer, as seen in the preceding program.
2. Creating a new field variable means that $0 has to be recomputed, slowing the execution of a program.
3. Creating a new field variable means that awk has to split each field variable higher than $0, once again further slowing execution.

Following are some of the advantages:

1. Fewer user-defined variables with shorter names mean decreases in the chance of programming errors.
2. Depending on the application, creating a new variable instead of a field using user-defined variables may make the program shorter. Consider that the following

```
awk '{product = $3 * $4
print $0, product
}' some-file
```

could have been written more concisely as:

```
awk '{$7 = $3 * $4
print $0
}' some-file
```

(Assume that six fields are in the input file.) Although this difference seems trivial, imagine if you had four, five, or more newly created fields. Using user-defined variables and having to list each when printing would be cumbersome and more error prone, especially when you have a long awk script spanning more than one page. You would have to flip and track down all user-defined variables.

3. Although we have not discussed loops (Chapter 14, "Awk Control Flow"), one could use an iterator to cycle through each field. This situation might happen if you are creating a table, and each column is a particular field value and each row is an input line.

The point of creating field variables is as a convenience mechanism. If it does not offer much convenience or slows down processing quite significantly, then refrain from using it.

 If you need to optimize the execution performance of your scripts, look at each statement that involves field variables and see whether there is an lvalue in any assignment. If yes, see whether you can instead use a user-defined variable.

**LAB
11.1**

LAB 11.1 SELF-REVIEW QUESTIONS

In order to test your progress, you should be able to answer the following questions.

1) A field variable can be both an lvalue and an rvalue.
   a) _____ True
   b) _____ False

2) A field variable can be assigned in a BEGIN pattern.
   a) _____ True
   b) _____ False

3) A field variable can be assigned in an END pattern.
   a) _____ True
   b) _____ False

4) The number of field variables created by awk depends on the number of fields that were split from an input line.
   a) _____ True
   b) _____ False

5) When a field variable is created by the user, it must have a number greater than the number that were split by awk.
   a) _____ True
   b) _____ False

6) A field variable is distinguished by a dollar sign prefixing a number.
   a) _____ True
   b) _____ False

Quiz answers appear in Appendix A, Section 11.1.

L A B 11.2

USER-DEFINED VARIABLES

LAB OBJECTIVES

After this Lab, you will be able to:

✓ Understand the Rules for Naming Variables

✓ Assign User-Defined Variables

**LAB
11.2**

An identifier is a name. A variable is an identifier that is used to identify a stored value. In the following assignment, the identifier and the variable are pi.

```
pi = 3.14
```

The variable `pi` is used to identify the stored value that pi contains—namely, 3.14. In awk, a subset of all valid characters may be used to construct identifiers. An identifier can be any sequence of letters (case-sensitive), digits, and the underscore character, but the first character cannot be a digit. The following are all valid identifiers:

```
pi
version_3_14
a2
```

This Lab is dedicated to user-defined variables. User-defined variables are variables that are created and named by the programmer. As stated in previous labs, a variable can contain a number or a string, or at times, both. Unlike other languages, in which you have to declare a variable as a certain type, which is strictly enforced, awk does not have any syntax to declare and define a variable.

To define a variable, all you have to do is name it and assign a value to it. In addition, unlike other languages in which you have to initialize a variable before using it, either during declaration or assignment, in awk, you do not have to explicitly initialize the variable when creating it. It can be used before an initialized value is given.

Once a variable has been assigned, it can be referenced any time in an awk program by using the named identifier.

Additionally, as stated before, because the type of a variable is not declared, awk infers the type of the variable by the context in which the variable is used. Thus, if awk expects a string variable for a string operator, awk infers that the variable's type is a string.

■ FOR EXAMPLE:

Consider the following awk program:

```
awk '{sum = sum + $1
      count = count + 1
     }
END {print "The average is ", sum/count}' some_file
```

This program calculates the average of all numbers contained in the first field of the input file some_file. The number of values that are averaged is determined by the number of lines in the input file some_file. Sum contains a total of all values in the first field up to the current line. Count contains the count of the number of input lines, up to the current line. At the end of processing, count contains the total number of input lines processed, and sum is divided by count to yield the average. The result is then printed in the END pattern after processing of input lines is completed. Notice that you have no reason to calculate the average in the END pattern by assigning the calculation to a variable and then printing the variable, as shown in the following segment:

```
awk '{sum = sum + $1
      count = count + 1
      }
      END { average = sum/count
            print "The average is ", average}' some_file
```

Awk allows you to perform the calculation and print the result using the `print` statement itself.

LAB 11.2 EXERCISES

11.2.1 UNDERSTAND THE RULES FOR NAMING VARIABLES

Which of the following identifiers are valid variable names in awk?

a) Name1

_____

b) 7Continents

_____

c) BEGIN

_____

d) PRINT

_____

e) street_address

_____

f) _pi

_____

g) `phone_+_number`

---

h) `begin`

---

i) What is the output of the following program?

`awk 'BEGIN {BEGIN=3}' courses.data`

Note that the file `courses.data` is presented entirely in Lab 9.3 of Chapter 9, "An Awk Program." You can also download it from the companion Web site to this book.

`http://www.phptr.com/phptrinteractive/`

11.2.2 ASSIGN USER-DEFINED VARIABLES

Unless instructed otherwise, use the `conf.data` file for the questions in this Exercise. The file is listed in Lab 4.1 (Chapter 4, "Grep Command Options"), and is available for download from the Web companion to this book.

`http://www.phptr.com/phptrinteractive/`

a) Write an awk program that outputs the number of people registered for the Adhesions conference.

---

b) What is the output?

---

c) Write an awk program that calculates the amount that was paid by each registrant (conference fee minus the amount owed). For each registrant, print out the name of the registrant, the amount paid, and the average amount paid by all registrants.

_____

_____

d) What is the output?

_____

_____

LAB 11.2 EXERCISE ANSWERS

This section gives you some suggested answers to the questions in Lab 11.2, with discussion related to those answers. Your answers may vary, but the most important thing is whether or not your answer works. Use this discussion to analyze differences between your answers and those presented here.

If you have alternative answers to the questions in this Exercise, you are encouraged to post your answers and discuss them at the companion Web site for this book, located at:

`http://www.phptr.com/phptrinteractive/`

**LAB
11.2**

11.2.1 ANSWERS

Which of the following identifiers are valid variable names in awk?

a) `Name1`

Answer: Valid.

A user-defined variable can include characters and numbers.

b) `7Continents`

Answer: Invalid.

A user-defined variable can include characters and numbers, but cannot start with a digit.

c) `BEGIN`

Answer: Invalid.

A user-defined variable can include characters and numbers but cannot have a name that is the same as a reserved word in awk. Reserved words are words that have special meaning to awk; `BEGIN` refers to the `BEGIN` pattern. See Appendix B for a complete list of reserved words.

d) `PRINT`

Answer: Invalid.

`PRINT` is reserved to awk.

e) `street_address`

Answer: Valid.

A user-defined variable may have an underscore in its name.

f) `_pi`

Answer: Valid.

A user-defined variable may begin with an underscore, and may contain characters and numbers, as long as it does not start with a number.

g) `phone_+_number`

Answer: Invalid.

A user-defined variable may contain characters, numbers, or the underscore, but the character must be from a-z or A-Z.

h) `begin`

Answer: Valid.

Although this may seem like a reserved word, it is not. Awk is case-sensitive, so `BEGIN` must be all uppercase. Still, to use reserved words for variable names in any form is not good practice.

i) What is the output of the following program?

```
awk 'BEGIN {BEGIN=3}' course.data
```

Answer: The output is a parse error. It is invalid because `BEGIN` is an awk reserved word and cannot be a user-defined variable.

11.2.2 ANSWERS

a) Write an awk program that outputs the number of people registered for the Adhesions conference.

Answer: The program is as follows:

```
awk '$2 == "Adhesions" { count = count + 1}
    END {print "Total people registered for Adhesions
is ", count}' conf.data
```

In this program, whenever the second field contains the string Adhesions, the action is executed. In the action, the variable `count` is assigned the previous value of `count` plus one. Therefore, `count` contains the number of lines that contain the string Adhesions.

b) What is the output?

Answer: The output for this program is:

Total people registered for Adhesions is 6

Note that the string "Total people registered for Adhesions is" within the print statement is optional. You can display any text you want in the print statement by enclosing the text string in quotes.

■ FOR EXAMPLE:

If the `print` statement had been written this way:

```
{print count, " people are registered for the Adhe-
    sions course."}
```

then the output would be as follows:

```
6 people are registered for the Adhesions course.
```

c) Write an awk program that calculates the amount that was paid by each registrant (conference fee minus the amount owed). For each registrant, print out the name of the registrant, the amount paid, and the average amount paid by all registrants.

Answer: The program is as follows:
```
awk {paid = $3 - $4
      sum = sum + paid
      count = count + 1
      print $1, paid
      }
      END {print "Average amount paid is ", sum/count}'
conf.data
```

d) What is the output?

Answer: The output is as follows:

The amount paid is the conference fee ($3) minus `amount_owed` ($4). This is added to `sum`, which contains a running total. This sum is divided by `count` (number of records seen), to calculate the average.

LAB 11.2 SELF-REVIEW QUESTIONS

In order to test your progress, you should be able to answer the following questions.

1) Which of the following are valid variables?
   a) _____h2
   b) _____virt_mem
   c) _____4W
   d) _____END
   e) _____These are all valid variables

2) A variable can appear in which of the following?
   a) _____BEGIN statement
   b) _____END statement
   c) _____main processing loop
   d) _____anywhere in an awk program

3) Before using a variable, you must do which of the following?
    a) _____declare it
    b) _____initialize it
    c) _____define it
    d) _____None of the above

4) A variable can be an rvalue and an lvalue.
    a) _____True
    b) _____False

5) A variable is first declared to awk when it is referenced.
    a) _____True
    b) _____False

Quiz answer appear in Appendix A, Section 11.2

**LAB
11.2**

L A B   11.3

BUILT-IN VARIABLES

LAB OBJECTIVES

After this Lab, you will be able to:

✓ Work with Built-In Field Variables

✓ Work with Built-In Record Variables

Awk provides a number of built-in variables that provide values that assist in performing various data manipulations during processing. This processing may occur while awk inputs lines from a file, or outputs lines. Because awk is used as a utility to create quick, terse, and easy-to-program solutions to a variety of problems, the fact that it provides built-in variables that would commonly be created by a user if awk did not provide them only makes sense. The objective of this Lab is to present the built-in variables, and to describe their functionality and what they contain, and the rules for their use.

Table 11.1 lists the built-in variables available in awk. We will not cover all these variables in this chapter. The rest of the variables that we do not cover here will be revisited in later chapters.

Table 11.1 ■ Awk's Built-In Variables

Variable	Contents	Default
ARGC	Number of command-line arguments	None
ARGV	Array of command-line arguments	None
FILENAME	Name of the current input file	None
FNR	Record number in current file	None
FS	Input field separator	" " (space)
NF	Number of fields in the current record	None
NR	Number of records read so far	None
OFMT	Output format for numbers	%.6g
CONVFMT	Conversion format	%.6g
OFS	Output field separator	" " (space)
ORS	Output record separator	"\n"
RLENGTH	Length of string matched by match function	None
RS	Input record separator "\n"	
RSTART	Offset of string matched by match function	None
SUBSEP	Subscript separator	"\0034"
ENVIRON	Array of environment variables	None

Remember, awk is case sensitive and will not recognize a built-in variable as such unless it appears in all uppercase letters.

Lab 11.3 Exercises

11.3.1 Work with Built-In Field Variables

The field separator, FS, is the delimiter that is used to determine when awk has encountered the end of a field, so it determines the way awk splits input lines into fields.

The default value for the field separator is the space and/or tab characters. You have seen examples in previous labs using the `conf.data` file where awk used the default FS value to delimit fields in that file, but that action was performed behind the scenes and so was invisible to you.

Here, you will change the value of FS explicitly at the command line. Suppose that in the `conf.data` file, your fields (or columns) were separated by semicolons instead of spaces, like so:

`Smith;Adhesions;700;200;081098;Digital`

Using this input line (or *record*—each line in an input file is referred to as a record), enter the following command:

```
awk -F; Smith {print $1, $2}
```

a) What is the result?

_____

_____

You can also change the value of FS in a BEGIN pattern (in fact, I recommend that you do so this way instead of at the command line). Suppose again that all of your fields in the `conf.data` file are separated by semicolons. Enter the following:

```
awk 'BEGIN {FS = ";"}
        {print $1, $2}' conf.data
```

b) What would the result be?

_____

_____

c) What would happen if you entered the following?
```
awk 'BEGIN {fs = ","}
        {print $1, $2}' conf.data
```

_____

_____

The output field separator, OFS, determines what character is inserted between each field as all fields are output. Like the FS, we have encountered the OFS many times in our examples without knowing it. By default, the value of OFS is a single blank space. The comma used to separate fields in the print statement tells awk to use the stored value for OFS; if no other value is defined for OFS, the default is used. For example, if you look at the results in question a of this Exercise, you'll note that the field "Smith" is separated from the field "Adhesions" by a single space because the print statement in the command is written as {print $1, $2}.

Here, you will change the value of OFS explicitly at the command line. The value of FS may be set to a value other than the default value using the -F option.

Using our revised input line from the conf.data file (semicolon-separated fields), enter the following command:

```
awk -F; Smith {print $1 ", " $2}
```

d) What is the result?

_____

_____

LAB
11.3

Now, enter the following command:

```
awk -F; Smith {print $1 $2}
```

e) What is the result?

_____

_____

Finally, enter the following command:

```
awk -F; Smith {print $0}
```

f) What is the result?

_____

_____

The NF variable contains the total number of fields that awk creates when splitting an input line (record) into fields. Therefore, using the default value for FS, the value of NF for each line in the conf.data file would be six.

 Be sure to understand that the value of NF can vary from line to line. In addition, each awk implementation limits the number of fields per line— usually to about 100.

Here are the first two lines from conf.data for use with the remaining questions in this Exercise:

| Smith | Adhesions | 700 | 200 | 081098 | Digital |
| Jones | Coatings | 900 | 0 | 081298 | Dow |

g) What is the difference in output between the following two programs?

```
awk '{print $1, NF}' conf.data
awk '{print $1, $NF}' conf.data
```

LAB
11.3

h) What is the output of the following program?

```
awk '{print $(NF-1), $NF}' conf.data
```

i) What is the output of the following program?

```
awk '{NF = 3; print $0}' conf.data
```

11.3.2 WORK WITH BUILT-IN RECORD VARIABLES

Two variables that are similar to FS *and* OFS *are* RS *and* ORS. *These represent the record separator and the output record separator, respectively. Remember, records and lines are one and the same, and both are terminated with a newline by default. These variables can be changed, but only in a limited way. You will see this in the "Test Your Thinking" section later in this chapter.*

The built-in variable NR specifies the number of records that have been processed so far.

The NR variable is set every time a new record is read. NR can be an lvalue or rvalue, and can be read or written. No default value exists for NR, a fact that makes sense because if no record has been input or processed, why have a default value for NR?

For the following three questions, use this input file named some_file:

```
10 nuts
15 bolts
16 screws
17 nails
19 tacks
```

Enter the following command:

```
awk '{print NR, $0}' some_file
```

a) What is the result?

_____

_____

For the next question only, use both the files some_file and some_file2, which contains the following data:

```
2 hammers
4 screwdrivers
1 pliers
```

**LAB
11.3**

Now, enter the following command:

```
awk 'END {print NR}' some_file some_file2
```

b) What is the result?

_____

_____

Finally, enter the following command:

```
awk '{sum = sum + $1}
        END {print NR, sum, sum/NR}' some_file
```

c) What is the result?

_____

_____

FNR, the file record number, is used to maintain a count of the number of input records that have been read in from the current file. Whereas NR keeps a running count from all files read so far, FNR maintains a count only for each individual file.

To demonstrate, enter the following command:

```
awk '{print FNR ".", $0}' some_file some_file2
```

d) What are the results?

_____

_____

e) What happens when you enter the following command?
```
awk '{print FILENAME, $0}' some_file some_file2
```

_____

_____

LAB 11.3 EXERCISE ANSWERS

This section gives you some suggested answers to the questions in Lab 11.3, with discussion related to those answers. Your answers may vary, but the most important thing is whether or not your answer works. Use this discussion to analyze differences between your answers and those presented here.

If you have alternative answers to the questions in this Exercise, you are encouraged to post your answers and discuss them at the companion Web site for this book, located at:

```
http://www.phptr.com/phptrinteractive/
```

11.3.1 ANSWERS

Using the given input line, enter the following command:
```
awk -F; Smith {print $1, $2}
```

a) What is the result?

Answer: The result is as follows:
Smith Adhesions

Remember, awk is case-sensitive. Do not confuse the −F with the −f option. The lowercase −f option specifies that the awk program is contained in a file. The uppercase −F command-line awk option specifies that the FS is the next character immediately following the −F option.

In fact, the user may specify a single character or may specify a regular expression or a string of characters as the FS value. The command-line awk option -F takes the character(s) immediately following (in this case, the semicolon) as the value to be used as the field separator. In the output here, awk has split the fields from the input line at the semicolon and output the results of fields one and two, as directed.

The two-step process by which awk splits an input line into fields is as follows:

Step 1: Search for the end of a field (i.e., the value of FS)

Step 2: Search for the start of the next field (i.e., any value that is neither FS nor the end of the line)

 You could specify multiple values for FS by enclosing the values in square brackets surrounded by quotes, like so:

```
awk -F'[; ]' Smith {print $1, $2} some_file
```

This program sets the value of FS to a semicolon or a space, or both. Remember to use the quotes, because the shell uses the brackets for file-name expansion.

Suppose again that all of your fields in the conf.data file were separated by semicolons. Enter the following:

```
awk 'BEGIN {FS = ";"}
           {print $1, $2}' conf.data
```

b) What would the result be?

Answer: The program would print the value of fields one and two, separated by a blank space, for the entire file.

**LAB
11.3**

Like the output in the previous question, awk would read each line in conf.data, break fields at the semicolon (as dictated in the BEGIN statement by {FS = ";"}, and print the first two fields of each line.

In awk, when FS is assigned a new value, it will affect the next input line read in. It will not affect the current input line. This fact is important to know because if a programmer wishes to change the default, then it should be set in a BEGIN pattern. If it was not set in the BEGIN pattern and instead was set in the main processing loop, then the first input line read in from the file would not have fields separated by the new value of FS.

c) What would happen if you entered the following?

```
awk 'BEGIN {fs = ","}
           {print $3, $5}' conf.data
```

Answer: This is sort of a trick question. Remember that awk is case-sensitive, so setting the value of variable fs—rather than the field separator FS—to a comma essentially does nothing.

Here, you will change the value of OFS explicitly at the command line.

Using our revised input line from the `conf.data` file (semicolon-separated fields), enter the following command:

```
awk -F; Smith {print $1 ", " $2}
```

d) What is the result?

> *Answer: The result is as follows:*
> **Smith, Adhesions**

The output fields are now separated by comma space, as dictated in the print statement {print $1 ", " $2}. What this says, essentially, is to print the value of field 1, print a comma and a space, and then print the value of field 2.

Now, enter the following command:

```
awk -F; Smith {print $1 $2}
```

e) What is the result?

> *Answer: The result is as follows:*
> **SmithAdhesions**

The fields are printed with no separators because nothing was used to separate them in the print statement. It did not default to a space, because the comma, which instructs awk to use the value stored in OFS—in this case, the default—was not used.

LAB
11.3

Finally, enter the following command:

```
awk -F; Smith {print $0}
```

f) What is the result?

> *Answer: The result is as follows:*
> **Smith;Adhesions;700;200;081098;Digital**

The $0 variable tells awk to print the entire input record as is, which in this case includes the semicolons separating the fields.

Like the value of `FS`, *the value of* `OFS` *can be changed within a* `BEGIN` *statement, like so:*

```
awk 'BEGIN {OFS=", "; FS = ";"}
      {print $1, $2}' conf.data
```

g) What is the difference in output between the following two programs?
```
awk '{print $1, NF}' conf.data
awk '{print $1, $NF}' conf.data
```

Answer: The first program outputs the value of the first field ($1) and the total number of fields (NF) in each input line, like so:

Smith 6

Jones 6

The second program outputs the value of the first field ($1) and the value of the last field ($NF) in each input line, like so:

Smith Digital

Jones Dow

Using the field operator with NF ($NF), you can specify that awk print the last field in the record, even if you don't know which field number that is. This possibility is useful, for example, if you want to print last names, zip codes, phone numbers, or whatever might typically be contained in the last field of a database file.

h) What is the output of the following program?
```
awk '{print $(NF-1) ", ", $NF}' conf.data
```

Answer: The output is as follows:

081098, Digital

081298, Dow

You see here how you can decrement the value of NF so that, for example, you can print only the last two fields in each record if you don't know how many fields you have, but note the syntax. In this example, NF is equal to six. The expression (NF-1) is thus equal to five, and so the value becomes $5, which prints the fifth field. Finally, a comma-space is inserted between the two fields in the output, as dictated by the ", ".

You can also increase the value of NF *to create new, empty fields. However, increasing or decreasing the value of* NF *sometimes has different effects in different implementations of awk, so use this practice with caution.*

i) What is the output of the following program?

```
awk '{NF = 3; print $0}' conf.data
```

Answer: The results of this program are machine dependent, so yours may vary. On my machine, the output is as follows:

Smith Adhesions 700

Jones Coatings 900

The reason that the print statement does not print fields one through six is that by reducing the value of NF to three, $0 is reconstructed. When the number of fields is decreased, $0 truncates the line and assigns the remaining fields with the null string.

11.3.2 ANSWERS

Enter the following command:

```
awk '{print NR, $0}' some_file
```

LAB
11.3

a) What is the result?

Answer: The result is as follows:

```
1 10 nuts
2 15 bolts
3 16 screws
4 17 nails
5 19 tacks
```

Here, each record (indicated by $0 in the print statement) is printed exactly as it is in the file, but is also preceded by the record's number, NR. According to this first program, NR clearly is useful if a programmer wishes to output line numbers in the output.

You can print any character(s) after printing the NR variable by enclosing that character in quote marks within the `print` *statement, like so:*

```
print NR ".", $0
```

Note the syntax of this command. The result here would be similar to a numbered list, as in:

```
1. 10 nuts
2. 15 bolts
3. 16 screws
```

Now, enter the following command:
```
awk 'END {print NR}' some_file some_file2
```

b) What is the result?

Answer: The result is as follows:

8

**LAB
11.3**

This program illustrates that NR can be used to determine and print the number of all records processed so far. Notice that NR keeps a running count of all records read and does not begin again at one once a new file is input.

Finally, enter the following command:
```
awk '{sum = sum + $1}
      END {print NR, sum, sum/NR}' some_file
```

c) What is the result?

Answer: The result is as follows:

5 77 15.4

This final program using NR calculates an average based on the total number of items in the first field ($1) divided by the number of records in the file. Here, the value of sum is incremented by the value of $1 in each record ({sum = sum + $1}), and then the average is printed in the END statement (sum/NR). Note that NR maintains its value in an END pattern.

To demonstrate, enter the following command:

```
awk '{print FNR ".", $0}' some_file some_file2
```

d) What are the results?

Answer: The results are as follows:

```
1.  10 nuts
2.  15 bolts
3.  16 screws
4.  17 nails
5.  19 tacks
1.  2 hammers
2.  4 screwdrivers
3.  1 pliers
```

When FNR reaches the end of the first file, some_file, its counter resets before the second file is read.

e) What happens when you enter the following command?

```
awk '{print FILENAME, $0}' some_file some_file2
```

Answer: The following output results:

```
some_file 10 nuts
some_file 15 bolts
some_file 16 screws
some_file 17 nails
some_file 19 tacks
some_file2 2 hammers
some_file2 4 screwdrivers
some_file2 1 pliers
```

The FILENAME built-in variable is useful in listings when you would like to prefix output lines with the file name to which they belong. This is especially useful when using multiple files.

LAB
11.3

LAB 11.3 SELF-REVIEW QUESTIONS

In order to test your progress, you should be able to answer the following questions.

1) The default for FS is multiple spaces and/or tabs.
   - **a)** _____True
   - **b)** _____False
   - **c)** _____Machine dependent

2) The default for NR is 0.
   - **a)** _____True
   - **b)** _____False
   - **c)** _____Machine dependent

3) When assigning NF, $0 is reconstructed.
   - **a)** _____True
   - **b)** _____False
   - **c)** _____Machine dependent

4) When reconstructing $0, FS is used.
   - **a)** _____True
   - **b)** _____False
   - **c)** _____Machine dependent

5) When decreasing the value of NF, $0 is reconstructed.
   - **a)** _____True
   - **b)** _____False
   - **c)** _____Machine dependent

6) The number 1 can be assigned to FS.
   - **a)** _____True
   - **b)** _____False
   - **c)** _____Machine dependent

Quiz answers appear in Appendix A, Section 11.3.

C H A P T E R 11

TEST YOUR THINKING

 The projects in this section are meant to have you utilize all of the skills that you have acquired throughout this chapter. The answers to these projects can be found at the companion Web site to this book, located at:

`http://www.phptr.com/phptrinteractive/`

Visit the Web site periodically to share and discuss your answers.

In Lab 11.3, we talked about field variables. We touched on the built-in variables RS and ORS. Throughout our discussion of awk, we have always used the default value for RS and ORS, which is the newline. Because each line in an input file is terminated by the newline, awk reads in a line at a time. Awk subsequently splits this input line into fields.

In this section, we explore changing the default value of RS and ORS. By doing so, multiple lines will very well read in and split into fields. Therefore, one record will consist of more than one input line. The processing steps of reading in a record from the input file will stop whenever the value for RS and ORS is encountered in the input file. Thus the term *multiline records* is used whenever we change the value of RS and ORS.

For these projects, use the file called `MailList.dat`, which contains the following data:

```
Kim Taylor
Compaq Corporation
21 Oceanview Terrace
Los Angeles, CA 90234

Peter Patsis
International Business Machines
23 Main St
Boston, MA 02321
```

```
Greg Kilroy
Sun Microsystems
45 South St.
New York, NY 12563

Jim Craig
Hewlett-Packard
75 Houser Rd.
Phillipstown, RI 10010

Fred Smucker
Raytheon Corporation
45 Wilson Lane
Chicago, IL 33465
```

1) What is the output of the following script, using the file `MailList.dat`:

```
BEGIN {RS = "" }
{ print "PRINTING NEW RECORD"
    for (i=1; i<=NF;  i++)
        print $i
    print "NF = ", NF, "NR = ", NR, "FNR = ", FNR
}
```

2) Write a mailing list program that prints out each address that contains the company name Hewlett-Packard.

3) Write a mailing list utility that sorts each mailing address according to zip code and prints out the sorted list.

OPERATORS

 Operators provide awk with more expressive power than sed and grep.

<table>
<tr><td colspan="2" align="center">CHAPTER OBJECTIVES</td></tr>
<tr><td colspan="2">In this chapter, you will learn about:</td></tr>
<tr><td>✓ Arithmetic Operators</td><td>Page 372</td></tr>
<tr><td>✓ The Assignment Statement</td><td>Page 382</td></tr>
<tr><td>✓ Logical Operators, and Relational and
    Conditional Expressions</td><td>Page 400</td></tr>
</table>

In this chapter, I will introduce and discuss the types of arithmetic operators awk provides and how they work. We'll also cover the use of various other concepts such as assignment operators, and logical and conditional testing to build powerful expressions you can use to write useful awk programs.

L A B   12.1

ARITHMETIC

OPERATORS

LAB OBJECTIVES

After this Lab, you will be able to:

✓ Understand the Results of Using the Arithmetic
  Operators

✓ Write Programs Using the Arithmetic Operators

Naturally, any programming language that is used to perform computations is going to provide a number of arithmetic operators. Awk provides a rich set of operators that may be used in computations. The goal of this Lab is to describe the operators, explain their use, and describe various rules regarding their use.

Awk provides six arithmetic operators to be used for performing various kinds of arithmetic on operands. The result of an arithmetic operation is a number. Any arguments used on either side of the operator will be coerced to a number. In addition, the result of performing the operation is a number. Therefore, any lvalue will have a number type. If the lvalue is a string, it is converted into a number.

Table 12.1 presents awk's arithmetic operators, with examples of their usage.

Table 12.1 ■ Awk Arithmetic Operators

Operator	Usage
Addition(+)	Awk `BEGIN {count = 4 END {print count + 1} some_file Result: 5 Awk performs floating-point addition using both operands when encountering the addition operator. We have already seen it used and seen the result of coercing operands on either side of the operator.
Subtraction (−)	awk `BEGIN {balance = 20; withdrawal = 10} END {print balance − withdrawal}' some_file Result: 10 The same rules for coercion apply to subtraction as they do to addition.
Multiplication (*)	awk `BEGIN { decimal = 0.34} END { print decimal * 100, "Percent" }' some_file Result: 34 Percent
Division (/)	awk `BEGIN { value = 20; divideBy = 2} END {print value / divideBy}' some_file Result: 10 An error results when the dividend is zero, called a *divide-by-zero* error.
Modula Operator (%)	awk `BEGIN {value = 7; divideBy = 2} END { print value % divideBy}' some_file Result: 1 This is also referred to as a remainder operator; in this program, the remainder when you divide seven by two is one. The modula operator calculates the remainder when y is divided by x. An error results if the dividend is zero. *Note that* the behavior when x or y is negative is machine dependent. Write a test awk program setting x and/or y to negative and print the result to see what your implementation does in this event.
Exponential Operator (^)	awk `BEGIN {value = 2; y = 3} END {print value ^ y} Result: 8 This operator raises a value y times. If $y=2$, it performs a square. If $y=3$, it cubes the value. Obviously, if $y=0$, the result is 1, and if the value is 0, the result is always 0.

**LAB
12.1**

All operators share the same rules for coercion as addition and subtraction. Also, all operations are done in floating point.

LAB 12.1 EXERCISES

12.1.1 UNDERSTAND THE RESULTS OF USING THE ARITHMETIC OPERATORS

Use the following file, called `input_file`, for Question a of this Exercise:

```
5
8
9
23
12
7
```

a) What is the output of the following program?

```
awk '{print $1%5}' input_file
```

b) What does the following program do?

```
ls -l | awk '$1 == "drwxrwxrwx" { count = count + 1}\
END '{print count}' input_file
```

12.1.2 WRITE PROGRAMS USING THE ARITHMETIC OPERATORS

Use the following data of times represented in hours, minutes, and seconds for Question a of this Exercise:

```
1:12:23
2:24:24
5:00:23
2:39:12
```

a) Write a program that prints out the total time elapsed.

_____

_____

Use the following file, called `transactions`, for the next question; this file contains three fields—starting balance, interest rate, and number of years:

```
1000.0 0.8 30
500.0 0.9 35
900.0 0.9 29
2000.0 0.6 33
```

Also use the following formula for calculating interest:

$$interest\_rate^{number\_years} \text{ x } starting\_balance$$

LAB
12.1

b) Write a program that calculates the ending balance, given the interest formula and the `transactions` file.

_____

_____

Use the following file, called `mortgage`, for the next question; this file contains two fields—interest rate and down payment:

```
0.07 10000
0.07 20000
0.07 30000
0.072 10000
0.072 20000
0.072 30000
0.08 10000
0.08 20000
0.08 30000
```

You will also use the following formula to calculate mortgage payments:

```
interest_rate + 1³⁰ x (100,000 - down_payment)
divided by (30 x 13)
```

c) Write a program that calculates the monthly payments of a loan amount of $100,000 over 30 years, given the mortgage formula and the `mortgage` file.

LAB 12.1 EXERCISE ANSWERS

This section gives you some suggested answers to the questions in Lab 12.1, with discussion related to those answers. Your answers may vary, but the most important thing is whether or not your answer works. Use this discussion to analyze differences between your answers and those presented here.

If you have alternative answers to the questions in this Exercise, you are encouraged to post your answers and discuss them at the companion Web site for this book, located at:

http://www.phptr.com/phptrinteractive/

12.1.1 ANSWERS

a) What is the output of the following program?

```
awk '{print $1%5}' input_file
```

Answer: The output is as follows:

```
0 - remainder of 5 divided by 5
3 - remainder of 8 divided by 5
4 - remainder of 9/5
3 - remainder of 23/5
2 - remainder of 12/5
2 - remainder of 7/5
```

The character percent, %, is the modula operator. Remember, it calculates the remainder when $1 is divided by 5. $1 is the first number in each line of the file.

b) What does the following program do?

```
ls -l | awk '$1 == "drwxrwxrwx" { count = count + 1}\
END '{print count}' input_file
```

Answer: This program prints out the total number of subdirectories in the current directory that allow read, write, and search permissions for everyone.

This program demonstrates that an awk program can have data piped to it as input. `ls -l` is a listing of all files in the current directory. The first field of that listing is the file permissions. If the permission for each file matches the string "drwxrwxrwx," then the action is executed. In the action, a count is kept of all files that are subdirectories with the file permission "drwxrwxrwx." In the END pattern, the count is printed. Pipes are covered in greater detail in Chapter 16, "Advanced Input and Output."

**LAB
12.1**

12.1.2 ANSWERS

a) Write a program that prints out the total time elapsed.

Answer: The program is as follows:

```
awk 'BEGIN {FS =":"; OFS=":"}
      { total_seconds = total_seconds + $3 }
    total_seconds >= 60 { total_seconds = total_seconds - 60
             $2 = $2 + 1
```

```
        }
        { total_minutes = total_minutes + $2 }
    total_minutes >= 60 { total_minutes = total_minutes - 60
            $1 = $1 + 1
        }
        { total_hours = total_hours + $1 }
        END {print $1, $2, $3}' input_file
```

This is a longer program than those to which we have been accustomed. The solution is also a little more difficult to think about and implement than in previous exercises. It requires a deeper understanding of the awk programming model and how to decompose problems within that model. The way it works is as follows. In the BEGIN pattern, FS is set to ":". The colon is used because the hours, seconds, and minutes are each separated by a colon. OFS is set to a colon so that when we output the elapsed time, it will be in the same form as the input line. The first statement after the BEGIN pattern keeps a running count of the total seconds seen so far. After this addition, a check is made to see whether that value is greater than 60. If it is, then you need to add one to the total minutes, $2 =$2 + 1, and subtract 60 from the total seconds (any second value equal to 60 means that another minute has passed; if it is greater than 60, then you need to find out how many more seconds have passed into the next minute to get the current value of total seconds). The reason one is added to $2 is just by choice; you could have easily added it to total_minutes and it would have produced the same result. The same logic is applied to total_minutes. Total_hours is just a running count, not clock time, so a check to reset the clock to 0 when hours is greater than 24 is not needed. Notice in this solution that we process the fields in reverse order. Seconds are processed first, which is $3. Minutes are processed next, which is $2. Hours are processed last, which is $1.

LAB
12.1

b) Write a program that calculates the ending balance, given the interest formula and the transactions file.

Answer: The program is as follows:
```
awk '{balance = ($2 ^ $3) * $1
        print "Ending balance is ", balance
        }' transactions
```

This is straightforward because the formula already dictates the arithmetic operators that will be used. All that is needed in the program is to

find the appropriate characters for each operator and use the appropriate
field variables for each variable in the formula:

Variables

> **$1 = starting balance**
> **$2 = interest rate**
> **$3 = number of years to calculate interest**

Operators

> **^ = exponential (raised to)**
> *** = multiplication**

The parentheses around the expression (`$2 ^ $3`) forces the operation
to be performed before the multiplication.

*Always use parentheses to force operations to be evaluated in correct
order.*

c) Write a program that calculates the monthly payments of a loan
amount of $100,000 over 30 years, given the mortgage formula and the
`mortgage` file.

**LAB
12.1**

Answer: The program is as follows:

```
awk '{rate = ((1+$1) ^ 30) * (100000 - $2)/(30 * 13)}
        print "The monthly payment is ", rate, "Interest
    = ", $1, "Starting balance: 100000"
        }' input_file
```

Again, this solution is straightforward because the formula already dictates the arithmetic operators that will be used. All that is needed in the
program is to find the appropriate characters for each operator and use
the appropriate field variables for each variable in the formula:

Variables

```
$1 = rate
$2 = down payment
```

Operators

```
^ = exponential (raised to)
* = multiplication
/ = division
+ = addition
```

The following solves each part of the problem:

```
((1+$1) ^ 30 = interest rate plus one raised to 30
(100000 - $2) = starting balance - down payment
(30 * 13) = total number of months in the lifetime of mortgage
```

LAB 12.1 SELF-REVIEW QUESTIONS

In order to test your progress, you should be able to answer the following questions.

1) If a string operand is used with an arithmetic operator, it will be coerced to a number.
   a) _____True
   b) _____False

2) The modulus operator is the same as the remainder when two operands are divided.
   a) _____True
   b) _____False

3) All arithmetic operations are done in floating point.
   a) _____True
   b) _____False

4) What is the result of 2 ^ 4?
   a) _____8
   b) _____12
   c) _____32
   d) _____16

5) What is the result of 5%3?

    a) _____1

    b) _____3

    c) _____2

    d) _____0

Quiz answers appear in Appendix A, Section 12.1.

LAB
12.1

L A B   12.2

THE ASSIGNMENT STATEMENT

LAB OBJECTIVES

After this Lab, you will be able to:

✓ Understand the Results of the Arithmetic, Increment, and Decrement Operators

✓ Write Programs Using These Operators

We talked about basic assignment statements in Lab 10.5. Here, we visit six available assignment statements that are used in conjunction with arithmetic operators. The goal of this Lab is to describe the uses of these operators and explain the rules regarding their use.

LAB 12.2

The six assignment operators covered in this Lab are as follows:

```
+=
-=
*=
/=
%/
^=
```

Each has the following form:

```
lvalue op= rvalue
```

We will distinguish between the assignment statement discussed in Lab 10.5 and these six assignment statements by referring to the former as the *assignment statement* and the latter as the *assignment operators*.

The way each assignment operator works can be functionally described if one expands the meaning of each:

```
x += 4     =>     x = x + 4
x -= 4     =>     x = x - 4
x *= 4     =>     x = x * 4
x /= 4     =>     x = x / 4
x %= 4     =>     x = x % 4
x ^= 4     =>     x = x ^ 4
```

So in our terminology, the lvalue of the variable on the left-hand side of the operator is used both as an lvalue and an rvalue on the right-hand side. In other words, it is used both as an assignment operand and an operator operand.

The rvalues of the assignment operators follow the rules for rvalues of an arithmetic operator. The lvalues of the assignment operators follow the rules for lvalues of the assignment statement. The rvalues of the operands are numbers, and the rvalue of the result is also a number. The lvalue of the assignment operator must be a variable, and the value assigned to that variable is the rvalue of the result of the arithmetic operation.

These operators cannot be chained. So the following assignment statement that was allowed in Lab 10.5 would not be allowed for the six assignment operators described in this Lab:

```
x = y = z
```

Therefore, the following is not legal:

```
x += y += 3
```

**LAB
12.2**

However, they can be chained, as follows:

```
x = y += 3
```

The following two programs illustrate the reason that these assignment operators are provided. Suppose that we have the following input:

```
peter 80
jim 100
greg 70
sam 90
```

Then the following awk program:

```
awk '{sum = sum + $2}
     END {print "The average is", sum / NR}' input_file
```

would produce the following output:

The average is 85

In other words, this program calculates the average of all the values in the second field. Using the assignment operator, we could have written the awk program as follows:

```
awk '{sum += $2}
     END {print "The average is", sum / NR}
```

This program would produce the following output:

The average is 85

These two programs are equivalent; each produces the same value. However, the second program is more concise, thereby saving programming time and reducing a chance of a programming error. Additionally, it is more efficient, because the retrieval of the address where the variable is stored is done once.

The other arithmetic operators are each used similarly.

INCREMENT AND DECREMENT OPERATORS

So far, we have two versions for incrementing a variable by 1:

```
count = count + 1
count += 1
```

The increment and decrement operators offer a third way to increment a variable by one. The increment and decrement operators come in two forms: prefix and postfix. The increment operator is usually written ++n or n++. The ++n version is called the *prefix notation,* and the n++ version is called the *postfix notation.* The increment operator can be an lvalue or an rvalue; it causes the variable used with the operator to be written and read.

 We discussed rvalues in Lab 10.5. We did not mention formally in that chapter that two types of rvalues always exist when evaluating an expression. The first type is the rvalues of each operand involved in the expression. The second type is the rvalue that results from executing the expression.

The prefix version ++n increments the current rvalue of n (type 1 rvalue) and then adds one to it. It then returns the value of this increment as the rvalue of the result of the operation (type 2), and finally assigns the value to n, as the new value of n. The postfix version n++ first returns n as the rvalue of the result of the operation, and then adds one to n and stores that result back into n as an lvalue. Therefore, the difference between prefix and postfix is only in what is returned by the operation. In prefix form, n + 1 is returned. In postfix form, n is returned. In both cases, after the operation is performed, n will be n + 1. The decrement operator differs from the increment operator in that the value of one is subtracted from n instead of added. All rules for using prefix and postfix work the same for both the increment and decrement operators.

**LAB
12.2**

■ *FOR EXAMPLE:*

In the following program, count is incremented by one for each input record.

```
awk '{sum+=$1
      count++
      }
      END {print "Average is ", sum/count}' some_file
```

It contains a running total of the number of records seen so far, and is used to calculate the average.

Be sure to understand the differences between the postfix variety and the prefix variety. This difference is recognized any time that the rvalue is to be used in some compound operation, such as a conditional or assignment statement. Consider the following example:

```
awk 'count++ < 6 {some action}' some_file
awk '++count < 6 {some_action}' some_file
```

If count was to be used in this hypothetical awk program and count was uninitialized (its value zero), the action in the first program would be executed six times. In the second version, the pattern would be executed five times. The reason is that in the first program, count is first returned as the rvalue of the expression count++, and then it would be incremented (postfix version). The rvalue of count before being incremented is used in the comparison. In the second, count would be incremented first, and the value of this increment would be the rvalue of the result. This rvalue would be used in the comparison.

Of the three methods for incrementing a number by one, the increment operator is the most efficient.

LAB
12.2

LAB 12.2 EXERCISES

12.2.1 UNDERSTAND THE RESULTS OF USING THE ARITHMETIC, INCREMENT, AND DECREMENT OPERATORS

Given that x=3 and y=3, determine the value of y after each of the following assignments:

a) y=x++

_____

b) y=++x

_____

c) y=--x

_____

d) y+=3

_____

e) y/=4

_____

f) y=x*=3

_____

Use the `courses.data` file from Lab 9.3 for the next question.

g) What is the output of the following programs?

```
awk '$6 == "Digital" {print $6++; print NF}' courses.data
```

_____

_____

```
awk '$6 == "Digital" {print ++$6; print NF}' courses.data
```

_____

_____

```
awk 'BEGIN {i=6}
     $6 == "Digital" {print $(i++); print $7, NF}' courses.data
```

_____

_____

```
awk 'BEGIN {i=6}
           {print ($i)++}' courses.data
```

12.2.2 WRITE PROGRAMS USING THESE OPERATORS

Use the following data file, called `input_file`, for the first three questions of this Exercise:

```
10 12 22
23 121 12
12 356 87
8 34 7
76 2 45
23 2 34
```

Write three programs that find the maximum number among all numbers in each column. Print out the column number and maximum number.

a) What is the program for column one?

b) What is the program for column two?

c) What is the program for column three?

Write a program, using the `courses.data` file from Lab 9.3, that does the following:

- Calculates and prints the number of people registered for conferences who come from Digital;
- Calculates and prints the total amount owed for people from Digital;
- Calculates the average amount owed for registrants from Digital.

d) What is the program?

_____

_____

e) What is the output?

_____

_____

Write a program that calculates the number of words and the number of lines from the following file of text (to make the program easier, I have left out quite a bit of punctuation; all you have to worry about is spaces and periods).

```
On the first day of his
visit to England the Grateful Deads
emissary went to meet the Beatles. He
met the band who had invited
him to a party they were having
at there pad. While there John Lennon
was engaged in a rather heated argument
with a Hells Angel who promptly
decked John on his keyster. John rather
bewildered asked the emissary what
was up with these dudes with Harleys.
```

LAB
12.2

f) What is the program?

_____

_____

g) What is the output?

_____

_____

LAB 12.2 EXERCISE ANSWERS

This section gives you some suggested answers to the questions in Lab 12.2, with discussion related to those answers. Your answers may vary, but the most important thing is whether or not your answer works. Use this discussion to analyze differences between your answers and those presented here.

If you have alternative answers to the questions in this Exercise, you are encouraged to post your answers and discuss them at the companion Web site for this book, located at:

`http://www.phptr.com/phptrinteractive/`

12.2.1 ANSWERS

Given that x=3 and y=3, determine the value of y after each of the following assignments:

a) y=x++

Answer: 3

Remember, postfix first returns the value, which is three, and then it increments. The final value for x is four.

b) y=++x

Answer: 4

Prefix increments first, and then it returns the incremented value. x is three before incrementing, and four after incrementing. Four is returned and assigned to y.

c) y=--x

Answer: 2

Prefix decrements first, and then the value is returned.

d) y+=3

Answer: 6

This expression expands to y = y + 3. Because y=3, the expression is y=3+3=6.

e) y/=4

Answer: 0.75.

This expression expands to y = y / 4 => 3 / 4 = .75.

f) y=x*=3

Answer: 9.

This expression expands to y = x = x * 3 => y = x = 3 * 3 => y = x = 9 => y= 9.

g) What is the output of the following programs?
```
awk '$6 == "Digital" {print $6++; print NF}' courses.data
```

Answer: The output is as follows:

0
6
0
6
0
6

... *and so on, printing 0 and then 6 on subsequent lines until all lines are processed.*

LAB
12.2

Why does the program output 0 and then 6? The printing of 0 is a little tricky. The statement $6++ is equivalent to:

```
print $6
```

followed by

```
$6 = $6 + 1
```

We are using the variable $6 to be used in the increment operation. Therefore, the rvalue of $6 will have one added to it. Because we are using postfix notation, the value of $6 (a company name) is returned as the rvalue result of the increment operation, and then the rvalue of $6 will be incremented. Remember that two types of rvalues exist; the first type is the rvalue of the operand and the second is the rvalue of the result. Remember also that a statement consisting solely of a primary expression and a statement separator is a valid statement. This fact is shown here:

```
$6
```

In this statement, no operators exist; therefore, the rvalue of the operand and the rvalue of the result are the same. Therefore, in any postfix increment operation, you can always expand it to the two following statements:

x   (x is a primary expression—field variable, variable, built-in variable, array element)

```
x = x + 1
```

where the value of x in the first statement is used as the rvalue of some other operation (in this case, a print statement). The only other point that needs mentioning is that the increment or decrement operation is considered a numerical operation. When we break the increment operation into two statements, the first statement simply returns the rvalue of the operand (this rvalue will be the result of the postfix notation). Even though this rvalue may be a string and no operator is associated with it, it is coerced to a number.

*If the value of the variable involved in the increment or decrement opera-
tor is a string, it will be coerced to a number before that value is returned
as the result of the increment or decrement operation. This fact is true of
both prefix and postfix notation.*

Therefore, the primary expression $6 will be coerced to a number. $6 is
the value "Digital." Because it is used in a numeric operation, $6 is first
converted to 0 and subsequently printed out. The value of NF remains six,
so its value is printed on the next line. Notice that the new incremented
value of $6 is no longer used. $6, as a result of executing this statement, is
1—0 (coerced value) + 1.

```
awk '$6 == "Digital" {print ++$6; print NF}' courses.data
```

Answer: The output is as follows:
```
1
6
1
6
1
6
```

... and so on, printing a one and a six on the next line for all courses.data
records.

The difference between this problem and the previous one is that the prefix operation is used instead of postfix. Therefore, the value is incremented first and the incremented value returned. In the prefix notation,
the rvalue of the operand and the rvalue of the result are not the same.
We can, however, break into two statements as follows:

```
x = x + 1
x          (x is a primary expression—field variable, user variable, built-in vari-
           able, array element)
```

In our case, the program equates to:

```
$6 = $6 + 1
print $6
```

**LAB
12.2**

The value of $6 is the string "Digital," which is coerced to the number 0. The number 0 is then incremented and $6 is then assigned 1. Its value is subsequently printed.

If you use the increment or decrement operator with a field variable, then $0 will be reconstructed, because the field variable is being assigned a value.

```
awk 'BEGIN {i=6}
          $6  ==  "Digital"  {print  $(i++);  print  $7,  NF}'
     courses.data
```

Answer: The output is as follows:
Digital
7

7

The difference between this program and the previous two is the difference between the following expressions:

```
$x
```

and

```
$(x),
```

Note that $3 and $(3) are the same; both refer to the third field.

LAB
12.2

The difference between the two of these is that in the first, x can be only a primary expression (which can refer only to a single field), and in the second, x can be any expression (which may refer to any field, depending on the value of x). Regardless of the parenthesized expression, what is returned from using the parenthesized expression depends on whether we are using the prefix or postfix notation. We are using postfix, so:

```
$(i++)
```

becomes

```
print $(i)            => print $(6) => print $6
i = i + 1             => i = 6 + 1  => i = 7
$i                    => $7
```

If we were using prefix, it would have been:

```
i = i + 1
print $(i)
```

print $(i++) outputs the value of $6, which is "Digital" (notice the pattern $6 == "Digital"). In the next statement, the print statement outputs print $7, NF. This tests whether NF is changed by the increment because the field number that is referenced is higher than the six that was broken up by awk when processing the input line. Indeed, NF changed; its value is 7. The effect of executing $(i++) is that i is no longer 6 but 7 (it is incremented). Therefore, the second time print ($i++) is executed, it prints $7, which is the null string. Because a null string outputs nothing and the side effect of a print statement is that it prints a newline, the output line is blank. NF is seven, and it is printed in the next line.

```
awk 'BEGIN {i=6}
     {print ($i)++}' courses.data
```

Answer: Results will vary depending on your implementation, but an error occurs on the RedHat linux distribution.

It physically performs the following assignment:

```
($i) => $i
($i) = ($i) + 1
```

The second statement is illegal. Why?

LAB
12.2

By definition, a parenthesized expression can be only an rvalue. It is used solely to force an ordering when operations are to be performed. Therefore, by definition, the parenthesized expression ($i) is evaluated first. ($i) is equivalent to $i, and i is 6. Therefore, ($i) is equivalent to $6. $6 is evaluated and the string "Digital" is returned. In the second statement, because "Digital" is a string constant and not a variable, and a string constant cannot be an lvalue, ($i) on the left-hand side of the assignment statement is illegal (i.e., "Digital" does not refer to a value; it is a value).

12.2.2 ANSWERS

Write three programs that find the maximum number among all numbers in each column in `input_file`. Print out the column number and maximum number.

a) What is the program for column one?

Answer: The program is as follows:

```
awk 'max > $1 { max = $1}
        { print "The max number of column 1 is ", max }' input_file
```

Because max is referred to in the pattern before a value is assigned to it, it is coerced to 0. Therefore, the first field of the first input line will be the max. All first fields of subsequent lines will be compared against this. If any subsequent first fields are greater than the max, the subsequent field will be the new max. At the end, max will contain the largest first field in the input file.

b) What is the program for column two?

Answer: The program is as follows:

```
awk 'max > $2 { max = $2 }
        { print "The max number of column 2 is ", max }' input_file
```

It is the same as the program for column one, but now the second field is used.

c) What is the program for column three?

Answer: The program is as follows:

```
awk 'max > $1 { max = $3}
        { print "The max number of column 3 is ", max }' input_file
```

Write a program, using the `courses.data` file from Lab 4.1, that does the following:

- Calculates and prints the number of people registered for conferences who come from Digital;
- Calculates and prints the total amount owed for people from Digital;
- Calculates the average amount owed for registrants from Digital.

d) What is the program?

Answer: The program is as follows:

```
Awk '$6 == "Digital" {count++
                      sum+=$4
                      print $1, $4
                     }
      END { print "Total Number Outstanding From Digital Is ", count
            print "Average amount owed is ", sum/count
          }' courses.data
```

The pattern checks whether the registrant is indeed from Digital. The action increments `count` (the number of people registered from Digital) by one. This example is one in which the prefix or postfix notation does not matter. If all you care about is to increment a variable by one and you do not care to use the increment operation as an operand to another operation, then it does not matter whether you use prefix or postfix. The field `$4` is the amount owed. `Sum` is used with the addition assignment operator to add the value of `$4` (amount owed) to the previous value of `$4`. Therefore, `sum` contains a running total of the amount owed for all people from Digital. The average amount owed is calculated using `count` and `sum`.

e) What is the output?

Answer: The output from this program is:

Leonard 200
Oreilly 0
Total Number Outstanding From Digital Is 2
Average amount owed is 100

Write a program that calculates the number of words and the number of lines from the given text file.

LAB 12.2

f) What is the program?

Answer: The program is as follows:

```
awk 'BEGIN {FS = [." "] }
     { count += NF }
     END { print "Number of lines is ", NR
           print "Number of words is ", count
         }' input_file
```

Because NF contains the number of fields in the current line, and if each word is split into a field, then NF contains the number of words in the current input line. If we add NF for every line, then we have the total number of words in the input line. Following this logic, all that is required is to have awk split the current input line into fields, by setting FS in the BEGIN pattern to characters(s) that signal the end of a word. A space or a period mark the end of a word (notice that the text passage was purposely written without correct punctuation). The number of lines is always contained within NR, so the value of NR is printed out in the end.

g) What is the output?

> *Answer: The output is as follows:*
> **Number of lines is 11**
> **Number of words is 71**

LAB 12.2 SELF-REVIEW QUESTIONS

In order to test your progress, you should be able to answer the following questions.

1) When using the increment operator, two types of rvalues exist.
  a) _____True
  b) _____False

2) The increment operator has two notations.
  a) _____True
  b) _____False

3) The statement x+=3 is equivalent to x = x + 3.
  a) _____True
  b) _____False

LAB 12.2

4) The first type of rvalue using the increment operator is the rvalue of the operand.
  a) _____True
  b) _____False

5) The second type of rvalue is the result of the value of i before or after the increment, depending on the notation.
  a) _____True
  b) _____False

6) The postfix notation returns the same value as the prefix notation.
    a) _____True
    b) _____False

7) The prefix notation ++i returns the value of i first, and then increments i.
    a) _____True
    b) _____False

8) The postfix notation i++ returns the value of i first, and then increments i.
    a) _____True
    b) _____False

Quiz answers appear in Appendix A, Section 12.2.

LAB
12.2

L A B   12.3

LOGICAL AND RELATIONAL OPERATORS, AND CONDITIONAL EXPRESSIONS

LAB OBJECTIVES
After this Lab, you will be able to: ✓ Understand the Results of the Conditional Expression and the Logical and Relational operators ✓ Write Programs Using the Logical and Relational Operators, and the Conditional Expression

So far, most of the operators we have seen have been used in an action. Relational operators are often, but not always, used in patterns, but they can be used in actions as well. Relational and logical operators are commonly seen in most general-purpose languages. Awk extends these operators to allow operators that can be used with regular expressions, called *regular expression matching operators*. These make sense because awk is a UNIX utility and regular expressions are common UNIX elements. In all previous chapters on awk, we have seen the use of relational operators. When we discuss control flow in Chapter 14, "Awk Control Flow," we will see relational operators used in actions. In this Lab, I explain relational operators in more detail, and discuss how they can be used and the rules regarding their use. Additionally, we discuss rules regarding logical operators and conditional expressions.

We define relational expressions as containing either a relational operator or a regular expression matching operator.

RELATIONAL OPERATORS

Relational operators are shown in Table 12.2.

Table 12.2 ■ Awk's Relational Operators

Sign	Comparison Function
==	Equals
!=	Not Equal
<	Less Than
<=	Less Than or Equal
>	Greater Than
>=	Greater Than or Equal

I will not go over the function of each one separately, because they are intuitive. I will go over just the use of one of them, the equals sign. But keep in mind that the discussion and statements made for the equals sign apply to all the other operators unless otherwise stated.

All the operators in Table 12.2 allow you to make a comparison between two expressions. The resulting value is either one if true, or zero otherwise. So the following comparison yields a 1 if $5 is indeed equal to 15, and a 0 otherwise:

**LAB
12.3**

```
$5 == 15
```

Remember that each side of the expression can be any allowable expression, including constants, user-defined variables, field variables, built-in variables, built-in functions, user-defined functions, and arrays—in other words, any expression that returns a value (an rvalue). Note that both arithmetic expressions and assignment statements may also be used with a relational operator; however, they may require the use of parentheses in the case of the assignment operator(s), and of the increment and decrement operator. The reason has to do with precedence of operators.

As with all relational expressions and logical operators that are used in patterns, if the result of the comparison is true (or more formally, one), then the action is performed. Otherwise, the action is not performed, and the next record processed. You have seen this pattern many times before.

■ FOR EXAMPLE:

We encountered the following awk program earlier:

```
awk '$6 == "Digital" {print $1, $6}' conf.data
```

If the value of $6 is the string "Digital," then the result of the comparison is 1, and the print statement in the action is executed. For all other values of $6, the result is 0 and the action is not performed.

For the equals relational operator only, be careful not to forget the double equals sign. A single equals sign is the assignment operator and is not the same as the assignment statement. Strange results and definite semantic errors will result.

RELATIONAL STRING MATCHING OPERATORS

Table 12.3 lists the relational string matching operators.

Table 12.3 ■ Awk's Relational String Matching Operators

Sign	Function
~	Is Matched By
!~	Is Not Matched By

Both of these operators enable the programmer to make a comparison using a regular expression. The value that results from a comparison using a string matching regular expression operator is 1 if the comparison is true, and a 0 otherwise. So the following comparison yields a 1 if $3 of the current record matches Phys as a pattern, and a 0 otherwise:

```
$3  ~  /Phys/
```

The right-hand side of the matching operator may include any expression that returns an rvalue. This include constants, user-defined variables, field variables, built-in variables, built-in functions, user-defined functions, and arrays. The various assignment statements and increment and decrement operators are not used often on the right-hand side of a matching operator. Awk will evaluate the expression, making a conversion into a string value if necessary, and will interpret the string value as a regular expression.

LOGICAL OPERATORS

Table 12.4 lists the logical operators and the function associated with them.

Table 12.4 ■ Awk's Logical Operators

Sign	Function
&&	And
||	Or
!	Not

The logical operators semantically work exactly as one would expect from a Boolean operator. Table 12.5 illustrates the result of using the three Boolean operators; T means true, and F is false.

Table 12.5 ■ Results of Logical Operators

	&&			||			!
A	**B**	**Result**	**A**	**B**	**Result**	**A**	**Result**
T	T	T	T	T	T	T	F
T	F	F	T	F	T	F	T
F	T	F	F	T	T		
F	F	F	F	F	F		

When using a logical operator, A and B are operands. The logical operators are used to create logical expressions by combining other expressions.

■ FOR EXAMPLE:

Most often, they are used in conjunction with relational expressions to
form a compound comparison, as follows:

```
age > 18 && age < 65
```

In this case, the operands A and B are each relational expressions. The
relational expression age > 18 is the A operand from Table 12.5, and age
< 65 is the B operand.

A logical operator is evaluated from the left-most operand (A in our case)
to the right-most. Therefore, age > 18 is evaluated first, and then age <
65 is evaluated. The order of evaluation can be important because,
depending on the operator, evaluation can be stopped if the result of the
whole expression can be determined from the operand A. This situation is
the case if we look at Table 12.5. In the And operator, &&, we can see that
if the first operand, A, is false, whether the second operand, B, is true or
false does not matter. Therefore, evaluation can stop and the B operand
does not need to be evaluated if A is false. The same is true with the Or
operator. If the first operand, A, is true, then the result will always be true
regardless of whether B is true or false. You can take this rule to your
advantage. If you know when using an && operator that one condition in
an expression will be more likely to be false than the second, then you
should use it as the first operand to reduce the number of comparisons.
Similarly, for an || operator, if the condition is more likely to be true,
make it the first operand. Secondly, one may perform an error check and
a comparison in the same statement.

```
NF >= 6 && $6 == "Digital"
```

**LAB
12.3**

If NF is false and a sixth field does not exist, then the operand B, $6 ==
"Digital," will not be performed.

Lastly, logical operators may be used in conjunction with parentheses to
enforce a strict ordering in evaluation of a logical operator. The following
awk excerpt illustrates this possibility:

```
company == "Digital && (age > 18 && age < 65)
```

This is also helpful to provide easier readability of a logical expression.

CONDITIONAL EXPRESSIONS

Unlike relational and logical expressions, conditional expressions are more likely to be used in actions rather than patterns. A conditional expression has the following form:

ComparisonExpr ? Expression1 : Expression2

The comparison expression is evaluated first. If the result or the expression is true, in other words, nonzero or non-null, then Expression1 is evaluated. Otherwise, Expression2 is evaluated.

■ FOR EXAMPLE:

Consider the following awk program:

```
awk '{$4 > 65 ? retired = "Is"   : retired = "Is Not"
        print $1, retired, "Retired"}' some_file
```

Assuming that $4 is an age and $1 is a last name, this program first prints out the name from each input record. Additionally, it prints out whether the individual is retired or not. The way this action is done is by using the conditional expression $4 > 65 ? retired = "Is" : retired = "Is Not." The expression that is being used, for Expression1 of the conditional, is the assignment statement retired="Is." The expression that is being used for Expression2 is retired="Is Not." If $4 is greater than 65, then Expression1 is evaluated; otherwise, Expression2 is evaluated. The assignment, therefore, assigns a string value of "Is" or "Is Not" to the variable retired. The assignment is based on the conditional. Therefore, the print statement outputs either of the following, based on whether Jones is older than 65 or is not older than 65:

LAB 12.3

```
Jones Is Retired
Jones Is Not Retired
```

The important point to note in this example is that the comparison expression can be any expression. The result of the expression will be tested to see whether it is zero, null, nonzero, or non-null. `Expression1` and `Expression2` can be any expression, so that any constant, variable, function, array value, or arithmetic or string operator, increment or decrement operator, or relational or logical expression can be used as an expression. The result of the conditional expression is the result of either `Expression1` or `Expression2`. Therefore, the result of the conditional expression is the result of an assignment statement (`retired = "Is"` or `retired = "Is not"`).

> *The result of a conditional expression is the result of* `Expression1` *or* `Expression2`.

Therefore, the conditional expression can be used as an operand to another expression. In this case, the value of `Expression1` or `Expression2` will be used as the rvalue to another expression. This circumstance is illustrated by rewriting the preceding example as follows:

```
awk '{print $1 ($4 > 65 ? retired = "Is"  : retired =
    "Is Not") "Retired"}' some_file
```

The output would be the same as before.

As a final note, a conditional expression can be thought of as follows:

```
if  ComparisonExpr is true
        evaluate Expression1
otherwise
        evaluate Expression2
```

LAB 12.3 EXERCISES

12.3.1 UNDERSTAND THE RESULTS OF THE CONDITIONAL EXPRESSION AND THE LOGICAL AND RELATIONAL OPERATORS

a) What is the final value of a after each of the following expressions?

```
a = "Digital" == "IBM"
```

_____

_____

```
a = "Digital" == "Digital"
```

_____

_____

Assume that $1 = 10, $2 = 20 for the following:

```
a = $1 == $2 ? "Equal" : "Not Equal"
```

_____

_____

Assume that $1 = 10, $2 = 10 for the following:

```
a = $1 == $2 ? "Equal: : "Not Equal"
```

_____

_____

Use the following file for the remaining questions in this Exercise:

```
Adh 10
Coa 20
Res 30
```

LAB
12.3

```
Adh 25
Sta 20
Coa 15
Res 30
```

What are the number of comparisons and the results of those comparisons for the next two statements?

b) `$1 == "Adh" && $2 == 25`

_____

_____

c) `$2 > 10 || $1 == "Coa"`

_____

_____

d) How would you optimize the comparisons?

_____

_____

12.3.2 WRITE PROGRAMS USING THE LOGICAL AND RELATIONAL OPERATORS, AND THE CONDITIONAL EXPRESSION

a) Write a program that prints the names of all Digital employees who have an amount-owed from the `courses.data` input file from Lab 9.3.

_____

_____

b) What is the output?

_____

_____

c) Write a program that finds out whether one column is equal to another column. Run the program comparing column one and column two of the following input file:

```
10 20
20 20
30 20
20 40
30 30
40 40
```

d) What is the output?

_____

_____

Analyze the following program for the next question:

```
awk 'BEGIN {expr = "(^[+-]?([0-9]+[.]?[0-9]*|[.][0-
9]+)([eE][+-]?[0-9]+)?$"}
      {$1 ~ expr {print $1, "  Is A Valid Number"}
           $1 !~ expr {print $1, " Not A Valid Number"}'
   input_file
```

e) How would you make the given program more efficient?

_____

_____

Use the following file for the next question, where column one contains a date, column two a company, and column three a whole number:

```
01/02/98 Digital 12
01/03/98 IBM 13
02/04/97 Sun 15
03/05/97 HP 24
04/09/98 TRW 20
04/10/97 Netscape 20
02/11/98 Compaq 10
```

**LAB
12.3**

f) Write a program that for each year will find out the total of all the numbers in field three for that year. Print each year out and its associated total. You can assume that no quantity in field three will equal the number for a year. Lastly, only the years 97 and 98 will be used.

_____

_____

For the next question, use the following file, which contains a customer name and a withdrawal amount:

```
Smith 500
Jones 7000
Jones 60
Smith 50
Jones 140
Jones 800
Smith 100
```

g) Write a program that figures out the ending balance for customer "Jones." Assume that the first time a customer's name is encountered, the second field is not a withdrawal amount but a starting balance.

_____

_____

LAB 12.3 EXERCISE ANSWERS

This section gives you some suggested answers to the questions in Lab 12.3, with discussion related to those answers. Your answers may vary, but the most important thing is whether or not your answer works. Use this discussion to analyze differences between your answers and those presented here.

LAB 12.3

If you have alternative answers to the questions in this Exercise, you are encouraged to post your answers and discuss them at the companion Web site for this book, located at:

```
http://www.phptr.com/phptrinteractive/
```

12.3.1 ANSWERS

a) What is the final value of a after each of the following expressions?

```
a = "Digital" == "IBM"
```

Answer: Null

A string comparison is made and a 0 or 1 is returned based on the comparison.

```
a = "Digital" == "Digital"
```

Answer: Non-null

A string comparison is made and a 0 or 1 is returned based on whether the comparison is true or false.

```
a = $1 == $2 ? "Equal" : "Not Equal"
```

Answer: "Not Equal"

Remember that if the conditional is false, the second statement gets executed and its result returned.

```
a = $1 == $2 ? "Equal: : "Not Equal"
```

Answer: "Equal"

In a conditional expression, if the conditional is true, the first statement gets executed and its result returned.

What are the number of comparisons and the results of those comparisons for the next two statements?

b) `$1 == "Adh" && $2 == 25`

Answer: Line 1: False, two comparisons

$1 = "Adh" and "Adh" == "Adh" are true, so $2 == 25 gets compared.

Line 2: False, one comparison

$1 = "Coa" is false, so the second comparison is not performed.

**LAB
12.3**

Line 3: False, one comparison

Line 4: True, two comparisons

Line 5: False, one comparison

Line 6: False, one comparison

Line 7: False, one comparison

A total of 9 comparisons

c) `$2 > 10 || $1 == "Coa"`

Line 1: False, two comparisons

`$2 > 10` is false, so `$1 == "Coa"` is evaluated, resulting in two comparisons.

Line 2: True, one comparison

`$2 > 10` is true, so `$1 == "Coa"` does not need to be evaluated.

Line 3:True, one comparison

Line 4: True, one comparison

Line 5:True, one comparison

Line 6:True, one comparison

Line 7:True, one comparison

A total of 8 comparisons

d) How would you optimize these comparisons?

Answer: The first could be optimized as follows:
`$2 == 25 && $1 == "Adh"`

The reason is that the number 25 occurs once, and it will be true only once, forcing the second comparison `$1 == "Adh"` to be evaluated only for the line that has the second field equal to 25. In all other lines, `$2 == 25` is false, so `$1 == "Adh"` is never evaluated for all other lines. The original expression performs the comparison `$1 == "Adh"` two times.

The result would be eight comparisons with the optimized solution.

The second comparison is already optimized.

12.3.2 ANSWERS

a) Write a program that prints the names of all Digital employees who have an amount-owed from the `courses.data` input file from Lab 9.3.

Answer: The program is as follows:
```
awk  '$6  ==  "Digital"  &&  $4  >  0  {print  $1}'
     courses.data
```

b) What is the output?

Answer: The output is as follows:
Leonard 200

We use a logical AND to test that both $4 is greater than zero and $6 == "Digital." Only if $4 == 0 do employees owe any money.

c) Write a program that finds out whether one column is equal to another column.

Answer: The program is as follows:
```
awk  '{print  $1  ==  $2  ?  "Equal"  :  "Not  Equal"}'
     input_file
```

d) What is the output?
Not Equal
Equal
Not Equal
Not Equal
Equal
Equal

We use a conditional expression to test whether the two columns are equal. If $1 == $2 then the first statement's value is executed, returned (remember, primary expression type 1 and type 2 rvalues are the same), and ultimately printed. Otherwise, the second expression is executed, returned, and printed.

e) How would you make the given program more efficient?

Answer: You would rewrite it as follows:
```
Awk '{$1 ~ (^[+-]?([0-9]+[.]?[0-9]*|[.][0-9]+)([eE][+-]?[0-9]+)?$ ?
    print $1, "Is A Valid Number" : print $1, "Not A Valid Number"}
```

By using a conditional expression and a regular expression matching operator, we can perform both tests in the two patterns in one statement.

f) Write a program that for each year will find out the total of all the numbers in field three for that year. Print each year out and its associated total. You can assume that no quantity in field three will equal the number for a year. Lastly, only the years 97 and 98 will be used.

Answer: The program is as follows:
```
awk '$1 ~ /98/ {year_98+=$3}
     $1 ~ /97/ {year_97 +=$3}
          END {print "Total for 98 is ", year_98
               print "Total for 97 is ", year_97
               }
```

The program uses two pattern-action statements. In the first pattern, we use a regular expression matching operator to test whether the $1 contains the text 98. If it does, then the number in $3 needs to be totaled with the previous total of year_98. This total is done in the action statement year_98+=$3.

g) Write a program that figures out the ending balance for customer "Jones." Assume that the first time a customer's name is encountered, the second field is not a withdrawal amount but a starting balance.

Answer: The program is as follows:
```
awk '$1 == "Jones" { total > 0 ? total-=$2 : total = $2 }
     END {print "Ending Balance = ", total}' input_file
```

In this program, if $1 == "Jones," then the action is performed. In the action, we use a conditional expression to determine whether this line is the first input line that contains Jones. If it is, the total is zero. Remember that a variable that has never been referenced is implicitly initialized with the value zero. Therefore, if this record is the first in which $1 == "Jones," then total will be zero. In this case, the second field is the starting balance. Otherwise, it is a withdrawal amount and must be subtracted from total. In the END pattern, total will contain the ending balance after all withdrawals. Notice that a potential error exists in this program. If the withdrawal amounts equal the starting balance, then total will once again be zero. Because the total is zero, the next withdrawal will be mistaken as a starting balance and the second statement in the conditional expression will be executed. The solution is to use an if statement, which we cover in Chapter 14, "Awk Control Flow."

LAB
12.3

LAB 12.3 SELF-REVIEW QUESTIONS

In order to test your progress, you should be able to answer the following questions.

1) The result of a conditional expression is 0 or 1.
    a) _____True
    b) _____False

2) The operands of the == operator are considered to be strings.
    a) _____True
    b) _____False

3) If at least one string operand exists for an == operator, then a string comparison is made.
    a) _____True
    b) _____False

4) The operands to a logical operator are considered to be numbers.
    a) _____True
    b) _____False

5) The rules for the == operator follow the rules for the rest of the relational operators.
    a) _____True
    b) _____False

6) A relational operator must appear in a pattern.
    a) _____True
    b) _____False

7) A logical operator must appear in a pattern.
    a) _____True
    b) _____False

8) The result of a relational or logical operator may be assigned to a variable.
    a) _____True
    b) _____False

**LAB
12.3**

9) A conditional and two expressions must appear in a conditional expression.
    a) _____True
    b) _____False
    Quiz answer appear in Appendix A, Section 12.3.

C H A P T E R   12

TEST YOUR THINKING

 The projects in this section are meant to have you utilize all of the skills that you have acquired throughout this chapter. The answers to these projects can be found at the companion Web site to this book, located at:

`http://www.phptr.com/phptrinteractive/`

Visit the Web site periodically to share and discuss your answers.

1) Try a couple of questions that test when rvalues or lvalues are used in the increment and decrement operators.

2) When do you think that the $0 is reconstructed with the following increment operation?

```
i = 6
$(i++); print $7, NF
```

When $(i++) is evaluated or when you print $7, NF or it is not reconstructed at all. If the input file has 10 lines, then i will be ten greater than its initial value of 6. Will NF be 10 + 6 after the program ends? Will $0 be reconstructed 10 times? Write a test program that tests these questions.

C H A P T E R 13

BUILT-IN FUNCTIONS, PRECEDENCE, ASSOCIATIVITY, AND MACHINE LIMITS

If I wrote titles that were any longer, I'd be in the record books.

CHAPTER OBJECTIVES

In this chapter, you will learn about:

This chapter covers a number of fundamental concepts you will use repeatedly in awk. We cover the types of built-in functions awk provides for arithmetic and string manipulation, review precedence of arithmetic and relational operators, and explain the order of evaluation. Finally, we present a few brief examples intended to give you an idea of how your hardware and operating environment contribute to the limits you may encounter when using awk.

L A B   13.1

BUILT-IN ARITHMETIC FUNCTIONS

LAB OBJECTIVES

After this Lab, you will be able to:

✓ Understand the Results of Using Built-In Arithmetic Functions

✓ Write Programs Using Built-In Arithmetic Functions

Built-in functions provide convenience to the user in making commonly used functions that would be arduous to implement yourself. Functions are discussed in more detail in Chapter 15, "Awk Arrays and Functions"; the goal of this Lab is simply to describe what each function does, and provide an example of how they may used.

The built-in functions are shown in Table 13.1.

Table 13.1 ■ Awk's Built-In Arithmetic Functions

Function	Description
`atan2(a,b)`	This function performs the arctangent of a/b, with the result in the range pi -pi. Atan2(0, -1) returns pi.
`cos(a)`	This function performs the cosine of a, where a is expressed in radians.
`exp(a)`	This function performs the exponential function of x. `exp(1)` is 2.7182..., the base of the natural logarithms, referred to as e. Therefore, `exp(a)` is e raised a times.
`int(a)`	Integer part of x. It is truncated toward zero when a is greater than zero. Therefore, if given 2.8, it will return 2. In other words, it always truncates to the digit on the left side of the decimal point.
`log(a)`	This function performs the natural (base e) logarithm of x.
`rand(), srand(a)`	This function returns a random floating-point number that is greater than or equal to zero and less than one. `srand` sets the seed or the starting point for the random generator with a. If `rand` is used in a program without using `srand`, then `rand` will start with the same value every time the program is run. If `srand` is used, then the starting value will change, determined by the seed. If `srand` is called without supplying a seed, then the time of day is used as the seed.
`sin(a)`	The `sin` function, like its `cos(a)` counterpart, performs the sine of a. The value a is in radians.
`sqrt(a)`	The `sqrt` function performs the square root of a.

These built-in functions can all be used in expressions as an rvalue. In other words, they can be used in assignment, relational, logical, and conditional expressions; in arrays; and as arguments to other functions.

As stated at the start of this section, you could implement these functions yourself, but to let awk do the work is more precise and easier.

LAB
13.1

LAB 13.1 EXERCISES

13.1.1 UNDERSTAND THE RESULTS OF USING BUILT-IN ARITHMETIC FUNCTIONS

a) What is the output of the following program?

```
awk 'END {print int(20/6)}' some-file
```


b) What is the output of the following program?

```
awk 'END {print cos(10)}' some-file
```


c) What is the output of the following program?

```
awk 'BEGIN {atan = 3}\
{print atan}' conf.data
```


13.1.2 WRITE PROGRAMS USING BUILT-IN ARITHMETIC FUNCTIONS

Write a program that returns a random roll of a pair of dice. For each roll, it returns a number from one to six, performs the same operation for the other die, then adds the two numbers for both dice, and outputs the result.

Run it using any file that you have that has more than one input record. What file you use doesn't really matter; you are not going to process it but need it merely to allow our program to generate a random roll more than once.

a) What is the program using `rand()`?

_____

_____

b) What is the program using `srand()`?

_____

_____

Try running it several times so that you can see whether your results differ from each run.

LAB 13.1 EXERCISE ANSWERS

This section gives you some suggested answers to the questions in Lab 13.1, with discussion related to those answers. Your answers may vary, but the most important thing is whether or not your answer works. Use this discussion to analyze differences between your answers and those presented here.

If you have alternative answers to the questions in this Exercise, you are encouraged to post your answers and discuss them at the companion Web site for this book, located at:

`http://www.phptr.com/phptrinteractive/`

13.1.1 ANSWERS

a) What is the output of the following program?
```
awk 'END {print int(20/6)}' some-file
```
Answer: The output is as follows:
3

The result of 20 divided by 6 equals 3.333. The `int` function truncates any digits to the right of the decimal point without rounding; thus, the result here is 3.

b) What is the output of the following program?

```
awk 'END {print cos(10) }' some-file
```

Answer: The output is as follows

-0.839072

The cosine function of 10 returns the result in radians.

c) What is the output of the following program?

```
awk 'BEGIN {atan = 3}\
    {print atan}' conf.data
```

Answer: You get a Parse Error. `atan` is the name of a built-in function, which is reserved.

13.1.2 ANSWERS

Write a program that returns a random roll of a pair of dice. For each roll, it returns a number from one to six, performs the same operation for the other die, then adds the two numbers for both dice, and outputs the result.

a) What is the program using `rand()`?

```
awk '{dice1 = int(6 * rand()) + 1
        dice2 = int(6 * rand()) + 1
        print dice1 + dice2
     }' input_file
```

b) What is the program using `srand()`?

```
awk 'BEGIN {srand()}
    {dice1 = int(6 * rand()) + 1
    dice2 = int(6 * rand()) + 1
    print dice1 + dice2
    }' input_file
```

Firstly, in b), we use `srand()` in the `BEGIN` statement so that each time this program runs, the values of `rand()` are different. By not providing an argument to `srand()`, the default value for a seed is used. this value is the time of day. The `rand()` function returns a floating-point number between 0 and 1. We multiply the result by six to get a number between 0 and 6. Since we want a whole number between 1 and 6, we use the `int()` function.

I have not listed the output in the first program, because each run will be different per machine and awk version. I have not given output for the second program, both because values will differ per machine and because the time of day will differ the time you run it and the time I ran it. You should notice different values for each run when using `srand()`. You should not notice differences per run when using `rand()`.

LAB 13.1 SELF-REVIEW QUESTIONS

In order to test your progress, you should be able to answer the following questions.

1) Which of the following functions performs the cosine?
   a) _____atan2
   b) _____exp
   c) _____cos
   d) _____sin

2) Which of the following functions returns the whole number of a decimal number?
   a) _____exp
   b) _____rand
   c) _____int
   d) _____log

3) Which of the following functions returns a random number?
   a) _____log
   b) _____srand
   c) _____sqrt
   d) _____rand

4) The operands to the arithmetic function must be a number.
   a) _____True
   b) _____False

Quiz answers appear in Appendix A, Section 13.1.

LAB
13.1

L A B 13.2

BUILT-IN STRING FUNCTIONS

LAB OBJECTIVES

After this Lab, you will be able to:

✓ Understand the Results of Using Built-In String Functions

✓ Write Programs Using Built-In String Functions

Awk string functions are similar to string functions used in other languages, but they also provide additional functions for string manipulation that are more common to other scripting languages like Perl. Again, we will talk about functions in more detail in Chapter 15, "Awk Arrays And Functions." The goal of this section is to instead describe built-in string functions, describe what each function does, and provide examples for how they are used.

INDEX(S, T)

Returns the left-most position where the string t begins in s, or zero if t does not occur in s. The beginning of the string is position 1. This is different from some programming languages, like C/C++, that use position 0 as the first string position. As an example,

```
index("The end is clear", "end")
would return five.
```

LENGTH(S)

Returns the leftmost position where the string t begins in s, or zero if t does not occur in s. The beginning of the string is position 1. This is different from some programming languages, like C/C++, that use position 0 as the first string position. As an example:

```
awk '{print length($0)}' some_file
```

As the program suggests, the number of characters that are in the current input record is given by `length($0)`.

The default and, hence, what gets evaluated when no argument is provided in the length function, is `$0`, the whole current input record.

One handy use of this function is to calculate total field lengths in a record in order to determine where to break output lines.

SUBSTR(S,P), SUBSTR(S,P,N);

The built-in `substr()` function offers the same functionality as most programming languages, namely returning a substring. Given the string s, the `substr(s,p)` function returns the substring starting at position p to the end of the string. The following program illustrates the `substr(s,p)` function.

```
awk '{print "Year is ", substr("01/04/98", 7)}'
```

The output of this print statement would be

Year is 98

The built-in `substr(s,p,n)` performs the same function as `substr(s,p)`, but instead returns the substr starting at position p plus n characters from p. So the following program

```
awk '{print "Month is ", substr("01/04/98", 1, 2)}'
   some_file
```

would print the first two characters from the string 01/04/98, which is the month. The program would produce the following output:

Month is 01

MATCH(S, R)

The built-in function match determines whether the regular expression r is contained or is matched within the string s. The function takes two arguments, the string s and the regular expression r. The match function returns the index where the substring begins or 0 if it is not matched in the string. For example, the excerpt

match("this is an example of match", /example/)

would return 12, which is where the regular expression /example/ appears in the string. As mentioned in the section on built-in variables (Lab 11.3), we skipped the discussion on the built-in variables RSTART and RLENGTH. The match function sets these variables when it is executed. RSTART is set to the same value as the return value of the function. Namely, it is set to the index where the substring begins or zero. RLENGTH contains the length of the substring in characters (not the ending position of the string). Remember, as with all built-in variables, RSTART and RLENGTH can appear as both an lvalue and an rvalue, i.e., they may be written to or read. When the regular expression does not match the current string, RSTART and RLENGTH are set to zero and –1. In the following example, we could use match to find for a given year all course subjects that a student took. The below awk program implements this problem:

```
awk 'match($0, /98/) {print $1, $2}' some_file
```

Given the following data:

```
01/04/96 Math
03/06/98 Physics
02/02/97 English
04/05/98 History
```

we would produce the following output:

```
03/06/98 Physics
04/05/98 History
```

GSUB(R, S), GSUB(R, S, T), SUB(R, S), AND SUB(R, S, T)

These functions perform string substitutions (much like the sed substitution command). The function `sub()` first finds the left-most, longest substring matched by the regular expression r, in the target string t. Next, it then replaces the substring with the substitution string s. The left-most, longest substring means that the left-most match is found first and extended as far as possible. For example, the left-most, longest substring using the string "proceed" and the regular expression (e)* is "ee." The `sub()` function returns the number of substitutions made. Therefore, the rvalue of the `sub()` function is a number, not the string replaced. Sub(r,s) is the same as sub(r, s, $0), so the default argument is $0. You can think of s and t in the argument list for sub(r, s, t) and gsub(r, s, t) as the source and target. The function gsub() is similar to sub(), except that it successively replaces each leftmost, longest overlapping substrings matched by the regular expression r within the string s in the string t. Again, gsub(r, s) is synonymous with gsub(r, s, $0).

The difference between the two functions is that `gsub()` performs its substitution globally on the input string, whereas `sub()` makes only the first possible substitution.

Both functions take at least two arguments. The first is a regular expression (enclosed within slashes) that matches a pattern. The second is a string that replaces what the pattern matches. A variable containing a regular expression may be used in place of the regular expression enclosed within slashes. Each may take a third argument, which is the target string to be replaced. If a third argument is not provided, then the target string is assumed to be $0. For example, the following statements

```
sub(/Coatings/, "Adhesion", "The Coatings conference
examines Coatings technology")
```

would result in the following target string

```
The Adhesion conference examines Coatings technology
```

whereas

```
gsub/Coatings/, "Adhesion", "The Coatings conference
examines Coatings technology")
```

would result in the following target string:

The Adhesion conference examines Adhesion technology

Gsub replaces every occurrence and sub replaces the first. Note that the actual result returned by the function is 1 for sub and 2 for gsub. Sub always returns either a 1 or 0; gsub returns n where n is some positive number or zero.

Since the result of the function that is returned is the number of substitutions made, it can be used in a comparison to determine whether the substitution occurred.

In a substitution made by either sub() or gsub(), any occurrence of the character & in s will be replaced by the substring matched by r. For example,

gsub(/d/, "&c&", "acacaaacaa")

would result in

adcdadcdaaadcdaa

In other words, every occurrence of "c" in the target will be replaced by "dcd."

The special meaning of & in the substitution string can be turned off by preceding it with a backslash, as in \&. This possibility is useful if the source string contains occurrences of &.

TOLOWER(T) AND TOUPPER(T)

These built-in string functions convert all characters in string t to lowercase or uppercase, respectively. For example, given the string

t = "This is an Example"

tolower(t) would result in

this is an example

toupper(t) would result in

THIS IS AN EXAMPLE

LAB 13.2 EXERCISES

13.2.1 UNDERSTAND THE RESULTS OF USING BUILT-IN STRING FUNCTIONS

 For this Exercise, use the `courses.data` file from Chapter 9, "An Awk Program," Lab 9.3. Alternatively, you can find the file at the Web site companion to this book, located at:

```
http://www.phptr.com/phptrinteractive/
```

a) What is the output for each of the following programs?
```
awk '{print substr(1,10)}' courses.data
```

_____

_____

```
awk '{print sub(/Coatings/, "Adhesions", $0)}' courses.data
```

_____

_____

```
awk '{sub(/Coatings/, "Adhesions", $0)
      print
     }' courses.data
```

_____

_____

```
awk '{print gsub(/200/, "400", $4)}' courses.data
```

_____

_____

13.2.2 WRITE PROGRAMS USING BUILT-IN STRING FUNCTIONS

Write a program that counts the number of lines, words, and characters in a file, and prints those totals out.

a) What is the program?

b) What is the output if the `courses.data` file is used?

In the `courses.data` file, we would like to add codes to the file. These codes are abbreviations of the course name. More specifically, the codes will be the first three letters of the course name.

Write a program that adds the code name for the Adhesions course. For example, the course name Adhesions will have the code Adh.

c) What is the program?

d) What is the output?

Rewrite the program to replace all course names.

e) What is the program?

f) What is the output?

_____

_____

The length function and the substr function could be used to split lines that are greater than x characters in length. The following program performs this task for lines greater than 80 characters in length:

```
awk 'length($0) <= 79 { print }
      length($0) >= 80 && length($0) <=159 {print sub-
   str($0, 1, 80)
         print "    ***", substr($0, 81)
                                            }
      length($0) > 159 {print "Line spans greater than
   two lines too long"} some_file
```

g) Analyze this program and explain how it works.

_____

_____

LAB 13.2 EXERCISE ANSWERS

This section gives you some suggested answers to the questions in Lab 13.1, with discussion related to those answers. Your answers may vary, but the most important thing is whether or not your answer works. Use this discussion to analyze differences between your answers and those presented here.

If you have alternative answers to the questions in this Exercise, you are encouraged to post your answers and discuss them at the companion Web site for this book, located at:

```
http://www.phptr.com/phptrinteractive/
```

13.2.1 ANSWERS

a) What is the output for each of the following programs?

```
awk '{print substr(1,10)}' courses.data
```

Answer: The output is as follows:

```
Leonard Ad
Johnson Co
Peters Sta
Koenig Coa
Moore Adhe
Oreilly Ad
Samuals St
Henry Coat
```

The program returns a substring of 10 characters, starting at position 1.

```
awk '{print sub(/Coatings/, "Adhesions", $0)}' courses.data
```

Answer: The output is as follows:

```
0
1
0
1
0
0
0
1
```

```
awk '{sub(/Coatings/, "Adhesions", $0)
      print
     }' courses.data
```

Answer: The output is as follows:

```
Leonard Adhesions 300 200 081098 Digital
Johnson Adhesions 200 0 081298 Dow
Peters Stabilizers 250 100 080198 Dupont
Koenig Adhesions 200 50 072898 Dow
Moore Adhesions 300 200 080198 IBM
Oreilly Adhesions 300 0 081198 Digital
Samuals Stabilizers 250 0 081098 Dupont
Henry Adhesions 200 100 080398 Shell
```

The first time the regular expression "Coatings" is matched in the record $0, it is replaced with the string "Adhesions." Remember, with sub, only the first occurrence of a match is replaced, and the output is always either 0 for no matches or 1 for the single match.

LAB 13.2

```
awk '{print gsub(/200/, "400", $4)}' courses.data
```

Answer: The output is as follows:

```
Leonard Adhesions 300 400 081098 Digital
Johnson Coatings 200 0 081298 Dow
Peters Stabilizers 250 100 080198 Dupont
Koenig Coatings 200 50 072898 Dow
Moore Adhesions 300 400 080198 IBM
Oreilly Adhesions 300 0 081198 Digital
Samuals Stabilizers 250 0 081098 Dupont
Henry Coatings 200 100 080398 Shell
```

Gsub performs the substitution globally for the specified field, so in this case whenever the expression 200 occurs in $4, it is replaced by 400. This occurs twice in the courses.data file.

13.2.2 ANSWERS

Write a program that counts the number of lines, words, and characters in a file, and prints those totals out.

a) What is the program?

Answer: The program is as follows:

```
awk '{words += NF
      chars += (length($0)+1)
      }
      END {print "Lines =", NR, "Words =", words, "Characters
 =", chars }' courses.data
```

The number of lines is contained in the built-in variable NR, so it does not need to be initialized. By default, each word in courses.data is split into a field (remember, the default field separator is a space), and NF will contain the number of words in the current input line. Therefore, the variable words keeps a running total of the number of words seen so far by adding the value of NF to the previous value of the variable words. The number of characters in the current line is the same as the length of $0. We add one to it to count the newline at the end of the record.

b) What is the output if the courses.data file is used?

Answer: The output is as follows:
```
Lines = 8 Words = 28 Characters = 171
```

Write a program that replaces the code name for the Adhesions course. For example, the course name Adhesions will have the code Adh.

c) What is the program?

Answer: The program is as follows:
```
awk '$2 == "Adhesions" {gsub(/Adhesions/, "Adh", $2) }
     {print $0}' courses.data
```

In the pattern, we check to see whether the second field, $2, is equal to Adhesions. If it is, then the action is performed. The gsub command then substitutes the string Adh for each occurrence of Adhesions. Notice that we did not perform the command print gsub(/Adhesions/, "Adh", $2). This would have printed the result of the gsub command, which is 0 if unsuccessful or the number of substitutions made. To see the effect of the change of a sub command, you need to print the target variable in a separate command.

d) What is the output?

Answer: The output is as follows:
```
Leonard Adh 300 200 081098 Digital
Johnson Coatings 200 0 081298 Dow
Peters Stabilizers 250 100 080198 Dupont
Koenig Coatings 200 50 072898 Dow
Moore Adh 300 200 080198 IBM
Oreilly Adh 300 0 081198 Digital
Samuals Stabilizers 250 0 081098 Dupont
Henry Coatings 200 100 080398 Shell
```

Rewrite the program to replace all course names.

e) What is the program?

Answer: The program is as follows:
```
awk '{ $2 = substr($2,1,3) }
     {print $0}' courses.data
```

Here we perform the substitution for all course names, so a pattern should not be included. I have demonstrated an alternative here, just using `substr()` and not `gsub()`, as I did before. I could have easily used `substr()` in the previous example. The first three characters are returned from the `substr` operation. Remember that the result of the `substr` function is a string, not a numerical result like `sub()` and `gsub()`.

**LAB
13.2**

The `substr` function extracts the first three characters from field number two, which is the full course name. So `Coatings` becomes `Coa`, which is the result we desire.

f) What is the output?

Answer: The output is

Leonard Adh 300 200 081098 Digital

Johnson Coa 200 0 081298 Dow

Peters Sta 250 100 080198 Dupont

• • •

and so forth.

```
awk 'length($0) <= 79 { print }
      length($0) >= 80 && length($0) <=159 {print sub-
   str($0, 1, 80)
       print "   ***", substr($0, 81)
                                            }
       length($0) > 159 {print "Line spans greater than
   two lines too long"} some_file
```

g) Analyze this program and explain how it works.

Answer: The explanation is as follows:

The first pattern determines whether the length of the line is less than 80. If it is, you have no need to split the line, and the line can be printed without splitting. The second pattern determines whether the line is greater than 80 and needs splitting. It also checks whether the length is less than 159; otherwise, you have three lines. For simplicity, we have limited the program to splitting into two lines. Otherwise, a pattern needs to be created for each additional line over 159 characters. The print statement then uses `substr(s, p, n)` to print the first line and `substr(s, p)` to print the rest of the line on the next line. A split line is prefixed by the substring " `***`" to distinguish it from a line that has not been split.

LAB 13.2 SELF-REVIEW QUESTIONS

In order to test your progress, you should be able to answer the following questions.

1) For each of the following, match the string function name to the description of what the function performs.

    a) `sub`   i) Searches for a pattern in a string and replaces the pattern for every occurrence of the pattern

    b) `substr` ii) Finds the character position in which a pattern occurs in a string

    c) `gsub`   iii) Extracts a string from another string

    d) `index`   iv) Searches for a pattern in a string and replaces the first occurrence of the pattern

2) The `index` function updates RSTART and RINDEX.
    a) _____True
    b) _____False

3) The `sub` function returns 0 or 1.
    a) _____True
    b) _____False

4) The `match` function and the `index` function both return the same result.
    a) _____True
    b) _____False

5) `$0` is used as an argument to the `length` function if no argument is supplied.
    a) _____True
    b) _____False

6) The `gsub` function returns 0, or the number of substitutions made.
    a) _____True
    b) _____False

Quiz answers appear in Appendix A, Section 13.2.

L A B   13.3

PATTERNS, PRECEDENCE, ASSOCIATIVITY, AND MACHINE LIMITS

LAB OBJECTIVES

After this Lab, you will be able to:

✓ Understand the Results of Precedence and Associativity

✓ Understand Machine Limits

In this Lab, I describe some rules regarding precedence, associativity, and machine limits. Knowing these rules and values can result in fewer errors, more concise code, and avoidance of extraneous parentheses. I also explore the BEGIN-END pattern in more detail.

BEGIN-END PATTERN

As we have seen many times before, the BEGIN and END pattern provides a major role in the awk programming model. The BEGIN and END pattern provides a preprocessing and postprocessing mechanism to perform some preliminary work and/or finish-up work before the main processing loop. Conceptually, when you decompose a problem into an awk program, you should think about three things:

1. What types of activities or operations need to be done before processing every input record?
2. What types of activities or operations need to be performed on every input record?
3. What types of activities or operations need to performed after every input record is processed?

Generally, the types of activities that need to be performed before any input record is operated on are shown as follows:

1. Initialize any user-defined variable that does not start at, or is initialized to, zero.
2. Initialize any field variables that should not start at their default value.
3. Change FS or OFS to change the way input lines are split into fields and output.
4. Process command-line arguments ARGV and ARGC.
5. Print headings for reports or output.

This list is short and obviously cannot encompass all the types of operations that might occur in a BEGIN pattern. The types of activities or operations that might occur in an END pattern are as follows:

1. Calculate and print totals.
2. Calculate and print averages.
3. Print footings for reports or output.

BEGIN and END patterns don't match any input records; in other words, the actions associated with them are always executed.

The statements in a BEGIN statement are always executed before any input records are read by awk, and the statements in an END statement are always executed after all input records are read by awk. If more than one BEGIN pattern exists, the associated actions are executed in the order in which they appear in the program, and similarly for multiple ENDs.

PRECEDENCE, ASSOCIATIVITY, AND MACHINE LIMITS

Precedence refers to the order in which multiple operations in a statement are executed. Table 13.2 lists operators in order of increasing precedence.

Table 13.2 ■ Expression Operators

Operation	Operators	Associativity
Assignment	=, +=, -=, *=, /=, %=, ^=	Right
Conditional	?:	Right
Logical OR	||	Left
Logical AND	&&	Left
Array Membership	in	Left
Relational Matching	~, !~	Left
Relational	<, <=, >, >=, ==, !=	Left
Concatenation	"a" "b"	Left
Arithmetic, Add, Subtract	+, -	Left
Arithmetic, Mult, Div, Mod	*, /, %	Left
Unary Plus, Minus	+, - -3 negation of 3	Left
Logical NOT	!	Left
Exponentiation	^	Right
Increment, Decrement	++, --	Left
Field	$	Left
Grouping	()	Left

Operators of higher precedence are evaluated before lower ones.

■ FOR EXAMPLE:

```
x + y * z
```

The `y * z` would be evaluated first, and the return value would be added to `x`.

Suppose that you have two or more operators in a statement with the same precedence. Associativity refers to the order in which these operators are evaluated.

Right associativity means that the right-most expression is evaluated first, then the second right-most expression is evaluated, and so on. Left associativity proceeds the opposite way. So consider the following two expressions:

```
x + y + z
```

Here, the expression `x + y` will be evaluated first (left associativity), and the result will be used to add with z. The opposite is true with assignments, or any other right-associative operation.

Precedence and associativity together uniquely determine the order of execution of an expression that has multiple operators.

Sometimes, a useful technique is to force execution of a lower precedent operator before a higher precedent operator by using the grouping operator, the parentheses. This is illustrated in the following example:

```
running_average = starting_value
running_average = (running_average + next_value) / 2
```

Note the use of parentheses to force execution of the addition operation before the division. The result would have been incorrect if the division had occurred first.

Use parentheses when using string concatenation and some other operator. Note the following:

```
awk '{print "The negation of x = " -x}'
```

This does not print the negation of x. Rather, it subtracts the string from x and prints the result as output. The reason is that subtraction has a higher precedence than string concatenation. It could have been written correctly as:

```
awk '{print "The negation of x = " (-x)}'
```

LAB 13.3 EXERCISES

13.3.1 UNDERSTAND THE RESULTS OF PRECEDENCE AND ASSOCIATIVITY

What is the result of the following operations? For these problems, `$2=3` and `i=2`.

a) `4 + 2 * 2 - 2`

_____

_____

b) `3 * 2 + (6 - 3) + i++`

_____

_____

c) `4 + $2 * 3 / 2`

_____

_____

13.3.2 UNDERSTAND MACHINE LIMITS

In this Exercise, run the following programs to find out the limits on your machine and awk implementation.

a) Test the number of fields with the following program:

```
{ for (i=1; i<100000; i++) {
  print i
  $i = i
  }
}
```

_____

_____

b) Test the number of characters per field with the following program:

```
{ for (i=1; i<100000; i++) {
    $1 = $1 "a"
                            }
}
```

_____

_____

LAB 13.3 EXERCISE ANSWERS

This section gives you some suggested answers to the questions in Lab 13.3, with discussion related to those answers. Your answers may vary, but the most important thing is whether or not your answer works. Use this discussion to analyze differences between your answers and those presented here.

If you have alternative answers to the questions in this Exercise, you are encouraged to post your answers and discuss them at the companion Web site for this book, located at:

`http://www.phptr.com/phptrinteractive/`

13.3.1 ANSWERS

What is the result of the following operations? For these problems, $2=3 and i=2.

a) `4 + 2 * 2 - 2`

Answer: The result is 6.

Multiplication has higher precedence than addition and subtraction, so it is performed first, and 2 * 2 = 4. Next we have addition and subtraction. Because addition and subtraction have equal precedence, we look at how they associate, which is left, so the addition is performed first. 4 + 4 = 8. Lastly the subtraction is performed, 8 – 2 = 6.

b) `3 * 2 + (6 - 3) + i++`

   Answer: The result is `11`.

The parentheses have the highest precedence of all the operators. They are evaluated first and yield 6 – 3 = 3. The increment operator has the next highest precedence. Furthermore, because we have postfix notation, the value of `i` is used and not its incremented value. Thus, the expression is 3 * 2 + 3 + 2. The next highest precedence here is multiplication, 3 * 2 = 6. The equation now becomes 6 + 3 + 2.

LAB 13.3

Because addition associates left, the addition 6 + 3 = 9 is performed, and finally 9 + 2 = 11 is performed.

c) `4 + $2 * 3 / 2`

   Answer: The result is `8.5`.

Based on precedence, this expression is evaluated in the following order:

```
$2 = 3
4 + 3 * 3 / 2
3 * 3 = 9       (* and / have equal precedence but asso-
ciate left)
4 + 9 / 2
9 / 2 = 4.5   ( / has higher precedence than +)
4 + 4.5 = 8,5
```

13.3.2 ANSWERS

In this Exercise, you ran the given programs.

a) Test the number of fields.

b) Test the number of characters per field.

   Answer: No correct answers exist, because limits are machine dependent.

Awk imposes the following machine limits: fields, characters per input record, characters per output record, characters per field, characters per printf string, characters maximum literal string, characters in character class, open files, pipes, and floating points.

LAB 13.3 SELF-REVIEW QUESTIONS

In order to test your progress, you should be able to answer the following questions.

1) A BEGIN pattern may occur more than once.
   a) _____True
   b) _____False

2) An END pattern must appear before a BEGIN pattern.
   a) _____True
   b) _____False

3) The number of fields allowed in awk is 100.
   a) _____True
   b) _____False

4) Precedence is considered before associativity when evaluating a statement with more than one operator.
   a) _____True
   b) _____False

5) Parentheses have the highest precedence.
   a) _____True
   b) _____False

6) Addition is always performed before subtraction.
   a) _____True
   b) _____False

7) Printing a header in a report is better to perform in a BEGIN statement than in an END statement.
   a) _____True
   b) _____False

8) Explicit initialization of variables is usually done in a BEGIN pattern.
   a) _____True
   b) _____False

Quiz answers appear in Appendix A, Section 13.3.

C H A P T E R   13

TEST YOUR THINKING

 The projects in this section are meant to have you utilize all of the skills that you have acquired throughout this chapter. The answers to these projects can be found at the companion Web site to this book, located at:

`http://www.phptr.com/phptrinteractive/`

Visit the Web site periodically to share and discuss your answers.

In this section, we will explore three more built-in variables that we did not cover: the ENVIRON, ARGC, and ARGV built-in variables. As the name suggests, the ENVIRON built-in variable is an array in which each array element is a UNIX environmental variable. For instance,

```
print ENVIRON["SHELL"]
```

outputs on my system

/bin/tcsh

As the example suggests, the name of each environmental variable is an index of the array. The ARGC and ARGV built-in variables perform the same functions as their C/C++ counterparts. They are both used to process command-line arguments. ARGV is an array that contains all the arguments and options that were specified and included at the command line when awk was invoked. The number of arguments is contained within ARGC, which is used as an index into ARGV. The first index in ARGV is 1. The total number of elements in ARGV is ARGC-1. You can think mnemonically of ARGV as an argument vector and ARGC as an argument counter. All the built-in variables that we have talked about here can be referenced or assigned anywhere in an awk program.

Create a file with any one line of input. Call it `some-file`.

Write the following program in a script called `arg.scr`:

```
BEGIN { for (i=0; i<ARGC; i++)
            print ARGV[i]
        print ARGC
      }
```

Execute the script with the following invocation at the command line:

```
awk -f arg.scr some-file "Jasper" n=15
```

1) What is the output?

2) What is ARGV[0[, ARGV[1]?

3) Does the -f or arg.scr argument in the invocation get printed?

Given the following file of withdrawals and deposits called trans.dat:

```
w 900
d 200
w 300
d 400
```

4) Write a program that calculates the final balance after the above transactions. Pass in a starting balance of 1200 at the command line to the program, and use ARGV and ARGC to process the transactions on the starting balance.

Enter the following program in a script called env.scr:

```
BEGIN { for (index in ENVIRON)
                    print ENVIRON[index]
        }
```

5) Using the file some-file that you created for questions 1 through 3, what is the output of the above program?

C H A P T E R 14

AWK CONTROL FLOW

 With the power of looping constructs and the conditional `if-else` *statement, you are able to express more involved algorithms into an awk program.*

In Chapter 12, "Operators," you were introduced to relational and logical expressions. Those expressions were mostly used in patterns. In this chapter, we explore additional comparison expressions, one of which (the `if` statement) is much like a conditional expression introduced in Chapter 12. The other two control flow statements, `while` and `for`, enable a programmer to program and utilize loops and looping statements. Unlike the relational and logical expressions, these control flow statements are mostly used in actions. They perform a useful task in that they allow common operations to be written once and potentially executed multiple times without the need to program the common operation for each repetition. With the power of looping constructs and the conditional `if-else` statement, you are able to express more involved algorithms into an awk program. Therefore, the examples and exercises will start to get a little more challenging in this chapter.

LAB 14.1

THE IF-ELSE STATEMENT

LAB OBJECTIVES

After this Lab, you will be able to:

✓ Understand the Syntax of an If-Else Statement

✓ Write Programs Using the If-Else Statement

SIMPLE SYNTAX

The `if-else` statement has the following form:

```
if (Expression)
        Statement1
else
        Statement2
```

In plain English, this example translates to "If `Expression` is true, perform `Statement1`; otherwise, perform `Statement2`."

The following are the syntactical rules to apply when working with the `if-else` statement:

- The `else` statement is optional, and thus `Statement2` in the preceding example is optional.
- Newlines are optional after the right parenthesis
- Newlines are optional after statement one.
- Newlines are optional after the keyword `else`.
- If `else` appears on the same line as statement one, then a semicolon must terminate statement one.

Use indentation and white space as much as possible to make code easier to read, and subsequently debug. I cannot emphasize this advice enough. As impossible as the scenario seems, someone down the road will read your code. Make it easier to read and debug for yourself by segmenting out branching and looping code from sequential code that is supposed to execute one statement after the other.

LAB 14.1

HOW AN IF-ELSE STATEMENT WORKS

If the expression in an `if-else` statement is true (non-null or non-zero), then statement one is executed. If it is false (null or zero) and you have an `else` statement, then statement two is executed. Otherwise, if no `else` is provided and the `if` expression is false, execution begins at the next statement after the `if` statement.

Examples of the most common structure of `if-else` statements are as follows:

```
1.  if (expr)
       x=3
2.  if (expr) x=3
3.  if (expr) x=5; else x=3
4.  if (expr)
       x=5
    else
       x=3
```

■ FOR EXAMPLE:

An example of a program that uses an `if-else` statement follows:

```
if ($2 == "Adhesions")
        register_adh = register_adh++
else
        not_reg_adh = not_reg_adh++
```

If the second field of the `courses.data` file for the current record is equal to "Adhesions," that is non-null, then statement one gets executed, incrementing the "registered in adhesions" counter (`register_adh`) by one. If $2 is not equal to "Adhesions," then statement two gets executed, incrementing the "not registered" counter by one.

GROUPING STATEMENTS WITHIN AN IF-ELSE STATEMENT

If more than one statement follows the `if` expression, and curly braces surround the statements; collectively they are known as a grouping statement. When grouping statements in an `if-else` statement, follow these syntactical rules:

- Either a semicolon or a newline can separate multiple statements.
- The group of statements must be contained within curly braces.
- The first statement can follow the opening brace or be placed on the next line.
- The closing brace is placed after the last statement either on the same line or on the next.
- Spaces and/or tabs may precede or follow an opening or closing brace.

■ FOR EXAMPLE:

The following is an example of the `if-else` syntax with more than one action statement:

```
if (expr) {
    action1
}
else {
    action2
}
```

This could also be written as:

```
if (expr)
{ action1
}
else
{ action2
}
```

`action1` and `action2` can be one statement or multiple statements, each of which is separated by a statement separator. These two forms are the most common conventions used by programmers when using braces. The use of braces tells the interpreter which statements you wish to execute as a group if the condition is true. For this same reason, a pattern is separated from an action using braces, as explained earlier in this book.

LAB 14.1 EXERCISES

14.1.1 UNDERSTAND THE SYNTAX OF AN IF-ELSE STATEMENT

a) Are the following valid `if-else` statements?

```
if (x>80)        y++
else y-
```

_____

```
if (x>80) y++
else
     y-
```

_____

```
if (x>80)        y++;
else y-
```

_____

```
if (x>80)
    y++
else y--
```

```
if (x>80)
    y++;
else y--;
```

Awk also allows multiple `if-else` statements in the same program. You can see the syntax for them in the next program.

b) What does the following program do?

```
{if ($2 == "Adhesions") count_adh++
        else if ($2 == "Coatings") count_coat++
        else if ($2 == "Resins") count_res++
        else count_stab++
}

END \{ print count_adh,count_coat,count_res,count_stab
    }/
```

---

c) What is wrong with the program?

14.1.2 WRITE PROGRAMS USING THE IF-ELSE STATEMENT

Write a program that calculates the ending balance for a customer, given a file of withdrawals and deposits. The first line of the file contains the numerical starting balance as the second field, with the letter b signifying the starting balance. Use the following example file:

```
b 1200
d 200
w 400
w 800
d 200
w 500
d 700
```

The d signifies a deposit, and the w signifies a withdrawal. The only other stipulation is that if the person has a negative balance due to withdrawing too much money, a service charge of $15 is levied against the account. Assume that all numbers represent dollars.

a) What is the program?

_____

_____

Use the following data for the next question:

```
33
27
7
15
8
12
28
15
16
6
11
```

b) Write a program that prints the following histogram. Given the data, each asterisk indicates that the input number falls in the appropriate range:

```
30-39 *
20-29 **
10-19 *****
 0-9 ***
```

The asterisks in this example indicate that one number fell into the 30-39 range, two numbers fell into the 20-29 range, five numbers fell into the 10-19 range, and three numbers fell into the 0-9 range.

LAB 14.1 ANSWERS

This section gives you some suggested answers to the questions in Lab 19.1, with discussion related to those answers. Your answers may vary, but the most important thing is whether or not your answer works. Use this discussion to analyze differences between your answers and those presented here.

If you have alternative answers to the questions in this Exercise, you are encouraged to post your answers and discuss them at the companion Web site for this book, located at:

```
http://www.phptr.com/phptrinteractive/
```

14.1.1 ANSWERS

a) Are the following valid `if-else` statements?

```
if (x>80)          y++
else y—
```

Answer: Yes

Spaces can occur between the right parenthesis and the statement. And the `else` can start on a new line.

```
if (x>80) y++
else
    y—
```

Answer: Yes

At least one space occurs between the right parenthesis and the state-ment. In addition, a statement can appear on the next line after an `else` statement.

```
if (x>80)          y++;
else y-
```

Answer: Yes

A semicolon can appear after any single statement.

```
if (x>80)
     y++
else y--
```

Answer: Yes

An `else` statement can follow a single statement in an `if` statement, even if the statement appears on a single line.

```
if (x>80)
     y++;
else y--;
```

Answer: Yes

Semicolons can terminate any statement. If multiple semicolons are immediately next to each other, then an empty statement is created by the translator. An empty statement performs no execution. A smart com-piler or interpreter will optimize any out.

b) What does the following program do?
```
{if ($2 == "Adhesions") count_adh++
        else if ($2 == "Coatings") count_coat++
        else if ($2 == "Resins") count_res++
        else count_stab++
}
END \{ print count_adh,count_coat,count_res,count_stab
    }/
```

Answer: The program prints out the number of people registered for each course.

In this example, we create multiple `if-else` statements because we want to increment a counter based on whether one of several possible conditions is true. Each conditional checks for which course the registrant is registered. If the course is an Adhesions course, then we want to increment the counter for Adhesions. Similarly, the other courses should be incremented based on the result of their conditionals. This example illustrates that multiple `if-else` statements may be nested. The innermost `if` statement is associated with the innermost `else` statement (i.e., `else count_stab++` is associated with (`$2 == "Resins"`). To avoid ambiguity, braces may be used to explicitly associate each `if-else` pair, as follows:

```
if ($2 == "Adhesions") {
        count_adh++
}
else {
        if ($2 == "Coatings") {
                count_coat++
        }
        else {
                if ($2 == "Resins") {
                        count_res++
                }
                else {
                        count_stab++
                }
        }
}
```

Multiple statements could also then be inserted within any of the braces.

c) What is wrong with the program?

Answer: The problem with this program is that if a course contained in the file has a course name other than Adhesions, Coatings, Resins, or Stabilizers, that course will be counted in the number of people registered for the Stabilizers course.

Let's use the example course name "Emulsions." Therefore, the value of `$2` is "`Emulsions.`" Let's analyze the conditionals:

1. `if ($2 == "Adhesions")` returns false, so it ignores the action and moves to the next statement;
2. `else if ($2 == "Coatings")` also returns false, so we move along;
3. `else if ($2 == "Resins")` also returns false;

4. The next statement, being `else count_stab++`, is thus executed because none of the other conditions were met, incorrectly incrementing the number of people registered for Stabilizers.

The problem of not checking for error conditions in processing input files can happen and can cause incorrect results. It may occur because you did not think that data other than what you expected would be in the file (the Emulsions course, for example). It may also occur because of typographical errors (i.e., entering "Stabolozers" in the input file for a course name).

Always check for error conditions in the last `else` statement that is part of a nested `if-else` statement. We call this last `else` statement the default action.

14.1.2 ANSWERS

Write a program that calculates the ending balance of a customer, given a file of withdrawals and deposits. Assume all numbers represent dollars.

a) What is the program?

Answer: The program is as follows:

```
{if ($1 == "b") balance = $2
 else if ($1 == "d") balance += $2
 else if ($1 == "w") {
          balance -= $2
          if (balance < 0)
              balance -= 15
          }
       else print $1, " Not Recognized"
}
END {print balance}
```

The output of this program is:
585

The program uses an `if` statement to check whether the transaction character is a b, w, or d. If the character is a b, then it assumes that the next field contains the starting balance. If it is a d, the program assumes that the transaction is a deposit and adds the second field to the balance. If it is a w, the second field is subtracted from the balance. Additionally, after subtracting the second field, an `if` statement checks whether the balance is less than zero. If so, then a $15 surcharge is subtracted from the balance. Notice three things about this program. First, if "b" occurs in the first field in a line other than line number 1, the second field of that line will be reassigned as the starting balance. We do not check for that error. Lastly, notice that we have multiple `if-else` statements. The rule is that the innermost `else` is associated with the innermost `if`. So in our example, the `else print $1 "Not Recognized"` statement is associated with `if ($1 == "w")`. Notice that it is not associated with `if (balance < 0)`, because that statement is enclosed in braces.

b) Write a program that prints the following histogram. Given the data, each asterisk indicates that the input number falls in the appropriate range:

```
30-39 *
20-29 **
10-19 *****
 0-9 ***
```

Answer: The program is as follows:

```
{ if ($1 > 29 && $1 < 40)
     count30 = count30 "*"
   else if ($1 > 19 && $1 < 30)
     count20 = count20 "*"
   else if ($1 > 9 && $1 < 20)
     count10 = count10 "*"
   else if ($1 > 0 && $1 < 10)
     count = count "*"
   else print "Error: Not in Range"
}

END {  print "30-39 ", count30
       print "20-29 ", count20
       print "10-19 ", count10
       print "  0-9 ", count
    }
```

The output is as follows:

```
30-39   *
20-29   **
10-19   *****
 0-9    ***
```

The program first determines to which range the number read in belongs. It then concatenates an asterisk to a counter variable corresponding to that range. It prints an error message if the number does not belong in any of the four ranges. The reason that we concatenate asterisks instead of incrementing numerically the counter variable is that we need to print asterisks at the end, and we have no way to determine how many that will be. So in our `print` statement, we don't know how many variables the print statement will contain. After determining the string count, the program in the END pattern prints the histogram out for each range.

LAB 14.1 SELF-REVIEW QUESTIONS

In order to test your progress, you should be able to answer the following questions.

1) The `else` clause of an `if` statement is optional.
    a) _____True
    b) _____False

2) A newline is optional after the right parenthesis.
    a) _____True
    b) _____False

3) A newline is required after statement one.
    a) _____True
    b) _____False

4) If an `else` part appears on the same line as statement one of the `if` clause, then the semicolon is optional after statement one.
    a) _____True
    b) _____False

5) If the conditional that is part of the `if` clause is true, then the `else` statement is executed.
  a) _____True
  b) _____False

6) If braces are part of an `if-else` statement, then the brace must appear on the same line as the `if` clause.
  a) _____True
  b) _____False

7) When nesting `if-else` statements, the innermost `else` clause is associated with the innermost `if` statement.
  a) _____True
  b) _____False

Quiz answers appear in Appendix A, Section 19.1.

L A B　14.2

THE WHILE AND DO STATEMENTS

LAB OBJECTIVES

After this Lab, you will be able to:

✓ Understand the Results of Using a While Statement
✓ Write Programs Using While and Do Statements

THE WHILE STATEMENT

Loops enable you to perform an action multiple times while an expression is true. The `while` statement has the following form:

```
while (expression)
     action
```

Basically, this says "While `expression` is true, perform `action` until expression is false"

The following are the syntactical rules to apply when working with the while statement:

- Newlines are optional after the right parenthesis.
- Statements may be indented if on a newline.
- As with the `if-else` statement, an action consisting of more than one statement must be enclosed in braces.

The same rules apply to braces as with an `if-else` statement:

- The first statement can follow the opening brace or be placed on the next line.
- The closing brace is put after the last statement, either on the same line or the next.
- You cannot avoid using braces by instead using semicolons to separate multiple statements on a single line. You must use braces.
- Spaces and/or tabs may precede or follow an opening or closing brace.

HOW A WHILE STATEMENT WORKS

**LAB
14.2**

The `while` statement evaluates the expression at the top of the loop, and if the expression is true (1), then the action is performed. After the action is executed, the expression is evaluated once again and continues to execute the action until the expression is false (0).

Examples of the most common structure of `while` statements are as follows:

```
1.   while (expr)
         statement
2.   while (expr) statement
3.   while (expr) {
         action

     }
4.   while (expr)
         { action
     }
```

■ FOR EXAMPLE:

The following program illustrates how it is used:

```
{i=1;
 while (i <= NF) {
     print $i
     i++
 }
}
```

This program prints out the value for each field in the current input record. As you recall, NF is the number of fields, and i is a counter that is used to reference each field. The while loop expression consists of a relational expression that checks whether i is less than the number of fields, NF. The counter is initialized with the value one. Let's say for illustrative purposes that NF is five. The first time through, NF is five, which is greater than the variable i, which is one. Therefore, the action enclosed within braces is executed. It prints out the value for the current field that is determined by the variable i. i is then incremented (i++), and the process is continued, printing the current field until i is equal to the total number of fields in the current input record.

DO LOOP

LAB 14.2

The do loop (or do-while loop) is similar to the while loop, except an action is first performed at least once before the condition is tested. The do loop has the following form:

```
do
    action
while (condition)
```

The following are the syntactical rules to apply when working with do loops.

- Newline is optional after do.
- Newline is also optional after the action.
- If while appears on the same line as the action, then the action must be terminated by a semicolon if it is a single statement.

In the do-while statement, the action is executed once, and then the expression is evaluated. If it is true, returns 1, then the action is executed repeatedly until the expression is false, zero.

The most common forms of the do-while statement are as follows:

```
1.  do
        statement
    while (condition)
2.  do statement while (condition)
```

3.  ```
    do {
       action
    } while (condition)
    ```
4.  ```
    do
    {
       action
    }
    ```

■ FOR EXAMPLE:

The following program is an example of how the do-while statement is used:

```
awk $1 ~ /^[0-9]+$/   '{ number = $1
                         do
                            number /= 10
                                     num_of_digits++
                                     while (number != 0)
                                     print "number of digits is ",
            num_of_digits
                         }
```

This program counts the number of digits that are found in a number. The pattern checks whether the first field is a number. If the pattern matches, then the action is executed. The first statement in the action assigns the number in the first field to the variable number. The next statement divides the number ten. If you had the number 150, then dividing by ten would result in the variable number containing the value 15. This shifts the number 150 one to the right and counts each least significant digit (in this case, zero). This process is continued until the most significant digit (one) is counted.

Why use a do-while statement in this case instead of a while statement? Consider the following program:

```
awk $1 ~ /^[0-9]+$/   '{ number = $1
                         while (number !=0) {
                            number /= 10
                                     num_of_digits++
                                     }
                                     print "number of digits is ",
            num_of_digits
                         }
```

The problem here is that if you are given the number zero, then you should get a count of 1 digit. However, this program would exit the loop before the increment to the num_of_digits.

LAB 14.2 EXERCISES

14.2.1 UNDERSTAND THE RESULTS OF USING A WHILE STATEMENT

Use the following file to answer the questions in this Exercise:

```
Jones 1000.00 w 200.00 w 100.00 d 500.00
Smith 5000.00 w 3000.00 d 300.00 w 1000.00
Taylor 3000.00 d 3000.00 w 2500.00
```

**LAB
14.2**

a) What output does the following program produce?

```
awk '{ print $1, "Beginning Balance Is ", $2
            i=3; balance=$2
            while (i <= NF ) {
                if ($i == "w")
                        balance-=$(i+1)
                else
                        balance+=$(i+1)
                i+=2
            }
            print $1, "Ending Balance Is ", balance
        }' input_file
```

_____

_____

b) What circumstances would make the program not work correctly?

_____

_____

14.2.2 WRITE PROGRAMS USING WHILE AND DO STATEMENTS

Use the following as input files for the first Exercise here.

The first file contains all the courses a student has taken, and all the test scores for those courses:

```
Fall98.dat

Calculus 50 78 83 88 90
PChem 90 92 97 88 85
Thermodynamics 77 89 93 75 70
```

LAB
14.2

The second file contains a breakdown of courses taken from a department, the grade point average (GPA) for courses related to that department, and the number of courses taken in that department:

```
OvGrades.dat

Mathematics 92 2
Physics 90 4
History 80 3
```

a) Write a program that calculates the grade average for each course, the GPA for that semester of courses, and the student's overall GPA.

_____

_____

b) Write a program that calculates the number of occurrences that a word appears in a file.

_____

_____

Assume that the first input record in the file contains the word to find. Use any text file that you have lying around and insert the word to be searched for in the first line of the text file.

LAB 14.2 EXERCISE ANSWERS

This section gives you some suggested answers to the questions in Lab 14.2, with discussion related to those answers. Your answers may vary, but the most important thing is whether or not your answer works. Use this discussion to analyze differences between your answers and those presented here.

If you have alternative answers to the questions in this Exercise, you are encouraged to post your answers and discuss them at the companion Web site for this book, located at:

LAB
14.2

http://www.phptr.com/phptrinteractive/

14.2.1 ANSWERS

Use the given file to answer the questions in this Exercise.

a) What output does the following program produce?

```
awk '{ print $1, "Beginning Balance Is ",  $2
           i=3; balance=$2
           while (i <= NF ) {
               if ($i == "w")
                     balance-=$(i+1)
               else
                     balance+=$(i+1)
               i+=2
           }
           print $1, "Ending Balance Is ", balance
       }' input_file
```

Answer: The output is as follows:

```
Jones Beginning Balance Is  1000.00
Jones Ending Balance Is  1200
Smith Beginning Balance Is  5000.00
Smith Ending Balance Is  1300
Taylor Beginning Balance Is  3000.00
Taylor Ending Balance Is  3500
```

b) What circumstances would make the program not work correctly?

Answer: *In the* else *statement, any character other than a "w" will be considered a deposit. Again, checking for an error condition should be included whenever possible.*

The program uses $(i + 1)$ to get the next field after the transaction character. The counter variable is incremented by two to position the counter variable to the next transaction character, because two fields are associated with each field: a transaction character and a numerical dollar value to be used in the transaction. The numerical value referenced by $(i+1)$ is added or subtracted according to whether the value referenced by (i) was a "w" or not.

**LAB
14.2**

14.2.2 ANSWERS

For this Exercise, you were given two files containing data related to courses and grades.

a) Write a program that calculates the grade average for each course, the GPA for that semester of courses, and the student's overall GPA.

Answer: *The program and its output are as follows:*

```
# if the filename is equal to fall98.dat then process
  then for each input line calculate

# the average for each class
FILENAME == "fall98.dat" { i=2; sum=0;

    # calculate each test score in current line
         while (i<=NF) {
             sum += $i
             i++

    }

# the average for the class is sum/NF -1 $1 is class name
```

```
              average += sum/(NF-1)
                      courses++
                                }

# if the filename is ovgrades.dat then total courses
     will be used in the final GPA calculation. Total_gpa

# is the total sum of all grades
FILENAME == "ovgrades.dat" {total_courses+=$3
              total_gpa += ($2 * $3)
                                        }
END { print "Semester GPA = ", average/courses
       print "Overall  GPA = ",  (average+total_gpa)  /
     (courses + total_courses)
          }
```

The output is:
Semester GPA =   83
Overall GPA =   86.0833

In the first pattern-action, the first pattern is matched when the file name is equal to `fall98.dat`. In this case, you then need to figure out the GPA of the student for all classes s/he is taken this current semester. The action calculates this by using a `while` statement to loop through all test scores. Each input line in this file is a course name and all test scores received in that particular course. The `while` statement adds up each test score until it has no more test scores to add, a point that is determined by the number of fields. The counter variable starts at two because field number one is the course name.

After the `while` statement, the GPA for the whole semester is first determined by keeping a running total of the sum of each course average. The variable `courses` is incremented, which contains the total number of courses the student is enrolled in for the current semester. These two variables average, and `courses` will be divided to get the GPA for the current semester. The second pattern-action statement is used to read in the courses and grades received by the student for all semesters. These are used to calculate the total GPA. `total_courses` keeps a running count of the total number of courses the student has taken in all semesters. The third field is the number of courses the student has taken in that department. This is added to `total_courses` to keep a running count. `total_gpa` tries to recreate a sum of all grades received by multiplying the department average of all courses with the number of courses taken in that department. In the end, the current semester grade is obtained by dividing the average (a sum of all grades calculated) by the number of courses taken in that semester. The overall GPA in all courses is taken by adding total_gpa to average and dividing by all courses taken to date, which is courses plus total_courses.

b) Write a program that calculates the number of occurrences that a word appears in a file. HINT: Assume that the first input record in the file contains the word to find.

Answer: The program is as follows:

```
{ if (NR==1)
      search_word=$1
   else {
      i=1
      while (i<NF) {
          if ($i == search_word)
              count++
          i++
      }
   }
}

END {print count}
```

The program works by first obtaining the search word that you wish to find. This is found in the first field of the input record read in. Therefore, the action first performs the if statement and checks whether the built-in variable NR is one, indicating that we are processing the first input record. If so, then the search word is assigned the first field of the first input record, which contains the search word. Otherwise, the else statement is executed. It sets the counter variable i to one. The while loop is then used to loop through all fields in the current input record (one through NF). If the current field, $i, contains the search word, then the if statement evaluates to true, and a count of the number of found search words is incremented to one.

LAB 14.2 SELF-REVIEW QUESTIONS

In order to test your progress, you should be able to answer the following questions.

1) If an action in a `do-while` statement has multiple statements, it must be enclosed in braces.
   a) _____True
   b) _____False

2) A `do` statement performs the same function as a `while` statement.
   a) _____True
   b) _____False

3) Space(s) and/or tab(s) must precede and follow the opening and closing brace in a `while` or `do` statement.
   a) _____True
   b) _____False

4) In a `do` statement, the action is executed at least once before the condition is tested.
   a) _____True
   b) _____False

5) An assignment may be made in a conditional of a `while` statement, as follows:
   ```
   while ((amount = $1) > 0)
   ```
   a) _____True
   b) _____False

Quiz answers appear in Appendix A, Section 14.2.

L A B   14.3

THE FOR STATEMENT

LAB OBJECTIVES

After this Lab, you will be able to:

✓ Understand the Results of Using the For Statement

✓ Write Programs Using the For Statement

The `for` statement provides another convenient looping mechanism, yet is more terse than its equivalent `while` statement. Its format is as follows:

```
for (counter; test; increment)
    action
```

The following are the syntactical rules to apply when working with the `for` statement:

- Newlines are optional after the right parenthesis.
- The statement may be indented if on a newline.
- As with the `if-else` and `while` statements, an action consisting of more than one statement must be enclosed in braces.

The same rules apply to braces as with an `if-else` and `while` statements:

- The first statement can follow the opening brace or be placed on the next line.
- The closing brace is put after the last statement, either on the same line or the next.

- You cannot avoid using braces by instead using semicolons to separate multiple statements on a single line. You must use braces.
- Spaces and/or tabs may precede or follow an opening or closing brace.

The `for` loop uses three expressions, `counter`, `test`, and `increment`, which are explained as follows:

- **counter**—Usually sets the initial value for a counter variable.
- **test**—States a condition that is tested at the top of the loop.
- **increment**—Usually increments the counter each time at the bottom of the loop, after the action and right before testing the condition.

Note the use of "usually" in the preceding list. All three statements are optional in a `for` statement.

LAB 14.3

Therefore, the `for` statement is a lot like the following `while` statement:

```
counter statement
while (test) {
        action
        increment statement
}
```

In the `for` statement, the `counter` statement is evaluated first. After this evaluation, the `test` statement is evaluated. If the comparison is true. (1) , then the action is evaluated. After the action is evaluated, the `increment` statement is evaluated last. These steps, except for the `counter` statement, will continually evaluate until the test statement is false, (zero).

The following are the most common forms of a `for` statement:

```
1.  for (counter; test; increment) action;
2.  for (counter; test; increment)
            action;
```

3. for (counter; test; increment) {
       action

   }
4. for (counter; test; increment)
   { action
   }

■ FOR EXAMPLE:

The following statement shows an example of the `for` statement:

```
for (i=0; i<NF; i++)
    print $i
```

This program initializes the counter variable i to 0 in the counter statement section of the `for` statement, before any other statement is evaluated in the `for` statement. The counter variable is then compared in the
test statement. If it is less than the number of fields, NF, and evaluates to
true, then the action is executed. Afterward, the counter is incremented.
The comparison is repeated, and the action is continually executed until
the comparison is false—the number of fields is equal to the counter i.
This program, therefore, prints all the fields in the current input record.

*I find that, once fixated on either prefix or postfix, programmers generally
continue that style throughout all `for` statements. I, like most programmers, tend to use the postfix notation in a `for` statement.*

LAB 14.3 EXERCISES

14.3.1 UNDERSTAND THE RESULTS OF USING THE FOR STATEMENT

a) Are the following valid `for` statements? What do they do?
```
For (i=1; i<=NF; i+=1)
    print $i
```

_____

_____

LAB
14.3

```
For (; i<=NF; i++)
    print $0
```

```
For (;;;)
    print "Start of Loop"
```

```
i=2
For (start_balance=$1*150; i<NF; i++)
    balance -= ($i * 150)
```

---

b) What does the following program do?

```
for (i=1; $i !~ /^[0-9][0-9]\/[0-9][0-9]\/[0-9][0-9]$
    && i<NF; i++);
if (i<NF) {
    month = 0 + substr($i, 0, 2);
    day = 0 + substr($i, 2, 2);
    year = 0 + substr($i, 4, 2);
}
print day, month, year
```

14.3.2 WRITE PROGRAMS USING THE FOR STATEMENT

To derive the factorial of a number, say six, you would perform the following multiplication:

```
6 x 5 x 4 x 3 x 2 x 1
```

As you can see, you would continually multiply by one less until you reach one.

a) Write a program that calculates the factorial of six.

_____

_____

LAB 14.3 EXERCISE ANSWERS

LAB
14.3

This section gives you some suggested answers to the questions in Lab 14.3, with discussion related to those answers. Your answers may vary, but the most important thing is whether or not your answer works. Use this discussion to analyze differences between your answers and those presented here.

If you have alternative answers to the questions in this Exercise, you are encouraged to post your answers and discuss them at the companion Web site for this book, located at:

```
http://www.phptr.com/phptrinteractive/
```

14.3.1 ANSWERS

a) Are the following valid `for` statements? What do they do?
```
For (i=1; i<=NF; i+=1)
     print $i
```

Answer: Yes, this is valid.

The program prints each field from the current input record, using the output field separator (`OFS`) (see Chapter 11, "Variables") as the output separator between fields. The `for` loop starts printing $1 first.

```
For (; i<=NF; i++)
     print $0
```

Answer: Yes, this is valid.

The `counter` statement is optional and is not provided in this example. The `for` loop prints $0 for every field in the input record. So the number of times that $0 is printed is NF*NR times.

```
For (;;;)
     print "Start of Loop"
```

Answer: Yes, this is valid.

All statements in a `for` loop are optional. Therefore, this `for` loop is an infinite loop. It has no test, so it will always evaluate to true. Therefore, this program prints "`Start of Loop`" forever.

```
i=2
For (start_balance=$1*150; i<NF; i++)
     balance -= ($i * 150)
```

**LAB
14.3**

Answer: Yes, this is valid.

The `counter` variable can be given an initial value as the result of an expression. Assuming that NF is greater than 301 (`start_balance` = 2 * 150), the balance is subtracted by the value of $i.

b) What does the following program do?
```
for (i=1; $i !~ /^[0-9][0-9]\/[0-9][0-9]\/[0-9][0-9]$
     && i<NF; i++);
if (i<NF) {
     month = 0 + substr($i, 0, 2);
     day = 0 + substr($i, 2, 2);
     year = 0 + substr($i, 4, 2);
}
print day, month, year
```
Answer: This program looks for a field in the current input record that looks like a valid date string. The field matches the following string:
dd/dd/dd   *where d is a digit between 0-9*

I emphasize *looks like a valid date string* (the date 34/99/99 will be matched). Notice that the `for` statement has a semicolon at the end. This is valid and means that no action will be performed in the `for` loop except for the `counter`, `test`, and `increment` statements that are part of the `for` statement. Specifying no action in a `for` loop is useful in situations where all you care about is cycling through a variable and positioning the counter variable at a certain position based on a test condition. This is what is done in our example. We cycle through the counter variable `i`, positioning `i` to the current field variable (this field is referenced by `i` and `$i`) in the input line. We do this based on the regular expression, which is a valid date. The other condition in the `for` statement, `i<NF`, is used so that the loop eventually terminates (the case that the current line contains no valid date).

If `(i<NF)` is found, then the loop terminates. We then test the condition `(i<NF)` to maintain that the `for` loop ended because a valid date was found and not because we could not find a valid date (if a date was not found, `i=NF`). Notice that when the `for` loop ends, we reference `i` in the `if` statement. This is valid because it retains its value after a `for` loop. If a date was found, the next three statements are executed. `$i` is then used to extract and convert the month, day, and year using the `substr` function.

**LAB
14.3**

Remember that the increment statement in a `for` loop is performed after the test statement of the loop.

The `print` statement prints the day, month, year instead of the input form of month, day, year.

14.3.2 ANSWERS

a) Write a program that calculates the factorial of six.

Answer: The program is as follows:
```
{ total =1
   for (i=6;  i>0;  i--)
      total *= i
}
END { print total }
```
The output is:
720

The program starts by setting the counter variable to six to hardcode the factorial of six. The `for` statement uses the autodecrement operator to reduce the counter variable by one. The action inside the `for` loop multiplies the current running total of the factorial of six by the counter variable. So after the first statement is executed, the total is 6 * 1 = 6. After the second iteration of the loop, the total is 6 * 5 = 30. After the third, the total is 30 * 4 = 120.

LAB 14.3 SELF-REVIEW QUESTIONS

In order to test your progress, you should be able to answer the following questions.

1) A `for` statement can equivalently be transformed into a `while` statement.
   a) _____True
   b) _____False

2) The increment part of a `for` statement is optional.
   a) _____True
   b) _____False

3) The counter part of a `for` statement is optional.
   a) _____True
   b) _____False

4) The action may not be indented if on a newline.
   a) _____True
   b) _____False

5) Semicolons must separate the counter, test, and increment part of a `for` statement.
   a) _____True
   b) _____False

6) The test part of a `for` statement is required.
   a) _____True
   b) _____False

Quiz answers appear in Appendix A, Section 14.3.

**LAB
14.3**

L A B   14.4

LOOP AND PROGRAM CONTROL

LAB OBJECTIVES

After this Lab, you will be able to:

✓ Understand the Results of Executing a Break, Continue, Next, or Exit Statement

✓ Write Programs Using These Statements

These statements in this Lab affect the flow of control of the looping structures we have seen so far. Each statement differs in two ways: the result of executing the statement and the looping structure it affects.

BREAK STATEMENT

A `break` statement causes an exit from the immediately enclosing `while`, `for`, or `do` statement. As a result, the loop exits, and no more iterations of the loop are performed.

■ *FOR EXAMPLE:*

An example is the following loop:

```
for (i=1; i<NF; i++) {
    if ($3=="Jones")
        break
    else
        print $i
}
print "Out of Loop"
```

Suppose that the record containing "Jones" is as follows:

```
066-98-0034 Fred Jones 200 20 Coatings
```

Then the output of the `for` statement on this line would be:

066-98-0034
Fred
Out of Loop

The important point to understand is that when the `break` statement is encountered, the loop is stopped and execution begins at the statement following the loop. In this program, all the fields for the current input record are printed one line at a time. A `for` statement is used to cycle through each field using the counter variable `i`. If the third field for the current input record has a value of "Jones," then the `for` loop encounters a `break` statement inside the `if` statement. The program's control resumes to the `print` statement after the loop as a result of executing the `break` statement. The program then prints the string `Out of Loop`. Notice that the first two fields of the current input record are printed. The value of the counter variable is 3 when the `break` statement is encountered. Therefore, the `else` part of the `if-else` statement was encountered two times before the `break` statement was executed. For that reason, two lines of output from the current input record contain `Jones` as the third field.

**LAB
14.4**

CONTINUE STATEMENT

The `continue` statement causes the next iteration of the loop to be executed. It causes execution to begin at the increment statement in a `for` loop, or the comparison expression in a `while` or `do-while` statement.

■ FOR EXAMPLE:

The following program excerpt is changed slightly from that shown in the break section:

```
for (i=1; i<NF; i++) {
    if ($2=="Fred")
        continue
    else
        print $i
}
print "Out of Loop"
```

Just as before, suppose that the record that contains "Fred" is as follows:

```
066-98-0034 Fred Jones 200 20 Coatings
```

Then the output of the for statement on this line would be:

```
066-98-0034
Jones
200
20
Coatings
Out of Loop
```

Again, inside the for statement, when the value for the second field of the current input record is equal to "Fred," then the continue statement is encountered. At that point, the counter variable i is equal to two, and the first field has been printed as a result when the counter variable was one. The continue statement causes control to pass to the increment statement in the for loop, i++. The counter variable, as a result of executing the continue statement, then becomes three and the loop is continued.

NEXT STATEMENT

When executed, the next statement causes awk to read in the next input record and begin matching patterns starting from the first pattern-action

statement in the program. Next performs the same functionality as continue when you consider the awk programming model of a main processing loop. Therefore, next transforms control back to the main
processing loop, and awk reads the next input record until no more
records remain to be read. After reading all records, control transfers to
the next pattern-action statement if more than one exists. If one does not
exist, then control transfers to the END pattern if one exists, or it exits.

■ FOR EXAMPLE:

A typical example of the next statement is as follows:

```
awk   FILENAME == "OneFileNameOutOfMany" {
        action
        next
        }
        {
        do something else
        }
```

While the built-in variable FILENAME is equal to the file name string in the
comparison, then the first pattern-action statement will be executed. In
the action statement, some action is performed and then the next statement is encountered. Awk then reads in the next input record and control
is then resumed at the first pattern-action. This pattern-action statement is
then repeatedly executed until the end of file is encountered and the next
file opened for reading. As a result, this generalized pattern-action can be
used when you want to read in a whole file and perform some action
before either processing another file or performing some calculation.

**LAB
14.4**

Understand that after the next statement is encountered and the next
input read in, the matching starts at the first pattern-action. However, if
the pattern does not match, processing continues with the second pattern-action if a second pattern exists.

EXIT STATEMENT

The exit statement acts differently, depending on whether it is encountered in an END statement or within a pattern-action statement. If the
exit statement is encountered within a pattern-action statement, control

passes to the END pattern if one is encountered. Otherwise, the program terminates and exits. If the `exit` statement is encountered in an END pattern, then the program simply exits. The `exit` statement can take an expression as an argument. The value of this statement is returned as the exit status as the result of running awk.

Lab 14.4 Exercises

14.4.1 Understand the Results of Executing a Break, Continue, Next, or Exit Statement

a) Does the number of comparisons differ if we process a file as follows?

```
{ if (filename == "xxxx")
        action
        next
    if (filename == "yyyy")
        action
        next
    if (filename == "zzzz")
        action
        next
}
```

or as follows?

```
filename == "xxxx" {action}
filename == "yyyy" {action}
filename == "zzzz" {action}
```

14.4.2 WRITE PROGRAMS USING THESE STATEMENTS

Use the following file for the first question in this Exercise:

```
# This program is an example

for (i=0; i<=NF; i++) {
        if (i == 3)                 # print the third field
                print $i
}
```

a) Using the given file, write a program that parses a line of text until it encounters a comment character, and outputs the line of text up to the comment character. The comment character for this program will be the character #. Use a `break` statement inside a `for` statement.

_____

_____

b) What is the output?

_____

_____

c) Write a program that checks whether any operands in a division are 0, prints an error message if any are zero, and then exits with a zero value.

_____

_____

LAB 14.4 EXERCISE ANSWERS

 This section gives you some suggested answers to the questions in Lab 14.4, with discussion related to those answers. Your answers may vary, but the most important thing is whether or not your answer works. Use this discussion to analyze differences between your answers and those presented here.

If you have alternative answers to the questions in this Exercise, you are encouraged to post your answers and discuss them at the companion Web site for this book, located at:

http://www.phptr.com/phptrinteractive/

14.4.1 ANSWERS

a) Does the number of comparisons differ between the two ways of processing a file?

Answer: Yes, the first program has fewer comparisons.

In the first program, "xxxx" gets compared each time for each record in "xxxx." Because the next statement begins execution at the top of the script, "xxxx" then gets compared again, once for each record in "yyyy" and each record in "zzzz." Similarly, "yyyy" gets compared for each record in both "yyyy" and "zzzz." The total number of comparisons in the first program is:

```
(3 * #records in "zzzz") + (2 * #records in "yyyy") +
(#records in "xxxx")
```

(3 * #records in "zzzz") is present because when the file "zzzz" is processed for each record in "zzzz," we have to evaluate the (file-name=="xxxx") and (filename=="yyyy") patterns. Therefore, three comparisons are performed for each record in "zzzz."

The total number of comparisons in the second program is:

```
(3 * #records in "xxxx") + (3 * #records in "yyyy") +
(3 * #records in "zzzz")
```

Because no `if` statements exist, every pattern gets evaluated for each input record of every input file.

14.4.2 ANSWERS

a) Using the given file, write a program that parses a line of text until it encounters a comment character, and outputs the line of text up to the comment character. The comment character for this program will be the character #. Use a break statement inside a for statement.

Answer: The program is as follows:

```
{ if ($0 !~ /#/)
      print $0
   else {
      outline = " "
      for (i=1; i<=NF; i++) {
          if ($i ~ /#/)
              break;
          else
              outline = outline " " $i
      }
      print outline
   }
}
```

The program first checks whether a comment character is contained in the current input line. If not, it just prints the entire line. If so, then it loops through the fields in the current line until the comment character is encountered, at which point the program breaks out of the loop and reads the next line, thus ignoring the comments.

**LAB
14.4**

b) What is the output?

Answer: The program prints the file without the comments (i.e., phrases preceded by the # character).

c) Write a program that checks whether any operands in a division are 0, prints an error message if any are zero, and then exits with a zero value.

Answer: The program is as follows:

```
{ if ($1 == 0 || $2 == 0)
      exit 0
   else
      print $1 /$2
}
```

This is a simple program that checks whether any operands are zero and exits with a zero result.

LAB 14.4 SELF-REVIEW QUESTIONS

In order to test your progress, you should be able to answer the following questions.

1) The break statement breaks out of the current iteration of a loop and continues with the next iteration.
   a) _____True
   b) _____False

2) The continue statement breaks out of the current iteration of a loop and continues with the next iteration.
   a) _____True
   b) _____False

3) If one pattern-action statement exists and no END pattern exists, then the exit statement exits the awk program.
   a) _____True
   b) _____False

4) An exit statement returns either a zero or one.
   a) _____True
   b) _____False

**LAB
14.4**

5) The next statement immediately reads in the next input line, splits up the input line into fields, and continues at the first pattern-action statement.
   a) _____True
   b) _____False

Quiz answers appear in Appendix A, Section 14.4.

CHAPTER 14

TEST YOUR THINKING

 The projects in this section are meant to have you utilize all of the skills that you have acquired throughout this chapter. The answers to these projects can be found at the companion Web site to this book, located at:

`http://www.phptr.com/phptrinteractive/`

Visit the Web site periodically to share and discuss your answers.

1) Why do you suppose that the grouping statement is introduced to an `if-else`, `while`, and `for` loop?

For the next Project, use the following line as input:

```
AddressHistory[1] = ASM I R
0x1:0x22222222..0x33333333 phys:44444444..55555555
```

The following should be the output of this Project:

```
1,0,1,1,22222222,33333333,44444444,55555555
```

2) Write a program that transforms the form of the input line to the form of the output line.

The output fields are transformed accorded to the following input fields:

Field 1: AddressHistory[1]

This is a dummy field; the text and value are skipped.

Field 2: =

This is a dummy field; the text and value are skipped.

Field 3: ASM Field

If the field contains the text ASM, then you are to output a 1.

If NoASM, then output 0.

Field 4: Instruction/Data Field

If the field contains an I, then it is an instruction access and you should output 0. If the next field contains D, then it is a data access and you should output 1.

Field 5: Read/Write Field

If the field contains an R, then it is a read access and you should output a 1. If the next field contains a W, then it is a write access and you should output a 0.

Field 6: ASN Field (Optional)

This field is the ASN (address space number). It is delimited by a colon character. It is a hex address and you should output the field as it is, except with the 0x that precedes the ASN stripped off.

Field 7: Virtual Address Span (Optional)

This field is the virtual address range of the memory access. It has a lower and upper address range. The range is represented in the following form:

```
0x33333333..0x77777777
```

The dots "..." separate the lower from the upper range.

You should output the lower address first as a text string with the 0x stripped off.

Field 8: phys

This is the text string that precedes the physical address span. It is delimited by a semicolon. It must appear before the physical address span to flag that a physical address span follows. It is not output when transforming the input line.

Field 9: Physical Address Span

This is the same as the virtual address, except that it is prefixed by the word phys. It should output the lower and upper addresses of the range as a text string with the 0x stripped off (as we did for the virtual address).

Therefore, the output should be as follows, with commas separating fields:

```
ASM,I_or_D,R_orW,ASN,VirtualAddrLo,VirtualAd-
drHi,PhysicalAddrLo,PhysAddrHi
```

Use the following file:

```
AddressHistory[1] = ASM I W
0x1:0x11111111..0x22222222 phys:aaaaaaaa..bbbbbbbb
```

```
AddressHistory[2] = ASM D R
0x1:0x22222222..0x33333333 phys:bbbbbbbb..cccccccc
AddressHistory[3] = ASM I R
0x1:0x33333333..0x44444444 phys:cccccccc..dddddddd
AddressHistory[4] = ASM D R
0x1:0x44444444..0x55555555 phys:dddddddd..eeeeeeee
AddressHistory[5] = ASM I W
0x1:0x55555555..0x66666666 phys:eeeeeeee..ffffffff
AddressHistory[6] = ASM D R
0x1:0x66666666..0x77777777 phys:11111111..22222222
AddressHistory[7] = ASM D R
0x1:0x77777777..0x88888888 phys:22222222..33333333
AddressHistory[8] = ASM I W
0x1:0x88888888..0x99999999 phys:33333333..44444444
AddressHistory[9] = ASM I W
phys:0xaaaaaaaa..0xbbbbbbbb
```

We will add the following stipulation. An asn and virtual address are optional. Therefore, the value `1:0x11111111..0x22222222` is optional. Therefore, the only requirement is that we must have a physical address range. The way we tell whether the asn and virtual address range have been left out is if after parsing the read/write field, the first field after the read/write field is the string "`phys`," then the asn and the virtual address range have been left out. What should be printed out as output will remain the same as described.

The Fibonacci series begins with 0 and 1, and has the property that each succeeding term is the sum of the previous two terms (i.e., in the following, the term that succeeds 8, which is 13, is the sum of the preceding two terms, 8 and 5):

```
0, 1, 1, 2, 3, 5, 8, 13, …
```

3) Write a program that calculates the Fibonacci series of n (Fibonacci(n)).
```
Fibonacci(0) = 1
Fibonacci(1) = 2
Fibonacci(2) = 3
Fibonacci(3) = 5
Fibonacci(4) = 8
```

C H A P T E R 15

AWK ARRAYS
AND FUNCTIONS

 Like variables, arrays come into existence simply by using them.

In this chapter, we will talk about awk arrays and user-defined functions. By the end of this chapter, you will be able to write almost all applications that you wish to implement using awk. Awk arrays provide a cohesive storage element, and awk functions enable us to execute common operations.

L A B   15.1

AWK ARRAYS

LAB OBJECTIVES

After this Lab, you will be able to:

✓ Understand the Results of Using Awk Arrays

✓ Write Programs Using Awk Arrays

Arrays provide a convenient mechanism by which multiple values may be referenced as a cohesive whole. As an example, each student may have multiple values representing grades that they have received for a course, yet we would like to treat all grades as a collective whole. An array of grades lets us do so. Therefore, like all other variables that we described in Chapter 14, "Awk Control Flow," arrays may be used to store or reference values, usually associated values. Like variables, they are also subject to initialization and declaration rules. Unlike variables, which are considered scalar in mathematical terms (they store one value), arrays store multiple values. Therefore, a mechanism must exist whereby their values can be accessed individually. Arrays also differ from variables in that they have specialized variables, control statements, and functions associated with their use. This Lab discusses these issues in detail.

**LAB
15.1**

■ FOR EXAMPLE:

An awk array is a built-in storage element, which is a one-dimensional array for referencing and storing array elements whose values can be any awk data type (string or number).

The syntax for storing a value into an array element is as follows:

```
array_name[subscript] = value
```

Here, `array_name` is the name, or identifier, of the `array` itself; subscript (also called *index*) is used to identify a particular array element; and `value` is the value associated with the array element. The following assigns values (each person's grade) to the array `History`:

```
History[1]=85
History[2]=95
History[3]=50
```

Here, the array name is `History`; each student is represented by the subscripts `[1]`, `[2]`, and `[3]`; and the values follow the equals signs. You can reference any element of this array by the array name, the subscript operator, and the subscript value—`History[1]`, for example.

The following syntax is used to reference an array element and retrieve the value associated with it:

```
array_name[subscript] = value
```

The subscript operator in awk is the square brackets. The subscript operator is used to index the subscript value and store it in a particular location in memory. You do not need to know where that particular value is actually stored. Conceptually, whether it is stored in disjoint or contiguous memory does not matter. All that matters is that we can use it as a collective whole by referring to it by its array name, or identifier, and can access each array element by using the subscript operator.

**LAB
15.1**

■ FOR EXAMPLE:

An example of using an array name (or identifier) and array element to reference the value associated with the array element is as follows:

```
x = History[1]
print x
```

This would print 85.

Therefore, an array name or identifier used with a subscript operator and subscript value can be either an lvalue or an rvalue. The following are all legal:

```
a[subscript] = length($0)
a[subscript] = $1
a[subscript] = $3 + count
a[subscript] = b[subscript]
a[subscript] = sqrt(b[subscript])
```

The characteristic that makes awk different from most other programming languages is that awk's array indices, or subscripts, are not numerical values as in most general-purpose programming languages, but rather are strings. So the following are all possible array indices:

```
array[1]
array["Jones"]
array[substr(1,3)]
array[count + 1]
```

Therefore, as we see, any expression that returns a string constant or number is a possible index. If the expression is a number, it will be converted into a string. Because awk arrays are associative arrays, we can think of array subscript values and the value associated with the subscript value as key-value pairs. The *key* is the subscript value, and the *value* is the value associated with the key.

■ FOR EXAMPLE:

So the following associates the key (last name) with the value (age):

```
array["Jones"]=85
```

Each key in an awk array is unique, and subsequent assignments to the same key override previous values. Therefore, the following assigns 34 to the array element "Jones" if the second assignment follows the first:

```
array["Jones"]=85
array["Jones"]=34
```

For now I will say that the following two array accesses are different:

```
array[USA]
array["USA"]
```

The first assumes that some variable USA exists that, if it is a number, must be converted into a string; otherwise, its value is to be used as the index into the array. The second assumes that the index is the string "USA" and this string should be looked up in the array to find the value represented by this location. Note that array subscripts can be used as sequential whole numbers and iterated through like other programming languages. This fact is demonstrated in the following two program excerpts:

```
for (i=1; i<=NF; i++)
    array[i] = i;
print array[2];

{ array[NR] = $0 }
```

The first excerpt uses a for loop and uses the counter variable i as an index into the array for storing the value of the counter variable i. The counter variable i is an index from one to the total number of fields. Therefore, print array[2] yields the value of the second array element, which is two. In awk, each array index that is used numerically starts at 0. Note, however, that the array subscript 1 and array subscript 10 would come before the array subscript 2. The reason is that when the array subscript 10 gets converted into its string equivalent "10," that string is less than the string equivalent of 2, which is "2." Also note that if subscripts are to be used as indices, then the index 4 is different from the index 04. Again, the reason has to do with awk rules for converting numbers into strings. The string "4" does not equal the string "04."

**LAB
15.1**

DECLARING AND INITIALIZING ARRAYS

Awk arrays, like all awk variables, are not explicitly declared and initialized. Awk arrays and array elements come into existence when they are referenced either as an lvalue or an rvalue. If an array element is not explicitly initialized by a previous assignment, then the default value is 0 for numeric or null for string. Therefore, the following statements each create or declare an array:

```
{ for (i=1; i<NF; i++)
       test[i] = $i
}

{ for (i=0; i<NF; i++)
       print array[i]
}
```

In the first excerpt, we initialize each array element with the value of each field read in. The last excerpt is a very strange program that results in finding out what value each array element contains when it was never assigned. The value of an array element that is accessed without explicitly being assigned an initial value is zero. Therefore, the program prints out zero NF times.

USING THE BUILT-IN LOOPING FOR STATEMENT

Consider the following array elements:

```
array["Jones"] = 13
array["Smith] = 12
array["Taylor"] = 11
array["Gregory"] = 16
```

How do you iterate through this array without remembering each name? Awk provides a built-in looping for statement for iterating through arrays. It has the following syntax:

```
for (value in array)
       x=array[value]
```

LAB
15.1

The syntactical rules are the same as a regular for statement, except the counter, test, and increment statements are not used. Instead, this for loop takes each subscript starting with the first and executes the action inside the for loop. This action is done repeatedly (assigning the string value for the subscript into the variable value) until all subscripts are exhausted.

■ *FOR EXAMPLE:*

So for our array of names-numeric values, we could write the following program to calculate the average of all numbers:

```
for (name in array) {
    total_names++
    sum += array[name]
}
END {print "average is ", sum/total_names}
```

The first time through the loop, the value of name is "Jones." The string "Jones" is then indexed as if the following had been explicitly written:

```
array["Jones"]
```

The value referenced by Jones (13) is then added to sum and the program continues. The second time through the loop, the value of name becomes Smith, and so forth.

The in operator can also be used to determine whether a particular index exists in an array. In other words, the in operator can be used to test for membership in an array. For example, we could have the following:

```
if ("Jones" in array) {
    print "Jones exists"
}
```

LAB 15.1

The value that the test ("Jones" in array) returns is 1 if that subscript does exist in an array, and 0 otherwise.

As opposed to most general-purpose programming languages, awk array indices are not numbers but rather strings. This fact has certain implications in awk programs. Because indices are not numerical indices, one cannot necessarily store each element at the next highest location in memory. In fact, awk uses some algorithm to store each string index into a numerical memory address. This algorithm does not store each element sequentially, so if you assign array["Jones"] before array["Peters"], when using the above for loop, "Jones" is not necessarily processed before "Peters" (i.e., "Jones" may not in fact be stored before "Peters").

I would like to emphasize that in these examples, I assumed that "Jones" would be the first element in each array, because "Jones" was the first record read in and stored. However, this choice was arbitrary and used for illustration purposes. The ordering in which array subscripts are stored is implementation dependent. Therefore, "Peters" could have easily been the first array element. The same is true for all other arrays that we use in future array examples. My choice of array subscripts is chosen arbitrarily.

THE DELETE STATEMENT

Awk provides a delete statement for deleting an element from an array. The statement has the following syntax:

```
delete array[subscript]
```

The brackets are required in this statement. The statement searches for the subscript in the array. If the subscript is found, then that subscript and its value are deleted from the array. If you subsequently perform an in test for membership in the array it would return false. So if we execute the following three lines in a program, the if statement returns false:

```
array["Age"] = 45
delete["Age"]
if ("Age" in array)
```

An array element cannot be deleted by assigning its value to null. The in test will still return true.

**LAB
15.1**

THE SPLIT FUNCTION

The built-in function split is used to parse a string, split the string into fields using a field separator as an argument to the function, and then store the fields as elements of an array. This function works as follows:

```
n = split(string, array, fs)
```

String is the input string that is passed into the split function. The split function takes this string and splits it up into fields according to the field separator. The fields are then stored in the array given by the second argument. The number of fields that were split and created as a result of executing this function is the return value that is assigned to n. For example, we split a person's full name into his/her first name and last name with the following excerpt:

```
z = split($1, fullname, " ")
```

This would split the full name, presumably residing in the first field variable $1, into a first name and last name. The first name is separated from the last name in $1 by a space. Therefore, two string values are created, first name and last name, both of which are stored in the array fullname. The function would return 2 as a result of executing this function, which corresponds to the number of fields split.

If no third argument is provided, then fs is assumed to be FS.

The subscripts to the array and the array element values that are stored as a result of the split function are described as follows:

- The subscript operator values start at 1 and go onward until n, the number of fields split.
- The array element values are the strings that were split as a result of the split function.

Therefore, the array fullname, if given "Peter Patsis" as the value of $1, would be as follows:

```
fullname[1] = "Peter"
fullname[2] = "Patsis"
```

Therefore, these two programs produce the same output:

```
for (i=1; i<=NF; i++)
    print $i
```

and

```
NF = split($0, array)
```

```
for (i=1; i<=NF; i++)
    print array[i]
```

In other words, because each array subscript is indexed from 1 to NF and each array element contains field number 1–NF, each produces the same output and both perform the same calculation.

LAB 15.1 EXERCISES

15.1.1 UNDERSTAND THE RESULTS OF USING AWK ARRAYS

Consider the following program:

```
awk '{array[2]=5}' some-file
```

a) What is array[0]?

_____

_____

b) What is array[1]?

_____

_____

**LAB
15.1**

Next, consider the following program:

```
awk '{print array[""]
      print array[0]
      array[""]=3
      array[0]=2
      print array[""]
      print array[0]
     }' some-file
```

c) What is the output?

_____

_____

d) What happens after the `delete` statements in the following programs?

```
awk '{ array["Smith"]=25
        delete array["Smith"]
     }' some-file

awk '{array["Smith"]=25
        delete array["Smith"]
        delete array["Smith"]
     }' some-file
```

_____

_____

e) What are the values of each array element in the following program?

```
awk '{array[""]=2
        array[1]=1
        array[var]=3
     }' some-file
```

_____

_____

15.1.2 WRITE PROGRAMS USING AWK ARRAYS

Use the following data for the first two questions in this Exercise, where the first field is the product number, the second is product name, and the third is the quantity ordered:

```
1234 Hammers 12
1456 Nails 11
1738 Saws 24
3215 Screws 44
1234 Hammers 13
```

```
1765 Bolts 29
1738 Saws 12
3215 Screws 13
```

a) Write a program that calculates the total number of items ordered for each product and prints the total as output.

_____

_____

b) What is the output?

_____

_____

In Chapter 14, "Awk Control Flow," we had an exercise that printed a histogram of the number of times that a number occurred within a range, using the following ranges:

```
30-39
20-29
10-19
0-9
```

It then printed the results in a histogram, which looked like the following:

**LAB
15.1**

```
30-39  ***
20-29  **
10-19  *
 0-9   **
```

So for this input file, three numbers were between 30–39, two between 20–29, and so on.

In that exercise, we worked on the following data:

```
33
27
7
15
```

```
8
12
28
15
16
6
11
```

The output produced for the program was

```
30-39 *
20-29 **
10-19 *****
 0-9 ***
```

c) Write a similar program using the same ranges, but use arrays instead of variables to store the ranges.

_____

_____

Use the following word-definition pair for Question d:

```
contradict, To assert the opposite of; To be con-
trary to or inconsistent with
flock, A group of people under the leadership of one
person
superfluity, Overabundance
suppurate, To form or discharge pus
filament, A fine wire heated electrically to incan-
descent in an electric lamp
extravagant, Excessive; Unrestrained
```

LAB
15.1

d) Write a program that, when given a word, returns the definition of that word. Use the following queries:
```
flock
filament
abstain
```

_____

_____

Bubble sorts enable you to sort an array of numbers. Suppose that you have the following four numbers:

```
1 = 4
2 = 8
3 = 6
4 = 3
```

A bubble sort program would compare each item of the array in turn and switch values if the value of position x-1 is greater than that of position x, where x refers to the index number, 1-4. So in position 1 (i.e., when x=1), the value is 4. In the second position (i.e., x=2), we encounter the value 8. The value of x-1 (4, in this case) is not greater than the value of x (8), so no action is performed. In the next position, we encounter a value of 6. This time, we switch values because the value of x-1 (8) is indeed greater than the value of x (6). The program continues until all values have been sorted in ascending order, performing as many passes as necessary. After the first pass, for example, we have the following sorted:

```
1 = 4

2 = 6

3 = 3

4 = 8
```

**LAB
15.1**

We continue until we perform x-1 passes of the algorithm for cycling through the list and switching numbers as appropriate. This example would perform three passes of the algorithm.

> **e)** Using a bubble sort, write a program that sorts the following numbers in ascending order.
> ```
> 5
> 13
> 11
> 67
> 5
> 10
> ```

22

20

19

3

LAB 15.1 EXERCISE ANSWERS

 This section gives you some suggested answers to the questions in Lab 15.1, with discussion related to those answers. Your answers may vary, but the most important thing is whether or not your answer works. Use this discussion to analyze differences between your answers and those presented here.

If you have alternative answers to the questions in this Exercise, you are encouraged to post your answers and discuss them at the companion Web site for this book, located at:

http://www.phptr.com/phptrinteractive/

15.1.1 ANSWERS

Consider the following program:
```
awk '{array[2]=5}' some-file
```

a)   What is array[0]?

Answer: Null

An array element that has not been explicitly initialized is null or zero if used in a numeric operation.

b)   What is array[1]?

Answer: Null

Next, consider the following program:

```
awk '{print array[""]
        print array[0]
        array[""]=3
        array[0]=2
        print array[""]
        print array[0]
        }' some-file
```

c) What is the output?

Answer: The output is as follows:

<blank line>

<blank line>

3

2

The first `print` statement prints the array element (`""`). This array element has not been explicitly initialized, so its value is also null. The `print` statement prints null, which is blank, and then prints a newline as a result of the default behavior of the `print` statement. The same is true of `array[0]`. After the first two `print` statements, `array[0]` and `array[""]` are assigned 3 and 2, respectively. Those values are subsequently printed out.

d) What happens after the `delete` statements in the following programs?

```
awk '{ array["Smith"]=25
        delete array["Smith"]
        }' some-file
```

```
awk '{array["Smith"]=25
        delete array["Smith"]
        delete array["Smith"]
        }' some-file
```

Answer: In both programs, the array element "Smith" is deleted.

You certainly can follow a `delete` statement with another `delete` statement that is exactly the same as the first. We see this in the second program. You do not have to worry whether you have deleted an array element at some previous time.

e) What are the values of each array element in the following program?
```
awk `{array["″]=2
        array[1]=1
        array[var]=3
      }' some-file
```

Answer: The values are as follows:
array["″]=3
array[1]=1
array[var]=3

Var is a variable that is being referenced without being explicitly initialized. A variable that is referenced but never explicitly initialized is initialized to null. Therefore, array[var] is the same as array["″], which
was previously assigned to 2. It is subsequently overwritten with 3.

15.1.2 ANSWERS

a) Write a program that calculates the total number of items ordered for
each product and prints the total as output.

Answer: The program is as follows:
```
{ if ($1 in product_name) {
    product_qty[$1]=$3 + product_qty[$1]
  }
  else {
    product_name[$1]=$2
    product_qty[$1]=$3
  }
}
END {for (name in product_name) {
        print name, product_name[name], product_qty[name]
    }
}
```

**LAB
15.1**

This program structurally consists of a single if-else statement. Let's
step through the program as follows:

```
if ($1 in product_name)
```

The if statement checks to see whether the particular product name (field number 1 in the input file) has been encountered before. This action is accomplished using the in operator and checking whether the array contains the subscript of the product name just read in.

```
product_qty[$1]=$3 + product_qty[$1]
```

If the test condition is true, then the array contains the product_name as a subscript. In this case, all that is required is to add the third field (quantity ordered) to the previous value of quantity ordered. The array product_qty contains a total quantity ordered for each product name.

If the condition is false, then this particular product has not been encountered before.

```
product_name[$1]=$2
```

In this case, we assign the product number associated with this product name into the array product_name. We did not have to do so, but to retain all the information read in from the input file is more correct. We could have also easily used product numbers as indexes into the arrays instead of product names. The choice was arbitrary.

```
product_qty[$1]=$3
```

Lastly, we initialize the quantity ordered for this product with the third field.

b) What is the output?

Answer: The output is as follows:
```
1234 Hammers 25
1456 Nails 11
1765 Bolts 29
3215 Screws 57
1738 Saws 36
```

In Chapter 14, "Awk Control Flow," we had an exercise that printed a histogram of the number of times that a number occurred within a range.

c) Write a similar program using the same ranges, but use arrays instead of variables to store the ranges.

Answer: The program is as follows:

```
{if ($1 > 29 && $1 < 40)
    histogram[3]=histogram[3] "*"
else if ($1 > 19)
    histogram[2]=histogram[2] "*"
else if ($1 > 9)
    histogram[1]=histogram[1] "*"
else if ($1 > -1)
    histogram[0]=histogram[0] "*"
else
    print "Number not in range 0-39"
}
END { for (i=3; i>-1; i--)
        print (10*i) "-" ((10*i)+9) " " histogram[i]
    }
```

The output is as follows:

```
30-39 *
20-29 **
10-19 *****
0-9 ***
```

Structurally, we use multiple `if-else` statements with a default `else` statement to cover the condition that a number read in does not fall into the range 0-39.

```
if ($1 > 29 && $1 < 40)
    histogram[3]=histogram[3] "*"
```

The `if` statement covers the condition that the number falls between the range 30-39. If so, then an asterisk is concatenated to the value that is currently contained in `histogram[3]`. Notice that the first time the statement `histogram[3]=histogram[3]` "*" is encountered, the value of `histogram[3]` is null because it was never explicitly initialized. Null concatenated with a single asterisk is a single asterisk, which we desire. Notice also that we must use the expression `$1 < 40` in the `if` statement to guard against the error condition that the number does not fall in the range 0-39. The rest of the `else-if` statements follow the same logic as the first `if` statement. The difference is that in the `if-else` statements that follow, no boolean "and" operator (`&&`) exists. Because we have an `else` statement following the first `if` statement (`if ($1 > 29 && $1 < 40`), the `else` statement will not be executed if the first `if` statement is true. If the first `if` statement is false, we know that `$1` is not greater than 29 and less than 40. If this condition is the case, all we have to do is check whether `$1` is greater than 19 to fall in the range 19-29, and we do not have to check whether `$1` is also less than 29 (`$1` cannot be greater than 29, so it must be less than 29).

```
END { for (i=3; i>-1; i--)
            print (10*i) "-" ((10*i)+9) " " histogram[i]
      }
```

In the END statement, we use a `for` loop to cycle through array elements whose values contain an asterisk for each occurrence of a number that falls in that particular range. The `for` loop uses the autodecrement operator because we wish to start at the 30s range down to the 0 range.

```
print (10*i) "-" ((10*i)+9) " " histogram[i]
```

The `print` statement multiplies 10 by the index of the `for` loop because the array index is a single digit, but the range header is in the tens digit.

d) Write a program that, when given a word, returns the definition of that word. Use the following queries:
```
flock
filament
abstain
```

**LAB
15.1**

Answer: The program is as follows:
```
BEGIN {FS = ","}
FILENAME == "words.dict" { dict[$1]=$2 }
FILENAME == "queries" { if ($1 in dict)
                            print $1, "--", dict[$1]
                        else
                            print $1, "--" "Word not found"
                      }
```

The output for this program is as follows:

```
flock  --   A group of people under the leadership of
one person
```

```
filament  --   A fine wire heated electrically to
incandescent in an electric lamp
abstain --Word not found
```

This program simply uses a pattern that checks for which file name is being processed. We use the BEGIN pattern to change FS to a comma, which separates a word from its meaning in words.dict. We use the check FILENAME== "words.dict" first so that the words and their meanings may be read and stored before processing queries. Each word ($1) is an index into the array dict, which contains all words in our dictionary. (We do not check whether the word is already contained in the array; it will simply be overwritten.) The second field ($2), which contains the meaning of the word, is stored at the position indexed by the word. The pattern FILENAME=="queries" processes the queries file. In the action for this pattern, we use an if statement and an in operator to see whether the word read in is contained within our words array. If so, we print its meaning by using the word as an index into our array (dict[$1]). Notice that a space exists before each meaning because we used a comma as the field separator. If we used the default space as the field separator, then we would have to remember to use a comma whenever we queried a word.

e) Using a bubble sort, write a program that sorts the given numbers in ascending order.

Answer: The program is as follows:
```
BEGIN { count = 0 }
{ array[count]=$1
  count++
}
END {
      for (i=count-1; i>-1; i--) {
       for (j=0; j<i; j++)
          if (array[j] > array[j+1]) {
             temp = array[j+1]
             array[j+1]=array[j]
             array[j]=temp
          }
      }
      for (i=0; i<count; i++)
         print array[i]
    }
```

**LAB
15.1**

In the main processing loop, each number is read in and stored in the array. The total number of numbers read in is stored in the variable `count`. Notice that `count` is initialized to zero in the `BEGIN` pattern. Therefore, the first number is stored in `array[0]`. This array is sorted in the `END` pattern.

```
for (i=count-1; i>-1; i--) {
```

This `for` loop determines how many elements are properly sorted and at which position. The first time through this loop, one element will be sorted and the position of the sorted element will be `array[count-1]`. The second time through, two elements will be sorted, and the position of the two sorted elements for our example are `array[9]` and `array[8]`. Therefore, at each iteration of the loop, array positions `array[i]` through `array[count-1]` will be properly sorted.

```
for (j=0; j<i; j++)
```

This `for` loop actually bubbles the next largest number up to its proper position, which is `array[i]`. This bubbling is done by comparing each element value `array[j]` with `array[j+1]` and exchanging if `array[j]` is larger than `array[j+1]`. Therefore, the largest number is pushed up to the next-highest array position continually until the `j` is equal to `i`, the current index. This `for` loop starts at zero and checks whether `array[0]` is greater than `array[1]`. If you are confused as to how this algorithm works, take the input file and go through this program using the actual numbers from the file.

**LAB
15.1**

LAB 15.1 SELF-REVIEW QUESTIONS

In order to test your progress, you should be able to answer the following questions.

1) An index in awk is considered a string.
   a) _____True
   b) _____False

2) A number value may be used as a subscript.
   a) _____True
   b) _____False

3) Array elements are stored in the order they were assigned.
  a) _____True
  b) _____False

4) The value associated with an array element must be explicitly initialized.
  a) _____True
  b) _____False

5) The `in` membership operator determines whether a value associated with an array element is contained in the array.
  a) _____True
  b) _____False

6) The delete statement deletes an array subscript from the array.
  a) _____True
  b) _____False

Quiz answers appear in Appendix A, Section 15.1.

LAB
15.1

L A B   15.2

AWK USER-DEFINED FUNCTIONS

LAB OBJECTIVES

After this Lab, you will be able to:

✓ Understand the Results of Using Awk User-Defined Functions

✓ Write Programs Using Awk User-Defined Functions

User-defined functions enable us to write more compact, understandable, and readable code. They enable us to write tasks that are performed multiple times into a single executable unit. A program that uses the function can then simply make a call to the function, and we do not have to write out all the instructions for it every time we wish to execute the function. The result is shorter programs that require less time to write. This was seen when we covered built-in functions. The built-in function sqrt() enables us to simply call the function name with an argument rather than having to write the sqrt() function out each time we wish to use it. Because functions have names, they enable us to understand and read the code more easily, since we do not have to analyze multiple lines of code to see what they are accomplishing. We can simply look at the function name, say, calculate 30YrMortgage, and understand its use. Some of the rules and ideas we express in this Lab apply to both user-defined and built-in functions. I will try to point this fact out whenever possible; however, you should think about how the information pertains to built-in functions as well.

As mentioned, a function is a convenient mechanism for creating and using useful tasks that may need to be performed several times. A function in awk can appear anywhere in the script that a pattern-action can appear. It is more easily read and noticeable if all functions are placed at the top of the script rather than the middle or the end of a script. The reason is that when the function is called, its definition (instructions that are part of the function), parameters passed to the function (i.e., in the sqrt(9) function, 9 is the parameter), and its implementation will have been seen before the call. In awk, as opposed to many general-purpose programming languages, a function call can be made before its definition is known. For example:

```
awk function sort(ARRAY, ELEMENTS, ...,) {
        ... .
    }
    { for (i=1; i<=NF; i++)
            array[i] = $i
        sort(array, NF)
    }
```

Again, this form is preferable in that the function definition and implementation are created before the call to the function. The syntax of a user-defined awk function is as follows:

```
function name(parameter list) {
    statements
}
```

Following are the syntactic rules for user-defined functions:

- The newline after the left brace is optional.
- The newline before the closing right brace is optional.
- You may have a newline after the closing parenthesis of the parameter list and before the left brace.
- A space may not be inserted between the function name and the opening parenthesis of the parameter list.

The following is also a valid form for a function:

**LAB
15.2**

```
function name(parameter-list)
{ statement
}
```

The name of the function follows the naming rules for any awk variable. The convention I typically use is to have the first letter of the function name lowercase and each letter that begins a new word in uppercase, as follows:

```
printTable(..)
calculateAvgPay(..)
```

I try to use the underscore for user-defined variables, as follows:

```
print_table = ...
average_pay = ..
```

The parameter list is a comma-separated list of variables that represent the formal arguments of the function. The actual arguments are supplied when the function is actually called. Therefore, in the sort example (shown earlier when discussing that a function definition can occur before a function call), the formal parameters are ARRAY and ELEMENTS. The actual arguments are `array` and NF. The actual argument values are passed to the formal arguments, and the formal arguments contain those values when control is passed to the function.

The body of a function contains one or more awk statements. Inside the body of the function and before the closing brace of the function, a `return` statement may appear, which returns control to the statement following the call that was made to the function in the awk script. Like an `exit` statement, the `return` statement is associated with an expression that returns a value as the result of executing the function. Thus, the `return` statement has the following form, where `expression` is any valid awk expression:

```
return expression
```

Thus, we may write a function that returns the maximum value of two variables as follows:

```
function max(a, b) {
    return a > b ? a : b
}
```

This function returns a if a > b, or b if b >= a.

If no `return` statement is provided, the `return` statement becomes the closing brace, and control is again returned to the statement that followed the function call in the calling body. The value of the return statement in this case is undefined.

LOCAL VS. GLOBAL VARIABLES

Programming languages generally speak of scope to talk about the lifetime that a variable exists. In language terms, this amounts to at what point in the program that is a reference to the variable valid. In other words, when is the variable created and the point it is destroyed? Two types of scopes for variables, local scope, and global scope exist.

In awk, user-defined variables, field variables, and body of a function have global scope. Global scope means that at any point in an awk program, these variables maintain their value throughout the awk program—that is, the variables values are never destroyed or deleted. This situation is not the case with local scope. When the local scope of a local variable is outside a function body, its value becomes NULL. The local variable does not assume the same value inside the function body as it does outside the function body. Local variables, in awk's case, are only the formal parameters in the parameter list, and they assume their value only inside the function. Once control is passed to the calling body, these formal parameter names, or local variables, can be referenced but their values are nonexistent or null. Everywhere else, a variable is a global variable. Therefore, inside the body of the function, a variable that is declared (and not a formal parameter) is not local to the function and is global; its value exists outside the function.

PASSING VALUES TO FUNCTIONS

**LAB
15.2**

Values are passed to functions in two ways: call by reference and call by value. We will talk more about call by reference a little later in this section.

CALL BY VALUE

When a variable is placed in a function call in the actual argument list, the following steps are performed:

1. The formal parameters in the parameter list that corre-
    spond to the position of the actual arguments in the func-
    tion call are created with the name that is given in the
    parameter list.
2. After creating the variable in the formal parameter list, the
    value that is contained within the actual argument is cop-
    ied to the formal parameter.

■ FOR EXAMPLE:

Consider the following call:

```
var1 = 3; var2 =4;
func1(var1, var2)
```

If the function `func1` has the following parameter list, the formal parameter `local1` is created with the name `local1`:

```
function func1(local1, local2)
```

The value of the actual argument `var1` is then copied to `local1`. Thus,
you can think of copy by value as creating a temporary variable that tem-
porarily holds a copy of the original value. The temporary variable can
then be used in assignments and can also be used as an rvalue, without
affecting the original value.

To illustrate awk's scoping rules, rules for passing values, and side effects
of assignment to variables within programs, consider the following:

```
awk 'function test_scope(local_var3)) {
              local_var3 = 4
              local_var4 = 5
              var2 = 8
              return local_var3 * 5
     }
     {

         var1 = 3
         var2 = 4
```

**LAB
15.2**

```
        print "After call to function return is ", test_scope
    (var3, var4)
        print "main var 1 ", var1
print "main var 2 ", var2
        print "local_var 3 ", local_var3
        print "local_var 4 ", local_var4
    }
```

The output of this program is:

```
After call to function return is 16
main var 1 Is 3
main var 2 Is 8
local_var 3 Is
local_var 4 Is 5
```

This program illustrates the following situations:

- The value of global variables within a function body and outside it
- The values of variables that are passed as parameters and their values within a function body and outside it
- The values of variables that are first declared inside a function body and their values within the function body and outside it
- The side effect of calling a function

A local variable can be any variable that is defined in the parameter list of a function; a global variable is defined everywhere else in the program.

Therefore, in this program, the local variable is local_var3. The global variables are local_var4 (defined in the function body), var1, and var2 (defined in the only pattern-action statement in the program).

**LAB
15.2**

Situation number 1 above is illustrated with the global variable var2. var2 is assigned 3 before the function is called. Inside the function, it maintains its value of 3 until it is assigned the value 8 inside the function. After the function, it maintains its value of 8 that was assigned inside the function. Therefore, 8 is printed.

Situation number 2 is illustrated when the function `test_scope` is called. The actual argument is `var1` (equals 3). The local variable `local_var3` is then assigned 3 when the value is passed. Within the function, `local_var3` is immediately assigned 4. Therefore, throughout the function, `local_var3` maintains the value 4. Its value is destroyed, and when the print statement is encountered in the pattern-action statement, it does not exist and is implicitly initialized by awk to null (uninitialized variable). `var1` was not affected when `local_var3` was assigned 4 in the function.

Situation number 3 is illustrated by `local_var4`, which is first declared inside the function and was not a parameter. Therefore, its value (5) is maintained throughout the function and outside the function, and 5 is printed in the pattern-action statement.

Side effects are illustrated by the assignment of `local_var4` and `var2`. By *side effect*, we mean situations 1 and 3 above. In both, either a global variable value is changed before and after the function is executed, or a global variable value is first defined in a function. This fact can cause potential problems. Using the above function, if we had the following `for` loop:

```
for (var2=1; var2<4; var2++) {
    sum += $(var2)
    test_scope(var1)
}
```

Because `var2` is changed in `test_scope` to 4, the `for` loop is executed once. This kind of mistake happens often.

To eliminate the side effect introduced by the situation of `var2` assigned eight inside the function body, do the following: Create another parameter in the parameter list and pass `var2` into the function by including it in the function call. You should not have a function change a global variable that was not passed in the parameter-list.

To eliminate the side effect of declaring local variables inside a function body that are to be used only inside the function, include another parameter in the parameter list and don't pass any value in the call to the function. This action creates a variable with the null value that can be assigned a value inside the function and that is destroyed when the function is exited. The convention is to separate parameters that are to be passed values in the function call from variables that are only to be declared and used within the function with multiple spaces, as follow:

```
test_scope (local_var3,globalvar2,                local_var4)
```

We will see more of this convention in the exercises.

CALL BY REFERENCE

In awk, arrays are always passed call-by-reference. As opposed to call-by-value, a temporary variable is not created and its value is initialized with the actual argument. Instead, with call-by-reference the actual argument's memory location is passed to the formal parameter. As a result, the actual argument and formal parameter access the same memory location for both lvalues and rvalues. Therefore, a change to the formal parameter will be seen to the actual parameter as well. In awk, arrays are passed call-by-value; therefore, any change to array elements or subscripts are seen throughout the program. Therefore, the following program will print 4:

```
awk 'function test(ARRAY, loc_var1, PI) {
                ARRAY[1] = 4
      }
      {
      array[1] = 1
      array[2] = 2
      PI = 3.14
      var1 = 2
      test(array, var1, PI)
      print array[1]
      }
```

The array is call-by-reference, so any change inside the function will be seen outside the function. Therefore, since ARRAY in `function test` is call-by-reference when it assigns four to ARRAY[1], the assignment is seen by both ARRAY[1] and array[1].

**LAB
15.2**

LAB 15.2 EXERCISES

15.2.1 UNDERSTAND THE RESULTS OF AWK USER-DEFINED FUNCTIONS

a) Is the following function call legal?

```
awk '{ print The max is ",  max($1, $2) }
        function max(a_loc, b_loc) {
             return a_loc > b_loc ? a_loc : b_loc
        }
     }' some-file
```

_____

_____

b) What is the result of executing the following program?

```
awk 'function func(var1) {
        var1 = 6
     }
     { var1 = 3
       func(var1)
       print var1
     }' some-file
```

_____

_____

c) What is the output of executing the following program?

```
awk 'function func(i_loc) {
         if (i_loc != 3)
             return i * i
         else
             break
     }
     { for (i=1; i<=6; i++)
           print func(i)
     }' some-file
```

_____

_____

15.2.2 WRITE PROGRAMS USING USER-DEFINED FUNCTIONS

Use the following three files for the first question in this Exercise:

The first, GradReq, contains the number of courses in each department that the student must take to graduate:

```
Computers 8
Math 4
Physics 3
SocialSciences 2
Psychology 2
English 3
```

The second, Fall98, contains the student name, ID, class, and grades for the current semester:

```
Jones 45634 Physics 75 87 90 82 90
Jones 45634 Computers 89 87 91 85 95
Jones 45634 Psychology 76 77 84 89 95
```

The last file, OverallGPA, contains the student ID, course department, the number of courses taken in the department, and the overall GPA in that department:

```
45634 Computers 4 3.8
45634 Math 3 3.6
45634 Physics 2 3.3
45634 English 1 2.9
```

LAB
15.2

a) Write a function that accomplishes the following:

Prints out a student's overall GPA for the current semester

Prints whether s/he is on the honor roll (GPA >= 3.5)

Prints how many courses the student needs to graduate with the current semester taken into account

_____

_____

b) Write a program that implements a postfix calculator. For addition, a postfix calculator's operands and operator would be placed as follows:

`a b +`

which is equivalent to

`a + b as a infix calculator`

a + b + c as a postfix calculator is a b + c +.

The calculator should perform addition, subtraction, multiplication, division, sqrt, the square of two numbers, and the remainder operator.

_____

_____

Implement a stack for the operands. If you do not know what a stack is, then you can reference a good data structures book. A stack is not required to solve this problem.

Use the following input file:

```
1 2 + 3 * sqr 2 /
4 sqrt 4 * 4 / 34 32 - *
4 sqrt 4 * 4 + 2 5 * %
```

c) What is the output?

_____

_____

LAB 15.2 EXERCISE ANSWERS

This section gives you some suggested answers to the questions in Lab 15.2, with discussion related to those answers. Your answers may vary, but the most important thing is whether or not your answer works. Use this discussion to analyze differences between your answers and those presented here.

If you have alternative answers to the questions in this Exercise, you are encouraged to post your answers and discuss them at the companion Web site for this book, located at:

```
http://www.phptr.com/phptrinteractive/
```

15.2.1 ANSWERS

a) Is the following function call legal?
```
awk '{ print The max is ", max($1, $2) }
        function max(a_loc, b_loc) {
            return a_loc > b_loc ? a_loc : b_loc
        }
    }' some-file
```
Answer: Yes it is legal.

A call to a function may occur before the actual function is defined. Each argument to the call to the function must be separated by a comma.

b) What is the result of executing the following awk program?
```
awk 'function func(var1) {
        var1 = 6
    }
    { var1 = 3
      func(var1)
      print var1
    }' some-file
```
Answer: 3

LAB 15.2

Var1 is contained in the parameter list of the function. As a result, it is a local variable that is destroyed when the function is exited. Whatever assignments are made to the variable inside the function body are not visible outside the function. `Var1` is initialized with the value of 3 in the main processing loop. After the call to the function `func` (just for your information, `func` is not a legal function name), the assignment inside the function body to `var1` is not seen outside the function, and the value 3 is printed in the `print` statement.

c) What is the output of executing the following program?

```
awk 'function func(i_loc) {
        if (i_loc != 3)
            return i * i
        else
            break
    }
    { for (i=1; i<=6; i++)
        print func(i)
    }' some-file
```

Answer: The output is as follows:

```
1
4
awk: ch20-3.scr:6: (FILENAME=some-file FNR=1) fatal:
use of `break' outside a loop is not allowed
```

An error results when `i` is 3 in the main processing `for` loop, because a break can be used only inside a loop. An `if-else` statement inside the function is not a loop, and the break statement inside the `if-else` is an error. Before that error results, the function `func` is called twice—first when `i` is 1 and second when `i` is 2. Therefore, 1 x 1 and 2 x 2 are printed.

15.2.2 ANSWERS

a) Write a function that accomplishes the following:

Prints out a student's overall GPA for the current semester

Prints whether s/he is on the honor roll (GPA >= 3.5)

Prints how many courses the student needs to graduate with the current semester taken into account

Answer: The program is as follows:

```
function convertGPA(avg_loc) {
   if (avg_loc>=90) return 4.0
   else if (avg_loc>=85) return 3.5
   else if (avg_loc>=80) return 3.0
   else if (avg_loc>=75) return 2.5
   else if (avg_loc>=70) return 2.0
   else if (avg_loc>=65) return 1.5
   else if (avg_loc>=60) return 1.0
   else return 0.0
}


function   calcAvg(tests_loc,                        i_loc,
   total_loc,FIELDS_LOC) {
   FIELDS_LOC=4
   for (i_loc=0; i_loc<tests_loc; i_loc++)
      total_loc+=$(i_loc+FIELDS_LOC)
   return convertGPA(total_loc/tests_loc)
}

function calcGPA(GRADES, courses_loc,   grade_loc, sum_loc) {
   for (grade_loc in GRADES) {
     sum_loc+=GRADES[grade_loc]
   }
   return (sum_loc/courses_loc)
}

function calcGrad(DEPT, GRAD,        dept_name_loc) {
   for (dept_name_loc in GRAD)
      if (dept_name_loc in DEPT) {
         if (DEPT[dept_name_loc] < GRAD[dept_name_loc])
                   print dept_name_loc, GRAD[dept_name_loc]-
   DEPT[dept_name_loc]
      }
      else
         print dept_name_loc, GRAD[dept_name_loc]
}
```

**LAB
15.2**

```
FILENAME == "Fall98" { cur_courses++
                       student_name = $1
                       student_id = $2
                       grades[cur_courses]=calcAvg(NF-3)
                       dept[$3]=dept[$3]+1
                     }
FILENAME == "overallgpa" {
```

```
                              courses+=$3
                              gpa[count]=$3*$4
                              dept[$2]=dept[$2]+$3
                              count++
                        }
      FILENAME == "gradreq" { grad[$1]=$2
                        }
      END { cur_gpa = calcGPA(grades, cur_courses)
            if (cur_gpa < 3.5)
                print student_name, student_id, cur_gpa, "NOT ON HONOR
      ROLL"
            else
                  print student_name, student_id, cur_gpa, "ON HONOR
      ROLL"
            print ""
            gpa[count]=cur_gpa*cur_courses
            courses+=cur_courses
            print "Overall GPA = ", calcGPA(gpa, courses)
            print ""
            print "Courses Needed To Graduate"
            print "-----------------------------------"
            calcGrad(dept, grad)
          }
```

The output is:

```
Jones 45634 3.16667 NOT ON HONOR ROLL

Overall GPA =   3.46154

Courses Needed To Graduate
------------------------------------
Computers 3
Math 1
Psychology 1
SocialSciences 2
English 2
```

Let's break this program down into its parts:

```
function convertGPA(avg_loc) {
   if (avg_loc>=90) return 4.0
   else if (avg_loc>=85) return 3.5
```

```
            else if (avg_loc>=80) return 3.0
            else if (avg_loc>=75) return 2.5
            else if (avg_loc>=70) return 2.0
            else if (avg_loc>=65) return 1.5
            else if (avg_loc>=60) return 1.0
            else return 0.0
     }
```

This function takes a grade in the range 0–100 and converts it into the 0.0–4.0 system. As per my coding convention, the first letter of a function name is lowercase, and each subsequent word starts in uppercase (convertGPA). Also to avoid confusion, I use the coding convention of ending each variable in the parameter list with the suffix loc (avg_loc). This function takes a single argument, avg_loc, which is a grade in the range 0–100. This grade is used in multiple if-else statements to determine which grade to give in the range 0–4.0. Therefore, if the grade is greater than or equal to 90, a 4.0 grade is received. The other else-if statements follow this logic. Notice that I used >=90 instead of greater than 89, because grades are decimal values and not whole numbers; otherwise a grade of 89.7 would be interpreted as a 4.0.

```
    function    calcAvg(tests_loc,                           i_loc,
        total_loc,FIELDS_LOC) {
        FIELDS_LOC=4
        for (i_loc=0; i_loc<tests_loc; i_loc++)
            total_loc+=$(i_loc+FIELDS_LOC)
        return convertGPA(total_loc/tests_loc)
     }
```

This function is used to take a bunch of test scores for a particular course and determine the average of all tests. Since the average will be in the range 0–100, a call is made to convertGPA to convert the average in the range 0–4.0. The coding convention follows the same logic as described above, with the additional property that multiple white spaces separate tests_loc with i_loc. The reason is that the variables i_loc, total_loc, and FIELD_LOC are not passed as arguments to the function but will be used locally inside the function body. To eliminate the possibility that these variables will be erroneously used outside this function, we declare them locally and include them in the parameter list. After the function is finished processing, they will be destroyed. FIELDS_LOC is also capitalized in that it is intended to be used as a constant. FIELDS_LOC is assigned four because we wish to access the first field that is a test score in the file Fall98. The first three fields are student name,

LAB
15.2

id, and course name. We then use a `for` loop to add all test scores in the accumulator variable `total_loc`. `Tests_loc` already contains the total number of tests taken.

```
function calcGPA(GRADES, courses_loc,    grade_loc, sum_loc) {
    for (grade_loc in GRADES) {
      sum_loc+=GRADES[grade_loc]
    }
    return (sum_loc/courses_loc)
}
```

This function is used to calculate the overall GPA of a student, given an array where each array element contains the value of a GPA grade in the range 0–4.0 times the number of courses that averaged that GPA. So in other words if you had three courses with an average of 4.0 and three courses with an average of 3.0, then each array element would be 12.0 (4.0 x 3) and 9.0 (3.0 x 3). These sums are used to calculate the overall GPA (i.e., 12 + 9 / 3 + 3 = 21/6= 3.5). The array `for` loop (`grade_loc` in GRADES) performs the sum of each average GPA in the file `overallGPA` for each department times the number of courses taken in that department. Each sum is stored in the accumulator `sum_loc`. `Courses_loc` contains the total number of courses taken in each department, and the return value is the overall GPA. Notice that the coding convention follows the same guidelines discussed in the previous two functions, with the additional property that an array is capitalized in the parameter list (GRADES).

```
function calcGrad(DEPT, GRAD,        dept_name_loc) {
    for (dept_name_loc in GRAD)
        if (dept_name_loc in DEPT) {
            if (DEPT[dept_name_loc] < GRAD[dept_name_loc])
                    print dept_name_loc, GRAD[dept_name_loc]-
        DEPT[dept_name_loc]
        }
        else
            print dept_name_loc, GRAD[dept_name_loc]
}
```

LAB
15.2

This function determines the number of courses that are needed to graduate. The coding convention follows the conventions used in the previous functions, with no new conventions used in this function that were not used in previous functions. The function uses two arrays, DEPT and GRAD. The array GRAD contains the number of courses needed to graduate within each department. The array is indexed by the string department name. DEPT contains the number of courses that the student has currently taken, including the current semester. All that is required is to cycle through each department in GRAD and see whether the number of courses taken in DEPT for that department is equal to or greater than the value for the department in GRAD. The array for loop (dept_name_loc in GRAD) is used to cycle through each department. The array membership operator in (dept_name_loc in DEPT) is used to check whether the student has taken any courses in that department. If so, then a check is made to see whether that value is less than the number required in GRAD, and the number of additional courses needed to graduate is printed. Otherwise, the student has not taken any courses in that department, and the number of courses that are required to graduate is printed from GRAD (print dept_name_loc, GRAD[dept_name_loc]).

```
FILENAME == "Fall98" { cur_courses++
                       student_name = $1
                       student_id = $2
                       grades[cur_courses]=calcAvg(NF-3)
                       dept[$3]=dept[$3]+1
                     }
```

This portion of the main processing loop processes each course and test score from the file Fall98. Each line contains a single course taken by the student for the current semester and the grades received for each test. We extract the student names and student id ($1, $2) for each line. Don't worry about the fact that this value does not change for each line yet we assign the same value multiple times. All we care about is that both contain the correct value at the end of processing this file (a more elegant solution could have been designed but is not worth the extra code). Cur_courses accumulates the total number of courses taken in the current semester. CalcAVG calculates the average GPA (0–4.0) for that course, and the result is stored in the array grades, which contains the averages for each course. For each course, the number of courses taken in the department is incremented by 1. Of course, since this number was never assigned previously, it contains 1 the first time it is assigned (note that the name of the department and the names of courses are the same, in order to simplify the programming).

LAB 15.2

```
FILENAME == "overallgpa" {
                           courses+=$3
                           gpa[count]=$3*$4
                           dept[$2]=dept[$2]+$3
                           count++
                         }
```

This portion processes the average GPA and the number of courses taken in each department. Courses accumulates the total number of courses taken by the student ($3 contains the number of courses taken in each department). The array gpa contains the sum (as described in the discussion of calcGPA) of the average GPA times the number of courses taken within the department for all departments. The total number of courses taken in that department is added in the array dept. After processing, dept will contain the total number of courses that were previously taken for that department, along with the current semester. (Notice the assignment dept[$3]=dept[$3]+1 in the pattern FILENAME=="Fall98" and dept[$2]=dept[$2]+$3 here. Whatever value was stored in dept for each department in "Fall98" will be added here.) The variable count contains the total number of departments that were processed. At the end of processing, count points to an array position in array gpa that is one greater than the last gpa that was stored. We will see how we use count being one greater than the last gpa in the END pattern:

```
FILENAME == "gradreq" { grad[$1]=$2
```

This portion is straightforward and stores the number of courses that are needed to graduate for each department.

```
END { cur_gpa = calcGPA(grades, cur_courses)
        if (cur_gpa < 3.5)
           print student_name, student_id, cur_gpa, "NOT ON HONOR
ROLL"
        else
             print student_name, student_id, cur_gpa, "ON HONOR
ROLL"
        print ""
        gpa[count]=cur_gpa*cur_courses
        courses+=cur_courses
        print "Overall GPA = ", calcGPA(gpa, courses)
        print ""
        print "Courses Needed To Take To Graduate"
        print "-----------------------------------"
        calcGrad(dept, grad)
    }
```

The END pattern prints out all the final values that we need to calculate. It first calls calcGPA to determine whether the student is on the honor roll for the current semester. We can use calcGPA because the sum that we discussed when describing the function is assumed to be the GPA times 1.

So if the student received a 4.0, 3.5, and 3.0 in three courses taken for the semester, then the sum would be 4.0 x 1 + 3.5 x 1 + 3.0 x 1/cur_courses (cur_courses is 1 + 1 + 1 = 3). Convince yourself that this processing is the same as will be done for overallGPA.

```
gpa[count]=cur_gpa*cur_courses
courses+=cur_courses
```

Here we calculate the sum that we calculated when processing over-allGPA, to take into account the current semester. We also add to the total number of courses taken by the student the number of courses taken in the current semester. We then have all the information we need to calculate the overall GPA (past courses and current semester) in the array gpa (notice that since count was one greater than the number of departments that were processed in the file overallgpa, we can store the current semester at the value that count indexes). All that is left to do is call calcGPA to calculate the overallgpa and calcGrad to calculate the number of courses required to graduate.

b) Write a program that implements a postfix calculator.

Answer: The program is as follows:

```
function printStack(STACK, i_loc) {
   print "PRINTING STACK *******"
   for (i_loc=0; i_loc<ELEMENTS; i_loc++)
     print STACK[i_loc]
   print "********************"
}

function stackEmpty(elements_loc) {
   return (elements_loc == 0)
}

function pop(STACK) {
   if (stackEmpty(ELEMENTS)) {
      print "ERROR POP:   STACK EMPTY"
      exit
   }
   else {
      ELEMENTS--
      return STACK[ELEMENTS]
   }
}

function push(STACK, value_loc) {
```

**LAB
15.2**

```
        STACK[ELEMENTS]=value_loc
        ELEMENTS++
}

function isOperator(op_char_loc) {
  if (OPERATORS ~ op_char_loc)
     return 1
  else
     return 0
}


function    calculate(op_char_loc,              op1_loc,    op2_loc,
    result_loc) {
   op1_loc=pop(STACK)
   if (op_char_loc == "sqr")
      result_loc=op1_loc*op1_loc
   else if (op_char_loc == "sqrt")
      result_loc=sqrt(op1_loc)
   else {
      op2_loc=pop(STACK)
      if (op_char_loc == "+")
        result_loc = op2_loc + op1_loc
      else if (op_char_loc == "*")
        result_loc=op2_loc*op1_loc
      else if (op_char_loc == "/")
        result_loc=op2_loc/op1_loc
      else if (op_char_loc == "-")
        result_loc=op2_loc-op1_loc
      else
        result_loc=op2_loc%op1_loc
   }
   push(STACK, result_loc)
}
```

```
BEGIN { OPERATORS = "[+-*/%]|sqrt|sqr"
        ELEMENTS=0
      }
{ for (i=1; i<=NF; i++) {
    if (isOperator($i))
      calculate($i)
    else
      push(STACK,($i+0))
  }
  print "RESULT OF ", $0, "IS  ", pop(STACK)
}
```

A stack in data structures is analogous to a stack of trays in a cafeteria. To take a tray off the stack, you take the tray off the top of the stack (called *popping the stack*). To put a tray back on the stack, you place it on the top of the stack (called *pushing the stack*). Thus, trays are put on or taken off the stack from the top. In data structures, in order to implement the stack, we use an array. Since we cannot use `array[0]`, the first position of the array, as the top of the stack, we instead use higher and higher indexes as the top of the stack (the reason is that since each element that needs to be pushed onto the stack is pushed on the top, we would over-write the previous value of the top of the stack since both would occupy `array[0]`). We could move each previous element that was on the top of stack to the next position, `array[1]`, but then we would have to move each subsequent element on top of the stack to its next-highest position. Instead, we use an array index counter variable that is incremented each time an element is pushed onto the stack. Therefore, the first time we push an element onto the stack, this index counter variable (arbitrarily called ELEMENTS) is zero. After pushing the element onto the stack, ELE-MENTS is 1, which represents the array position that is currently the top of the stack. Whenever we pop an element off the stack, we decrement the counter by 1. Therefore, two variables are needed to implement a stack, an array (the stack) that is used to store the elements that are pushed onto or popped off the stack, and an index variable that points to the top of the stack. We use the stack data structure so that we may push and pop operands onto or off the stack when needed. When we encounter an operator, we pop the number of operands needed to perform the opera-tion off the stack. Otherwise, we push onto the stack the operand encountered in the arithmetic expression.

The stack and the functions that we wish to perform on the stack are given below:

```
function printStack(STACK, i_loc) {
  print "PRINTING STACK *******"
  for (i_loc=0; i_loc<ELEMENTS; i_loc++)
    print STACK[i_loc]
  print "********************"
}

function stackEmpty(elements_loc) {
    return (elements_loc == 0)
}

function pop(STACK) {
```

**LAB
15.2**

```
        if (stackEmpty(ELEMENTS)) {
            print "ERROR POP:   STACK EMPTY"
            exit
        }
        else {
            ELEMENTS--
            return STACK[ELEMENTS]
        }
    }

    function push(STACK, value_loc) {
        STACK[ELEMENTS]=value_loc
        ELEMENTS++
    }
```

printStack is never used in the program but is used for debugging to print out the contents of the stack. stackEmpty is used by pop to make sure that we do not attempt to take an element off an empty stack (an annoying error). Pop is used to take an element off the top of the stack. The variable STACK is an array that is used to store the elements that are on the stack. The variable ELEMENTS is a global variable that is used to index the top of the stack. It always contains a value that is one greater than the indexed position of the top of the stack. If ELEMENTS is 0, then we know that the stack is empty. Therefore, to pop the stack, we first decrement ELEMENTS to point to the array element that is currently at the top of the stack, and we then return the element that is indexed by STACK[ELEMENTS]. To push an element onto the top of the stack, we first take the element that we wish to push (value_loc) and store that value into the array position indexed by ELEMENTS. We then increment the top of the stack array index ELEMENTS by one to get ready for the next push. We are now ready to discuss the postfix calculator.

```
    function isOperator(op_char_loc) {
      if (OPERATORS ~ op_char_loc)
         return 1
      else
         return 0
    }
```

This function is used to determine whether the current field in the arithmetic expression is an operator. We use the regular expression matching operator OPERATORS ~ op_char_loc to determine whether the current character contained in the current field is an operator. The OPERATORS value is "[+-*/%}|sqr|sqrt," which contains all the characters that represent arithmetic operators for our calculator. If it is an operator, we return 0; otherwise, we return 1. Notice that we do not have an equivalent function isOperand, because if a field contains a nonnumber that is also not an operator, then we will use awk's built-in coercion rules to convert a string into a number. This is what awk would perform when evaluating an arithmetic operation.

```
function calculate(op_char_loc,   op1_loc, op2_loc, result_loc) {
    op1_loc=pop(STACK)
    if (op_char_loc == "sqr")
        result_loc=op1_loc*op1_loc
    else if (op_char_loc == "sqrt")
        result_loc=sqrt(op1_loc)
    else {
        op2_loc=pop(STACK)
        if (op_char_loc == "+")
          result_loc = op2_loc + op1_loc
        else if (op_char_loc == "*")
          result_loc=op2_loc*op1_loc
        else if (op_char_loc == "/")
          result_loc=op2_loc/op1_loc
        else if (op_char_loc == "-")
          result_loc=op2_loc-op1_loc
        else
          result_loc=op2_loc%op1_loc
    }
    push(STACK, result_loc)
}
```

The function calculate is the function that actually controls the evaluation of an arithmetic operation. It is called whenever an operator is encountered in the arithmetic expression that was read in. It first pops an operand from the stack. It does not pop two operands just yet, because the sqr and sqrt operators do not work on two operands. We therefore check whether the operator is either sqr or sqrt, and if so, we perform either operation and store the result into the variable result_loc. If the operator is not sqr or sqrt, then we pop another operand from the stack. We then use multiple if-else statements to determine the operator and perform the operation. We store the result into the variable result_loc. Notice that op2_loc, not op1_loc, is always the first operand in each subsequent operation (postfix). After calculating the result, we then push result_loc back onto the stack. We do not return the value of result_loc to the calling program, because we need to store intermedi-

**LAB
15.2**

ate results before the final result so that we may use these results as operands for subsequent operations. At the end of processing, the top of the
stack contains the final value.

```
BEGIN { OPERATORS = "[+-*/%]|sqrt|sqr"
          ELEMENTS=0
       }
  { for (i=1; i<=NF; i++) {
     if (isOperator($i))
        calculate($i)
     else
        push(STACK,($i+0))
   }
     print "RESULT OF ", $0, "IS  ", pop(STACK)
   }
```

The main processing loop is fairly straightforward once we have created
all our functions. All we have to do is cycle through each field and determine whether the field is an operator or not. If it is an operator, then we
call `calculate` to evaluate the operation. Otherwise, we assume that it is
an operand and we push the operand onto the stack. At the end of
cycling through each field, the top of the stack should contain the final
result (a major assumption that we do not check). Notice that in the call
to `push`, I coerce the operand by adding zero to it. I do so to make sure
that the operand will be a number when it is pushed onto the stack.

c) What is the output?

Answer:

RESULT OF   1 2 + 3 * sqr 2 / IS   40.5
RESULT OF   4 sqrt 4 * 4 / 34 32 - * IS   4
RESULT OF   4 sqrt 4 * 4 + 2 5 * % IS   2

LAB 15.2 SELF-REVIEW QUESTIONS

In order to test your progress, you should be able to answer the following questions.

1) A function name follows the same naming conventions as a variable.
    a) _____True
    b) _____False

2) A function call must have the same number of arguments as contained in the parameter list.
    a) _____True
    b) _____False

3) A parameter in the parameter list is local to the function.
    a) _____True
    b) _____False

4) An array is passed call-by-value.
    a) _____True
    b) _____False

5) A variable first referenced in the function body is global.
    a) _____True
    b) _____False

6) A parameter that is not passed a value in the function call is assigned the null value.
    a) _____True
    b) _____False

7) A return statement may return a value.
    a) _____True
    b) _____False

8) A function definition can occur anywhere in an awk program.
    a) _____True
    b) _____False

Quiz answers appear in Appendix A, Section 15.2.

**LAB
15.2**

C H A P T E R   15

TEST YOUR THINKING

 The projects in this section are meant to have you utilize all of the skills that you have acquired throughout this chapter. The answers to these projects can be found at the companion Web site to this book, located at:

http://www.phptr.com/phptrinteractive/

Visit the Web site periodically to share and discuss your answers.

In the section on arrays, each array was one-dimensional. In this section, we explore multidimensional arrays. The extension to three or more dimensions is not used very often, so in the following discussion we will use two-dimensional arrays. In a two-dimensional array, each element is defined by a row and column as follows:

```
array[2, 3]=45
```

This would assign 45 to row number 2, column number 3. Awk does not truly support two-dimensional arrays but simulates two-dimensional arrays. Because awk uses strings and associative arrays as one-dimensional indexes, awk must provide a mechanism to transform a two-dimensional index into a one-dimensional index. It does so by transforming `array[2, 3]` into a one-dimensional array index.

Whenever awk encounters the comma in a 2-D array, it substitutes the comma with the built-in variable SUBSEP. The default value for SUBSEP is \034. It then interprets the row and columns as strings (i.e., "2" and "3"). Finally, it concatenates all three arguments together, like so:

```
[2, 3] = ["2" \034 "3"] = ["2\0343"]
array["2\0343"] = 45
```

In this fashion, you can still process the rows and columns of the 2-D array without having to know how awk actually indexes the array.

Use the following file, called `rowcol`:

```
1 2 3
3 4 5
6 7 8
```

1) Execute the following program:

```
BEGIN { row = 1 }
{ for (i=1; i<=NF; i++)
      array[row, i] = $i
  row++
}
END { for (i=1; i<NR; i++) {
        for (j=1; j<=NF; j++)
        print "Row =", i, "Col =", j, "Value =", array[i, j]
        }
     }
```

What is the output?

In the following program, use the following file called `gridPath`:

```
0  3  9  7
2  34 12 6
4  7  6  2
23 11 6  9
7  2  16 11
```

Each number is measured in hours. Each number represents the number of hours needed to get from point a to point b. So the value for row 1 column 2 is 3. This means that to get from row 1, column 1 to row 1, column 2 takes 3 hours. To get from row 1, column 1 to row 2, column 1 takes 2 hours, and 34 hours are needed to get from row 1, column 1 to row 2, column 2. Don't worry about exactness; the measurements are not exact but just randomly chosen.

In the following program, we want to find the smallest time needed to get from a starting point in the grid to an ending point in the grid using a *greedy* algorithm.

A greedy algorithm for any point always chooses the smallest number from all the available choices. So if our starting point was row 1, column 1, a greedy algorithm would choose row 2, column 1 as the next path to take, because it is the smallest time in hours from the available choices. The available choices and their values are:

From row 1, column 1, we can go to:

row 1 column 2 = 3

row 2 column 1 = 2

row 2 column 2 = 34

In other words, we can traverse only to a grid position that is adjacent to the current position. A restriction to the problem is that you can go only to a point in the grid that has a row position that is one greater than the current row in the grid or a column position, that is one greater than the current column number, or that has a row, column number that is both one greater than the current row, column number. In other words, we always move forward, never backwards.

Use the following file, called `startend`, which contains the row and column of the starting position and row and column of the ending position:

```
1  2  4  3
2  2  5  3
```

The output of the program should print the time to get from the start to the end and print the path it took.

2) What is the program?

C H A P T E R 16

ADVANCED INPUT AND OUTPUT

So far, you have seen the `print` function used to print simple output that does not require formatting. The `printf` and `sprintf` statements give you greater control over the format of your output. You will see how in the first Lab of this chapter.

Although we have seen the use of pipes as input and output to awk at the command line, we have not seen that pipes may be used within an awk program. In addition, although we may use the redirection symbols > and >> at the command line, awk allows the redirection symbols to be used within an awk program to redirect output to a file. We will cover pipes and redirection of output into files in this chapter. We will also see how to circumvent the normal processing steps of reading in one input line at a time from a file and instead process the file by using the `getline` function.

L A B   16.1

THE PRINTF AND SPRINTF STATEMENTS

LAB OBJECTIVES

After this Lab, you will be able to:

✓ Understand the Results of Using the Printf and Sprintf Statements

✓ Write Programs Using These Statements

In all the previous awk chapters, we exclusively used the print statement. While more general than the printf statement, the print statement did not allow us to produce output formatted exactly as we desired for all output. The printf statement provides such enhanced capability. The limitations of the print statement are as follows:

- It always produces a newline after it is executed.
- The comma is replaced in output by the value of OS.
- It does not allow us to specify formatting of numbers.

LAB 16.1

All these limitations are avoided when using the printf statement. The two forms of the printf statement are:

```
printf string, expr1, …, exprN
printf (string, expr1, …, exprN)
```

As you can see, the use of parentheses is optional. In addition, the `expr1, ..., exprN` argument is optional. You will see this argument after we discuss the `string` argument.

THE STRING ARGUMENT

The `string` argument is the string to be output and must be enclosed in double quotes. Therefore, the simplest form of the `printf` statement is:

```
printf "This is an example string"
```

This outputs the following:

This is an example string

Note that the `printf` statement does not output a newline after its execution. If you desire to print a newline, then the newline character must explicitly be included in the string, as shown in the following example:

```
printf "This is an example string\nIt uses a new-
line\n"
```

This outputs the following:

This is an example string
It uses a newline

Note that the same output could be produced by the following two `printf` statements in the order they appear, as follows:

```
printf "This is an example "
printf "string\nIt uses a newline"
```

Because `printf` does not automatically output a newline after its execution, the next character to be printed will be printed on the same line as the previous `printf` statement if a newline is not provided in the string.

LAB
16.1

THE EXPR1, ... , EXPRN ARGUMENT

expr1, .. , exprN are any number of string or number variables and/or arithmetic, string, or relational operations, and/or function calls (i.e., anything that produces a value and is an rvalue). These are used when you desire to output any variable and/or expression that yields a value inside the string. expr1, ... , exprN produces a value to be output, but does not specify where in the string that you would like to output the value. The means by which you specify where in the string you would like to output an expression is by using a format specifier, which is recognized by the percent character (%). The printf statement is more versatile than the print statement in that the format specifier is followed by a character that additionally specifies the data type with which the value of the expression is to be associated. The format specifiers are listed as follows:

%c—an ASCII character (i.e., a, or b, or x, etc.)
%d—a whole number (i.e., 1, 40, -5)
%e—[-]d.dddddE[+-]dd
%f—[-]ddd.dddddd
%g—e or f, whichever is shorter, with nonsignificant zeros suppressed
%o—an unsigned octal
%s—a string
%x—unsigned hexadecimal
%—a percent character

Therefore, an example of the printf statement with an expression is as follows, assuming that gpa is 3.14:

```
printf "GPA = %f\n",gpa
```

This would output:

GPA = 3.14

As you can see, the variable gpa is printed as a decimal number indicated by the %f format specifier. It is printed exactly at the position in the string in which the format specifier was encountered. It is important to note that if more than one expression is provided in the printf statement, then more than one format specifier should be provided. Each expression matches a format specifier in order. In other words, the first expression is matched with the first left-most format specifier in the string. The second expression is matched with the second format specifier, and so on.

■ FOR EXAMPLE:

Assume in the following that gpa is 3.14 and name is "Jones":

```
printf "%s GPA = %f\n", name, gpa
```

This example outputs the following:

Jones GPA = 3.14

Here, name was matched with the first left-most format specifier and gpa with the second.

In addition to specifying the data type of a format specifier, you may additionally specify the precision with which you desire the expression value to be output. For example, assume in the following that amount = 1200.1234:

```
printf "The balance due is %7.2f\n", amount
```
The balance due is 1200.12

The precision before the decimal point and percent sign (7) specifies the total width in spaces that you wish to print the number (including the decimal point). In our example, the number 1200.1234 is to be printed seven columns long. The number 2 after the decimal point specifies the number of digits after the decimal point of a real number that are to be printed. The decimal point and the number after the decimal point are optional. Therefore, we can specify the precision of a whole number by the following (assume that income is 1000000):

```
printf "Annual income = %6d\n", income
```
Annual income = 100000

Always remember to include the newline character \n in the string whenever you wish to start output on the next line. Otherwise, all output will appear on the same line.

**LAB
16.1**

SPRINTF

Sprintf is exactly like `printf`, except that output is not directed to the screen. The syntax of the `sprintf` statement is:

```
sprintf string, expr1, ... , exprN
```

`sprintf` returns the string that was constructed as a result of the format specifier and optional precision directive. For example, assume that bal-ance is 1200.1234:

```
amount = sprintf ("%7.2f", balance)
```

Here, `amount` will equal 1200.12.

Sprintf is useful when you would like to format input and/or variables for processing.

LAB 16.1 EXERCISES

16.1.1 UNDERSTAND THE RESULTS OF USING THE PRINTF AND SPRINTF STATEMENTS

For this Exercise, assume that:

```
First_Name = "Peter"
Last_Name = "Patsis"
Name = "Peter Patsis"
Char = "Y"
Number = 101
Real_Number = 98.6
```

**LAB
16.1**

a) What is the result of the following statements?
```
printf "%c", Char
```

```
printf "%c", Number
```

```
printf "%d", Number
```

```
printf "%6d", Number
```

```
printf "%f", Real_Number
```

```
printf "%6.2f", Real_Number
```

```
printf "%-6.2f", Real_Number
```

```
x = sprintf("%s %s", First_Name, Last_Name)
```

```
printf "%s", Name
```

```
printf "%15s", Name
```

```
printf "%-15s", Name
```

**LAB
16.1**

```
printf "%.4s", Name
```

```
printf "%15.4s", Name
```

```
printf "%-15.4s", Name
```

```
x = sprintf("%s %d", (Real_Number > 98.6 ? "Fever" :
    "Normal"), Real_Number
```

16.1.2 WRITE PROGRAMS USING THESE STATEMENTS

a) Write a program that outputs the conf.data file from Lab 4.1 as a table. Use whatever spacing you like for the table. Just make sure that you use more than one space to output each field in the file. Also, print out a column header for each field. Output the sum of all the amount-owed fields as a footer under the amount-owed column.

In Exercises 14.1.2.b and 15.1.2.b, we printed a histogram of the number of times that a number occurred within a range. Refer to those Exercises for the data and output.

b) Rewrite the program so that the first asterisk in each range starts at the same column. In addition, make sure that the text specifying the range (i.e., 30–39, 20–29, 10–19, 0–9) ends on the same column.

For the next question, you will write a program that prints out a three-by-three tic-tac-toe board. Use the following input file, called moves, for this question:

```
X 1 1
O 3 1
X 2 1
O 1 1
```

The first field contains the player (X or O) who is making the move. The second is the row in which the move is to be made. The third is the column in which the move is to be made. Skip moves that already have an X or O in that row or column. The board would look like the following after the file is processed

```
|x| | |
|x| | |
|o| | |
```

Each row and column starts at 1. Print a space in empty cells. Also, prefix and suffix each cell with "|".

c) What is the tic-tac-toe program?

_____

_____

LAB 16.1 EXERCISE ANSWERS

This section gives you some suggested answers to the questions in Lab 16.1, with discussion related to those answers. Your answers may vary, but the most important thing is whether or not your answer works. Use this discussion to analyze differences between your answers and those presented here.

If you have alternative answers to the questions in this Exercise, you are encouraged to post your answers and discuss them at the companion Web site for this book, located at:

```
http://www.phptr.com/phptrinteractive/
```

LAB 16.1

16.1.1 ANSWERS

a) What is the result of the following statements?
   printf "%c", Char

Answer: Y

   printf "%c", Number

Answer: e

The ASCII value of 101 is e. Whenever %c is used, any numeric value that is provided as an argument will be interpreted as an ASCII value.

   printf "%d", Number

Answer: 101

   printf "%6d", Number

Answer: " 101"

The number is three characters long. The format specifier specifies that the number be printed six columns long. Therefore, the number is pre fixed with three spaces.

   printf "%f", Real_Number

Answer: 98.600000

The default precision after the decimal point is six. This is machine dependent.

   printf "%6.2", Real_Number

Answer: " 98.60"

The real number is four characters long, including the decimal point. One digit is supplied with the real number but the precision is two. Therefore the number is first suffixed with a zero. This makes the real number five characters long. The format specifier specifies that the number occupy six columns. Therefore, it is prefixed with a space.

   printf "%-6.2", Real_Number

Answer: "98.60 "

This is the same as the previous specifier. The difference is that the specifier is −6.2 instead of 6.2. Therefore, the number is not prefixed with a space but suffixed.

```
x = sprintf("%s %s", First_Name, Last_Name)
```
Answer: x = "Peter Patsis"

The strings "Peter" and "Patsis" are concatenated according to the format specifier. The result is assigned to the variable x.

```
printf "%s", Name
```
Answer: "Peter Patsis"

```
printf "%15s", Name
```
Answer: "   Peter Patsis"

A string format specifier may also use a precision argument. The precision specified is 15 characters long. The string "Peter Patsis" is twelve characters long and therefore is prefixed with three spaces.

```
printf "%-15s", Name
```
Answer: "Peter Patsis   "

This is the same as before, except that the negative precision number causes three spaces to be suffixed.

```
printf "%.4s", Name
```
Answer: Pete   "

A decimal number with a string format specifier determines the number of characters that will be taken from the string and output. If the number following the decimal number is less than the string length, the output will cause the string to truncate.

```
printf "%15.4s", Name
```
Answer: "   Pete"

LAB 16.1

```
printf "%-15.4s", Name
```
Answer: Pete   "

```
x = sprintf("%s %d", (Real_Number > 98.6 ? "Fever" :
    "Normal"), Real_Number
```

Answer: x="Normal 98.6"

16.1.2 ANSWERS

a) Write a program that outputs the conf.data file
from Lab 4.1 as a table. Use whatever spacing
you like for the table. Just make sure that you
use more than one space to output each field in
the file. Also, print out a column header for
each field. Output the sum of all the amount-
owed fields as a footer under the amount-owed
column.

Answer: The program is as follows:

```
BEGIN { printf "%15s %15s %15s %15s %15s %15s\n", "Name", "Con-
    ference Name", "Conference Fee", "Amount Owed", "Date Regis-
    tered", "Company"
        for (i=0; i<95; i++)
            printf "-"
        printf("\n")
}
{ printf "%15s %15s %15d %15d %15d %15s\n", $1, $2, $3, $4, $5,
    $6
    sum+=$4
}
END { for (i=0; i<95; i++)
        printf "-"
        printf "\n%64d\n", sum
    }
```

To make life easier, we use 15 characters as a precision for all fields. This
assures that all headers, data, and footer will line up.

```
BEGIN { printf "%15s %15s %15s %15s %15s %15s\n", "Name", "Con-
    ference Name", "Conference Fee", "Amount Owed", "Date Regis-
    tered", "Company"
```

The BEGIN statement is used to print the header for the table. It uses the
printf statement with the format specifier %15s to print the constant
strings in its argument list.

```
for (i=0; i<95; i++)
        printf "-"
    printf("\n")
```

It then uses the `for` loop to print a dash to separate the header from the data. It prints 95 dashes. It does not print a newline within the `for` loop, so that each dash will appear on the same line. Finally, a newline is printed.

```
{ printf "%15s %15s %15d %15d %15d %15s\n", $1, $2, $3, $4, $5,
    $6
    sum+=$4
}
```

The main processing loop consists of two statements. The first uses a `printf` statement with a format specifier of `%15s` or `%15d` to print each field of the `conf.data` file. The second statement sums all the amounts owed for all registrants.

```
END { for (i=0; i<95; i++)
        printf "-"
      printf "\n%64d\n", sum }
```

Finally, we print 95 dashes to separate the data from the footer. The last statement prints the sum of all amount-owed by all registrants. We know that amount-owed is the fourth column, so it is 15x4 characters away from the first column position. We use 64 to indent a little.

b) Rewrite the program so that the first asterisk in each range starts at the same column. In addition, make sure that the text specifying the range (i.e., 30–39, 20–29, 10–19, 0–9) ends on the same column.

Answer: The program is as follows:

```
{ array_index = int($1/10)
  if (array_index < 4)
     histogram[array_index]++
  else
     print "Number out of range"
}
END { for (i=3; i>-1; i--) {
         header = (10*i) "-" ((10*i)+9)
         printf "%5s  ", header
         for (j=0; j<histogram[i]; j++)
```

**LAB
16.1**

```
                              printf "*"
                         printf "\n"
                  }
            }
```

The expression array_index = int($1/10) takes the number that is input and indexes it into the appropriate range—3, 2, 1, or 0. The number of numbers encountered in this range is incremented by one with the expression histogram[array_index]++.

```
      END { for (i=3; i>-1; i--) {
                  header = (10*i) "-" ((10*i)+9)
                  printf "%5s   ", header
                  for (j=0; j<histogram[i]; j++)
                        printf "*"
                  printf "\n"

            }
      }
```

For each range 0–3, we cycle through the histogram array, printing the appropriate number of asterisks given by the value of array element his-togram[0], [1], [2], or [3]. First, the header string is created by concat enating i*10 (30, 20, 10, or 0) with a dash and i*10+9 (39, 29, 19, or 9). We use the format specifier %5 with three spaces to make sure that the headers line up.

The output is:

```
      30-39   *
      20-29   **
      10-19   *****
       0-9    ***
```

c) What is the tic-tac-toe program?

Answer: The program is as follows:
```
function printBoard(BOARD,    i_loc, j_loc) {
for (i_loc=1; i_loc<4; i_loc++) {
    for (j_loc=1; j_loc<4; j_loc++)
        printf "|%c", BOARD[i_loc*10+j_loc]
    printf "|\n"
}
printf "\n\n"
return
}
```

```
BEGIN { for (i=1; i<4; i++) {
          for (j=1; j<4; j++) {
              board[i*10+j]=" "
          }
        }
        printBoard(board)
      }
{ array_index = $2*10+$3
  if (board[array_index]==" ")
    board[array_index]=$1
  printBoard(board)
}
```

The output is

```
| | | |
| | | |
| | | |
```

```
|x| | |
| | | |
| | | |
```

```
|x| | |
| | | |
|o| | |
```

```
|x| | |
|x| | |
|o| | |
```

```
|x| | |
|x| | |
|o| | |
```

The board is printed in the BEGIN pattern before any moves are made. [ ] is printed once again after each move is read in. I chose to use an array which is a one-dimensional storage element, to store each board position which is a two-dimensional abstraction. The main challenge was how to index a one-dimensional storage element that represents a two-dimensional object. I did this by multiplying 10 by the row and adding the column number to it. Therefore, my indexes are 11, 12, 13, 21, 22, 23, 31, 32, and 33. Therefore, when I read in a move, say X 3 1, I multiply $ (3) by 10 and add $3 (1) to it. So X 3 1 indexes 31. Printing the board is easy once we fixate on a storage strategy. All we need to do is create double for loop. The first for loop cycles through 1–3 for each row. The second for loop cycles through each column. Thus, in the printBoard function, we see the following loops:

```
for (i_loc=1; i_loc<4; i_loc++)
    for (j_loc=1; j_loc<4; j_loc++)
            printf  ....
```

All that is left in the program is to determine whether the move is valid. [ ] so, we store $1 (X or O) into the array position indexed by $1, $2 a described. If the position of "indexed by $2, $3" is blank (we assigned a array elements to blank in the begin pattern), then the position is no occupied and it is a valid move. Otherwise, if it is X or O, we are attempting to either overwrite our previous move or overwrite an opponent move. Either case does not matter; both are invalid.

LAB 16.1 SELF-REVIEW QUESTIONS

In order to test your progress, you should be able to answer the following questions.

1) The number of format specifiers must be the same as the number of expressions in the expression list.
   a) _____True
   b) _____False

2) A format specifier is optional in the string of a printf statement.
   a) _____True
   b) _____False

3) A newline is always printed as a result of executing a `printf` statement.
  a) _____True
  b) _____False

4) An optional precision may be specified, in addition to a format specifier.
  a) _____True
  b) _____False

5) A negative sign provided with a format specifier left-justifies the specifier.
  a) _____True
  b) _____False

6) A real number may be provided as a precision.
  a) _____True
  b) _____False

Quiz answers appear in Appendix A, Section 16.1.

**LAB
16.1**

L A B   16.2

OUTPUT INTO PIPES, FILES, AND THE GETLINE FUNCTION

LAB OBJECTIVES

After this Lab, you will be able to:

✓ Understand the Results of the Getline Function, and Direct Output into Pipes and Files

✓ Write Programs, Using the Getline Function, That Direct Output into Pipes and Files

OUTPUT INTO FILES

In awk, output may be directed into a file instead of to the screen, by using the redirection operators > and >> within an awk program. This possibility is illustrated by the following program:

```
awk '$2 == "Coatings" || $2 == "Adhesions" { print $0 > "Inter-
   national.dat"\
$2 == "Resins" || $2 == "Stabilizers" {print $0 >"Domes-
   tic.dat"\
}' conf.data
```

This program prints $0 into the file `international.dat` if the confer-
ence name is equal to "Coatings" or "Adhesions." Otherwise, it prints $0
into `domestic.dat` if the conference name is equal to "Resins" or "Stabilizers." The file redirection operator is used to redirect $0 into the appro-
priate file. The file that will be used as output must be enclosed within
double quotes. If not, the filename will be assumed to be a normal uninitialized variable and not a file. The difference between the > redirection
symbol and >> is that when >> is used, the output is appended to the file
surrounded in double quotes. If > is used, then the file is overwritten. The
name of the file may also be contained within an awk variable.

■ FOR EXAMPLE:

Consider the following:

```
BEGIN {outfile = "RegNames.dat" }
{ print $1, $2 > outfile }
```

This program prints the first and second fields of an input file into the file
`RegNames.dat`. Be sure to distinguish, when using a relational operator
with a redirection operator, the order in which you intend each to be
used—by using parentheses as in the following:

```
awk '{print ($1, $4) > ($4 > 0 ? "confOwed.dat" : "Conf-
    Paid.dat")}' conf.data
```

Here, the conditional expression returns a file name based on the conditional $4>0. The file name is returned to the redirection symbol, which
prints the first and fourth fields of the `conf.data` file.

OUTPUT INTO PIPES

In the previous discussion, we redirected output into a file by using the
redirection symbol. We may instead redirect the output into a pipe by
replacing the file redirection symbol with the pipe symbol (|). This
option is illustrated as follows:

```
awk '{print ($2, $1) | "sort"}' conf.data
```

**LAB
16.2**

Here, the output produced by the print statement, which prints the conference name followed by the registrant's name, is piped into the sort routine, which sorts according to the conference name. The same rules apply as with the file redirection symbols. The pipe expression (sort) must be enclosed in double quotes. The pipe expression may be contained in a variable. Because the pipe symbol (|) is not used by awk for any other operator, parentheses are not needed, as they were with the redirection symbol, in order to distinguish the pipe symbol from a relational operator.

THE GETLINE FUNCTION

The getline function is used to instruct awk that we wish to read in an input line from a file. This circumvents the normal processing step in which awk reads in an input line, splits the input line into fields, and processes each pattern that is not a BEGIN or END pattern using this input line. The getline function causes a line of input from an input file, standard input, or pipe to be immediately read in. The line that is read in for most versions of getline is still split up into fields $0, $1, .. , $NF as it normally is. The value of FS is still used, and NF, NR, and FNR are updated as normal. Processing continues at the next awk statement following the getline function. The various forms of the getline are shown in Table 16.1.

Table 16.1 ■ Forms of Getline

Expression		Action
getline	- reads in a line into $0	Sets $0, NF, NR, FNR
getline var	- reads in a line into var instead of $0	Sets var, NR, FNR
getline <file	- reads in a line from file	Sets $0, NF
getline var <file	- reads in a line from file into var	Sets var
cmd | getline	- pipes cmd into getline into $0	Sets $0, NF
cmd | getline var	- pipes cmd into getline into var	var

Each version of getline determines where getline is to read in its input (file, pipe, or as part of the awk "program" input-file command-line invocation), and after reading the line, whether to store the line read in into $0 or a variable. The getline function returns a 1 if it successfully reads in an input line, a 0 if it encounters the end of the file, and a –1 if the file cannot be found or opened for input.

An example of the two most common forms of `getline` is as follows:

Given the file

```
12000.23
w  3000
d  2000
```

we can determine an ending balance with the following awk program:

```
{ balance = $1
    while (getline) {
        if ($1 == "w")
            balance-=$2
        else
            balance+=$2
    }
}
```

Remember that when we encountered this program as an exercise without the `getline` function, we had to use `NR==1` to store the first record into balance. Because the `getline` function by itself with no arguments reads in the next line of input from the file specified in the awk invocation, we do not need the pattern-action `NR==1` {balance = $1}. Because awk automatically opens the input file and reads in the first line, `getline` by itself in an action will read in the second line. We cannot circumvent this action by using `getline` by itself. Therefore, we may manipulate the first line read in by awk and process subsequent lines with `getline`. `Getline` continues reading in lines within the `while` loop until the end of file is reached. When end of file is reached, `getline` returns 0. `While(0)` is false, and the `while` loop is exited.

The second common form of `getline` is to input the line read in into a variable instead of $0, as the following illustrates:

```
{ printf "Enter the starting balance "
    getline balance < "-"
```

```
     printf "\nEnter a transaction w - withdrawal d -
   deposit ctrl-d to end"
    while (getline trans_type < "-") {
        printf "\nEnter a transaction amount"
        getline trans_amt < "-"
        if (trans_type == "w")
            balance-=trans_amt
        else
            balance+=trans_amt
        printf "Enter a transaction w - withdrawal d -
   deposit
   }
}
```

In this example, getline inputs a line into the variable trans_type or trans_amt. The input file is determined by the file name "-", which is a symbol used to specify standard input. In other words, getline and "-" are used to perform interactive input from the user. The input that is entered by the user is stored into the variable trans_type or trans_amt. Not all versions of awk will use "-". See whether this program works on your machine.

LAB 16.2 EXERCISES

16.2.1 UNDERSTAND THE RESULTS OF USING THE GETLINE FUNCTION, AND DIRECT OUTPUT INTO PIPES AND FILES

a) What is a potential problem with the following getline statement?

```
while (getline <"input-file")
```

_____

_____

b) How do you make the preceding while statement less problematic

_____

_____

For the next question, assume that we have the following file called `input-file`:

```
w  1
x  2
y  3
z  4
```

Further, the values of $0, NF, NR, and FNR are the following before the `getline` function is called:

```
$0  = x 2
NF  = 2
NR  = 2
FNR = 2
var = " "
```

Finally, assume that if getline is called without a filename argument, the file `input-file` was provided at the command line to the awk program.

What is the value of $0, NF, NR, FNR, and `var` after the execution of each of the following `getline` functions?

c) `getline`

_____

_____

d) `getline var`

_____

_____

e) `getline <input-file`

_____

_____

f) `getline var <input-file`

---

g) What does the following program do:

```
awk '{while ("who" | getline) {\
if ($1 < "p") print $1\
}' some-file
```

16.2.2 WRITE PROGRAMS, USING THE GETLINE FUNCTION, THAT DIRECT OUTPUT INTO PIPES OR FILES

a) Write a program that converts the current system date from a format that prints the month in text and the year as 19xx to a mm/dd/yy format. For example, Sep. 14, 1969 would be printed as: **9/14/69**

---

b) Write a program that outputs the registrants who owe money for each conference into a separate file for each conference. For example, all people who owe money for the Adhesions conference would be placed into `Adhesions.dat`, and so forth. Include in the file the name of the registrant, the amount owed, and the amount paid.

LAB 16.2 EXERCISE ANSWERS

This section gives you some suggested answers to the questions in Lab 16.2, with discussion related to those answers. Your answers may vary, but the most important thing is whether or not your answer works. Use this discussion to analyze differences between your answers and those presented here.

If you have alternative answers to the questions in this Exercise, you are encouraged to post your answers and discuss them at the companion Web site for this book, located at:

```
http://www.phptr.com/phptrinteractive/
```

16.2.1 ANSWERS

a) What is a potential problem with the following getline statement?
```
while (getline <"input-file")
```

Answer: The problem is that if the file is not opened (either because it does not exist or we don't have permission to open it), then getline returns −1. While(-1) *is interpreted as true (non-zero), and we are in an infinite loop.*

b) How do you make the preceding while statement less problematic?

Answer: You would rewrite it as follows:
```
while ( (getline <"input-file) > 0).
```

You should technically add >0 whenever processing getline functions that open or pipe a file as input.

What is the value of $0, NF, NR, FNR, and var after the execution of each of the following getline functions?

c) getline ==> sets just $0, NF, NR, and FNR

Answer: The values are as follows:
```
$0 = y 3    (the next is read in and since FNR and NR
= 2 the third line is read)
NF = 2
NR = 3
FNR = 3
```

```
var = ""
```

d) `getline var ==>sets just var, NR, and FNR`

Answer: The values are as follows:
```
$0 = x 2
NF = 2
NR = 3
FNR = 3
var = "y 3"
```

e) `getline <input-file ==> sets just $0, NF`

Answer: The values are as follows:
```
$0 = y 3
NF = 2
NR = 2
FNR = 2
var = ""
```

f) `getline var <input-file ==> sets just var`

Answer: The values are as follows:
```
$0 = x 2
NF = 2
NR = 2
FNR = 2
var = "y 3"
```

g) What does the following program do:
```
awk '{while ("who" | getline) {\
if ($1 < "p") print $1\
}' some-file
```

Answer: It prints out all users who are logged in who have a user name that is less than p.

Here we use a pipe as input to the awk program. The pipe executes the UNIX command who, which returns all users that are logged in. We use getline function by itself, which awk splits into fields. The first field i the user's name. We then use the conditional to test whether $1 (user) i less than p and print $1 if the conditional is satisfied.

16.2.2 ANSWERS

a) Write a program that converts the current system
date from a format that prints the month in text
and the year as 19xx to a mm/dd/yy format. For
example, Sep. 14, 1969 would be printed as:
9/14/69

Answer: The program is as follows:

```
BEGIN { month["Jan"]=01
        month["Feb"]=02
        month["Mar"]=03
        month["Apr"]=04
        month["May"]=05
        month["Jun"]=06
        month["Jul"]=07
        month["Aug"]=08
        month["Sep"]=09
        month["Oct"]=10
        month["Nov"]=11
        month["Dec"]=12
      }
{ "date" | getline
  printf "%2d/%2d/%2s\n", month[$2], $3, substr($6, 3,
  2)
}
```

We hardcode the numeric equivalent of the month into the array
month. I know of no fancy algorithm that will do this without hardcod-
ing the month. We then use the UNIX system date command to pipe
the date into the program. Its format contains the month in the second
field, the day in the third field, and the year in the last field, $6. We use
the substr function to convert a date in *1998* form to *98* form. The rest
is straightforward.

The output when I ran the program on September 22 is:

9/22/98

b) Write a program that outputs the registrants who owe money for each conference into a separate file for each conference. For example, all people who owe money for the Adhesions conference would be placed into Adhesions.dat, and so forth. Include in the file the name of the registrant, the amount owed, and the amount paid.

Answer: The program is as follows:
```
$2 == "Adhesions" { if ($4 > 0) printf ("%s %s %s\n", $1, $3,
    $4) >"Adhesions.dat" }
$2 == "Coatings" { if ($4 > 0) printf ("%s %s %s\n", $1, $3,
    $4) >"Coatings.dat" }
$2 == "Stabilizers" { if ($4 > 0) printf ("%s %s %s\n", $1, $3,
    $4) >"Stabilizers.dat" }
$2 == "Resins" { if ($4 > 0) printf ("%s %s %s\n", $1, $3, $4)
    >"Resins.dat" }
```

First, we use the following pattern-action statement to process the Adhesions conference:

```
$2 == "Adhesions" { if ($4 > 0) printf ("%s %s %s\n", $1, $3,
    $4) >"Adhesions.dat" }
```

`$2 == "Adhesions"` is the conditional that we use to process the Adhesions conference. If true, then the action checks whether `$4 > 0`. If so, then this registrant owes money for the conference. We then use the `printf` statement to print the registrant name, conference fee, and amount owed. This printout is redirected by using the redirection symbol (`>`) into the `Adhesions.dat` file.

The remaining lines follow the same logic.

After processing, these files contain the following:

```
Adhesions.dat
Smith 700 200
Patsis 700 350

Coatings.dat
Kenny 900 450
Mack 900 100
Patterson 900 450
Bostic 900 900
```

```
Stabilizers.dat
Phillips 850 100
Denny 850 200
Donaldson 850 200
Federicks 850 100

Resins.dat
Jackson 800 200
Harrison 800 800
Quinn 800 500
```

LAB 16.2 SELF-REVIEW QUESTIONS

In order to test your progress, you should be able to answer the following questions.

1) Getline called without any additional arguments does not update NF.
   a) _____True
   b) _____False

2) Getline var called without any additional arguments does not update $0.
   a) _____True
   b) _____False

3) If the redirection symbol is used, the filename does not have to be enclosed in double quotes.
   a) _____True
   b) _____False

4) If the < redirection symbol is used with getline without additional parameters, it updates $0.
   a) _____True
   b) _____False

5) If the >> redirection symbol is used, then it overwrites the file's contents.
   a) _____True
   b) _____False

Quiz answers appear in Appendix A, Section 16.2.

LAB
16.2

C H A P T E R   16

TEST YOUR THINKING

The projects in this section are meant to have you utilize all of the skills that you have acquired throughout this chapter. The answers to these projects can be found at the companion Web site to this book, located at:

`http://www.phptr.com/phptrinteractive/`

Visit the Web site periodically to share and discuss your answers.

In Lab 11.3, we talked about built-in variables. The only built-in variables that we have not discussed is OFMT and CONVFMT. Throughout the chapters on awk, we have seen how to use the print statement. In this "Test Your Thinking," we will go over the use of the built-in variable OFMT, which is used in conjunction with the `print` statement. In the introduction to the `printf` statement in Lab 16.1, we mentioned that one limitation of the `print` statement was that it did not allow us to specify the formatting of numbers. Although this is still true, with the use of the OFMT variable, awk allows us to give some specification over the formatting of numbers. OFMT is used to determine how to convert a number to a string when the number is to be output with the `print` statement. For example, if avg = 93.14, OFMT = "%d", and we encountered the print statement below:

```
print "The value is = ", avg
```

The output would be

The value is = 93

We specify the value of OFMT in this same fashion as we specified a format specifier in a `printf` statement. OFMT may assume any of the formats that were used for numbers in a `printf` statement (I say "that were used for numbers," because to convert a number to a string with %s would not make much sense, since that would be redundant).

CONVFMT is similar to OFMT in every respect except that CONVFMT is not used only within a `print` statement but anywhere in an awk program that a string is to be converted to a number.

Enter the following program using any file that has a single line of input (we do not care about the contents of the input file for this program but need to use a file when invoking awk).

```
BEGIN  {  OFMT  =  "%4d";  avg  =  34.1234;  prevAvg  =
   120.0234 }
{value = "The value of CurrentAvg = " avg "Previ-
   ousAvg = " prevAvg }
END { print "CurrentAvg = ", avg, "PreviousAvg = ",
   prevAvg
      print value
      }
```

1) What is the output?

2) Run the program again but assign different format specifier values for OFMT in the BEGIN pattern. Try using various precision values along with the format specifiers.

3) What are potential limitations of using OFMT with a print statement?

4) Run the program again but use CONVFMT in the BEGIN pattern instead of OFMT.

5) In the exercises of Lab 16.1, we wrote a program that printed out a tic-tac-toe board given a file of moves. For this program, write an awk program that plays an interactive game of tic-tac-toe. By "interactive," we mean that the input will come from standard input. After each correct move, print out the contents of the board. Determine when the game is finished and print the winner (X or O), or a tie if no one wins.

A P P E N D I X A

ANSWERS TO SELF-REVIEW QUESTIONS

CHAPTER 1

Lab 1.1 ■ Self-Review Answers

Question	Answer	Comment
1)	b	
2)	a	
3)	a, b, and c	
4)	a, b, and c	
5)	a	

CHAPTER 2

Lab 2.1 ■ Self-Review Answers

Question	Answer	Comment
1)	c	
2)	None	
3)	a, b, and d	
4)	b and d	
5)	d and e	
6)	a and d	

CHAPTER 3

Lab 3.1 ■ Self-Review Answers

Question	Answer	Comment
1)	c	
2)	a	
3)	d	
4)	e	An error results because it needs to be quoted.
5)	d	No output occurs because no matching lines exist.

CHAPTER 4

Lab 4.1 ■ Self-Review Answers

Question	Answer	Comment
1)	b and d	
2)	b	
3)	b	
4)	d	

Lab 4.2 ■ Self-Review Answers

Question	Answer	Comment
1)	c and d	But note that using these might result in unexpected output.
2)	b and d	Again, using these might result in unexpected output.
3)	a	
4)	b	

Lab 4.3 ■ Self-Review Answers

Question	Answer	Comment
1)	b and d	
2)	a	
3)	b	

CHAPTER 5

Lab 5.1 ■ Self-Review Answers

Question	Answer	Comment
1)	b	
2)	a	
3)	a, b, and d	
4)	d	It's an error because the last slash is not provided. If it were provided, the answer would be c.

CHAPTER 6

Lab 6.1 ■ Self-Review Answers

Question	Answer	Comment
1)	a, b, c, and d	
2)	c	
3)	e	
4)	c, d, and e	
5)	a, b, c, and d	

CHAPTER 7

Lab 7.1 ■ Self-Review Answers

Question	Answer	Comment
1)	a - iv; b - i; c - iii; d - ii	
2)	c and d	
3)	c and d	
4)	f	The correct answer is 650.
5)	d	
6)	e	

Lab 7.2 ■ Self-Review Answers

Question	Answer	Comment
1)	b	
2)	a	
3)	b	
4)	a	
5)	a	

Lab 7.3 ■ Self-Review Answers

Question	Answer	Comment
1)	a	
2)	b	
3)	a	
4)	b	
5)	b	
6)	b	

Lab 7.4 ■ Self-Review Answers

Question	Answer	Comment
1)	b	
2)	b	
3)	b	
4)	a	

Lab 7.5 ■ Self-Review Answers

Question	Answer	Comment
1)	b	
2)	a	
3)	a	
4)	b	
5)	b	
6)	b	

Lab 7.6 ■ Self-Review Answers

Question	Answer	Comment
1)	b	
2)	b	
3)	b	
4)	b	
5)	b	

CHAPTER 8
Lab 8.1 ■ Self-Review Answers

Question	Answer	Comment
1)	a	
2)	d	
3)	a	
4)	d	

CHAPTER 9
Lab 9.1 ■ Self-Review Answers

Question	Answer	Comment
1)	a	
2)	a and c	
3)	e	

Lab 9.2 ■ Self-Review Answers

Question	Answer	Comment
1)	b	
2)	a	
3)	a	
4)	c	
5)	b	
6)	a	

Lab 9.3 ■ Self-Review Answers

Question	Answer	Comment
1)	b and c	
2)	a, b, c, and d	

CHAPTER 10

Lab 10.1 ■ Self-Review Answers

Question	Answer	Comment
1)	a and c	
2)	a and d	
3)	a and d	
4)	a	
5)	d	This is machine dependent.

Lab 10.2 ■ Self-Review Answers

Question	Answer	Comment
1)	b	
2)	e	String concatenation does not have an operator.
3)	c	

Lab 10.3 ■ Self-Review Answers

Question	Answer	Comment
1)	a	
2)	e	This is machine dependent.
3)	c	

Lab 10.4 ■ Self-Review Answers

Question	Answer	Comment
1)	Either	It is undetermined. It could be a (number) or b (string).
2)	a	
3)	a	
4)	b	

Lab 10.5 ■ Self-Review Answers

Question	Answer	Comment
1)	a and c	
2)	b and d	
3)	a, c, and d	
4)	c and d	

CHAPTER 11

Lab 11.1 ■ Self-Review Answers

Question	Answer	Comment
1)	a	
2)	b	
3)	a	
4)	a	This one can also be answered false if you consider that you may create field variables in addition to the ones awk created when splitting the input line.
5)	a	Otherwise, you would overwrite the field value from the input line.
6)	a	

Lab 11.2 ■ Self-Review Answers

Question	Answer	Comment
1)	a and b	
2)	d	Keep in mind, though, that BEGIN statements, END statements, and main processing loops are all part of an awk program.
3)	d	
4)	a	
5)	a	

Lab 11.3 ■ Self-Review Answers

Question	Answer	Comment
1)	b	
2)	a	
3)	c	

Lab 11.3 ■ Self-Review Answers (Continued)

4)	b	OFS is used when reconstructing $0.
5)	c	
6)	a	

CHAPTER 12

Lab 12.1 ■ Self-Review Answers

Question	Answer	Comment
1)	a	
2)	a	
3)	a	
4)	d	
5)	c	

Lab 12.2 ■ Self-Review Answers

Question	Answer	Comment
1)	a	
2)	a	
3)	a	
4)	a	
5)	a	
6)	b	
7)	b	
8)	a	

Lab 12.3 ■ Self-Review Answers

Question	Answer	Comment
1)	b	
2)	b	
3)	a	
4)	a	
5)	a	
6)	b	

Lab 12.3 ■ Self-Review Answers (Continued)

7)	b
8)	a
9)	a

CHAPTER 13

Lab 13.1 ■ Self-Review Answers

Question	Answer	Comment
1)	c	
2)	c	
3)	d	
4)	b	

Lab 13.2 ■ Self-Review Answers

Question	Answer	Comment
1)	a-iv; b-iii; c-i; d-ii	
2)	b	The index function updates RSTART and RLENGTH.
3)	a	
4)	a	
5)	a	
6)	a	

Lab 13.3 ■ Self-Review Answers

Question	Answer	Comment
1)	b	
2)	b	
3)	b	
4)	a	
5)	a	
6)	b	
7)	a	
8)	a	

CHAPTER 14

Lab 14.1 ■ Self-Review Answers

Question	Answer	Comment
1)	a	
2)	a	
3)	b	
4)	b	
5)	b	
6)	b	
7)	a	

Lab 14.2 ■ Self-Review Answers

Question	Answer	Comment
1)	a	
2)	b	
3)	a	
4)	a	
5)	a	

Lab 14.3 ■ Self-Review Answers

Question	Answer	Comment
1)	a	
2)	a	
3)	a	
4)	b	
5)	a	
6)	b	

Lab 14.4 ■ Self-Review Answers

Question	Answer	Comment
1)	b	
2)	a	
3)	a	

Lab 14.4 ■ Self-Review Answers (Continued)

    4)   b

    5)   a

CHAPTER 15

Lab 15.1 ■ Self-Review Answers

Question	Answer	Comment
1)		
2)		
3)		
4)		
5)		
6)		

Lab 15.2 ■ Self-Review Answers

Question	Answer	Comment
1)		
2)		
3)		
4)		
5)		
6)		
7)		
8)		

CHAPTER 16

Lab 16.1 ■ Self-Review Answers

Question	Answer	Comment
1)		
2)		
3)		
4)		

Lab 16.1 ■ Self-Review Answers (Continued)

5)

6)

Lab 16.2 ■ Self-Review Answers

Question   Answer   Comment

1)

2)

3)

4)

5)

AWK, SED, AND GREP REFERENCE

AWK PROGRAMMING MODEL

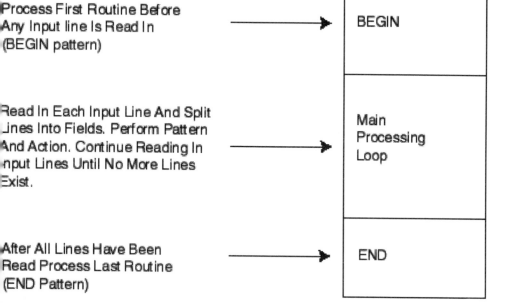

Process First Routine Before Any Input line Is Read In (BEGIN pattern) → **BEGIN**

Read In Each Input Line And Split Lines Into Fields. Perform Pattern And Action. Continue Reading In Input Lines Until No More Lines Exist. → **Main Processing Loop**

After All Lines Have Been Read Process Last Routine (END Pattern) → **END**

After the system invokes awk, awk executes the statements within the BEGIN pattern if a BEGIN pattern is provided. Awk then takes the first input line and splits it into fields. After splitting the line into fields, awk examines the pattern on the split input line. An awk pattern is the part after the beginning quote up to the opening brace.

If the pattern is true (evaluation of the expression in the pattern results in a non-zero or non-null value), then awk executes the action. An action may contain multiple steps. Each step may involve many operations, print statements, and so forth. Awk then continues with the next line until all the lines have been processed. Once all input lines have been read, awk then executes the END pattern if an END pattern exists, and then it exits.

COMMENT

A comment in awk begins with the # sign and ends at the end of a line. The comment character can appear on a line by itself or it can be used at the end of a statement.

PATTERN

A pattern can be any of the following:

- BEGIN
- END
- expression
- /regular expression/
- pattern && pattern
- pattern || pattern
- !pattern
- (pattern)
- pattern, pattern

Some patterns are given as follows.

1. BEGIN PATTERN

A BEGIN pattern is executed before the first line of input is read and before the END pattern is executed. A BEGIN pattern can appear anywhere in an awk program, but is more commonly placed after all function definitions and before the END pattern and any other pattern. Field variables may not be accessed within a BEGIN pattern. An action must be specified with a BEGIN pattern.

2. END PATTERN

The END pattern is executed after the last line of input is read and the last pattern executed. An END pattern can appear anywhere in an awk program but is more commonly placed after all function definitions, the BEGIN pattern, and any other pattern. All variables may be accessed in an END pattern. An action must be specified in an END pattern.

3. EXPRESSION

A pattern is optional. If no pattern is provided, then an action must be present, which is executed for every input record. A pattern can be any expression (primary) or an operator that combines expressions. If the expression yields a non-zero or non-null value, then the pattern is assumed to be true and the action is executed if provided. Otherwise (zero or null), the action is not executed. If a single pattern is provided in an awk program, then it must be placed after the opening quote on the command line and before the opening brace of an action. Each subsequent pattern must be placed at the start of a newline. Patterns usually consist of a relational expression.

4. /REGULAR EXPRESSION/

A pattern can be a regular expression enclosed in slashes. If the regular expression matches the input line $0, then the action will be executed.

5. PATTERN1 && PATTERN2, PATTERN1 || PATTERN2

Any of the patterns 1–8 may be used in conjunction with a boolean operator that combines patterns (&&, and ||) to form a complex pattern. If && is used, then if pattern1 and pattern2 are true, the action will be executed. If || is used, then if pattern1 or pattern2 is true, then the action will be executed.

6. !PATTERN

Any of the patterns 1–8 may be used in conjunction with the negation operator to negate the result of the pattern. If the pattern is true, then the negation is false and the action is not executed. If the result of pattern is false, the negation of the pattern yields true and the action is executed.

7. (PATTERN)

Any pattern may be enclosed within parentheses to force the ordering of evaluating a pattern. This option is especially useful for complex patterns that include a combining operator such as && and/or ||. This is shown in the following:

```
($1 > 3 && FNR < 7) || $2 > 7
$1 > 3 && (FNR < 7 || $2 > 7)
```

8. PATTERN, PATTERN

A range may be used to specify a pattern. This works exactly as it did in sed (Chapter 6, "Sed Syntax and Addressing"), activating or deactivating ranges. An example is the following:

```
$2 == "Coatings", $2 == "Stabilizers"
```

When $2 is equal to "Coatings," the range is activated. When $2 == "Stabilizers," the range is deactivated and will not activate until $2 == "Coatings" once again.

ACTION

An action is optional. If it is not provided, then a pattern must be provided. If no action is provided, then if the pattern is true, the action will be to print $0. An action is enclosed within a pair of braces. If a pattern is provided, then the opening brace must appear on the same line as the pattern it accompanies. The rest of the action and closing brace can appear on the same line as the opening brace or on any subsequent line. If no pattern is provided, then the opening brace can appear anywhere on a line and must be the first non white-space character encountered. An action is zero, one, or more statements (described next) in any combination.

STATEMENT

A statement consists of one of the following followed by a statement separator:

1. A primary expression (described below)

2.   An operator that combines primary expressions (described below)
3.   One of the following:
```
break
continue
next
exit [Expression]

if (Expression) then
    action
[else action]

while (Expression)
    action

do
   action
while (Expression)

for (counter; test; increment)
    action

for (variable in array)
    action

delete array-element

return [Expression]

input-output statement

empty statement
```

STATEMENT SEPARATOR

Statements are separated by a semicolon, a newline, or both. A statement that has two statement separators next to each other creates an empty statement. A statement may be typed over several lines by escaping the end of each line with a backslash. A statement may be typed on a subsequent line without a backslash, after a comma, left brace, &&, ||, do, else, and the right parentheses in an if or for statement.

AWK PROGRAM AND PROGRAM FORMAT

An awk program is everything between the opening quote and ending quote of an awk invocation. An awk program contains one or more pattern-action statements and function definitions. A pattern-action statement has the following form:

```
pattern {action}
```

Patterns and actions are described previously, and either, but not both, may be omitted.

A function definition has the following form:

```
function name(parameter-list) statements
```

A function definition (described below) should, but does not have to appear before any pattern-action statement.

An awk program has the following format:

```
function name(parameter-list) Statement
...
BEGIN {action}
pattern {action}
...
END {action}
```

The dots suggest that more than one of the immediately above items may follow the item. In other words, more than one function may appear and more than one pattern {action} may appear. Any of the above items are optional. Multiple statements may be put on the same line within a pattern, action, or function if each statement is separated by a semicolor. Blank lines may be placed before or after any statement, pattern-action statement, or function definition.

DATA TYPES

Two data types are in awk—strings and numbers.

STRINGS

A string in awk is defined as a sequence of zero or more characters. Note that a string with zero characters is the null string, which is empty (i.e., it contains no characters).

Examples of various string representations are as follows:

"Hello, World"	a string with 12 characters
"\t"	a string with 1 character
"John Smith\n"	a string with 11 characters
" "	a string with zero characters, the null string
"0123"	a string with four characters, the digits 0123
"(-|+)?[0-9]*"	a string containing 12 characters, a regular expression

As the example "\t" suggests, a string may contain escape sequences. The following is a list of the escape sequences.

■ Awk Escape Sequences

Character	Function
\b	backspace
\f	formfeed
\n	newline (line feed)
\r	carriage return
\t	tab
\ddd	octal value ddd, where ddd is 1 to 3 digits between 0 and 7
\c	any other character c where c is interpreted literally (e.g., \\ for backslash)

STRING INITIALIZATION If a variable is involved in an operation that expects a string, and the variable is referenced before it was explicitly given a value by an assignment statement, then the string is initialized to the null string.

NUMBER

In awk, numbers can be represented in one of three ways:

As an integer, or whole number, preceded by an optional sign value, as shown below:

```
1
+5
001
```

As a real number (decimal and fractional part) preceded by an optional sign value, as shown below:

```
10.12
+5.3
```

In scientific notation—an example is shown below:

```
-5.2e-1
```

The scientific notation may have a decimal and fractional part preceding the letter e. These are seen in the above example with the number 5.2. In addition, an optional sign may appear before the digit after the letter e. This may be seen with the negative sign before the number 5.2 and after the letter e. The letter e may be in either upper- or lowercase.

INITIALIZATION OF NUMBERS   If a variable is involved in an operation that expects a number, and the variable is referenced before it was explicitly given a value by an assignment statement, then the number is initialized to 0.

COERCION

A number's representation when coerced to a string remains the same, but the number is its ASCII equivalent. In other words, the number 10 becomes "10" when coerced to a string; however, the 1 and 0 are the ASCII equivalent 48 and 49.

A string is coerced to a number by the following rule:

1. If the first character is not a digit 0–9, then the number is 0 (including the null string).
2. If the first character is a digit, then the longest string of digits 0–9 starting from the first character forms the number (i.e., "104" is the number 104, and so is "104abc").

The following table describes the situations in which a coercion will be made. Following the table is a description of how it is used.

Operation	Operator	Type Of Operand	Operation Result
Assignment	=	U	U
Assignment	=, +=, -=, *=, /=, %/, ^=	N	N
Conditional	?:	U	U
Logical OR	||	U	N
Logical AND	&&	U	N
Array Membership	in	S	N
Relational Matching	~, !~	S	N
Relational	<, <=, ==, !=, >=, >	U	N
Concatenation	"a" "b"	S	S
Arithmetic, Add, Subtract	+, -	N	N
Arithmetic, Mult, Div, Mod	*, /, %	N	N
Unary Plus, Minus	+, -	N	N
Logical NOT	!	U	N
Exponential	^	N	N
Increment, Decrement	++, --	N	N
Field	$	N	N
Grouping	()	Doesn't Apply	Doesn't Apply

In this table, a U stands for undetermined, an S stands for string, and a N stands for a number.

If the operand and the operation result are of the same type (e.g., for addition, both are N), then if one or both of the operands is of a different type, a coercion will be performed. The rules described here for converting from a string into a number or a number into a string will be applied. In the assignment operator, the type of operand may be either a string or a number and the type of the result of the assignment is determined by the type of the right-hand side of the assignment statement. A relational operator may take a string or number, but only if both operands are number will a numerical comparison be made. Note that regardless of the type of the comparison, the result will be numerical. The same is true for the logical operators as is for the relational operators. The conditional operator is a little bit trickier and we talk about it in Lab 12.3. We talk about the rest of the operators in more detail in Chapter 12, "Operators."

EXPRESSIONS

An expression can consist solely of a primary expression or more than one primary expression with an operator that combines expressions.

PRIMARY EXPRESSIONS

CONSTANTS   Two types of constants exist: strings and numbers. Strings must be enclosed in quotes; numbers are not. (Strings and numbers are described earlier in this appendix.) A string or number constant may be assigned to a variable and may occur anywhere that an operand is required.

USER-DEFINED VARIABLES   User-defined variables come into existence whenever the variable is first used as an rvalue or an lvalue. A user-defined variable is thus defined when it is named and/or assigned. A user-defined variable does not have to be explicitly declared and/or assigned. A user-defined variable name can be any sequence of letters (case-sensitive), digits, and the underscore character, but the first character must always be a letter. Awk-reserved words cannot be the name of a user-defined variable. A list of reserved words is given in the following table:

■ Awk-Reserved Words

function	break
continue	next
exit	if
else	do
while	for
delete	return
in	any built-in (string or arithmetic) function name
getline	print
printf	sprintf
system	close

A user-defined variable that is referenced before it is assigned is implicitly initialized by awk to zero if used as a number operand, or to null if used as a string operand.

A user-defined variable may be used (either assigned or accessed) anywhere in an awk program (in any pattern, action, or function).

BUILT-IN VARIABLES   Built-in variables are distinguished in that they all have uppercase names. The following table describes each.

Variable	Default	Description
ARGC	None	The number of command-line arguments passed into awk
ARGV	None	The array that stores each command-line argument
FILENAME	None	The name of the file awk is currently processing
FNR	None	The number of records that have been processed from the file that is being read
FS	`" "`	The field separator used to break up the input line read in

Variable	Default	Description
NF	None	The number of fields that have been
NR	None	The number of records that have been read in from all files processed so far
OFMT	%.6g	The output format for numbers
CONVFMT	%.6g	The string conversion format for numbers
OFS	" "	The output field separator, used in the print statement for each comma encountered and in constructing $0
ORS	"\n"	The output record separator is used in constructing $0; it is used as a result of executing the print statement
RLENGTH	None	The length of the string matched by the regular expression in the match() function
RS	"\n"	The record separator, used to determine when the end of a record is encountered in splitting input records into fields, and to stop splitting the record into fields
RSTART	None	The beginning position of the string matched by the match() function
SUBSEP	"\0034"	The separator character for array subscripts, separating a row index from a column index in a multidimensional array
ENVIRON	None	An array used to store UNIX environmental variables

Increasing the value of NF creates empty values (null) for field variable $(old value of NF + 1) to $(new value of NF). The result of decreasing the value of NF is machine dependent. Some versions will set the field variables above the new value of NF to null, whereas some will recreate $ with a field variable of one to the new value of NF. The ENVIRON variable is indexed by the name of the UNIX environmental variable. For example, ENVIRON["SHELL"] for my system is /bin/tcsh.

FIELD VARIABLES   Awk automatically creates field variables when splitting the input line into fields as described above in the awk programming model. The fields are split according to the values of FS and RS. A field variable is distinguished from other variables in that it is prefixed by the dollar sign ($) and followed by a number. Each time awk encounters the field separator, FS, in the input record, awk assigns the field into a field variable. The first time awk encounters the field separator, it assigns the field to $1, the second to $2, and so forth, until the record separator is encountered. $0 contains the value of the entire input record. The total number of fields split from the input record is given by the value of NF. Following are some rules for field variables:

- Field variables may be assigned and referenced.
- Every time a field variable is assigned, $0 is reconstructed using the value of OFS and ORS.
- Because it is numeric, a field variable may be referenced by $(expr) where expr yields a number.
- A field variable may be assigned anywhere in an awk program except in a BEGIN pattern.
- Field variables may be created above the number of fields originally split by awk.
- Creating a field variable is done by prefixing the variable with a dollar sign ($) and following it with a number greater than the number originally split up into fields by awk (the value of NF). This increases the value of NF. See the earlier discussion about built-in variables (NF) for the implications of increasing NF.

ARRAYS   Following are some rules regarding arrays:

- An awk array is a storage element like a variable that is used to store multiple values as a cohesive whole.
- An array in awk is an associative array. In other words, an awk array is a set where each element in the set is associated with an array index, which uniquely identifies the array element.
- An associative array has indexes that are strings. Therefore, array indexes are strings in awk.
- An array element may be assigned by:
  array[index]=value
- An array element may be referenced by:
  var_value = array[index]
- An array element may be deleted by:
  delete array[index]

- A test can be made to determine whether an index is contained within an array by the array membership test operator, `in`. This is shown as follows:
  ```
  if (index in array)
  ```
- You can use the special array `for` loop to cycle through all elements of an array, as follows:
  ```
  for (variable in array)
  ```
- The index of each array element is given by `variable`, and each element can be accessed by `array[variable]`.

BUILT-IN ARITHMETIC FUNCTIONS

`atan2(a, b)`	arctangent of a/b
`cos(a)`	cosine of a in radians
`exp(a)`	exponential of a
`int(a)`	integer part of a
`log(a)`	natural log of a
`rand()`	pseudorandom generator, between 0 and 1
`sin(a)`	sin of a in radians
`sqrt(a)`	square root of a
`srand(a)`	pseudorandom generator, between 0 and 1 (a is the starting seed)

BUILT-IN STRING FUNCTIONS

`index(s,t)`	Return the character position in which string t occurs in s; return 0 if t is not in s
`length(s)`	Return the total number of characters in s
`match(s, r)`	Return character position in which regular expression r is matched in s; return 0 if regular expression r does not occur in s; sets RLENGTH and RSTART
`substr(s,p)`	Returns a `substr` starting at character position p to the end of s
`substr(s, p, n)`	Returns a `substr` starting at character position p, n characters long
`split(s, a)`	Split string s into array a using the value of FS as the field separator
`split(s, a, fs)`	Split string s into array a using FS as the field separator
`sub(r, s)`	For the first occurrence of regular expression r in $0, substitute the longest substring in $0 with string s; return the number of substitutions made (0 or 1)

`sub(r, s, t)`	For the first occurrence of regular expression r in t, substitute the longest substring in t with string s; return the number of substitutions made (0 or 1)
`gsub(r, s)`	Substitute string s globally for every occurrence of regular expression r in $0; return the number of substitutions made
`gsub(r, s, t)`	Substitute string s globally for every occurrence of regular expression r in t; return the number of substitutions made

USER-DEFINED FUNCTIONS   A user-defined function can be defined an appear anywhere in an awk program. It should be placed before any pattern-action statement is defined by convention.

A user-defined function definition has the form:

```
function name(parameter-list) {
    statement(s)
    [return expression]
}
```

The name of a function follows the same conventions as user-define variables.

The formal parameters of variables in the parameter list are passed int the function call-by-value. Call-by-value makes a copy of the value passe into, and are temporary values that are destroyed when the function exi (i.e., they are no longer recognized outside the function). The exception an array that is passed call-by-reference (i.e., the array element values th were assigned outside the function are recognized inside the functio and the array elements that are assigned inside the function are reco nized outside the function).

Variables that are defined outside the function can be referenced withi the curly braces (called the function body) of the function.

Variables that are assigned within the function exist and maintain the value outside the function.

The function body may contain a return statement (optional). The return statement is accompanied with an expression that yields a value that is returned.

To avoid side effects, any variables that are used within the function body that were not passed into the function by the call should be included in the parameter list so that they are not accidentally accessed outside the function.

A function call has the form:

```
return = name(arg1, arg2, ..., argN)
```

Each argument's value (arg1, .., argN) is assigned in the same positional order as is defined in the parameter list (i.e., arg1's value is assigned to the first parameter in the parameter list, arg2 to the second, and so on). Any additional parameters in the parameter list that were not provided in the call are assigned the null value.

OPERATORS THAT COMBINE EXPRESSIONS

ARITHMETIC OPERATORS

Name (Symbol)	Form (a and b are any expressions that yield a result)
Addition (+)	a + b
Subtraction (–)	a – b
Multiplication (*)	a * b
Division (/)	a / b
Modulus (%)	a % b, the remainder when a is divided by b
Exponential (^)	a ^ b, a raised b times

ASSIGNMENT OPERATORS

Symbol	Form	Description (b can be any expression that can be an rvalue; a must be an lvalue)
a = b	a = b	value of b (rvalue) assigned to a (lvalue)
a += b	a = a + b	value of a (rvalue) added to b (rvalue) and assigned back to a (lvalue)
a -= b	a = a - b	value of a (rvalue) subtracted by b (rvalue) and assigned back to a (lvalue)
a *= b	a = a * b	value of a (rvalue) multiplied by b (rvalue) and assigned back to a (lvalue)
a /= b	a = a / b	value of a (rvalue) divided by b (rvalue) and assigned back to a (lvalue)
a %/ b	a = a % b	value of a (rvalue) modulus b (rvalue) and assigned back to a (lvalue)
a ^= b	a = a ^ b	value of a (rvalue) raised b (rvalue) times and assigned back to a (lvalue)

INCREMENT/DECREMENT OPERATORS

Form, Name	Result Value	Value of i After Evaluating
i++, Auto Increment, Postfix	i	i + 1
++i, Auto Increment, Prefix	i + 1	i + 1
i--, Auto Decrement, Postfix	i	i - 1
--i, Auto Decrement, Prefix	i - 1	i - 1

CONDITIONAL EXPRESSION

```
(conditional) ? Statement1 :   Statement2
```

If conditional is true, then `Statement1` is evaluated and returned; other-wise, `Statement2` is evaluated and returned.

LOGICAL OPERATORS

Symbol	Form	Description (a and b are any expressions)
||	a || b	If a or b is true (non-zero or non-null), then the result is true (non-zero, non-null). Otherwise, the result is false.
&&	a && b	If a and b are true (non-zero or non-null), then the result is true (non-zero, non-null). Otherwise, the result is false.
!	!a	If a is false (zero or null), then the result is true. Otherwise, the result is false.

MATCHING OPERATORS

Symbol	Form	Description
~	a ~ b	returns true if regular expression b is contained in string expression a
!~	a !~ b	returns true if regular expression b is not contained in string expression b

RELATIONAL OPERATORS

Symbol	Form	Description (a and b are any expression that yields a result)
<	a < b	if a is less than b, then the result is true (non-zero or non-null)
<=	a <= b	if a is less than b, then the result is true (non-zero or non-null)
==	a == b	if a is less than b, then the result is true (non-zero or non-null)
=	a != b	if a is less than b, then the result is true (non-zero or non-null)
	a > b	if a is less than b, then the result is true (non-zero or non-null)
=	a >= b	if a is less than b, then the result is true (non-zero or non-null)

CONCATENATION (NO EXPLICIT OPERATOR)   Concatenation is performed by placing two expressions side by side with a space separating them. If op1 and op2 are expressions, then the following performs string concatenation and places the result in var:

```
var = op1 op2
```

The result of a string concatenation appends op2 onto op1 and returns the concatenated string. If either expression op1 or op2 yields a non-string result, then the result will be coerced into a string.

PRECEDENCE AND ASSOCIATIVITY

In the following table, the operators are listed in order of increasing precedence. Therefore, assignment has the lowest precedence.

Operation	Operator	Associativity
Assignment	=, +=, -=, *=, /=, %/, ^=	Right
Conditional	?:	Left
Logical OR	||	Left
Logical AND	&&	Left
Array Membership	in	Left
Relational Matching	~, !~	Left
Relational	<, <=, ==, !=, >=, >	Left
Concatenation	"a" "b"	Right
Arithmetic, Add, Subtract	+, -	Left
Arithmetic, Mult, Div, Mod	*, /, %	Left
Unary Plus, Minus	+, -	Left
Logical NOT	!	Left
Exponential	^	Right
Increment, Decrement	++, --	Left
Field	$	Left
Grouping	()	Left

LOOPING AND CONTROL STATEMENTS

IF-ELSE STATEMENT

```
if (expression)
    statement1
[else
    statement2]
```

The brackets indicate that the `else` part is optional. If `expression` is true (non-zero, non-null), then `statement1` is executed. Otherwise, if an `else` part is provided, then `statement2` is executed. If more than one statement is to be executed, then curly braces must be provided.

```
if (expression) {
    statements
}
[else {
    statements
}
```

Each statement must be separated by a statement separator.

WHILE-DO STATEMENT

```
while (expression)
    statement
```

```
while (expression) {
    statements
}
```

If `expression` is true (non-zero, non-null), then `statement1` is executed. The statement is continually executed until `statement` is false (zero or null). In the second form, more than one statement can be included in the `while` statement if each statement is separated by a statement separator and all statements are surrounded by curly braces.

```
do
    statement
while (expression)
```

```
do {
    statement
} while (expression)
```

Statement is executed once. If expression is true, then statement is continually executed until statement is false (zero or null). In the second form, more than one statement can be included in the do-while statement if each statement is separated by a statement separator and all statements are enclosed within curly braces.

FOR STATEMENT

```
for (counter; test; increment)
    statement

for (counter; test; increment) {
    statements
}
```

In the second form, more than one statement can be included in a for statement if each statement is separated by a statement separator and all statements are enclosed within curly braces.

An example of the for statement is:

```
for (i=0; i<6; i++)
    print i
```

the counterpart of the for statement is i=0;
the test part is i<6;
the increment part is i++
the statement is print i

The for statement works by first executing the counter expression. The test part is executed and if the expression is true (non-zero, non-null) then the statement is executed. Finally, the increment expression is executed last.

All three statements are optional, and all three statements can be an expression.

INPUT-OUTPUT

INPUT

Expression	Function	
`getline`	Reads a line into `$0`	Sets `$0`, NF, NR, FNR
`getline var`	Reads in a line into `var` instead of `$0`	Sets `var`, NR, FNR
`getline <file`	Reads in a line from `file`	Sets `$0`, NF
`getline var <file`	Reads in a line from `file` into `var`	Sets `var`
`cmd | getline`	Pipes `cmd` into the `getline` function, which reads a line of input into `$0`	Sets `$0`, NF
`cmd | getline var`	Pipes `cmd` into the `getline` function, which reads a line of input into `var`	`var`

The `getline` command returns 0 when the end-of-file is reached, –1 if an error occurs—some examples are: Cannot open file (permissions, file doesn't exist), pipe error. If a pipe or file redirection symbol (<) is not used, then the input comes from the awk invocation line. The awk invocation line specifies that standard input or a user-supplied file is to be used. The following indicates two ways to specify input at the awk invocation line (see "Command-Line Invocation" later in this appendix):

1. Standard Input => awk `'program'`
2. User-Supplied File => awk `'program'` some-file

OUTPUT

Statement	Action
`print`	Print an entire record
`print expr-list`	Print `expr-list`
`print expr-list >file`	Print `expr-list` into `file`; if `file` exists, it will be overwritten
`print expr-list >>file`	Append `expr-list` onto the end of `file`; if `file` does not exist, it is created
`print expr-list "| cmd"`	Pipe `expr-list` into `cmd`; use quotes to specify the pipe symbol and `cmd`
`printf frmt-expr, expr-list`	Print `frmt-expr` using `expr-list`
`printf frmt-expr, expr-list >file`	Print `frmt-expr` using `expr-list` into `file`; if `file` exists, it is overwritten
`printf frmt-expr, expr-list >>file`	Append `frmt-expr` using `expr-list` onto `file`; if `file` doesn't exist, it is created
`printf frmt-expr, expr-list "| cmd"`	Print `frmt-expr` using `expr-list` into `cmd`; use quotes to specify the pipe symbol and `cmd`

- `expr-list`—a list of any expression (primary or operator that combines expressions)
- `frmt-expr`—a list of character literals (string) together with format specifiers surrounded in double quotes

If no file redirection symbol (`>`, `>>`) or pipe is used, then the output will be directed to standard output (the screen).

If a string is used (as a constant or string variable), it may contain an escape sequence to be printed. (The definition of a string includes the use of an escape sequence as a character literal.)

PRINT AND PRINT EXPR-LIST Expr-list is optional in the print statement. Both print the value of ORS as an end result of executing the print statement. If expr-list is left out, then an entire record is output followed by ORS. Expr-list is a single expression or any number of expressions separated by commas. For each comma, the value of OFS will be printed. The expressions can be constants, variables, array elements, function calls, and the value of an operation, as mentioned below the table. Each expression will be converted to a string. If a number is to be converted into a string, then the value of the output format specifier (OFMT) will be used. If no value for OFMT exists, then awk will use its default action, as described earlier in "Coercion."

PRINTF FRMT-EXPR, EXPR-LIST The expr-list in the printf statement is a list of any expression, as described in the print statement and below the table above; however, a format specifier in the frmt-expr specifies how to print each expression. A format specifier for each expression exists in the expr-list. As described below the table above, the frmt-expr is a list of literal characters together with format specifiers (if an expr-list is provided). The expr-list is optional. If it is left out, then the frmt-expr contains no format specifiers and is just a string of character literals. Therefore, printf uses a user-supplied list of format specifiers to print each expression in the expression list and does not coerce each expressions into a string or use the output format specifier for printing numbers. It also does not use the value for ORS after executing the printf statement. The following is a list of format specifiers:

- %c—an ASCII character (i.e., a or b or x, etc.)
- %d—a whole number (i.e., 1, 40, -5)
- %e—[-]d.ddddddE[+-]dd
- %f—[-]ddd.dddddd
- %g—e or f, whichever is shorter, with nonsignificant zeros suppressed
- %o—an unsigned octal
- %s—a string
- %x—an unsigned hexadecimal
- %—a percent character

Additional parameters may be used between the % symbol and above format specifier character that specifies the precision and width with which you specify, along with the format specifier. These are optional and are listed below:

- – specifies that you wish to print the expression left-justified.
- width pads the field with blanks (string, char), or 0s (everything else) to the width provided as needed.
- .prec is the maximum width to the right of the decimal point for real numbers.

So an example of a format specifier that uses all three is:

```
%-5.2f
```

COMMAND-LINE INVOCATION

```
awk [-v variable=value] [-Fvalue] [--] 'awk program'
   variable=value [datafile(s)]
awk [-v variable=value] [-Fvalue] [--] -f
   scriptfilename variable=value [datafile(s)]
```

The difference between the two forms is that in the first, the awk program is provided at the command line. In the second, the -f awkscript parameter instructs awk that the awk program is contained within the file called scriptfilename.

Anything surrounded within brackets is optional.

The awk program is described earlier in this appendix, in "Awk Program and Program Format."

The datafile(s) is optional. If none is provided, then input comes from standard input.

The rest of the parameters are described below:

- [--]—is another way to specify that input comes from standard input (make sure that your version allows this).
- [-v variable=value]—sets an awk variable on the command line that enables the variable to be used within the

awk program. The variable name is listed after the -v, followed by the equals sign and the value for the variable. (i.e., -v balance=3400.00). You cannot set the value of a built-in variable (FS, NF, OFS, etc.) using the -v option. See whether this works on your version.

- -Fvalue—sets FS to value. No space occurs between the -F option and the value following the -F option. An example of using this option is -F" , ".
- variable=value—provides the same function as the -v option, except with some differences. The -v option specifies that variable is to be set to value before the BEGIN pattern is even executed. Without the -v option, the value is set after the first line of input is read. Therefore, in the -v option, a built-in variable cannot be used, but setting the variable on the command line without the -v option allows you to set the value of any variable. The value without the -v option can be any value or shell variable of the pipe value. It must be quoted if it contains spaces or tabs.

INDEX